ORIGINS AND DESTINATIONS

ORIGINS AND DESTINATIONS

The Making of the Second Generation

Renee Luthra, Thomas Soehl, and Roger Waldinger

Russell Sage Foundation
New York

The Russell Sage Foundation

The Russell Sage Foundation, one of the oldest of America's general purpose foundations, was established in 1907 by Mrs. Margaret Olivia Sage for "the improvement of social and living conditions in the United States." The foundation seeks to fulfill this mandate by fostering the development and dissemination of knowledge about the country's political, social, and economic problems. While the foundation endeavors to assure the accuracy and objectivity of each book it publishes, the conclusions and interpretations in Russell Sage Foundation publications are those of the authors and not of the foundation, its trustees, or its staff. Publication by Russell Sage, therefore, does not imply foundation endorsement.

BOARD OF TRUSTEES
Claude M. Steele, Chair

Larry M. Bartels
Karen S. Cook
Sheldon Danziger
Kathryn Edin
Michael Jones-Correa

Lawrence F. Katz
David Laibson
Nicholas Lemann
Sara S. McLanahan
Martha Minow

Peter R. Orszag
Mario Luis Small
Shelley E. Taylor
Hirokazu Yoshikawa

Library of Congress Cataloging-in-Publication Data

Names: Luthra, Renee, author. | Soehl, Thomas, author. | Waldinger, Roger David, author.
Title: Origins and destinations : the making of the second generation / Renee Luthra, Thomas Soehl, and Roger Waldinger.
Description: New York : Russell Sage Foundation, 2018. | Includes bibliographical references and index.
Identifiers: LCCN 2018013855 (print) | LCCN 2018015207 (ebook) | ISBN 9781610448758 (ebook) | ISBN 9780871549129 (pbk. : alk. paper)
Subjects: LCSH: United States—Emigration and immigration—Social aspects. | Children of immigrants—United States—Social conditions. | Immigrants—United States—Social conditions. | Immigrants—Cultural assimilation—United States. | Transnationalism.
Classification: LCC JV6475 (ebook) | LCC JV6475 .L88 2018 (print) | DDC 305.9/069120973—dc23
LC record available at https://lccn.loc.gov/2018013855

Copyright © 2018 by Russell Sage Foundation. All rights reserved. Printed in Canada. No part of this publication may be reproduced, stored in a retrieval system, or transmitted in any form or by any means, electronic, mechanical, photocopying, recording, or otherwise, without the prior written permission of the publisher.

Reproduction by the United States Government in whole or in part is permitted for any purpose.

The paper used in this publication meets the minimum requirements of American National Standard for Information Sciences—Permanence of Paper for Printed Library Materials. ANSI Z39.48-1992.

Text design by Suzanne Nichols.
Cover photo by Mirko Vitali.

RUSSELL SAGE FOUNDATION
112 East 64th Street, New York, New York 10065
10 9 8 7 6 5 4 3 2 1

Contents

	List of Illustrations	vii
	About the Authors	xiii
	Acknowledgments	xv
Chapter 1	Origins and Destinations	1
Part I	Perspectives	25
Chapter 2	Bringing the International Back In: A New Perspective	27
Chapter 3	The International Perspective	49
Part II	Transmission	85
Chapter 4	The Importance of Context	87
Chapter 5	Getting Ahead: Institutions, Ethnicity, and International Influences	118
Part III	Transformations	151
Chapter 6	Acquiring Citizenship	153
Chapter 7	Exercising Citizenship	177

Chapter 8	Cross-Border Connections	202
Chapter 9	Ethnicity: Crossing Blurry Boundaries	226
Part IV	Conclusion	259
Chapter 10	Conclusion: The Making of the Second Generation	261
	Appendix	283
	Notes	305
	References	313
	Index	325

List of Illustrations

Figure 1.1	Schematic Summary of the Explanatory Approach	5
Figure 3.1	Location of Immigrant-Sending Countries in the Traditional Versus Secular-Rational and the Survival Versus Self-Expression Value Space	57
Figure 3.2	Relationship Between Value Orientation Scales and Number of Books in Household, Average Years of Education, and Polity III Scores	59
Figure 4.1	Predicted Changes in Educational Attainment and Occupational Status Associated with Changes in Group- and Individual-Level Variables	115
Figure 5.1	Select Coefficients from Hierarchical Linear Regression Models Predicting Educational and Occupational Attainment for the Children of Immigrants	126
Figure 5.2	Expected Years of Education, by Parental and Group Educational Quintiles	130
Figure 5.3	The Interaction of Supplementary Education, Parental Education, and Traditional Versus Secular-Rational Scores	133

Figure 5.4	Hierarchical Linear Regression Model Predicting High School Quality for the Children of Immigrants in Public Schools in New York City	138
Figure 5.5	School Quality and Educational and Occupational Attainment of Immigrant Offspring in New York City	140
Figure 5.6	Cross-Border Ties and Educational and Occupational Attainment of Los Angeles Immigrant Offspring	143
Figure 5.7	Legal Status of Los Angeles Immigrant Parents at Arrival and Socioeconomic Outcomes for Their Children	145
Figure 6.1	Cumulative Probability of Naturalizing for 1.5-Generation Los Angeles Respondents by Status of Entry	157
Figure 6.2	Citizenship Density (Number of Citizens in Child-Parent Groupings) by Select Group-Level Characteristics	166
Figure 6.3	Naturalization Trajectories for 1.5-Generation Los Angeles Respondents by Select Group-Level Variables	168
Figure 6.4	Effects of Select Individual-Level Variables and Measures of Context of Immigration and Emigration	170
Figure 7.1	Predicting Participation of Los Angeles Respondents in Civic or Non-electoral Political Activities: Summary of Key Regression Results	187
Figure 7.2	Predicting Aggregate Measures of Los Angeles Respondents' Civic and Political Engagement: Summary of Key Regression Results	188

Figure 7.3	Predicting Engagement of Los Angeles Respondents in Electoral Politics: Summary of Key Regression Results	189
Figure 7.4	Predicted Marginal Probability of Party Registration Varying Average National-Origin Group Skin Color and Sending-Country Traditionalism	197
Figure 8.1	Regression Results: Effects of Group-Level Variables on Remitting and Visits to the Parental Home Country	215
Figure 8.2	Regression Results: Effects of Parental Location and Family Structure on Cross-Border Ties in the Los Angeles Second Generation	217
Figure 8.3	Regression Results: Effects of Parental Cross-Border Activities on Cross-Border Ties in the Los Angeles Second Generation	219
Figure 8.4	Regression Results: Effects of Language Spoken at Home, Generation, Citizenship Status, and Parental Education on Cross-Border Activity in the Los Angeles Second Generation	222
Figure 9.1	Mentions of Ethnic Labels and Importance of Ethnic Labels Among Los Angeles Respondents	234
Figure 9.2	Select Regression Coefficients for the Ethnic Categorization Preferences of Los Angeles Respondents: Parental Origin Status at Arrival, Respondents' Generational and Citizenship Status, and Language Practices in the Household	236
Figure 9.3	Los Angeles Respondents' Preferred Ethnic Label by Generation and Naturalization (Regression-Adjusted Predicted Probability)	237

Figure 9.4	Predicted Probability of Los Angeles Respondents' Preferred Ethnic Label by Parental Legal Status at Arrival	237
Figure 9.5	Coefficients from Linear Regression Predicting Mother-Tongue Proficiency (Scale) and Preference for English	243
Figure 9.6	Predicting Los Angeles Respondents' Preference for English	247
Figure 9.7	Acculturation Type by Generation	251
Figure 9.8	Difference in Predicted Probability of Acculturation Type by Remittance Behavior of Parents, Parental Education, and Group-Level Variables	252
Figure 9.9	Predicted Probability of Selective and Consonant Acculturation by Parental and Group-Level Education	254
Figure A.1	Correlations of Traditional Versus Secular-Rational Values with GDP, Number of Books in the Household, Average Levels of Education, and Literacy	286
Figure A.2	Correlations of Survival Versus Self-Expression Orientations with GDP, Number of Books in the Household, Average Levels of Education, and Literacy	288
Figure A.3	Correlations of Survival Versus Self-Expression Orientations with the UN Gender Empowerment Index, the Human Development Index, Polity Scores, and Contraceptive Use	290

Figure A.4	Correlations of Traditional Versus Secular-Rational Value Orientations with the UN Gender Empowerment Index, the Human Development Index, Polity Scores, and Contraceptive Use	292
Figure A.5	Importance of God in One's Life by Country and Education Level	295
Figure A.6	Acceptance of Homosexuality by Country and Education Level	296
Figure A.7	Difference from U.S. Average by Size of City for WVS Value Orientations	298
Table 3.1	The Status Prevalence Scale	66
Table 3.2	Indicators of Cross-Border Activities in the IIMMLA and ISGMNY Surveys	69
Table 4.1	Conceptualizing and Measuring Contexts of Immigration and Emigration	88
Table 4.2	Context of Immigration for Immigrant Groups in the IIMMLA and ISGMNY: Immigration Policy, Societal Reception, and Coethnic Community	98
Table 4.3	Descriptive Statistics of Second-Generation Immigrants, Ages Twenty-Three and Older	100
Table 4.4	Correlation Among Multiple Dimensions of Context, Years of Education Completed, and Occupational Status	102
Table 4.5	Detailed View of Cells Adjacent to the Reception Contexts Under Comparison	104
Table 4.6	Contextual Variables Predicting Educational and Occupational Attainment: Summary of Hierarchical Linear Regression Models	105

Table 5.1	Hypothesizing Sources of Intergroup Differences	120
Table 5.2	Interaction Effects Between Highest Parental Educational and Occupational Attainment and Context Characteristics When Predicting Educational and Occupational Attainment of the Second Generation	134
Table 5.3	Interaction Effects Between Second-Generation Educational Attainment and Context Characteristics When Predicting Second-Generation Occupational Attainment	136
Table 5.4	Summary of Findings on Educational and Occupational Attainment Among Immigrant Children	147
Table 7.1	Dependent Variables, Labels, and a Summary of Survey Items	186
Table 8.1	Comparative Cross-Border Behavior: Immigrants Ages Thirty-Five to Sixty (Latino National Survey) Versus Immigrant Offspring Ages Twenty to Thirty-Two (IIMMLA and ISGMNY)	209
Table 9.1	Level of National Pride and Suspicions of Foreigners in Select Sending Countries	228
Table 9.2	Generational Language Knowledge and Types of Acculturation	249
Table 9.3	Distribution of Acculturation Types	250
Table 10.1	Summary of Key Theoretical Approaches and Their Empirical Treatment in This Book	265

About the Authors

RENEE LUTHRA is senior lecturer in the Department of Sociology at the University of Essex.

THOMAS SOEHL is Canada Research Chair in International Migration and assistant professor of sociology at McGill University.

ROGER WALDINGER is Distinguished Professor of Sociology at the University of California Los Angeles.

Acknowledgments

JUST LIKE THE respondents whose tales will be told in the pages to follow, this book is a story of origins and destinations. It began in an office on the University of California, Los Angeles, campus with a proposal for an edited book that, if plausible at the time, was rightly rejected, though with sufficient kindness that revision was requested. At that moment, we three, all transplants from elsewhere—Renee from Houston, Thomas from Bavaria, Roger from New York—were based in Los Angeles. But as time marched on, and as this book took shape, the configuration changed. As we write these acknowledgments, only Roger is still standing at the point of departure; Renee was first to go, heading across the pond to the University of Essex, to be followed by Thomas, who, recruited to McGill University, crossed the northern U.S. border. Thus, as this book headed toward its conclusion, it hurtled back and forth across half the globe: when Roger sent a late evening email, Renee responded to it at the crack of dawn minutes before Roger fell asleep, and then Thomas interjected sometime before Renee went to bed and Roger returned to consciousness. In a sense, this book is a by-product of the very same globalization that produced the immigrant offspring about whom we write. Whether that globalization made this book better or worse is a question that we leave for readers to decide. What we can say is that we were friends at the start of this intellectual journey and so we very much remain—geographic distance notwithstanding.

First, our deepest thanks go to the Russell Sage Foundation. The foundation patiently nurtured a proposal that eventually proved significantly better than our initial try; generously funded our research; patiently waited until we completed a manuscript; and then obtained a sterling set of critical reviewers whose skeptical reactions to our original submission pointed the way to improvements that we believe have made for a much better book. Special thanks go to Aixa Cintron, who worked with us at the proposal stage; to Eric Wanner and Sheldon Danziger, presidents of the foundation, for their support of this project; and to Suzanne Nichols, the foundation's publications director, whose confidence in our effort never flagged, even as the delivery date was further and further postponed. Roger Waldinger expresses his deep appreciation for the foundation's continuing support, which now goes back almost a quarter century; he hopes that the foundation and its staff find that this investment proved worthwhile.

We also express our most profound gratitude to the Russell Sage Foundation for its long-term investment in immigration research, which in turn made possible the two heroic data collection efforts on which our work builds: the Immigrant Second Generation in Metropolitan New York (ISGMNY) survey and the Immigration and Intergenerational Mobility in Metropolitan Los Angles (IIMMLA) survey. For their breadth, depth, and quality, these two surveys are truly unique. Consequently, we owe a great debt to the colleagues who captained these efforts: John Mollenkopf, Mary Waters, and Philip Kasinitz, the principal investigators of the New York City study; and Rubén Rumbaut, Frank Bean, Leo Chavez, Jennifer Lee, Susan Brown, Louis DeSipio, and Min Zhou, the members of the Los Angeles team.

This book also owes much to the uniquely stimulating and supportive environment that we encountered in the UCLA Department of Sociology, Roger as a faculty member, Renee and Thomas as graduate students. The perspective developed in this book and the tools that we have implemented are largely the legacy of the intellectual currents we found in Haines Hall, where UCLA Sociology makes its home.

Russell Sage's generosity notwithstanding, some additional financial assistance helped us bring this project to a close. In particular, we wish to thank the Fonds de Recherche de Québec Societé et Culture, as well as the Canadian Social Science and Humanities Research Council and the Research Centre on Micro-Social Change of the Economic and Social Research Council (ESRC).

This book has also benefited from reactions we received at a variety of workshops and conferences where portions of the project were presented, and we thank both the organizers of these events and those who attended them. We are also most thankful to John Hall, Jennifer Elrick, Lauren Duquette-Rury, Lucinda Platt, Sarah Carol, and Merlin Schaeffer, who read earlier versions of the manuscript and provided invaluable feedback. Thanks also go to Peter Catron, Sakeef Karim, and Ali Zeren, who helped with producing tables, figures, and the analyses behind them; without their help, our journey would have lasted still longer. Our gratitude goes as well to the excellent statistical consultants at UCLA's Institute for Digital Research and Education.

Beyond the collective gratitude, we each have our own personal thanks to express:

Renee thanks dear colleagues and friends on both sides of the pond who provided intellectual and moral support during this long process. Jennifer Flashman and Vikki Katz have been there since the very beginning, reading her work and sharing their ideas as fellow graduate students at UCLA—and beyond. Lauren Duquette-Rury and Annie Ro provided camaraderie as new postdocs when she returned as a visiting scholar, quickly becoming sounding boards for both scholarly and personal decisions. Colleagues at the University of Essex were a source of support and many helpful conversations both before and after the move from the Institute for Social and Economic Research to the Department of Sociology; Renee particularly thanks her very first friend at ISER, Tina Haux, and Neli Demireva and Ayse Güveli in Sociology. She also owes a great debt to Lucinda Platt—for providing the first research position post-PhD, for her mentorship, and for her friendship. Renee's very deepest gratitude goes to her husband and best friend, Yannig Luthra, whose insights shape all of her work and whose loving care for their family forms the base of her life. Finally, Renee wishes to thank the delightful Michele-Christine, a constant source of wonder, laughter, and light—and who at five years old knows to tell her mama to stop talking about work.

Thomas thanks his colleagues at McGill University, who made him feel instantly welcome and eased the transition from life as a graduate student to one that includes a regular paycheck but also a broader set of responsibilities. For stimulating conversation, much-needed distraction, and lovely company during long days at the office, Thomas thanks his neighbors on the seventh and eighth floors of the Leacock Building: Sarah Brauner-Otto, Matt Lange, Eran Shor, Barry Eidlin, Jan Doering, and Jennifer Elrick. For generous friendship and support, the occasional game of chess, and advice on how to choose good titles, a special thank-you to John Hall. Most importantly, Thomas's deepest appreciation goes to Yvonne Hung for being a wonderful and inspiring partner in their own migration and migrant family project. Emilia and Luisa joined the party in California—as 2.5-generation Americans. Now 1.5-generation Canadians, they are enthusiastically showing how to make one's way in a destination country. Emilia and Luisa, you are an endless source of joy.

Roger's thanks begin with his institutional and intellectual home, UCLA, which assembled and supported a splendid Department of Sociology and more recently a superb, cross-campus group of migration scholars whose presence has made UCLA an especially stimulating environment for migration studies. A special note of gratitude goes to the departmental colleagues who have been Roger's closest intellectual and institutional collaborators for the past twenty-seven years: César Ayala, Rogers Brubaker, Rubén Hernández-León, Gail Kligman, David Lopez, Robert Mare, Jeffrey

Prager, Emmanuel Schegloff, Judith Seltzer, and Min Zhou. These past years were also leavened by the wit and wisdom of the late Mel Pollner. Thanks also to Lauren Duquette-Rury for her friendship and the many stimulating conversations during her years at UCLA, both of which now continue long-distance. Beyond the precincts of Haines Hall, Roger also thanks Hiroshi Motomura and Marjorie Faulstich Orellana for their colleagueship, insights, and steadfast commitment to building a campus-wide interdisciplinary community of migration scholars. As a second-generation American, Roger is also indebted to his first-generation parents, who set the scholarly example: the late Hermann Waldinger and Renee Waldinger, whose difficult twilight years have darkened the years in which the writing of this book has come to a close. Last but not least, Roger's very deepest notes of appreciation go to his immediate, beloved family: his wife Hilary; children Max, Mimi, and Joey; and the newest arrivals, grandchildren Sky and Shay. The best of times were had with you!

And one final note of thanks—to each other!—for the friendship and commitment that have made this long and sometimes difficult journey from origin to destination a source of continuing stimulation.

Chapter 1 | Origins and Destinations

IMMIGRANTS ARE REMAKING America, from bottom to top. At the bottom stand the workers doing the difficult, dangerous, and dirty work that most native-born shun, whether picking crops, cleaning toilets, or slaughtering and carving up the animals that appear on the American dinner table. At the opposite end of the spectrum, one finds the immigrant overachievers, who, as inventors, corporate moguls, financiers, or Nobel Prize winners, often leave the native-born population far behind.

The mass arrival of the foreign-born can be transformational, and nowhere is the legacy of immigrants more lasting than in their descendants, starting with their children—the second generation. This second generation is the inevitable by-product of immigration itself: since the young are the people most likely to leave their old home in search of a better future elsewhere, immigrants reach their new home at precisely the age when family formation usually begins. Consequently, their arrival yields large numbers of children born in the host society yet socialized by parents who were raised in a different environment, one with expectations and orientations typically foreign to the place that their children experience as their native world. In beginning again, the parents start out in a new, strange country that must be learned, triggering a process of adaptation that even when successful is almost always error-prone and transmits the signal—to the immigrants themselves, to their children, and to the outsiders around them—that perhaps profoundly, perhaps ineffably, they remain out of place. Moreover, moving in a world where no one is free to cross state borders simply as he or she wishes, all immigrant parents commence anew as aliens, lacking the full rights enjoyed by the citizens of their adopted country and often enough discovering that the route to joining the citizenry is arduous, long, and sometimes impossible to successfully traverse.

This common background provides the scaffolding from which the children of immigrants are launched into the world. Despite these salient features shared by almost all immigrant offspring, they nonetheless do not turn out the same. Even as they contribute to the greater diversity of the societies that their parents decided to join, these immigrant offspring are themselves incredibly diverse, standing out from their fellow second-generation counterparts on myriad dimensions.

That simple straightforward observation motivates this book: we seek to understand the origins of the many differences among today's second generation, looking for sources stemming from countries of origin, immigrant groups' experience in the United States, and the characteristics of immigrant households and individuals. We provide new questions to guide our exploration, introduce a novel perspective for framing our inquiry, import a methodology used elsewhere in the social sciences but rarely applied to these issues, and engage with the scholars who have gone before us so as to provide a systematic assessment of the many hypotheses generated by the past quarter century of research.

THE QUESTION

The central question animating this book is purposefully broad and aims to demonstrate the utility of our methodology and our perspective across a variety of domains: *What are the primary individual- and group-level determinants of second-generation variation in school, work, ethnic attachment, and political life?*

The foreign-born in the United States truly represent the world, providing a cross-section of the globe's economic and cultural diversity. Today's newcomers arrive from both the planet's poorest states and its richest, from not only deeply religious societies, such as those in Central America or the Philippines, but also the most dramatically secular, such as the former Soviet Union and China. That diversity is fully reflected in the immigrant home, making for a set of socialization experiences that are far more variegated than those among the children of native-born Americans. And yet, while parents' foreign origins affect the destinies of their offspring, those progeny themselves follow a life course that unfolds in a setting very different from that experienced by their parents. That new context tends to diminish the yawning social and economic gaps among the foreign-born, largely because the wealth and institutional framework of the society of arrival improves conditions for even the least fortunate of those residents who started out abroad. Since society-wide investments in public goods in the United States greatly outdistance the levels attained in the poorer countries of emigration, and since the everyday environment provides a higher level of security and stability than the parents could have found at the point of origin, the children of immigrant farm and factory workers typically follow career and educational pathways that increasingly resemble those of their counterparts from wealthier nations as well as the native-born.

Movement toward convergence with the standard of the society of arrival provides the telltale sign that assimilation, as defined by the textbooks, is well under way. Thanks to that same tendency, the distance between high and low immigrant origin achievers somewhat diminishes from first to second generation. Nonetheless, a very significant gulf remains. On average, for example, the children of Chinese immigrants in Los Angeles complete sixteen years of schooling, as opposed to thirteen among their Mexican-origin counterparts. Likewise, the offspring of Filipino migrants are far more likely to work as professionals or managers than their Salvadoran-origin peers. These intergroup disparities catch the eye of both amateur and professional students of migration and ethnicity, yet represent only one axis of variation in second-generation experiences and trajectories. Despite everything that might separate the offspring of immigrants originating in one country from those of another immigrant group, the gaps separating persons who share the same national roots turn out to be no less important—and are sometimes even more important. Of course, in this respect, the children of immigrants are just like their counterparts among the children of natives: U.S.-born parents are not all cut from the same mold, and more importantly, as parents do not all possess the same resources, some are more equipped to help their children than others. But the children of immigrants are all the offspring of people who grew up in foreign places and who had to somehow adapt to a country that was initially unfamiliar and not their own; thus, on this count, the children of immigrants are *not* just like their counterparts among the children of natives.

Parents' common international experiences—their exposure to different economic and social conditions in their home country, their continuing ties to significant others there, and their lengthy, perhaps permanent, experience as aliens living among citizens in a foreign land—shape their lives in a variety of ways. Even so, the course of parental adaptation does not follow a single path: as some quickly abandon homeland loyalties and practices while others instead hold fast to them, their children are given different models to follow that might—or might not—prove of use. Immigrant parents further depart from their native-born counterparts in that they belong to family networks that stretch across national boundaries.

As previously noted, migration is a selective process that leads some—typically young adults—to depart and others—often children and parents—to stay in place. Because that very selectivity internationalizes kinship ties, the children of immigrants often grow up in households with a foreign connection that may serve as either a recipient of help or a focus of concern, activities that could then have an influence on the resources available to immigrant offspring and the orientations that they adopt.

As the reader will soon see, we follow the scholars in our field by searching for the roots of intergroup variation; however, we depart from the researchers who have gone before us in that determining the source of intragroup variation ranks equally high on our agenda. At the intergroup level, we seek to understand how population-wide disparities in the contexts of emigration and immigration yield population-wide disparities among immigrant offspring, whether seen through their achievements or their behavior. By contrast, our quest at the intragroup level requires that we assess how differences in parental starting points and parental responses to the constraints and opportunities offered by the new environment produce new lines of distinction among their offspring. Once we delineate the sources of inter- and intragroup differences, as well as the outcomes affected by those differences, we then strive to discover whether differences among immigrant nationalities or differences within those same groups have the greater effect on today's second generation.

A NEW PERSPECTIVE

With few exceptions, as scholars examine the unfolding of the destinies of the second generation after migration, they do so with their backs to the receiving-country border. By contrast, we adopt an international perspective that keeps both the origin and destination country in view as we contend that the influences related to both the spanning and the delimiting of national political boundaries comprise the salient traits distinguishing the children of immigrants from all others. We underscore the shared conditions linked to place of origin that produce interethnic differences while also highlighting the household-level at-entry characteristics and subsequent life-course decisions that produce intraethnic, family-level variation. As we proceed, we bring together place of origin and place of destination, as well as identities rooted in the former and those that develop in the latter. The trajectories recounted and analyzed in the chapters that follow involve the encounter with multiple boundaries—territorial, political, and social—and the various social and political spaces within which the adult children of immigrants pursue their lives.

Figure 1.1 Schematic Summary of the Explanatory Approach

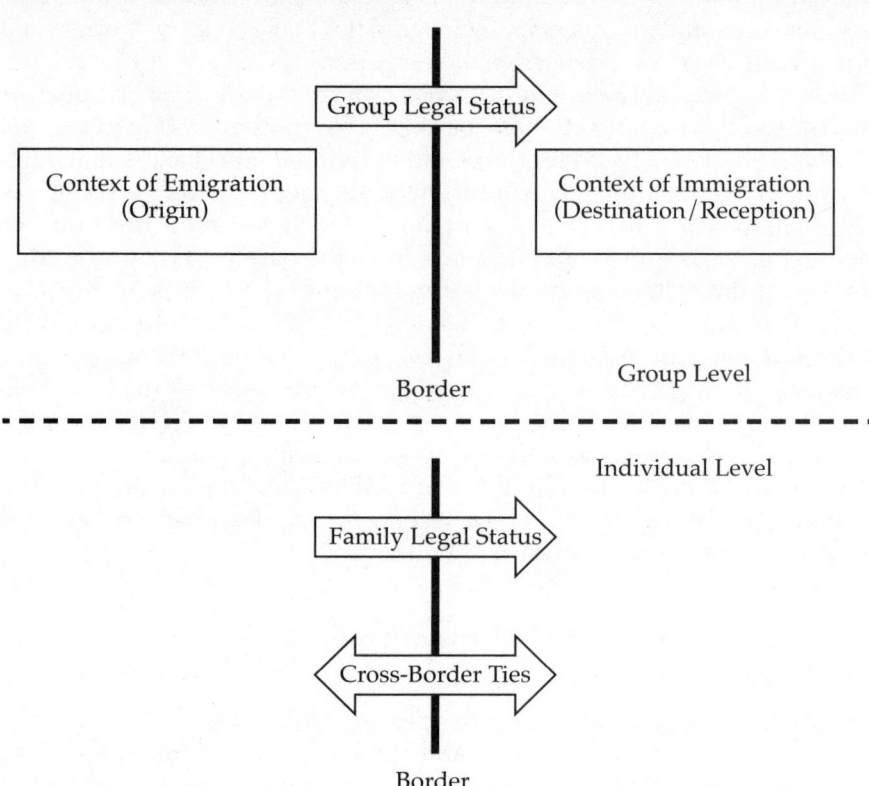

Source: Authors' compilation.

Taken together, our explanatory model includes determinants of second-generation difference that we map in a two-dimensional space, visualized in figure 1.1. On the vertical axis, we consider the *level* of influence: what are the most important characteristics of the immigrants themselves, and of the national-origin groups to which they belong, in determining a range of socioeconomic, political, and cultural outcomes? On the upper half of this axis, which we conceptualize as the contexts of emigration and immigration, lie group-level traits: the salient attributes prevalent in the sending country and in the coethnic community in the United States. The lower half includes individual factors central to the perspective advanced in these pages. Consequently, we abstract other relevant variables—all to be discussed at later points of the book—to single out only those influences that uniquely shape the experience of immigrants and their descendants, namely, their social ties to the country of origin and their family-level experiences of alien status.

On the horizontal axis of figure 1.1, we consider the *location* of influence: unlike the children of U.S.-born parents, the children of immigrants are likely to be shaped by both group- and individual-level factors that operate on *both* sides of the U.S. border. At the top right stands the context of destination factors that arise within the United States; at the top left is the context of the origin factors deriving from the parents' home countries. In the bottom half, denoting the individual-level characteristics, are individual- and family-level traits that extend across places: the international locations of significant others and the ensuing cross-border engagements, as well as the legal status at arrival, which reflects decisions made by both immigrants and states when the former are still living in the origin country.

The relative importance of these influences varies depending on the outcome under consideration. In the next section, we provide a brief general overview of these characteristics and the ways in which they are expected to impinge upon the children of immigrants.

Intergroup Differences: Contexts of Emigration and Immigration

The lives of immigrants are deeply shaped by influences that derive from the country of emigration and separate their experiences from those of all others in the country of immigration whose lives unfold entirely within the boundaries of the state where they were born and subsequently remained. First comes the simple fact that immigrants start out from someplace else: born and educated in another country, immigrants were socialized in a political, cultural, and economic system different from the one they encounter after migration. Upon their arrival in the receiving country, the lessons they learned and the orientations they absorbed in that earlier context, in tandem with their individual-level resources, then influence their understanding of their new environment and their reactions to its demands. As such, group-level variation early in immigrant parents' life course deeply affects variation in outcomes later in their lives. As those variations extend to how parents go on to raise their children, we expect that socioeconomic and cultural characteristics of the context in their home countries will influence the outcomes realized by that second generation.

Thus, unlike their U.S.-born and U.S.-bred counterparts, immigrant parents are socialized abroad, albeit in national contexts that systematically differ from each other. Upon arrival, immigrant parents and children also encounter contrasting contexts of immigration that can either constrain or facilitate their pursuit of the good life in their new home. Those contexts involve conditions that immigrants share with their conationals and that vary across groups: in the resources potentially available from coethnics, which we define as "ethnic capital"; in the degree of societal acceptance, which we conceptualize as location in the American system of "skin-color stratification"; and in exposure to the differential effects of migration policies, which we conceptualize as "migration-status disparities."

Only the last of these contextual features is distinctive to international migrants, who, unlike ethnically or racially distinctive groups of U.S. nationals, begin their American lives as foreigners starting out with at best limited rights to continued residence and social membership. International migration, unlike internal migration, involves traversing territorial borders that are gated so as to separate the relatively few who are wanted or tolerated from the far more numerous who are seen as undesirable or unacceptable. In today's globalized economy, however, the demand for migrant workers—whether of the high- or low-skilled sort—almost always supersedes the levels of permanent migration that receiving-country nationals are prepared to accept. In their efforts to reconcile the conflicting pressures of business demand for labor and consistently negative popular views of immigration, states implement migration control policies that yield a proliferation of legal statuses, ranging from the tolerated but unauthorized, at the most disadvantaged end, to those lucky enough to eventually cross the internal border of citizenship, at the most advantaged end.

For several reasons, the prevailing legal status varies from one nationality to another, furnishing an influence on intergroup differences that stems not from the place of origin but from the receiving society. From the outset, the incidence within a nationality of more protected status (refugee) or more vulnerable status (asylum seeker or unauthorized resident) affects both societal perception and the overall level of resources on which coethnics can draw if and when they turn to one another for support. Members of groups most likely to enter with rights of permanent settlement are put on the quickest path to citizenship, while groups among whom unauthorized migration is common or even prevails count many fewer members who are even eligible for citizenship; hence, group-level differences in legal status and citizenship prevalence widen over time. Although any individual immigrant may enjoy a legal status more or less advantageous than that of the median member of his or her group, that median status will still affect population-wide resources and standing, thereby yielding impacts at the individual level, with further consequences for the ways in which immigrant parents' resources affect second-generation outcomes. Thus, regardless of individual attributes, the contexts of emigration and immigration yield long-lasting effects on the experiences of the foreign-born as well as their descendants.

Intragroup Differences: Cross-Border Connections and Civic Stratification

Every immigrant is also an emigrant, simultaneously getting oriented to the place of reception while retaining ties to the people and places left behind. That duality between immigration and emigration results from the political and social logic of international migration. Since migration is selective, as we have already noted, it inevitably produces international families by pulling kinship networks apart. Over time the core network often shifts location, but rarely completely, with the inertia experienced by the elderly causing others to stay in place. In today's world, moreover, the internationalization of families reflects the additional impact of receiving states' intensifying efforts to police national boundaries. Because gaining entrance into the developed world is so hard, the people who emigrate are those who can get through or across obstacles, inevitably leaving at home those who cannot traverse the political barriers to mobility.

Thus, in departing from one country and moving to another, migrants ironically and unintentionally tie those two countries together. The migrants and their descendants reside on the *immigration*-country side of the territorial border. Yet their continuing connections to the *emigration*-country side extend their social ties across that same frontier. And because those social ties connect to significant others, they remain meaningful, yielding influence even on experiences undergone in the country of reception.

Homeland ties are pervasive, motivating both immigrant parents and offspring to expend resources and time to keep up with and possibly support the relatives and communities left behind. However, the quotidian experience of those connections varies across groups and families, with implications for their transmission from one generation to the next. On the one hand, immigrant agency matters. Immigrant parents decide whether to cut homeland ties or instead continue to remit, to call, to visit, to engage in homeland politics, or some combination of these. These efforts then serve as a model for children to follow, who then have to decide whether to follow the parental example or not. On the other hand, the maintenance of cross-border ties depends on a complex set of factors related to the location of core family members, the options and appeal of family reunification, and the communication efforts of those left behind, all of which are largely beyond the control of immigrant parents or their second-generation children. Hence, differences in the persistence of the homeland tie and its importance range widely among the adult children of immigrants, with consequences for outcomes unfolding in the country where they actually reside.

After crossing the territorial boundary, every newcomer starts as an alien confronting a series of other internal, often invisible, but vitally important boundaries, each one of which demarcates a zone corresponding to a distinctive set of rights. The first stages of a migrant's life—and more often than not, the entirety of the migrant's experience in the new country—take place in that conceptual space between the external territorial boundary and the internal boundary demarcating citizens from aliens. Consequently, immigration yields additional migrations, this time not spatial but rather political as the migrants move from one status to another. Unlike the move that brought them to the United States, impelled by their own initiative and their willingness to sacrifice for a better life, migrants have limited control over their ability to cross status boundaries. Moreover, the resources that helped them get from there to here—whether their willingness to assume risk or their ability to gain help from relatives and friends already present in the United States—prove much less useful when politicians and state officials are the people determining who can cross over status boundaries and under what conditions.

Presence in that liminal zone between citizenship and the territorial boundary does not prevent migrants to the United States from enjoying many of the advantages of life there. Yet, as long as they persist in that space, they are still foreigners, lacking the standing of "new Americans," with consequences that ramify widely and take myriad form. International migration inherently generates civic stratification as the newcomers are sorted into different statuses, each with a distinctive set of entitlements, depending on the legal circumstances under which they gained entry into their new environment.[1] Since upon-arrival rights differ, so too do the resources that immigrant parents can mobilize for the benefit of their families and transmit to their children. Those starting out furthest from the inner circle of citizenship enjoy the fewest protections, experience the greatest vulnerability to territorial expulsion, and need to leap over multiple hurdles before citizenship becomes an option. By contrast, for those beginning with rights of permanent residence, citizenship can be accessed without excessive difficulty, allowing status advantages to cumulate over time. Of course, since, for the eligible, citizenship acquisition is optional, choice comes into play, widening disparities among persons who started out with the same options. These first-generation discrepancies in legal status and citizenship all have second-generation effects, but their impacts work through different channels, depending on whether the offspring were themselves born abroad, and thus experience civic stratification directly, or instead, if born in the United States, undergo its effects indirectly via their parents.

These boundaries within and between states, the spaces between them, and the bridges across them define the terrain covered in this book. We train our focus on the adult children of immigrants, a population made up of two related, yet different groupings. One consists of those children of immigrants who were themselves born abroad but were brought to the United States as young children and raised there. For these adult children of immigrants—often labeled the 1.5 generation—the trajectories limned in the previous paragraphs provide a close match with their own personal experiences, as they too began as emigrants and became immigrants, embarking on the extended process of becoming an American, in both its formal and informal senses. But for those adult children born in the United States—let's call them the "true" second generation—the process is somewhat different.[2] The origin country and alien status lie in the background. Directly experienced by immigrant parents, those realities are often, though not always, conveyed to the children through household practices and socialization, yielding impacts that affect the children's own ability to function as full-fledged Americans who are accepted as such without a moment's hesitation. But if the children are born "here," they nonetheless grow up with relatives—sometimes their own parents—still residing "there." If they come into the world as American citizens, they usually grow up in households where at least one parent lacks that status and may have begun his or her sojourn in America in a much more precarious legal condition. If the children speak flawless English, they may nonetheless retain some facility—perhaps even complete fluency—in their parents' native tongue. On the other hand, precisely because they are Americans in fact, as well as in head and heart, they are especially attuned to the differences among the various types of ethnic Americans. Moreover, regardless of whether the children are born or just raised in the United States, they are affected by the broader social context in which they come of age.

MULTILEVEL MODEL AND ANALYSIS

Our conceptual model thus operates at two levels: at the group level of *interethnic* effects, and at the individual or family level of *intraethnic* effects. Throughout this book, in order to properly model these conceptually distinct levels, we use multilevel analysis, a statistical technique equipped with the power to assess effects generated by factors that simultaneously operate at these two levels. On the one hand, we know that the children of immigrants from some origin countries may be more or less alike compared to the children of immigrants from other countries: as an example, we hypothesize that immigrants and their offspring with roots in poorer societies may maintain stronger links to the homeland than those who come from richer societies. At the same time, we also suspect that even within the national group disposed toward tighter homeland connections, the children of parents who frequently travel back to the homeland may remain more closely tied to the sending country than those whose parents never or rarely return home. Multilevel models allow us to simultaneously test for country of origin and individual-level differences such as these. Moreover, by using multilevel models, we gain the capacity to distinguish how much of the variation in second-generation outcomes can be linked to each level separately. In other words, how well does the analysis explain differences *between groups*—those with tighter or looser homeland connections—and how successfully does it perform in explaining those same differences *between individuals*? Gaining traction over these two dimensions generates significant intellectual rewards, as the scholarship with which we will engage attacks sources of both inter- and intragroup differences. And yet, as the reader will soon see, it does so without explicitly identifying the focal level of interest and never seeks to assess the relative importance of one level as compared to the other.

The strengths of multilevel analysis are threefold. First, the unit of analysis in the second level of a multilevel analysis becomes the national origin itself. But whereas nationality is just a name—a nominal variable lacking in rank order—we can unpack theoretically relevant characteristics pertaining to both the place of origin and the population of immigrants who started out from there and turn them into measurable variables, the consequences of which can then be assessed. The growing national-origin diversity of America's foreign-origin population, which encompasses far too many national-origin groups to meaningfully compare one at a time, makes this property especially important. Thus, looking at a large number of groups, we can compare outcomes—whether involving schooling or the acquisition of citizenship or political participation—across groups among whom advantageous legal statuses are prevalent versus those among whom less-advantaged statuses, such as lack of authorized presence, are more common. And if we can identify relevant aspects of the home-country context, we can also assess the impact of differences in the prevalence of one legal status or another, controlling for those very same home-country attributes. As we will shortly explain, these two shared, contextual features—one related to the context of immigration and the other to the context of emigration—belong at the center of any effort to understand the sources of intergroup difference, as they involve the distinctive and enduring characteristics of population movements across state boundaries. And since those dimensions can also be measured—in ways that we shall soon describe—they can be converted into variables, which in turn provide the means for determining just when differences in context matter and, when they do, with what impact.

Second, multilevel models allow us to simultaneously measure the effect of individual- or family-level variation while controlling for contextual factors. They also enable us to separate the individual- and group-level influences of the same concept—for instance, educational attainment. We know that the children of highly educated parents achieve higher levels of education themselves; we also expect that, regardless of parental resources, the children belonging to immigrant populations with higher average levels of education will attain higher levels of schooling. Simultaneously modelling both parental and group-level resources in a multilevel framework allows us to separate the variation explained by a characteristic at the group and individual level. For instance, we can assess how much variation in educational attainment is explained by the average education level of the group, holding constant the education of the parent. We can also examine how much variation is explained by the educational resources of the parent while holding constant the education level of the group.

Finally, multilevel models enable us to test for interactions across levels. Keeping with the example, does parental education matter more or less in determining second-generation schooling for immigrants from coethnic communities with high levels of education, or among those immigrants from communities where the average level of education is low? On the one hand, we might anticipate that parental education will matter more when the coethnic community has fewer resources and thus less to give; on the other hand, parental education may matter more in contexts where the presence of other highly educated coethnics generates pathways by which foreigners can translate their educational knowledge into the new U.S. environment. In chapter 5, our modeling strategy enables us to properly assess the cross-level hypotheses that are a central part of existing explanations of second-generation variation.

We note that we are not the first to employ multilevel analysis to plumb the sources of difference among the second generation; indeed, European scholars have led the way, though that research has examined neither a similar set of group-level influences nor individual-level influences.[3] But following the example from the other side of the Atlantic allows us to significantly improve on previous U.S.-centered scholarship, for which the search for the sources of national-origin disparities has typically defined the overriding intellectual goal. The most innovative of recent U.S. approaches explicitly sought to move away from the old-fashioned group-by-group comparisons that almost always ended up producing an ethnoracial Olympics—this one excels, that one lags behind.[4] Instead, those investigations aspired to shed light on the way in which differences in a shared variable—a context that cumulated advantages for some groups and disadvantages for others—affected a broad range of second-generation outcomes. Unfortunately, practice diverged from theory as researchers, failing to isolate the relevant attributes of the shared context, fell back on group-specific comparisons—comparing the children of the Chinese to the children of the Mexicans, for instance, which in turn led back to generalizations about entire populations.

To be sure, these current efforts are careful to avoid anything that might smack of a cultural explanation, contending that differences between groups arise in the context of reception that immigrants encounter at arrival. Yet such scholarship is stymied by its research design, which seeks answers by pursuing pairwise group comparisons: A versus B. However, while the members of immigrant-origin group A may indeed fare differently from the members of immigrant-origin group B, the one-by-one comparison precludes the possibility of explanation: since so many attributes distinguish A from B—whether those related to the point of departure or of reception or those related to the circumstances of emigration or those involving the resources harvested before departing—the comparison of two cases leaves the grounds for adjudicating among the varying sources of influence inherently wanting. And regardless of the specific attributes that distinguish A from B, those traits are unlikely to be unique to these two groups alone; rather, if particular sets of attributes truly matter, they should be present to varying degrees across a wider set of populations. But to distinguish the relevant features, one has to abstract from the singularities associated with a particular group and identify the variables that are likely to count among immigrants coming from a broad set of countries. Doing so is all the more important now that the number of immigrant populations in the United States has multiplied: at the turn of the twentieth century, one might reasonably have asked why Jews were different from Italians, who were in turn different from Poles. However, because the immigrants and immigrant offspring of the early twenty-first century come from an ever-growing number of countries located around the globe, that exercise defies completion, necessitating the multilevel model used in this book.

Unlike other researchers, we focus only on the adult children of immigrants and do not extend the lens to later-generation members of the native population. The rationale for our self-limiting approach stems from considerations of both an intellectual and practical nature. Intellectually, we seek to understand the impact of the distinctively international influences of population movements across borders. Although we have yet to show how much those international influences matter, we can assure the reader that the demonstration will appear again and again in the pages to follow. But there is every reason to assume that the impacts of those influences will be greatly attenuated among the children of the children of immigrants, who will all be born American citizens, will be raised by parents who are all de facto Americans and mainly de jure Americans as well, and will grow up with the country of origin as an increasingly distal presence in their lives. Yet even if international factors are of much diminished importance, it follows that the differences found among second-generation adults will leave at least some imprint on the third generation. And though even further decay of international influence is likely among the great-grandchildren of immigrants, they too are likely to bear slight, but detectable, signs of it.

Demonstrating both decay and persistence among these later generations requires the appropriate data, however, whether for second-generation parents or for first-generation grandparents, and that information is nowhere available. Alternatively, one could take the standard approach, which assumes that among the native-born children of the native-born or native-raised, neither generation nor contexts of immigration and emigration nor any of the other traits associated with a foreign origin yields differences that matter. But in that standard approach, the very factors that lie at the source of heterogeneity among the second generation disappear in the comparison to a generationally undifferentiated population of the native-born children of the native-born. Since the contrast group then becomes one in which there is no variation in the relevant factors—*all* parents are citizens, *all* speak English at home, *none* retain ties to the country of origin, and indeed, country of origin cannot even be traced—the capacity to assess the impact of disparities in parental legal status, language used in the parental household, ties to home-country relatives, or home-country culture is lost.

SECOND-GENERATION DESTINIES: THE NEED FOR A SYSTEMATIC ASSESSMENT

The following pages implement the agenda sketched out here, while maintaining dialogue with the work of the insightful scholars who have gone before us and the influential books that they have written. The destiny of today's second generation has ranked high on the immigration research agenda for roughly twenty-five years, an interest first triggered by Alejandro Portes and Min Zhou's pathbreaking 1993 article on "segmented assimilation."[5] There, Portes and Zhou announced that the offspring of the new immigrants of the turn of the twenty-first century would cleave from the pattern of the past, following not one but several trajectories of adaptation. In this view, success would attend some groups, while others would be more likely to encounter a dead end; moreover, for members of the materially less advantaged groups, the road to progress would be unlocked by retaining home-country loyalties and values, in contrast to what the conventional wisdom had long maintained.

That article did not just excite the field: it served as the manifesto for an empirical research project launched in San Diego and Miami by Alejandro Portes, working in harness with Rubén Rumbaut; that work eventuated in the award-winning book *Legacies*, published in 2001.[6] Not surprisingly, so controversial an approach quickly prompted reactions, of which the most influential was probably Richard Alba and Victor Nee's book *Remaking the American Mainstream*.[7] A work of synthesis, not original research—and thus unlike *Legacies*—that book sought to update assimilation theory for the twenty-first century; naturally enough, responding to the claims of segmented assimilation ranked high among these authors' objectives. Whereas Portes and his collaborators emphasized the importance of group membership, Alba and Nee instead focused on the individual. For these proponents of "neo-assimilation" theory, the key driver of assimilation lay in the ways in which the individual search for the better life simultaneously weakened group attachments and increased the capacity to transmit resources, thereby bettering the life of the next generation, notwithstanding any prejudice or discrimination that might be encountered along the way.

Thus, these competing perspectives projected two very discrepant second-generation futures, one more pessimistic, one more optimistic. Their differing forecasts also corresponded to a divergence in views regarding the central axis of variation: did it lie *between* groups, as contended by segmented assimilation, or among individuals *within* groups, as argued by neo-assimilation theory? In breaking open the debate, these critical contributions provided the ammunition for the next round of empirical assessments, this time based on new data collection efforts conducted in the leading urban centers of immigrant America—New York and Los Angeles. In a curious way, the researchers who studied the New Yorkers—Philip Kasinitz, John Mollenkopf, Mary Waters, and Jennifer Holdaway—provided an account that echoed both segmented assimilation and neo-assimilation theory.[8] Like Portes and his collaborators, they organized their inquiry around the structuring power of groups. And yet like Alba and Nee, they perceived the advent of the second generation as pointing in a positive direction, in contrast to the gloomier view adopted by segmented assimilation theory. As Kasinitz and his coauthors saw it, second-generation New Yorkers were "inheriting the city" and benefiting from second-generation advantages linked to immigrant selectivity, the immigrants' optimism, the hybrid culture produced by the multiethnic metropolis, and the institutional legacy left by past immigrations, which would facilitate the immigrant offspring's efforts to get ahead.

Whereas this perspective born on the East Coast emphasized the advantages shared by today's immigrant offspring, the scholars who focused on the southern California scene highlighted the disparities in second-generation resources and experiences, albeit while advancing very different perspectives and using contrasting methodologies. In *Parents Without Papers*, Frank Bean, Susan Brown, and James Bachmeier brought the obstacles to second-generation progress front and center: advancing a "membership exclusion" model, these scholars underscored the ways in which differences in parental legal status—and in particular, undocumented status—shaped second-generation trajectories.[9] Though the book's subtitle—*The Progress and Pitfalls of Mexican American Integration*—pointed toward an account of intergroup differences, as a study of a single group it could only illuminate the sources of *intragroup* differences. And by emphasizing the weight of differences among individuals belonging to the same population, *Parents Without Papers* implicitly worked with the same perspective as neo-assimilation theory, albeit while introducing a variable left out of Alba and Nee's account.

By contrast, Jennifer Lee and Min Zhou sought to understand the intergroup differences lying behind the "Asian American Achievement Paradox," a puzzle that provided the title for their book.[10] Though their raw material came from qualitative interviews drawn from a selected subsample of the same large-scale survey that informed *Parents Without Papers*, Lee and Zhou chose not to engage with the "societal exclusion" model. Instead, they sought to explain the factors propelling the rapid integration of Chinese and Vietnamese immigrant offspring, contending that a complex of factors—the hyperselection of immigrant parents; their import, not of home-country values, but of specific institutions; a "success frame" endorsed by students and parents; and a "stereotype promise" maintained by teachers—led to extraordinary achievement in the narrow span of two generations, even among those immigrant offspring raised by unskilled parents lacking in English-language facility. Thus, whereas *Parents Without Papers* highlights the ways in which legal-status *disparities* among immigrant parents stemming from the same country led to educational and occupational *differences* among their children, *The Asian American Achievement Paradox* roots the *commonalities* among Chinese and Vietnamese immigrant offspring—in this case, their success—in the *shared* attributes and behaviors of their parents.

These thumbnail sketches will be elaborated at greater length in the next chapter, but for the moment they suffice to demonstrate the lively nature of the debate fostered by a quarter century of scholarship on the second generation. However, the picture we have traced here also shows that the authors of these influential works are not truly in dialogue with one another. For instance, a central divide among these works involves the emphasis that some put on the differences *between* groups versus the focus in others on the differences among individuals *within* the same group. Yet, as no major work has thus far sought to disentangle the factors that make for intergroup disparities from those that produce intragroup differences, scholars are often talking past one another. Similarly, researchers have not yet sought to systematically weigh the relative importance of variations between national-origin groups as opposed to those found within a group of people originating in the same place, nor have they assessed how the sources of difference may vary from one dimension of social life to another.

Moreover, each successive work, while building on the contribution of a predecessor, generates a new set of hypotheses, but without fully scrutinizing claims put forward at an earlier stage in the debate. Consequently, the field is long overdue for a systematic assessment of the many plausible, indeed deeply insightful, hypotheses generated by these earlier efforts to understand the experiences of today's second generation. Since that assessment hinges on a clear delineation of the issues in question, we carefully sift through the accumulated literature to spotlight the specific claims in contention and then subject those claims to the thoroughgoing test that they deserve.

THE PATH AHEAD

It is with this background in mind that we have written the pages to follow. We begin the first part of the book, "Perspectives," with a chapter that engages with the works just mentioned in a way that specifies the hypotheses advanced in each book, brings out the fundamental contrasts among these authors, and identifies the gaps remaining in this existing scholarship. Chapter 3 details our own approach, which we refer to as the "international perspective." We explain how the distinctive characteristics of international migrations—population movements across state boundaries occurring in the face of migration control systems designed to sift, select, and exclude—yield fields of influence that span international borders. We also describe how international migration creates *internal* borders that separate newcomers from native-born citizens as well as immigrants of different legal statuses. These influences specific to the immigrant experience distinguish the socioeconomic and political trajectories of the second generation from those of native-born minorities, simultaneously shaping intergroup differences while producing new forms of variation among immigrant offspring with origins in the same place. We then present our plan for putting that approach into action. We introduce objective indicators of the characteristics of the contexts of emigration and immigration that are theorized to underlie national-origin differences. We then build these attributes into a two-level model containing family-level predictors of second-generation outcomes at one level, nested within countries of origin at a second level.

The rest of the book falls into two further parts. Part II, "Transmission," engages with the theme that dominates the writings in this field: namely, the acquisition of the education, skills, and resources needed to fulfill the "American dream" to which so many of the immigrants and their descendants aspire. The focus of the two chapters in Part II will be familiar, but not so the mode of analysis. Chapter 4 contrasts our approach to the practices prevailing in the field, demonstrating the shortcomings of nationality-based comparisons and showing how our two-level approach can distinguish specific contextual effects that lie behind intergroup differences in educational and occupational attainment. In these pages, we tackle the enduring question of how best to understand intergroup differences in socioeconomic attainment by considering the impact of those shared contextual factors deriving from the context of immigration—a long-standing issue in migration scholarship—as well as those that stem from the context of emigration, which migration researchers have tended to neglect.

The following chapter drills down in greater detail, showing that second-generation schooling and occupational experiences reflect the influence of the migration process both as linked to shared, group-wide contexts of immigration and emigration and as connected to factors operating at the individual and household levels. Chapter 5 explores the sources of intra-group differences, systematically testing the hypotheses advanced in the literature discussed in chapter 2 as well as the perspective that we elaborate in chapter 3. Chapters 4 and 5 show that a consideration of contexts of emigration alters our understanding of second-generation socioeconomic attainment. Moreover, these two chapters demonstrate the value of a more disaggregated approach that opens up the black box of nationality so as to identify the specific characteristics shared among persons of common national background that are relevant to educational and occupational attainment.

The third part of the book, "Transformations," looks at the processes and impacts of boundary-crossing and boundary-straddling as well as the consequences of the time spent in that liminal social space between the boundaries of the territory and the citizenry. Chapter 6 examines the acquisition of citizenship, unraveling the features that lead some foreign-born immigrant offspring to cross the internal boundary of citizenship status while making it impermeable to others. Chapter 7 then considers political participation, a particularly strategic research site, as it gives us leverage for understanding a question that is increasingly important as the noncitizen population grows: how can noncitizens engage in citizenship, if not necessarily in the same way as status citizens?

Whereas earlier chapters treated parental and familial cross-border connections as determinants of different outcomes, chapter 8 addresses ties to the parental country of origin as outcomes in their own right and tries to explain the factors accounting for the prevalence and persistence of cross-border connections in the second generation. Looking at ethnicity, chapter 9 examines how and with whom these immigrant offspring choose to affiliate, from whom they opt to differentiate themselves, and how these patterns are affected by their distinctive backgrounds. This chapter also considers language change, detailing the shifts in language competence and preference and accounting for the sources of language retention and loss.

We conclude with a final chapter reviewing the lessons learned as this book has progressed, drawing out implications for the next generation of research and for the new America unfolding before our eyes.

SOURCES

This book mainly draws on two exceptionally valuable, indeed unique, sources of data: the Immigrant Second Generation in Metropolitan New York (ISGMNY) survey, conducted in 1998 and 1999, and the Immigration and Intergenerational Mobility in Metropolitan Los Angeles (IIMMLA) survey, conducted in 2004. These two ventures were both funded by the Russell Sage Foundation (which has also supported the writing of this book and the research on which it is based), as part of the foundation's long-term investment in the data and intellectual resources needed to understand contemporary immigration and its consequences. As the outgrowth of a single ongoing effort, these two surveys overlap in significant ways: they sought to answer similar questions, and hence both queried respondents in similar, sometimes identical, ways. Moreover, they adopted similar methodologies, namely, telephone surveys of young adult immigrant offspring ages eighteen to thirty-two in the greater New York area and ages twenty to forty in the LA metropolitan area.

In design and choice of locale, these two surveys also illustrate the promise and perils of research on this topic. In 2004, when the IIMMLA was fielded, 13 percent of the adult civilian population had at least one foreign-born parent. Although that percentage translates into a huge population, from a research standpoint, the people in that population remain relatively hard to find with an instrument like a survey. Making the highly improbable assumption that every person contacted would agree to an interview, one would have to call nearly eight thousand people in order to get a sample of just one thousand. Moreover, the geography of second-generation America makes the numbers still more unfavorable: while 13 percent of persons may be the offspring of an immigrant, that population is strongly concentrated in a handful of states, so generating a nationally representative sample of one thousand members of the second generation would require screening calls far beyond that eight-thousand-person threshold.

For these very practical reasons, the researchers responsible for these studies wisely decided to focus their efforts on the two metropolitan capitals of immigrant America, Los Angeles and New York, where the second-generation population has expanded to truly impressive numbers. Of course, that sensible choice also entailed a cost, namely, that the lessons learned from these surveys cannot be fully generalized to the national second-generation population. On the other hand, because a disproportionate share of that population resides in these two places and very sizable fractions live in similar large metropolitan areas, such as Miami, San Francisco, and Chicago, information gathered in Los Angeles and New York is likely to tell us much of what we need to know about today's emerging second generation.

Nonetheless, zooming in on New York and Los Angeles presents challenges if the goal is to capture the diversity of today's second generation. For instance, a representative survey of one thousand immigrant offspring living in Los Angeles would generate a nicely sized subsample of Mexican-origin respondents, but far too few persons of Korean, Chinese, or Filipino background for accurate subgroup analysis. And given the greater national-origin spread of New York's immigrant population, a representative survey of immigrant offspring would probably yield so much ethnic heterogeneity that subgroup analysis would be almost impossible. Consequently, both surveys engaged in quota sampling of second- and 1.5-generation groups. In total, the ISGMNY interviewed 3,415 young adults in New York City and its surrounding suburbs. The survey targeted second-generation Chinese, Dominicans, former Soviet Jews, West Indians, and Latin Americans from Colombia, Ecuador, and Peru, and it also included comparison groups of native-born blacks, Puerto Ricans, and non-Hispanic whites. The IIMMLA conducted 4,655 interviews in the Los Angeles metropolitan area—comprising Los Angeles, Orange, Ventura, Riverside, and San Bernardino Counties. Like the ISGMNY, the IIMMLA engaged in quota sampling, including Mexicans, Vietnamese, Filipinos, Koreans, Chinese, Central Americans from Guatemala and

El Salvador, and a catchall category of "all other" as well as three native-parentage comparison groups comprising third- and later-generation Mexican Americans, non-Hispanic whites, and blacks. The IIMMLA thus provides 3,309 respondents with at least one foreign-born parent, and the ISGMNY 2,430.

Though quota sampling is an imperative for the reasons noted, it has both virtues and vices. On the one hand, it generates national-origin subsamples large enough for reliable analysis; on the other hand, the result is less heterogeneity in national origin than might have been yielded by a representative survey. Fortunately, both surveys generated a good deal of national-origin heterogeneity, and more than one might have expected based on the limited number of groups for which the survey researchers aimed. Most valuable has been the IIMMLA "all other" category for some immigrant offspring respondents. This target yielded over six hundred respondents with immediate or parental backgrounds from Canada, a variety of European countries (Germany, the United Kingdom, Italy, France), and numerous Latin American countries (most notably, Costa Rica, Cuba, Honduras, and Nicaragua). Other such categorizations were less clearly of a miscellaneous nature but nonetheless involved targets more properly thought of as categories than as groups. In seeking to interview a certain quota of West Indians, for example, the New York researchers captured persons originating in a variety of different countries of origin (Jamaica, Trinidad, the Bahamas, Barbados, Guyana, and so on). Other respondents categorized alike in the sampling strategy were nonetheless diverse in their national origins: the Chinese respondents came from Taiwan, Hong Kong, and mainland China, and the Soviet Jews originated in Russia, Ukraine, Uzbekistan, and Belarus. Greater national-origin variance is of course a source of greater analytic leverage. And as we will explain in chapter 3, the capacity to make many fine-grained national-origin distinctions helps shed significant light on the ways in which contexts of emigration affect outcomes in the society of reception.

Both the IIMMLA and ISGMNY are cross-sectional surveys that provide a snapshot of this population at one point in time. As survey researchers know, the liability of the cross-sectional approach lies in the difficulties it poses to the drawing of causal inferences. For example, in this field we are often interested in the relationship between some behavior that is thought of as "ethnic"—such as retaining fluency in the tongue of one's own or one's parent's country of origin—and some other outcome, such as obtaining U.S. citizenship. But with cross-sectional data, it is hard to determine whether it was the preference for maintaining mother-tongue fluency that led someone to refrain from obtaining U.S. citizenship, or whether concern about the symbolic importance of citizenship acquisition led that person to make the effort to retain mother-tongue fluency. Thus, with information of this sort, the best we can say is that there is an association between language and citizenship (at this point, an utterly unfounded hypothesis), but not that one causes the other.

We have looked to chronology to gain leverage on causality: that a preceded b does not mean that a caused b, but it certainly precludes the possibility that causality could have gone the other way around. When some of the chronologically prior events of interest to us were not precipitated by the people whom we are analyzing but by someone else, we rule out reverse causality. As we examine, for example, the influence of place of birth—whether in the United States or abroad—we recognize that the relevant decision was made by parents, not children; hence, we need not worry that a child's preference for being born in the United States or elsewhere influenced some later outcome. Since the large majority of the foreign-born persons found in these surveys arrived in the United States at a very young age (75 percent arrived by age ten), we can also preclude the possibility that their preference for life in the United States might have provided the motivation for their migration. In the analyses to follow, we are particularly interested in the influences transmitted from parents to children, whether related to the parents' immigration experiences and statuses, aspects of their socioeconomic characteristics, or the household practices to which our respondents were exposed as children. Given this concern, we have tended to rely more on the IIMMLA than the ISGMNY, as the former provides greater in-depth information on events occurring prior to adulthood as well as parental attributes of importance. Moreover, the IIMMLA collected particularly detailed information on both parents' and, for the foreign-born members of the sample, respondents' legal status at the time of entry into the United States as well as at the time of the survey. With this information in hand, we can then begin to understand how the distinctively political nature of international migration influences second-generation trajectories, which is another reason why the chapters to follow make special use of the IIMMLA.

We are greatly indebted to the social scientists who designed and implemented these pathbreaking surveys: Philip Kasinitz, John Mollenkopf, and Mary Waters, who fielded the ISGMNY; and Rubén Rumbaut, Frank Bean, Leo Chavez, Jennifer Lee, Susan Brown, Louis DeSipio, and Min Zhou, who were responsible for the IIMMLA. Compounding our debt to these scholars has been our reliance on the issues that they deemed important and the questions that they decided to ask, which, by and large, have proved exceptionally wise, as we believe readers will come to agree as they read the pages to follow.

We note that considerable time has elapsed since the ISGMNY and IIMMLA were fielded, and in a social world in constant flux—all the more so on our ever more globalized planet—the picture captured toward the beginning of the millennium is likely to be somewhat different from what we would see if we could return to the field now, toward the end of the twenty-first century's second decade. Nonetheless, the changes that have transpired since immigrant-origin New Yorkers and Angelenos were interviewed for the ISGMNY and IIMMLA are modest when considered in the light of the recurrent fundamentals—displacement, the internationalization of families, adaptation, alien status—that shape the process of migration and settlement. Moreover, the important differences that might distinguish the present moment from the years when the ISGMNY and IIMMLA were conducted do not represent novel features, absent at that earlier time, so much as the further development of tendencies already then in place. To be sure, legal status now has a more powerful impact than it did at the turn of the twenty-first century, and the liabilities experienced by undocumented immigrants have surely grown. Yet these aspects of today's immigrant experience are fully incorporated into our analysis, as our perspective emphasizes the centrality of status prevalence at the intergroup level and citizenship and status on arrival at the intragroup level. Furthermore, the bias produced while using data collected at an earlier time when migration controls were not enforced as severely as they are today is downward, a shift that should be concerning only if the variables related to legal status consistently prove irrelevant. As the reader will see, the analysis recurrently demonstrates the importance of status-related variables, providing reason to think that we would find similar, though probably stronger, results were we able to access more recent data.

The ISGMNY and IIMMLA represent the last major effort to survey America's second generation and thus provide the best opportunity to demonstrate the utility of the international perspective we develop and the multilevel models we employ. Because so many of the previous major works have been based on these same data, returning to these sources provides an excellent opportunity to test competing hypotheses. We now move on to the next chapter, which takes stock of the current field before illustrating the ways in which the model outlined in figure 1.1 complements and extends these existing perspectives, the task to which we turn in chapter 3.

Part I | Perspectives

Chapter 2 | Bringing the International Back In: A New Perspective

MIGRANTS SHARE THE common experience of leaving home to settle in a foreign land, but they depart for a myriad of reasons. Some move abroad simply to support a survival strategy back home that takes advantage of global inequality: they work where wages are high to maintain family members residing where the costs of living are low. Others depart with plans to relocate permanently, whether to improve their lifelong earnings, to benefit from public goods, like education, that are more available in the country of destination, or simply to enjoy the safety and security experienced by all the residents of the developed world, including foreigners. Still others are compelled to move, forced out by war, persecution, or natural disaster. But whatever their motivations, the majority of migrants choose to adjust to a world different from the world they knew before departure; their adaptations, in turn, affect the possibilities available to the next generation.

On the one hand, the twin decisions made by immigrants—opting first for displacement and then for adaptation to the new context—yield a second-generation landscape that looks vastly different politically, socially, and economically from the setting confronted by the first generation: typically, when compared to their parents, the children of immigrants more closely resemble the children of natives. On the other hand, the narrowing of difference goes hand in hand with enduring heterogeneity, involving persistent intergroup disparities as well as the intragroup differences that make for diverging trajectories among immigrant offspring sharing the same national origin. To a large extent, these inter- and intragroup differences stem from the point of departure: immigrant offspring resemble the native-born children of native-born parents at least to the extent that parental disparities in resources, skills, and interpersonal competencies shape the lives of all children. Despite this similarity, an essential background difference separates the children of immigrants from their native-origin counterparts. Most importantly, elements inherent to the migration experience structure their destinies: the cultural and economic development of their parents' countries of origin; the social and legal context of their parents' departure from their original home and their entry into their new home; their ties to family members and significant others remaining in the home country; and the decisions that they and their parents make in adjusting to a different and initially strange environment. The lasting legacy left by all of these distinctly international elements of immigrants' lives results in second-generation life trajectories that unfold differently from the life trajectories of children of the native-born.

In the previous chapter, we briefly introduced the conceptual model we use to explain the divergent pathways taken by the children of immigrants—pathways determined in part by circumstances linked to their specific national origins and in part by features shared by all those whose parents crossed international boundaries in search of a better life. The international perspective that we advance is meant to synthesize and extend—rather than replace—existing scholarship on the second generation in two ways. First, we seek to build on the insights generated by the researchers who have come before us, incorporating them into a multilevel model that simultaneously takes into account group-level and individual-level sources of differences. Second, we do so in a way that keeps in view the persisting intergenerational legacy of population movements across borders, the characteristics of the society of origin, and the influences of the new context into which immigrant parents enter.

In this chapter, we review the works of the key scholars on whom we build and consider the most influential book-length analyses of second-generation trajectories and their determinants. As we show here, these previous works have pursued one of two goals: either using national-origin comparisons to explain intergroup sources of difference or providing in-depth case studies of specific national-origin groups to uncover intragroup sources of variation. Although both are worthy goals whose pursuit has resulted in valuable findings, all of the studies to be discussed in this chapter have employed research designs that leave their accounts of second-generation variation incomplete. Comparing a handful of national-origin groups can provide qualitative accounts of interethnic difference, but as with any small-N sample, too many variables lie behind observable differences and too few cases are available to establish the needed controls. Case studies of individual nationalities can similarly reveal mechanisms that lie behind intergenerational continuity and change for any one specific group, but they do not allow generalization to the second-generation population as a whole. Only one previous effort, *Legacies*, displayed the needed sensitivity to the differences between inter- and intradimensions; yet this application of the hypothesis of segmented assimilation failed to explicitly recognize the distinctive nature of these two dimensions and did not implement the multilevel model needed to examine them.

In this chapter, we return to the key prior works briefly discussed in chapter 1, reviewing the lessons they have taught, highlighting the issues they have elided, and explaining how these contributions fit into a more comprehensive multilevel model of individual- and group-level variation in second-generation outcomes. Chapter 3 explains how we implement that model.

SECOND-GENERATION TRAJECTORIES: THE PLAY OF THE DEBATE

Legacies and the Hypothesis of Segmented Assimilation

Controversy has swirled over the destiny of today's second generation, ever since the early 1990s, when Alejandro Portes and Min Zhou published a now-famous article claiming that assimilation could have both positive and, more startlingly, negative consequences. The hypothesis of segmented assimilation advanced by Portes and Zhou provided the guiding framework for Portes and Rumbaut's pioneering Children of Immigrants Longitudinal Study (CILS), which surveyed a group of foreign-origin middle school students in Dade County, Florida, and in San Diego in 1992, surveyed them again as high school students in 1996, and met up with them a third time in 2000–2001, when they were young adults. The results from the first two waves provided the raw material for Portes and Rumbaut's book *Legacies: The Story of the Second Generation*.

The electric effect of the hypothesis of segmented assimilation stemmed from three related claims: (1) that assimilation could have both negative and positive consequences; (2) that the most vulnerable immigrant offspring would achieve better outcomes if full assimilation was delayed by at least one generation; and (3) that those who failed to delay full assimilation would experience downward assimilation into an underclass. While such iconoclasm had the positive consequence of generating immense interest among researchers, it also directed their attention to the most inflammatory but also most elusive claims. "Downward" assimilation is inherently difficult to conceptualize, much less demonstrate, in regard to the children of immigrant parents who already stand at the bottom of the social structure.

And the notion of an "underclass," drawn from the worlds of journalism and politics, is inherently contested, making it very difficult to assign the concept any neutral, commonly agreed upon definition.[1]

Nonetheless, when stripped to its essential elements, the hypothesis of segmented assimilation offers a coherent and plausible account of the sources of interethnic differences: it is a two-level model that emphasizes the impact of context, on the one hand, and the role of family-level strategies, on the other. The second, "higher" level places mode of incorporation—a contextual variable shared by all members of the group—at the heart of the process. Understanding it as comprising three dimensions—migration policy, reception by the native population, and characteristics of the coethnic community—Portes and his collaborators hypothesized that the mode of incorporation would yield varying effects: if positive, it would enhance the benefits of immigrants' individual-level resources or compensate for their deficiencies; if negative, it would override the benefits of individual-level resources and enlarge the fallout from any deficiencies. To quote Portes and Rumbaut, the mode of incorporation

> condition[s] the extent to which immigrant human capital can be brought into play to promote economic and social adaptation. No matter how motivated and ambitious immigrants are, their future prospects will be dim if government officials persecute them, natives consistently discriminate against them, and their own community has only minimum resources to offer.[2]

In thus setting the conditions for first-generation settlement, the mode of incorporation would in turn influence the options available to immigrants' children, either providing immigrant parents with the material and social resources needed to navigate the difficulties caused by adaptation to a new, strange, and sometimes threatening environment or depriving them of those resources.

Nested within the second contextual level of the mode of incorporation is the first, lower level consisting of individual immigrant families and the strategies they deploy to facilitate or hinder successful adaptation. In considering this level, the hypothesis of segmented assimilation focuses on those familial practices or characteristics that could either offset or exacerbate the problems associated with a negative mode of incorporation operating at the intergroup level. The reasoning is straightforward: in the encounter with a difficult and foreign environment, internal cohesion becomes of paramount importance for immigrant families, especially for those with few material resources at hand. Yet the situation confronted by immigrant parents invariably generates threats to family unity: the children grow up as natives in an environment that parents find at least somewhat strange. Not fully understanding that environment, and often not fully mastering the language needed to navigate it, the parents lack the tools for guiding their children, a deficiency aggravated when parental skills or earnings are low. Brought up in the society of immigration, the children later develop desires, expectations, and behavioral patterns that the parents neither share nor have the material capacity to meet. Additional stresses to familial cohesion come from the external environment. Like all other children, immigrant offspring grow up exposed to the consumerist, hedonistic, individualistic ethos of the contemporary world, which universally erodes children's respect for authority and hierarchy both within the family and beyond it. Unlike many other children, however, the offspring of working-class or poor immigrant parents grow up in neighborhoods where local solidarity is limited, other families are likely to be fragmented, institutional resources are few, and problems abound. Within the neighborhood and beyond, authorities and gatekeepers treat the offspring of working-class immigrants with suspicion; the experiences of prejudice and discrimination in turn erode commitment to the search to get ahead.

Under these conditions, the hypothesis of segmented assimilation contends that immigrant children of working-class parents are most likely to fare well when parents pursue "selective acculturation," a strategy that facilitates the transmission of familial values from parents to children and increases parents' capacity to usefully assist their children. The key is a household environment that produces shared parent-child experiences and greater intergenerational continuity; a home in which the mother tongue prevails exemplifies such a cohesion-producing setting. The critical role played by selective acculturation in reinforcing familial cohesion lies behind the seemingly paradoxical claim advanced by the hypothesis of segmented assimilation: that under certain conditions, slower, more selective acculturation proves more advantageous than the type of continuous, across-the-board adaptation forecast by assimilation theory, whether in classical or neoclassical form.

In this book, we take this two-level hypothesis seriously, using the appropriate statistical techniques to examine the effect of group-level constraints and opportunities, family-level processes of acculturation, and the interaction between the two. In so doing, we demonstrate, for instance, that family-level strategies—such as use of the parents' language in the childhood home—do *not* yield an appreciable effect on second-generation progress; however, we also show that access to certain ethnic resources, such as after-school foreign language schools, *can* yield positive effects, albeit only for the children of less-educated parents. By allowing the impact of individual-level strategies and characteristics to vary with the characteristics of groups through cross-level interactions—while embedding these characteristics in a larger model that seeks to understand variation across a range of second-generation outcomes—we substantially improve upon previous empirical tests of these claims. The chapters to follow will provide a complete assessment of this two-level hypothesis, but here we linger on the ambiguities and contradictions found in the key texts associated with segmented assimilation to explain why scholars have had such difficulty in subjecting this approach to an adequate evaluation.

Portes and his various coauthors advanced the concept of "mode of incorporation" in order to abstract from nationality and identify the underlying variable by which nationalities get sorted into more or less advantageous contexts. They presented the three dimensions of the mode of incorporation as aspects of a reception context that immigrants encounter as "an objective reality."[3] Although immigrants neither set immigration policy nor determine the ethnic and racial attitudes of the native-born population, the same cannot be said for the coethnic community, which is likely to have imported at least some relevant aspects from the society of emigration. Indeed, the point is implicitly recognized when *Legacies,* for example, finds a negative association between West Indian nationality and children's residence in two-parent households and ascribes it to a "trait of the societies of origin," in this case "the relative family instability in the English-speaking Caribbean."[4] Likewise, *Legacies* notes immigrant parents' discomfort with "the permissiveness of U.S. culture," which in turn leads them to think that "'becoming Americanized' is a negative"—perceptions necessarily requiring a contrast to a home-country culture where different norms prevail.[5] Similarly in emphasizing the mechanisms that link parents' desire to educate children in "home-country ways" to the avoidance of "dissonant acculturation," Portes and his collaborators again highlight a legacy of home-country orientations almost surely acquired before emigration, which in turn affect second-generation experiences.[6] Thus, despite the repeated emphasis on the context of reception, home-country culture creeps in through the back door, a tendency that also appears in the other books that we review here.

Notwithstanding this conflation of contexts of emigration and immigration (or origin and reception), the concept of mode of incorporation moved beyond previous ad-hoc comparisons of selected nationalities and thus represented a large conceptual leap forward. Yet rather than operationalizing and measuring the concept, Portes, Rumbaut, and their coauthors fell back on the conventional method of pairwise national-origin comparisons, contending that national origin is "a suitable empirical proxy for modes of incorporation."[7] Thus, in *Legacies* the authors maintain that "dichotomous variables representing major individual nationalities . . . provide direct indicators of modes of incorporation, since the history of early reception and settlement of each of these groups is known."[8]

That procedure might work if the number of groups were very small and their histories were so clearly discrepant that an analyst could accurately situate them in modes that were more or less advantageous. Yet it fails for the larger purpose of developing a more general model of second-generation outcomes in a society with an increasingly diverse immigrant-origin stock. The proliferation of groups and the fine differences among them make it impossible to use nationality as a reliable indicator of the underlying concept; in such a case, either disparate groups are collapsed together (as with "Asians" or "Latinos") or only a small number of national-origin groups are examined in any detail, with the rest relegated to a residual, catchall "other" category. Although these strategies provide important insight on some key comparisons, neither can satisfactorily test the concept. For example, how are we to know that it is actually the more positive governmental reception that resulted in superior outcomes for the children of Cubans compared with the children of Mexicans, when the Cuban advantage could also derive from the strong middle-class tilt of their coethnic community, as opposed to the predominantly working-class immigrant Mexicans, or the more positive societal reaction to the differences in skin tone between the two populations, Mexicans being somewhat darker than the generally lighter-skinned Cubans? Without a large number of countries that differ across these dimensions, how can we systematically assess the effect of one dimension while holding the others constant? Consequently, the proponents of segmented assimilation have been caught in a circular loop, contending that knowledge of each nationality's mode of incorporation provides the basis for predicting nationality effects, but then using the coefficients from dummy variables for specific nationalities as evidence of the importance of mode of incorporation.

Another source of ambiguity involves the conditions under which strategies of selective acculturation are likely to yield positive results, a question never fully clarified in the relevant writings. One might argue that these strategies will prove advantageous under all conditions, regardless of whether the mode of incorporation is positive or negative or whether parental resources are high or low. Yet the logic of the overall framework works against this possibility, as material success allows immigrant parents, like their native counterparts, to turn to the market—acquiring therapy or tutoring or private college advisers or moving to a superior school district—to offset difficulties or inadequacies found in the home environment. By contrast, materially constrained parents need to find solutions by using informal, nonmaterial, though not necessarily ineffective, resources.

Therefore, insofar as ethnic strategies represent a tool for guarding against the threats to familial cohesion, their impact is most likely to kick in when the context is unfavorable or parental resources are few. Hence, the appropriate hypothesis forecasts that when a negative mode renders a group's circumstances unfavorable, practices that sustain familial cohesion will produce offsetting effects. Put somewhat differently, at the intergroup level, the hypothesis of segmented assimilation advances mode of incorporation as a *main effect* that has a positive, negative, or neutral impact on the resources available to *all* members of an ethnic population and in turn generates *interethnic* differences. By contrast, at the intragroup level, the hypothesis emphasizes the *interactions* between cohesion-producing family strategies and group-level modes of incorporation, such that the impact of a negative mode of incorporation could be either blunted or enlarged depending on whether or not families choose to implement strategies that promote parent-child cohesion. It is this interaction that should lie at the source of *intraethnic* disparities, with the impact of the mode of incorporation varying across immigrant families who come from the same origins but differ in the extent to which they use those ethnic strategies to promote intrafamilial cohesion. Though this interaction between the first level involving familial and individual traits and the second level pertaining to group characteristics lies at the heart of the hypothesis of segmented assimilation, it too has never been comprehensively tested.[9] The chapters to follow will provide a long overdue assessment of this influential approach.

Inheriting the City and the Second-Generation Advantage

The hypothesis of segmented assimilation launched the debate over the destiny of the second generation on a note of inflected pessimism: *Inheriting the City*, an award-winning 2008 book coauthored by Philip Kasinitz, John Mollenkopf, Mary Waters, and Jennifer Holdaway, sought to respond to this bleak prognosis. Based on a mixture of qualitative and quantitative data and focusing on the experiences of Chinese, Russian Jews, Anglophone Caribbeans, Dominicans, and Latin Americans from Colombia, Ecuador, and Peru in New York, this book made the case for a "second-generation advantage." In the main, that second-generation edge is *not* the product of the strategies of ethnic retention so strongly foregrounded by the hypothesis of segmented assimilation. Rather, the advantage possessed by these immigrant offspring New Yorkers in part reflects the processes that selected their own parents for migration. It also results from the environment encountered in New York: post–civil rights institutions promoting diversity and constraining discrimination as well as the hybrid culture produced by the encounter between the global and the local that turns the in-between status of the second generation into a plus.

Although the concept of second-generation advantage appeals, the sources of that advantage are shared by all second-generation New Yorkers; consequently, the authors struggle to explain interethnic differences. High levels of parental human capital, they contend, account for the strong performance of the Russian Jews, and yet the Chinese, who are equally if not more successful, are more likely to come from more humble origins. The latter, the authors suggest, succeed for a variety of reasons: family strategies involving the pooling of income and high rates of labor force participation provide resources for children; a high level of social class diversity combines with cross-cutting ethnic networks to circulate information and social support throughout the community; a positive context of reception yields diminished discrimination, especially in the housing market; and imported cultural orientations reinforce familial cohesion. Ironically, these latter mechanisms actually bear a remarkable resemblance to those singled out in *Legacies:* it is precisely by maintaining some elements of their homeland culture that certain immigrant parents provide their children with options that mainstream peers may not find open to them or may not accept as feasible choices.

These hypotheses are certainly plausible, but as the Chinese are the only group in the study to share all of these positive features, we cannot know if their impact would be generalizable to other groups, nor which particular combination is necessary for second-generation success. Like *Legacies*, *Inheriting the City* explores only a portion of the possible national-origin comparisons. Thus, though the authors present the Chinese as the group with the greatest immigrant advantage and express a good deal of disquiet regarding the future of Dominicans, the authors neither systematically describe the pattern of intergroup differences that distinguish all five of the groups under study nor inquire into the factors that might make the experience of the Latin Americans different from that of the West Indians, who in turn might not undergo the same trajectory as the Dominicans. Last, as in *Legacies*, home-country culture enters through the back door, with speculations regarding its effect on the Chinese having no parallel in the treatment of other groups.

At the core of the book, moreover, lies an argument about groups:

> We hope that our evidence will convince the reader that these groups are in some sense real, not just our own nominal creation. Indeed, we think that the data make clear how group membership shapes people's lives. Time after time in the pages that follow we will present evidence that even after controlling for all the other relevant variables we have measured in our study, there is still a group effect that we cannot explain away.[10]

Although not inherently objectionable, this contention that the group effect cannot be explained away nonetheless begs the key question: Yes, the group effect stands in for *something*. But what exactly that something might be is difficult to determine. To be sure, the authors of *Inheriting the City* do consider the factors that may underlie group differences. For instance, they argue (correctly in our view) that "it is better to be part of a poor group that has some well-off members than a uniformly poor group," and similarly, that effects are likely to follow from group-level differences in legal status.[11] But in the absence of an effort to rank nationalities according to these (or any other) criteria, the systematic evidence needed to support these claims never appears.

We also note that the populations profiled in *Inheriting the City* are characterized by a good deal of heterogeneity. The Chinese, for example, stem from Hong Kong, Taiwan, and mainland China, each of which has generated migration streams with distinct social class characteristics; though ethnicity may be shared, spoken languages differ such that the Cantonese-speaking garment worker from Hong Kong will be unable to communicate effectively with the Mandarin-speaking doctor from Taiwan. The West Indians are an even more heterogeneous group: more respondents had roots in Jamaica than in any other Caribbean country, but the Jamaicans still made up a minority of this subsample. Though the West Indians share some important commonalities, the repeated failures at forming a federated state among the Anglophone Caribbean nations suggests that the differences among the nationalities are unlikely to be trivial. And there is certainly no evidence to suggest that persons from Ecuador, Colombia, and Peru think of themselves as part of a single collectivity.

On the other hand, in its critique of the hypothesis of segmented assimilation, *Inheriting the City* does highlight a mismatch between the theory's emphasis on individual-level strategies aimed at cohesion—such as transmitting fluency in the parents' mother tongue—and the actual record of success: the Chinese, the most successful of the second-generation New Yorkers, were actually the most likely to lose mother-tongue competency. Yet this point conflates the group level and the family or individual level: it may well be that most Chinese immigrant offspring lost fluency in Chinese with no adverse effects on their education or occupation. However, that finding does not speak to the relevant segmented assimilation claims regarding family-level strategies and responses to disadvantage, claims that involve intragroup, *not* intergroup, differences. Consequently, the issue in question concerns the impact of strategies aimed at familial cohesion where other resources, whether at the group or family level, are lacking. In contexts of deprivation and disadvantage—such as those experienced by the offspring of low-skilled garment and restaurant workers from Hong Kong, which contrast with the experience of children of college-educated Taiwanese engineers or doctors—do efforts that strengthen the ethnic bond, such as transmitting the parental language to children, yield positive impacts or not? Answering questions of this sort requires clearly distinguishing between group- and individual- or family-level characteristics and using the statistical techniques that allow one to appropriately do so—precisely the goals pursued in this book.

Parents Without Papers and Membership Exclusion

Two books published in 2015 provide the view from the West Coast, both drawing on data collected from the 2004 Immigration and Intergenerational Mobility in Metropolitan Los Angeles survey, on which our book draws as well. *Parents Without Papers,* written by Frank Bean, Susan Brown, and James Bachmeier, uses quantitative data from the large-N survey to explain "the Progress and Pitfalls of Mexican American Integration."[12]

These authors advance a new perspective, labeled the "membership exclusion" model, which moves away from the conventional assimilation approach with its emphasis on the differences between strangers and natives. Instead, they emphasize the ways in which the distinctively political nature of international migration yields migrants who not only fall outside the circle of citizenship but differ in legal status and entitlements from the get-go: "right from the beginning, legal status—or, more generally, societal membership—is crucial for integration." Although sensitivity to the impact of migration policy is not totally new, the authors contend that "formal lack of societal membership reflects such a powerful force adversely influencing integration that it warrants its own designated perspective." For Bean and his coauthors, undocumented status exemplifies membership exclusion and its effects. Analyzing the first-, second-, and third-generation Mexican-origin respondents surveyed by IIMMLA, they show that parents' unauthorized status yields long-lasting effects, most importantly among those Mexican immigrants whose mothers arrived without authorization and never succeeded in gaining legal permanent residence. Transitioning from unauthorized to legal status, however, represented a turning point that "forestall[ed] the scarring of immigrant families" and allowed the children of legalized immigrants to perform comparably to those of their peers born to parents who entered legally.[13]

This book provides powerful insight into the way in which undocumented status shapes *intragroup* heterogeneity within a specific group: Mexican immigrants and their descendants. Although the book's subtitle—*The Progress and Pitfalls of Mexican American Integration*—suggests that the prevalence of unauthorized status distinguishes the Mexican American experience from the experience of groups among whom unauthorized status is uncommon, it is actually a case study of a single group; as such, its main contribution is at the intragroup level, explaining the sources of difference among those of a single national origin. We learn that among Mexican Americans, individual-level differences in legal status matter above and beyond the standard variables related to assimilation, such as years of residence or generation, and acculturation, such as language practices in the home.

Moreover, the book tells us that membership exclusion is just one, albeit powerful, component of a broader sociocultural complex, partly rooted in the country of origin, that shapes the attainment of Mexican immigrants and their offspring. The decision to depart made by these migrants, who came mainly from rural Mexico, was one element of a family strategy designed, at least in part, to diversify sources of income and minimize risks. After they arrived in the United States, their obligations to family members still residing in Mexico continued to shape their behavior; the cultural model imported from a scarcity-conscious rural environment inclined these immigrants toward interdependence rather than the autonomy valued by middle-class American culture. Consequently, the migrants' unauthorized status fostered the "development of family-related cultural repertoires," which were accentuated by the resemblance between circumstances at the point of origin and those at the destination. In sum, low wages, instability, and vulnerability to exploitation "combine to create an overwhelming need to rely on and provide for one's family."[14]

Thus, although it emphasizes the "made in the U.S." impact of legal status, this book, just like the other works reviewed in this chapter, acknowledges the home-country legacy, but without foregrounding it. While the findings reported in *Parents Without Papers* are intriguing, as a case study the book simply cannot shed empirical light on which of the traits—the high level of membership exclusion, Mexicans' strong familial orientation, or some other characteristic such as their long history in the United States or geographic proximity to the country of origin—most powerfully distinguishes Mexican immigrants from other groups, which might also share some, but not all, of these features. Answering these more general questions requires a very different approach, namely, a comparison of numerous immigrant-origin populations differing in their degree of membership inclusion, whether high, medium, or low. We implement precisely that strategy in this book.

The Asian American Achievement Paradox and Minority Cultures of Mobility

Jennifer Lee and Min Zhou's *The Asian American Achievement Paradox*, another award-winning book, draws on the qualitative interviews collected as part of the IIMMLA project. The paradox to which the authors address their book concerns the exceptional achievement of the children of Asian immigrants, "including those whose parents were penniless immigrants and refugees when they arrived in the United States, have only an elementary school education, do not speak English, and work in ethnic restaurants and factories."[15] Much of the literature contends that the values imported by parents offset other resource deficiencies, but Lee and Zhou argue instead for a more limited conceptualization of sending-country culture, highlighting the ethnic resources and institutions, such as after-school programs, that spring up in immigrant communities in the United States. Although these ethnic resources, as well as an orientation that Lee and Zhou call the "success frame," represent imports from the country of origin, the hyperselectivity of the immigrant flow ensures that these ethnic institutions provide the toolkit needed for academic success. Elaborating a "model of minority cultures of mobility," Lee and Zhou contend that when combined with the "stereotype promise" that Asian immigrant children encounter in schools and other mainstream institutions, hyperselectivity, ethnic resources, and the success frame yield exceptional academic performance.

Thus, while drawing from the very same research project that informed *Parents Without Papers*, Lee and Zhou develop an argument focused at the intergroup level, emphasizing the distinctive combination of imported cultural expectations, parental socioeconomic resources, and the social context encountered by Asian American immigrants and their offspring. These expectations and resources are contrasted to those of Mexican Americans, who serve as a foil against whom the high-achieving Chinese and, especially, Vietnamese are compared. In particular, their identification of the stereotype promise for Asian Americans, entailing privileged expectations and treatment by educators and peers, marks a break with the hypothesis of segmented assimilation, which underscores the importance of the policy context and posits that the societal reaction to all non-European migrants is negative.

However, while *The Asian American Achievement Paradox* claims to explain an Asian American phenomenon, it examines the experiences of immigrant offspring from just two countries of origin, Vietnam and China, a surprising lacuna considering that the IIMMLA contained abundant information about two other Asian American populations, Koreans and Filipinos. Despite the vast heterogeneity in the socioeconomic and migration histories of the Vietnamese and Chinese, the authors claim that their success can be explained by a common set of factors, at least some of which arise from majority-group perceptions of Asian Americans. Yet Filipinos, whose Asian-origin group has been similarly positively selected and who enjoy a professional profile like that of the Vietnamese and Chinese, do not experience the same kind of exceptional success. With this group left out of view, one wonders which of the ingredients that make for Chinese and Vietnamese achievement—stereotype promise, ethnic institutions, the success frame—may be missing among the Filipinos. Or is some other group-level cultural indicator, such as religion (82 percent of the Filipinos surveyed by the IIMMLA were raised as Catholics, a trait they shared with the most-disadvantaged Central American groups, in contrast to only 6 percent of the Chinese and 29 percent of the Vietnamese), a potential cause?

Moreover, in emphasizing what sets the Vietnamese and Chinese apart from the Mexicans, the book fails to probe the ways in which the Chinese and Vietnamese on whom they focus might not all be the same. For instance, we read that "*nearly all* of the [Chinese and Vietnamese respondents] framed success in terms of a good education; *nearly all* used the same markers to frame a good education."[16] That could well be so, yet the disparity between the reported view that an "A minus is an Asian fail" and respondents' actual reports of school performance—their high school average GPA was not an A but rather a B (3.4)—provides further reason to think that these Chinese and Vietnamese immigrant offspring were far from homogeneous.[17] Similarly, an account more attentive to intragroup differences might explain why, for instance, one in eight Chinese and nearly one in three Vietnamese in the IIMMLA sample had failed to obtain a university degree by age twenty-five.

The purported consensus, among parents as well as children, also stands in contrast to the underlying demographic and national-origin diversity of the respondents. In both New York and Los Angeles, these immigrants and immigrant offspring from Southeast Asia and East Asia were not all the same, reflecting only inconsistent evidence of hyperselectivity and significant variation in parental educational resources depending on whether they originated in Taiwan, Hong Kong, mainland China, or Vietnam. Indeed, since most of the ethnically Chinese respondents surveyed in Los Angeles were the children of college-educated Mandarin speakers from Taiwan, it is not clear that their academic achievement, while impressive, in any way poses a paradox. That paradox could have been more fruitfully explored had Lee and Zhou instead focused on the New Yorkers, among whom a substantial proletarian segment was to be found. Yet even in New York City, though the children of working-class immigrants did remarkably well, their performance fell far short of exceptional. Only a minority of the most positively selected Taiwanese ethnic respondents (21 percent) had attended (or were attending) the highest-prestige universities, and there were far fewer among those from Hong Kong (9.6 percent), the most proletarian group. These disparities among the New Yorkers of varying origins in China would seem to underscore the importance of exploring the sources of intraethnic as well as interethnic differences.

Finally, Lee and Zhou emphasize that the combination of selectivity, ethnic capital, and public institutional resources explains the success of the Chinese and Vietnamese they interview. Unlike the Mexican-origin respondents interviewed, these groups demonstrate a high prevalence of the success frame—and the ethnic resources to scaffold it. Yet, while this combination of factors seems to come together perfectly in the young second-generation groups they study—and is generally absent, according to the authors, from their Mexican-origin peers—what effects might we anticipate if a success frame were found among almost all immigrant groups, but in greatly varying degree? And if the authors of *Parents Without Papers* are right about the powerful negative impact of membership exclusion, can we not anticipate that the membership *inclusion* experienced by the Chinese and Vietnamese would yield correspondingly strong positive effects? The answer to questions of this type can only be found with the variation present in a more comprehensive sample of origin countries— precisely the approach we take.

Remaking the American Mainstream and Neo-assimilation Theory

Thus far, we have focused on works of empirical scholarship that used qualitative and quantitative techniques to analyze data collected from immigrant offspring. This section pivots to a discussion of Richard Alba and Victor Nee's now-classic book, *Remaking the American Mainstream*. Though a work of synthesis, not original analysis, this book has been deeply influential, and because it arose in response to the hypothesis of segmented assimilation and sought to provide an alternative direction, its consideration is directly relevant to our intellectual goals.

Assimilation has long provided the master concept for understanding the transformations undergone by immigrants and their descendants. Yet, until recently, the most influential contribution provided no more than a typology of the different dimensions of assimilation, leaving the underlying force behind the process largely untheorized.[18] In 2003, however, publication of *Remaking the American Mainstream* finally provided the compelling, coherent perspective that the field had long needed. Since dubbed "neo-assimilation" theory, this effort drew power from its apparent parsimony. As most recently summarized by Richard Alba:

> In the contemporary institutional context, a principal mechanism of assimilation is simple enough: minority and immigrant-origin Americans seek to improve their social and material circumstances, and some assimilation often occurs as an unintended consequence of their efforts. The perception of opportunities motivates individuals to undertake changes that have assimilatory consequences, whether they are understood that way or not. And since, on average, opportunities are greater in the mainstream than they are in ethnic communities, individuals are also motivated to attempt to enter mainstream settings—in residence, in the labor market, and in other ways. It is useful to think of these opportunities in a broader way than the concept of upward socioeconomic mobility. For the second generation, improvement in social and material circumstances might translate into the ability to avoid an immigrant job (with its humiliations and incessant demands) or to own a home in a neighborhood suitable for raising one's family.[19]

In this rendition, purposive, rational choice constitutes the motor force of assimilation. Moreover, the nature of the decisions made after migration stem from the very considerations that led migrants to leave home in the first place: namely, the search for a better life.

This view positions immigrants as strangers confronting a strange environment; because the needs of survival force them to learn to adapt to that new world, the immigrants increasingly become like the people among whom they have chosen to live. Impelled to pick up competencies that diminish the costs of strangeness, immigrants slowly, almost imperceptibly, change their behavior in small, incremental steps, each one of which makes the next advance a bit easier. Thus, the cumulative, continuous nature of the process renders the strange familiar, while yielding results that validate the original search for a better life. As time passes, immigrants steer their way through the formerly foreign world without thought, using newly acquired skills to demonstrate competence in ways that bring recognition and reward and yield exposure to an entirely different mix of people than those known before leaving home.

Because assimilation so perfectly matches the immigrants' fundamental goals, few of them can escape it, even those who do not embrace assimilation and in fact may wish to avoid it altogether. Yet, as depicted by Alba and Nee, immigrants' adaptive strategies are merely the proximate causes of assimilation, yielding results only if and when they encounter an environment that rewards them and their descendants for connecting with the mainstream and adopting its practices.

Earlier waves of immigrants—most notably those from Mexico, Asia, and the Caribbean—were not greeted by such an environment and instead found that discrimination by the majority thwarted ethnic minority effort and mobility. In the post–civil rights era, contend Alba and Nee, changes in U.S. policies "extending civil rights to minorities and women have increased the cost of discrimination in non-trivial ways."[20] Consequently, by switching to English, acquiring higher-level skills, or moving to a safer neighborhood where out-group contacts are more plentiful, all immigrants and their offspring can now access a better future. Since acting otherwise imposes unacceptable costs, most new Americans select "mainstream strategies," thereby progressing toward assimilation. Hence, the institutional environment provides the distal causes of assimilation, steering the immigrant search for progress in ways that gradually but inexorably produce the decline of an ethnic difference.

Neo-assimilation theory compellingly explains the mechanisms that transform migrants and their descendants, leading them to increasingly resemble the people among whom they have chosen to live. Yet neither immigrants nor their descendants are all the same, and so we still have to ask whether this theory can account for both inter- and intragroup differences and, if so, how. Indeed, a careful reading of *Remaking the American Mainstream* reveals Alba and Nee to be grappling with just these questions, though in ways that significantly complicate the perspective they seek to advance.

For the most part, their book emphasizes the importance of the intragroup, individual, or household characteristics. Though immigrants and their children, as well as native-born Americans, may all engage in the purposive search for a better life, just as Alba explained, *Remaking the American Mainstream* makes it clear that they are likely to do so in different ways, in large measure as a result of disparities in the human and cultural capital that immigrant parents import from the place of origin. Unlike the mass migrations of the turn of the twentieth century, made up overwhelmingly of unskilled laborers, socioeconomic diversity is the distinctive characteristic of today's newcomers. Some degree of heterogeneity in education and occupational experience is found among almost all immigrant populations, regardless of whether they are mainly composed of highly educated professionals or unskilled laborers. Whereas the hypothesis of segmented assimilation contends that the coethnic community, a stand-in for group-level cohesion and educational and occupational resources, will shape the ability of all members of the group to realize their goals, Alba and Nee take the opposing view. Instead, they argue that the "forms of capital" model advanced in their book "predicts that immigrant professionals and their children, whether Chinese [a mainly high-skilled migration] or Mexican [a mainly low-skilled migration], are likely to have a similar pattern of entry into the American mainstream."[21]

Though this emphasis on the centrality of intragroup, individual, or household variables aligns with their overall approach, Alba and Nee also observe that entire "ethnic groups can be seen as broadly differentiated from one another on the basis of the forms of capital they typically bring." Moreover, nodding in the direction of segmented assimilation and invoking its vocabulary, they note that trajectories of adaptation may actually correspond to differing, group-level socioeconomic profiles: "For some groups, especially human-capital immigrants, assimilation is shaped mainly by individualistic adaptation. Others—traditional labor migrants with a low stock of human and financial capital in particular—follow a collectivist pattern in which network mechanisms shape the trajectory of adaptation."[22]

Alba and Nee also observe that migrants' purposive activity is context-bound, which is why their pursuit of self-interest is not simply propelled by the abstract utility maximization of economics but also shaped by culturally propelled perceptions and beliefs. As illustration, they sketch the portrait of an undocumented Mexican immigrant whose migration was

> shaped relationally, motivated by concern for his family as opposed to his immediate self-interest . . . [and whose] choices are not well accounted for by the "thin" rationality assumptions of neoclassical economics, as they are embedded in the cultural belief that a man ought to be willing to sacrifice for the well-being of his family. The normative content of such cultural beliefs imparts direction and purpose to the rational action of individuals . . . young Mexican people who cross the border at night and experience the uncertain circumstances of underground lives as illegal aliens in migrant labor camps have more than their own immediate self-interest in mind, as reflected in the high volume of remittances sent by undocumented migrants to their families.[23]

Thus, as with the other authors whom we have reviewed, Alba and Nee invoke home-society culture while only allowing it to enter through the back door. Yet, whether home-society culture is an intragroup variable—pertaining only to those immigrant households in which migration was launched in order to support the survival of core family members still living back home—or whether it might also be an intergroup variable—reflecting a broadly shared home-country propensity to view family life as fundamentally interdependent—is never addressed. By contrast, cross-border ties clearly belong to the family of individual or household variables. Yet in noting that kinship relationships can extend across borders, Alba and Nee never consider the implications of those persistent loyalties—as manifested in the sending of remittances—for the trajectories that unfold after migration. Since survival migrations usually lead to two-way exchanges—migrants send remittances while stay-at-homes care for children, elderly parents, and property—the rational choice for migrants with cross-border ties may not entail entry into "the mainstream" but rather continued investment in ties to stay-at-homes and coethnics. By contrast, the newcomer who has moved with core family members in tow may be prone to focus on the single-minded search for a better life in the place of destination.

Ultimately, in attempting to disentangle the proximate causes of assimilation, Alba and Nee evoke both intergroup and intragroup dimensions, though an intragroup model emphasizing the importance of household and individual characteristics provides the best fit for the neo-assimilation theory that they elaborate in their book. By contrast, in rooting the distal causes of assimilation in the institutional environment that immigrants encounter in the labor market, they are less attuned to the distinctive institutions produced by a system of migration control.

Alba and Nee see labor market institutions as monitoring discrimination, whether based on race, religion, or gender, and enforcing norms of fairness and equal opportunity. The institutions of migration control similarly engage in monitoring and enforcement. However, the latter institutions are designed to discriminate in favor of citizens and against foreigners, regardless of the country from which newcomers arrive. Moreover, since developed states simultaneously want to exclude most foreigners while admitting certain selected types, who in turn enter with greatly varying residence rights and differing entitlements for employment and social provision, systems of migration control inherently produce categorical differences that cannot simply be changed through immigrants' purposive behavior but require the intervention of state agents whose actions lie beyond immigrants' control. Those same conflicting pressures lead developed states to tolerate the presence of a large noncitizen population that gets turned into de facto citizens precisely by the process of social assimilation that Alba and Nee describe. Yet native-born citizens insist on keeping de jure citizenship hard for foreign-born de facto citizens to obtain; in turn, citizens use the barriers to citizenship acquisition as instruments of discrimination against people whose residence should give them the right to join the people of the state in which they have chosen to live. And by impeding naturalization, citizens reinforce the stigma inevitably associated with a foreign status. Thus, in the language of statistics, migration control institutions comprise omitted variables, which is why straightforward application of neo-assimilation theory, as presented by Alba and Nee, is likely to produce biased results. Indeed, *Parents Without Papers* implicitly advances just this argument: while resembling *Remaking the American Mainstream* in that it emphasizes the importance of intragroup variation, this book differs from *Remaking the American Mainstream* in contending that parents' exclusion from political membership proves deeply consequential for their children. We similarly correct for the omission of migration control institutions, though, like Alba and Nee and unlike *Parents Without Papers,* our scope extends to a broad cross-section of the immigrant population and not just a single nationality.

EXTENDING THE CANON: TOWARD AN INTERNATIONAL, MULTILEVEL PERSPECTIVE

Though a critical assessment, this review also shows how much we have learned from the research on which we build. Portes and Zhou's 1993 article on segmented assimilation remains a seminal work, both because it launched a new research field and because it advanced an entirely new, and hence stimulating, perspective. As applied in *Legacies*, the idea of context of reception provides an ingenious way of conceptualizing the substantive content of nationality, even if the application of the idea leaves something to be desired. Though departing from segmented assimilation in significant ways, *The Asian American Achievement Paradox* furnishes a new way of thinking about the concept of "coethnic community"—one component of the context of reception—and insightfully identifies the psychosocial elements that might underlie group-level differences. Whereas the hypothesis of segmented assimilation contends that differences in the reception context generate intergroup differences, *Remaking the American Mainstream* cogently identifies the individual-level mechanisms that can flatten those differences, whether they derive from place of origin or reception. In many ways, *Inheriting the City* demonstrates the power generated by the assimilative processes theorized by Alba and Nee, though the book's emphasis on the tenacity of group membership cuts against the grain of the model developed by the authors of *Remaking the American Mainstream*. *Parents Without Papers* adds specificity to the concept of policy context by zeroing in on one specific aspect to show how legal status differences can yield disparities even within a population encountering a negative reception context. Yet, in highlighting the importance of legal status as a source of intragroup difference, the authors of *Parents Without Papers* also introduce a variable at once missing from, and orthogonal to, the approach taken by neo-assimilation theory.

The remainder of the book builds on these foundational contributions. We adapt the idea of context of reception elaborated by Portes and Rumbaut in *Legacies* and other works by developing new concepts that correspond to the different components of the context of reception and define these components in ways that allow us to identify objective, fine-grained measures of the features that combine to create the context of immigration. Our implementation of the indicators that align with each feature—the group-level prevalence of legal statuses, whether favorable or unfavorable; potential access to coethnic resources, understood as ethnic capital; and a group's position in a skin-color stratification system that reflects the degree of societal acceptance—feeds into our systematic assessment of the theoretical approaches summarized in this chapter. Using objective, standardized measures of the culture of origin, we assess directly the role of the specific ethnic institutions underscored by Lee and Zhou, and we similarly search for the cultural features that might facilitate second-generation mobility, as proposed by *Inheriting the City*. Finally, as already mentioned, we apply the insights of the social exclusion model developed in *Parents Without Papers* to the full range of immigrant groups in the New York and Los Angeles surveys. Thus, in some sense, our work is a work of synthesis, bringing together many different viewpoints in a first comprehensive assessment.

However, this book seeks to do more. We also aim to *extend* the current canon through an international perspective that accounts for both intra- and intergroup variation. As this extensive review has shown, our current understanding of differences among the children of immigrants in the United States suffers from two crucial gaps. First, the literature has yet to conceptually recognize and empirically analyze the multilevel structure of second-generation inequality. On the one hand, outcomes for the children of immigrants, like those for all children, are shaped by the characteristics of their family and home environments. On the other hand, unlike the children of the U.S.-born, the children of immigrants are clustered within a higher level of national origins, the characteristics of which directly affect their opportunities and constraints while also potentially determining how family-level processes will unfold for them.

Second, all of the books that we have discussed take a view that never extends beyond the country of immigration. Consequently, the frameworks they advance leave their analyses limited to social ties and statuses held in the United States while ignoring the characteristics of the countries of origin and the persistent ties linking those places to immigrant parents and their offspring. Moreover, in standing with their backs to the border, these authors similarly neglect the transition from sending-country national to receiving-country foreigner, and finally to receiving-country permanent resident and citizen. Only *Legacies* and *Parents Without Papers* begin to consider the ways in which migration control strategies affect second-generation outcomes, and neither does so comprehensively: *Legacies* attends only to group-level effects, and *Parents Without Papers* looks only at effects operating at the family or individual level. Neither book considers the impact of sending-country characteristics and cross-border ties.

In the following chapter, we outline the ways in which we will aim to close these two gaps, employing a multilevel conceptual and empirical model of second-generation variation that includes characteristics of both the receiving and sending contexts, as well as individual-level ties between the two, and that can be applied to a variety of domains. Building on the knowledge imparted by the existing scholarship, we work with a more comprehensive model that includes contexts of both emigration and immigration, cross-border ties, and civic stratification, all working as independent variables to explain variation across socioeconomic, sociocultural, and political outcomes. We have also benefited from the primary data gathered by other scholars. Combining two excellent second-generation surveys that allow, for the first time, sufficient variation in national origins has enabled us to employ the multilevel statistical models we use here. As the next chapters will show, our approach yields new insight into the importance of cross-border ties and sending-country culture in the lives of the second generation, as well as the ways in which legal status impinges on the lives of immigrants of many different national origins across a variety of domains.

Chapter 3 | The International Perspective

THIS BOOK PRESENTS an expanded model of the approaches reviewed in the previous chapters, seeking to incorporate the strengths of those approaches while addressing their weaknesses. Our model centers on four understudied concepts: two at the first level of intragroup difference, and two at the second level of intergroup difference. We include both sending-country characteristics (the context of emigration) and group-level legal status prevalence as second-level predictors of second-generation outcomes and as potential confounders and moderators in observed relationships that unfold within the receiving country. Then we predict intragroup variation in cross-border ties in the second generation that not only are outcomes of interest in their own right but may explain intragroup differences in status attainment and in political and social outcomes. Finally, we acknowledge the influence of first-level variation in both parental and own legal status and citizenship on second-generation outcomes.

When modeling the impact of these variables on outcomes of interest, we rely on temporal ordering to better capture causal effects. Having been socialized in the country of origin, parents depart home, leaving part of the kin network behind. They then learn to make their way in a new environment, forming families and raising children who subsequently progress through school and later begin independent lives, creating new families and embarking on careers of their own. Each prior event in the chain affects the next, though in highly contingent, indeterminate ways. Parental education, the context of emigration, and the reception context at the point of parental entry affect the resources available to immigrant children and the experiences they undergo in the households in which they are raised. These at-entry conditions retain their influence over subsequent developments, but in more distal ways, with more proximate effects exercised by the circumstances confronted by children in their parents' household as they grow into maturity. Some conditions are shared by immigrant parents of a common origin—the prevailing culture of the society of origin, the home country's polity, the warmth (or chill) of the receiving-society welcome, and the overall selectivity of the migration.

Alongside the shared at-entry conditions producing *intergroup* differences, however, are those that create family-level variation *within* groups—most importantly, parents' socioeconomic level and legal status and their connections to kin, both those in the new home and those in the old one. At the group level, the contextual characteristics facing immigrants either constrain or enable the trajectories of their children; similarly, entry into the United States initiates a process of status attainment for immigrant parents that shapes the trajectories of both their children and the children of U.S. natives in similar, though not identical, ways. These parameters of constraint nonetheless leave considerable room for individual agency and choice. In particular, parent and child life course decisions related to maintaining or severing ethnic ties—such as whether to retain or abandon the home-country language, or whether to seek a coethnic spouse or cross ethnic lines—furnish a further source of *intragroup* differences in social boundaries, possibly moderating the impact of at-entry conditions on intergroup disparities.

The international perspective we introduce here is both expansive and comprehensive; however, advancing such a broad conceptual framework poses the added challenge of operationalization in the analysis stage. Proponents of the prevailing approaches—whether neo-assimilation or segmented assimilation—have relied on nationality as an indicator for developing between-group comparisons. Yet nationality is a name, not a variable. To be sure, nationality may be deployed as if it were a variable, but in that case the distinctions made between one nationality and another are purely nominal, as nationality itself offers no basis for ranking. That deficiency might matter less for a two-group comparison, especially if the nationalities differ significantly on either some premigration or postmigration attribute. Yet, since nationality inherently conflates aspects related to *emigration* and *immigration*, such carefully controlled comparisons are the exception, not the rule. The problem is only exacerbated when the migrations become more diverse, not only in terms of a growing number of source countries but also with respect to the increasingly differing circumstances under which migrants enter the country. Consequently, we offer a different approach, one that uses variables instead of names and that disaggregates the theoretically relevant, different features of nationality.

In the remainder of this chapter, we elaborate on the key variables that initiate and then propel the process outlined in the previous paragraphs, focusing on the core elements of the international perspective that we advance to explain second-generation outcomes: the context of emigration, legal status, and cross-border ties. These elements constitute the main contributions of this book. Rather than provide a new theory of assimilation or integration, we show that consideration of the specifically international aspects of population movements across boundaries yields effects not just before and during but also *after* migration. We explicitly model influences stemming from both the source and destination countries, as well as the ties between them, to shed new light on the experience of the children of immigrants and on the trajectories they follow.

CONTEXTS OF EMIGRATION

Prevailing approaches, as we saw in the previous chapter, take migrants' arrival in the country of destination as the point of analytic departure. Yet the adult immigrants who were the parents of the children we study did not arrive in the United States as blank slates, indistinguishable except for their context of reception. Rather, they came from specific places, with specific cultural, political, and economic conditions. No one can be thought of as a perfect representative of the norms and values of their country of origin.[1] All immigrants, however, will have been socialized in a context that was not of their choosing, and thus we can conceptualize the characteristics of the country of origin—the context of *emigration*—as an exogenous influence on the lives of immigrants. Although this influence may vary in its strength, it is a rare person who can completely escape the forces of socialization in her country of birth. In much the same manner, children do not choose their parents, and thus children's socialization is heavily influenced by the behavior and expectations of their parents, who themselves grew up and were socialized in an environment very different from that encountered by their children. To some extent, parents are likely to impart the same lessons they learned as youngsters, without necessarily knowing how well the lessons they absorbed in the origin country are likely to apply to the world in which their children will mature. Consequently, we expect associations between origin-country conditions and second-generation outcomes for two main reasons.

First, the largest benefits to migration accrue to those leaving poor countries in order to capture the higher wages, greater safety, and superior amenities to be found in rich ones. Thus, the socioeconomic differences between countries that send the most immigrants and the countries that generally receive them tend to be large. In moving from the developing to the developed world, migrant parents arrive with models of behavior and interpersonal relations that fit conditions at the point of departure, but that may be at variance with the models prevailing in the place where they settle, and which their children rapidly absorb. Even though we know that immigrants from more socially traditional countries, such as Poland, tend to be more liberal in their values and orientations than the average nonmigrant, they generally are far less liberal on issues such as homosexual rights or gender equality than the average receiving-country native in wealthier western Europe.[2]

Given potentially large differences between conditions in sending and receiving countries, it is unlikely that the parenting and home environments of the children of immigrants of different origins and the native-born can realistically be assumed to be similar. To be sure, not all foreign-born parents will maintain mind-sets that are equally foreign: those with more education, greater dominant-language capacity, and higher incomes are likely to have had more exposure to their native-born counterparts and therefore to be somewhat more similar to them. By contrast, the imprint of the home-society culture is likely to linger longer and to be transmitted with greater force by those immigrants who, for reasons of skill, language, or legal status, live and work in ethnically encapsulated worlds. It may also be the case that the cultural norms of the context of emigration are actually beneficial—a hypothesis central to both *Inheriting the City* and *The Asian American Achievement Paradox*. Moreover, parenting generally begins relatively early in an immigrant's sojourn; typically immigrant children are being raised at a time when the receiving society still seems strange to their family and the imprint of the home society remains powerful. And of course, socialization for many of the foreign-born immigrant offspring studied in this book began outside U.S. boundaries and hence before U.S. tastes and models of behavior had begun to influence their parents.

The second reason why we expect to find associations between origin-country conditions and second-generation outcomes is that national histories affect the origin-country orientations that migrants may take with them. Though countries may currently share similar levels of economic development, history yields substantial cultural differences related to earlier influences, whether distal or relatively proximate, or whether based in prior religious traditions or political regimes. For instance, eastern European and East Asian countries with Communist histories were secularized much more rapidly than other sending countries, and one result is that immigrants from these countries tend to be less traditional than the average U.S. citizen, as reflected in lower rates of religiosity, higher rates of female labor force participation, and higher academic performance after adjustments for economic standing.[3] On the other hand, immigrant-sending countries with Catholic backgrounds, such as those in Latin America, and highly observant Muslim societies in Africa and the Middle East display stronger gender differences and greater adherence to traditional patriarchal structures than might be expected from their economic standing alone. Similarly, experiences with democracy and transparent governance only imperfectly vary with economic well-being. Once again, many of the former satellite nations of eastern Europe stand out for their histories of repression and foreign control, with lasting impacts on levels of trust and political participation.[4] By contrast, many immigrants from Central America, whether official refugees or not, fled countries characterized by civil unrest, high levels of political repression, and corrupt, unrepresentative regimes, and hence they are also likely to bring different experiences of political participation and attitudes toward official authorities.

Acknowledging the likelihood of such heterogeneity, popular culture and political discourse commonly link sending-country orientations and values to different outcomes among the children of immigrants within the receiving country. The attribution of the higher attainments of Asian Americans to "superior" cultural traits is perhaps the most common example, as evidenced in the writings of popular and controversial authors such as Amy Chua.[5] More insidious and less open, but perhaps just as influential, is the reverse attribution, as when poorer outcomes—for instance, those among Mexican Americans—are linked to cultural deficiencies. Mainstream social scientists have reacted skeptically, correctly viewing this popular discourse surrounding immigrant culture and second-generation outcomes as rooted in political agendas. Yet, as we saw in chapter 2, scholarship on the second generation repeatedly, though usually implicitly, invokes the importance and influence of the context of emigration in explaining mobility patterns that deviate from the general norm. Rarely, however, does the scholarship identify the explicit characteristics of sending countries that are likely to explain differences across different origin groups.

Hence, the task before us is to develop a wider account of origin contexts, one that can travel across myriad source and destination countries and that can explain how disparities in origin characteristics systematically yield differences among members of the second generation. Such a systematic account of origin effects on second-generation outcomes requires standardized information on a large number of sending countries that displays the necessary variation in sending-country characteristics anticipated to affect second-generation outcomes. Prior research has often been unable to identify a sufficiently large number of source countries and the necessary variation; even when the appropriate data are available, deciding which measures to use in order to capture the impact of sending-country cultural background is difficult. Scholars have used indicators ranging from the level of globalization to the religious background of the origin country, to the degree of democratic expression as shown by indices such as the World Bank's Worldwide Governance Indicators (WGI) of Political Stability and Absence of Violence.[6] Of course, some characteristics of the sending country—for instance, its political stability—should be more likely to influence political participation or naturalization, whereas other indicators—such as mean level of education—should be more closely linked to the academic performance of the second generation.[7] Ideally, we would wish for a parsimonious yet comprehensive measure of sending-country culture that would exert an impact across a variety of domains.

In this book, we conceive of origin-country variations in culture as origin-country variations in *values*. Cultural values can be loosely defined as identifying those objects, conditions, or characteristics that members of a society consider important, or valuable. We expect the strong heterogeneity in the economic standing and religious and political traditions of the many sending countries to the United States to result in important differences in the values that immigrants bring with them and later impart to their children. For instance, immigrants to the United States tend to come from countries where physical well-being is less taken for granted, and hence objects, conditions, and characteristics that ensure survival are expected to be more strongly valued among these immigrants. Economic scarcity promotes a value system that privileges internal solidarity and discourages autonomy and self-expression.[8] Where the household remains a unit of production, as in rural communities, individual existence outside the household is tenuous; the household's survival itself requires respect for parents, loyalty to the family, and responsiveness to its needs. In developing countries, even those living in urban areas exhibit family patterns rooted in agrarian structures, since parents and children may still work alongside one another in small units of production. Thus, immigrants from more survival-oriented societies are likely to model stronger familial interdependence and reciprocity than the average U.S. parent. The outcomes are potentially advantageous, as when children study hard and excel at schooling as part of an "immigrant bargain" with their parents.[9] They could also be disadvantageous, however, as when parents' expectations of financial support from children detract from the time the children can invest in education, or when parents pull children out from schooling altogether.

Similarly, the children of immigrants from countries that place more—or less—value on religion and other forms of traditional authority may experience a different form of socialization than U.S. natives, with lasting effects on their social, political, and economic outcomes. The United States is somewhat of a religious outlier among highly developed countries in that, unlike more secular European receiving societies, immigrant religiosity has traditionally served as a "bridging" mechanism to the mainstream.[10]

This may not be the case, however, with other traditional values: with its early expansion of mandatory primary and secondary schooling alongside intense investment in higher education and, most recently, its fervor for technological change, the United States has shifted away from traditional forms of respect for the elderly and long-established authorities. Consequently, the children of immigrants from more traditional cultures may experience greater emotional difference from their parents and frequently clash with them, with repercussions for the transmission of ethnic attachments as well as for socioeconomic achievements.[11]

In short, we anticipate that immigrants will bring with them more than just a set of unique toolkits specific to a single outcome such as educational attainment; rather, we conceptualize the broader context of emigration as a key source of differences in the values that orient the lives of immigrant parents and therefore as an influence that shapes the lives of their U.S.-raised children, across a wide variety of domains. To provide a framework for conceptualizing such differences in cultural values, we draw on two measures from the World Values Survey (WVS), a massive data-gathering effort of harmonized measures of cultural indicators from around the world. In particular, we rely on the most influential discovery deriving from decades of research with the WVS: the existence of a high degree of correlation in a wide range of values and orientations at the country level. As it turns out, a large portion of the world's variation in values across a variety of dimensions (see the appendix for demonstrations) can be mapped across only two dimensions, which can be concisely described as orientations toward self-expression and free thought, on the one hand, and toward rational and secular values, on the other. These two underlying value dimensions are captured by two scales derived by Ronald Inglehart and his collaborators from the World Values Survey and widely used as summary measures of both individual-level and macro-level value orientations.

The scale measuring orientations toward the traditional versus the secular-rational reflects the contrast between societies in which religion is very important and those in which it is not. Strongly linked to this dimension are a range of values associated with deference to authority—whether that of God, the government, or the father—the importance of child-parent ties, and standards based in traditional family values. Traditional societies value religion and authority, and they condemn euthanasia, divorce, and abortion; secular-rational societies take the opposite view.

The second scale measures a country's location on the continuum between survival and self-expression values. This second major dimension is linked to the transition from industrial to postindustrial societies and includes items on democratic self-expression (for example, signing a petition) and the level of priority given to economic and physical safety relative to self-expression and quality of life. Self-expression-valuing societies include developed countries where there is less familial interdependence and emphasis is given to individual choice, autonomy, attention to the environment, and increased tolerance for diversity.

Together, these two dimensions explain 71 percent of the variation in the ten variables used by Inglehart and his collaborators to construct them (see appendix) and are highly correlated with a variety of other values, making them ideal summary measures. The country-level variation in these two scales is summarized in Inglehart and Welzel's global "Cultural Map," which displays ninety-seven countries in two-dimensional space, the x axis representing the movement of societies from more traditional toward more rational and the y axis movement from more survival-oriented toward more self-expressive.[12] Figure 3.1 reproduces that map, with points for all of the countries represented in Inglehart and Welzel's work; the major U.S.-sending countries present in our data are drawn as circles scaled according to the number of respondents in our data. Circles without shading are countries where data from the WVS are not available and we rely on multiple imputation (for more information on the imputation process, see the appendix).

As displayed in figure 3.1, self-expression tends to rise with secular-rationalism, largely because both orientations are driven by economic development. However, for a variety of historical reasons, most societies fall at some distance off the diagonal, as exemplified by both the United States and many of the most prominent immigrant-sending countries. In the United States, economic development has generated a relatively strong (though by no means the strongest) predisposition toward self-expression, yet a much lower level of secularism than that experienced in most other countries of the developed world, which are clustered in the upper right-hand quadrant. Indeed, the United States is a "deviant case, having a much more traditional value system than any other postindustrial society except Ireland."[13] This "exceptionalism" has been noted by other political scientists and sociologists, who observe that the United States is characterized by a greater level of political conservatism that emphasizes a minimal state and voluntary rather than state organization, coupled with weak working-class organization and strong approval for laissez-faire capitalism.[14] The persistence of religious beliefs and traditional attitudes toward inequality in the United States aligns it with many Latin American countries on the traditional versus secular-rational scale, even as it falls along the same lines as many western European countries in values toward self-expression.

Historically specific factors have similarly produced great variance among the societies of *emigration:* both Confucianism and communism

Figure 3.1 Location of Immigrant-Sending Countries in the Traditional Versus Secular-Rational and the Survival Versus Self-Expression Value Space

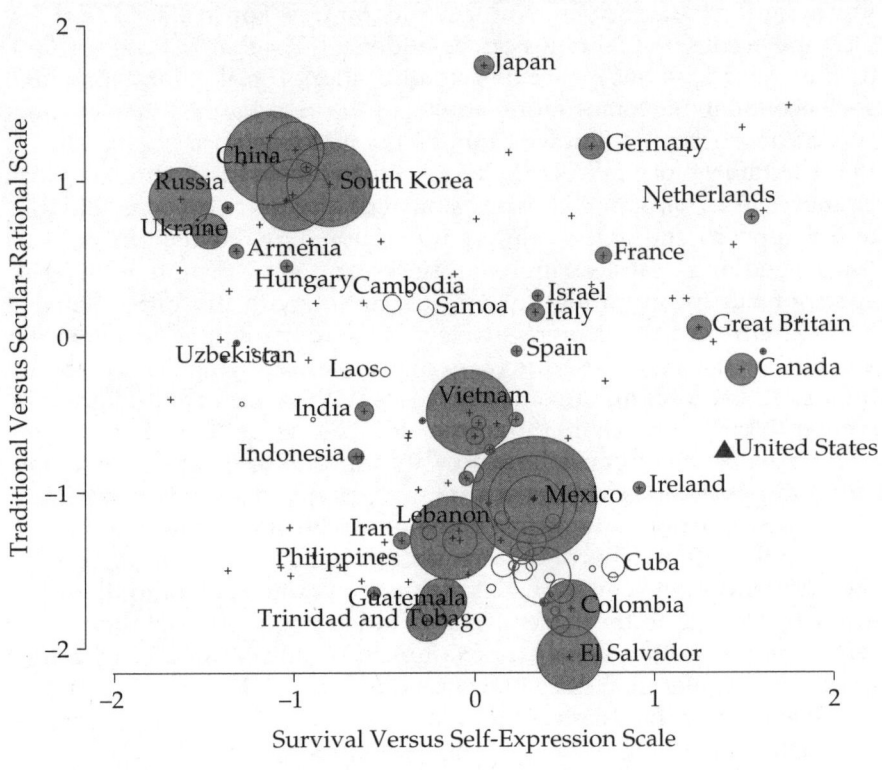

Source: Based on Inglehart and Welzel 2005 using multiple imputation at the country level.

promoted a secular-rational outlook, but both also constrained the growth of self-expression. By contrast, Catholicism proved less conducive to secularism, but more permissive of self-expression. Although survival orientations are almost always stronger in the major sending countries than in the United States, the map shows that they are characterized by both higher and lower levels of secularism than the United States: some countries are clustered in the upper left-hand quadrant of the value space (China, South Korea, Taiwan, Russia) and others in the central/lower left-hand quadrant (Vietnam, Mexico, the Philippines, Colombia, El Salvador).

These summary scales provide a parsimonious measure of sending-country values and cultural orientations, which are continuous, quantifiable, and substantiated through decades of research. They also offer insights not immediately apparent from readings of the traditional "Asian advantage" or "Latino disadvantage" literatures. For instance, Anthony Ocampo argues that Filipinos can be understood as the "Latinos" of Asia, as they tend to show patterns of acculturation, social assimilation, and socioeconomic outcomes more similar to those of Latinos than of other Asian Americans.[15] When we examine the map in figure 3.1, we can see that the Philippines falls squarely within the cluster of Latin American countries in terms of its self-expression and secular orientations, and thus at the opposite end of the value space occupied by the majority of other Asian sending countries. Similarly, we see a strong variation in the value space of European immigrant-origin groups, with those from former Soviet-controlled states more strongly clustered among Asian countries and those (relatively few) from western Europe occupying the upper right quadrant, comprising the only countries with levels of self-expression similar to (or greater than) those prevailing in the United States.

As already mentioned, we know that migration is selective, across value dimensions as well as demographic and socioeconomic dimensions: the value orientations of those people who opt to emigrate may differ from the orientations of those who choose to stay. On the other hand, the differences between countries, as shown in figure 3.1 (and discussed at greater length in the appendix), are indeed very large; similarly, the within-country differences—for example, by education—are typically a good deal smaller than the between-country disparities.

We anticipate that this variation in value orientations in the countries of socialization of immigrant parents will influence a range of outcomes, especially, but not only, educational attainment. Greater orientations toward secularism and rationalism are strongly associated with the average level of educational attainment of a sending society, with more educated societies espousing more secular values. In figure 3.2, we plot the relationship between the score on the traditional versus secular-rational scale and the score on the survival versus self-expression scale against the average years of educational attainment for each of the immigrant-origin countries in our sample.[16] As the figure shows, the relationship between secular-rational values and the average level of education for the countries present in our surveys is very strong—and weaker, but still present, for survival versus self-expression values.

Moreover, this value domain still more strongly links specifically to "scholarly culture," as measured by the number of books in the parental household. Recent scholarship has demonstrated that the number of books

Figure 3.2 Relationship Between Value Orientation Scales and Number of Books in Household, Average Years of Education, and Polity III Scores

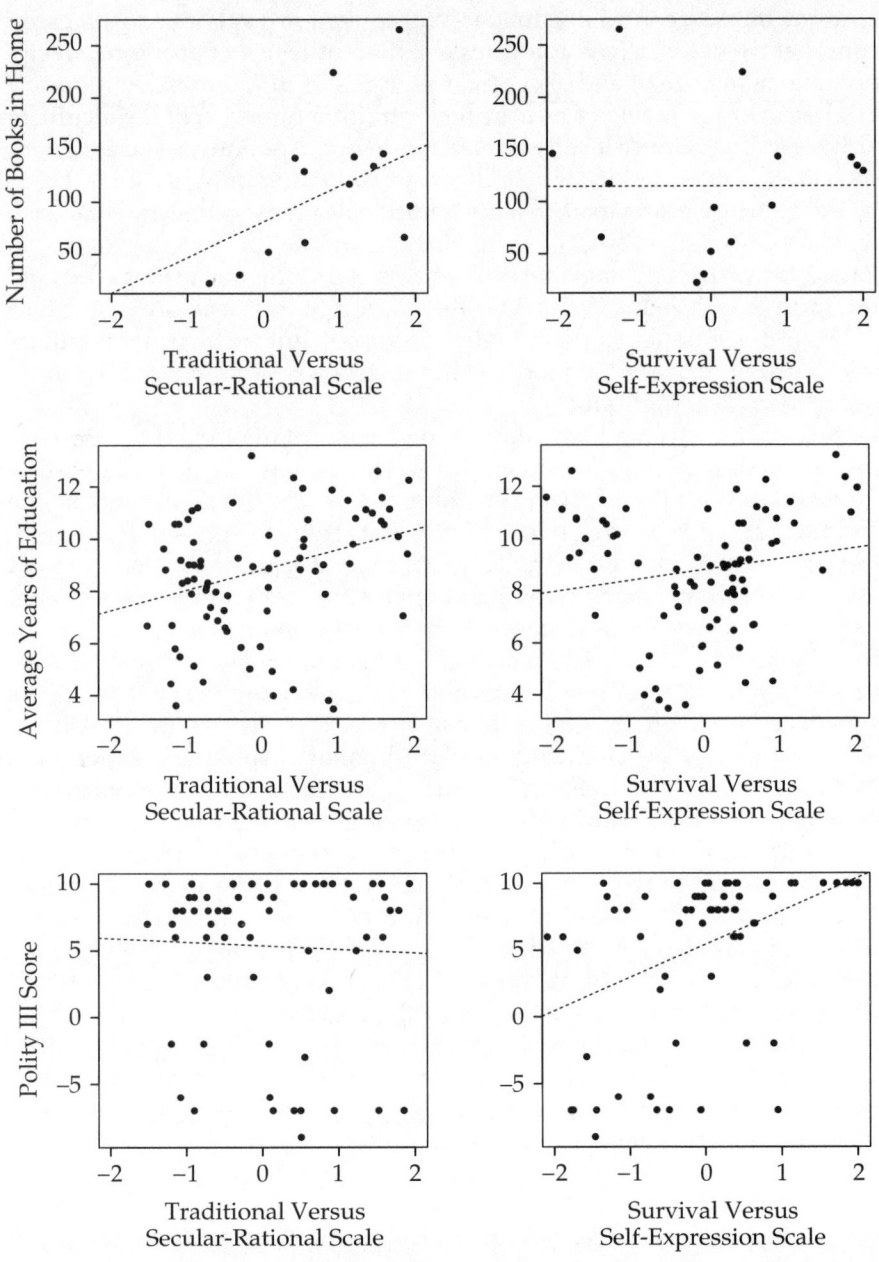

Source: Inglehart and Welzel 2005; Jaggers and Gurr 1996; Evans et al. 2010; Barro and Lee 2013.

in the parental household is independently associated with educational attainment, even controlling for parental education levels: this relationship consistently holds across countries at different levels of economic development, across time, and also across children of different backgrounds.[17] Higher average levels of educational attainment and scholarly culture at the sending-society level, moreover, are independently associated with second-generation educational outcomes, even after individual-level controls.[18] Hence, we anticipate that the traditional versus secular-rational scale will be associated with socioeconomic outcomes in the second generation. Particularly given the fact that secular-rational values are stronger among the more highly educated *within* the United States (as well as in other countries), we anticipate that higher socioeconomic achievement will be associated with origins in more secular societies as opposed to those more oriented toward tradition.[19]

Although a stronger orientation toward secular-rational values may promote educational attainment, these values may not actually predict *convergence* with the values prevailing among the "mainstream" in the United States. On the one hand, immigrants from societies that are more secular-oriented may prove more supportive of educational achievement for their children. On the other hand, their lower adherence to traditional values may permanently distance them from the mainstream in their political alignments, in their feelings of being at home in the United States, or in their ability to form friendships and partnerships with U.S. natives. As shown in the WVS data, while espousing self-expressive values, the United States is much less secular and more traditional in value orientation than many of the immigrant-sending countries. Friendship and partnership formation are predicated on homophily—preferences for shared understandings and values. If the children of immigrants from more secular countries find themselves surrounded by U.S. natives espousing more traditional beliefs, the expected positive association between structural and social assimilation may not materialize.

While immigrant-sending countries may lie on both the more traditional and the more secular-rational ends of the spectrum, the survival versus self-expression dimension more clearly defines the axis of variation separating countries of emigration from countries of immigration. The largest benefits to migration accrue to those migrating from poorer to richer countries, and thus most immigrants to the United States come from countries that are materially less secure and frequently offer fewer political liberties. Many of the Latin American and Asian sending countries populating the left-hand side of figure 3.1 have had recent experience with authoritarian governments and civil unrest. This negative correlation between democracy and state functioning and survival orientations can be seen in figure 3.2, which plots the traditional versus secular-rational and survival versus self-expression scale orientations of the countries in our sample against their Polity scores—a measure of regime authority on a 21-point scale ranging from −10 (hereditary monarchy) to +10 (consolidated democracy). As the figure shows, there is no relationship between traditional orientations and political regime. However, the figure clearly displays the expected positive relationship between open and democratic political institutions and self-expression, as well as a movement away from survival orientations as political systems become more transparent and fair. Many countries of emigration are characterized by an absence of political expression and low levels of material well-being; such conditions encourage strong orientations toward kin and local collectivities in order to ensure survival.

Conditions in the developed societies of immigration, by contrast, breed a propensity for self-expression. In a sense, the gap between survival and self-expression orientations sums up the difference between immigrant parents and immigrant children: the former were raised in societies emphasizing interdependence, whereas the latter grow up in a society promoting individualism. In the survival-oriented societies often found in the developing world, the household is a unit of production in which parents supervise children whose work role comes to reproduce that of an earlier generation; by design, the household in self-expression societies is instead a short-term way-station. States in the developed world prohibit child labor, mandate secondary schooling, and make postsecondary schooling increasingly normative. In so doing, developed states effectively discourage children from contributing to the household economy, all the while providing them with the competencies that will free them from dependence on their parents, namely, those derived from formal education—which, in turn, facilitates the geographic mobility that further weakens family ties.

A survival background may therefore be at odds with the expectations of the society that immigrants and their children encounter, one in which everything around them—schools, media, peers—encourages individualism and self-expression, orientations facilitated by the easy availability of consumer goods, even to the most modest. On the one hand, this mismatch may prove protective. Some forms of autonomy, such as those emphasized in schools, may foster independence in ways that converge with parents' goals, whereas others, such as those sometimes found in the street, encourage detachment in ways that conflict with parental objectives. Since the challenge is to encourage children to achieve independence without breaking ties to parents and kin, a parental strategy of combining education and *educación*—that is to say, formal schooling and skill acquisition *in tandem with* a moral orientation emphasizing greater respect for parents and familial unity—may prove protective.[20] Similarly, the traits emphasized by Lee and Zhou in their account of the Asian Academic achievement paradox—most notably, children's adherence to the "success frame" cultivated by their Chinese and Vietnamese parents—can be read as testimony to the survival orientation that these parents imported with them at the time of migration.[21] On the other hand, a survival orientation might hold back second-generation progress. For instance, expectations for material support from children may encourage work early in adolescence or discourage moves to pursue opportunities further afield; these expectations, in turn, may restrict the high school options of the children of more survival-oriented immigrants to poorer-quality schools close to immigrant neighborhoods or later discourage their pursuit of higher education at top-tier universities in distant states. Nevertheless, although origins in survival-oriented societies can cut both ways, overall we anticipate that such origins will be an asset, reinforcing cohesion among immigrant families vulnerable to the strains resulting from both material difficulties and the orientation toward self-expression that prevails around them.

CONTEXTS OF IMMIGRATION

The contexts of emigration represent one salient axis of intergroup variation; no less important are the contexts of immigration encountered upon arrival. These shared, population-wide conditions take three forms: the migration-status disparities produced by policies of migration control; the resources that migrants can find among their coethnics (conceptualized in this book as "ethnic capital"); and migrants' susceptibility to discrimination by the majority (which we conceptualize as "skin-color stratification"). However, as these latter two axes of variation can be experienced by any population, whether migrant or not, they fall outside the distinctively international influences lying at the heart of the perspective we advance. Hence, we return to the conceptualization and operationalization of ethnic capital and skin-color stratification in the next chapter.

In contrast, population-wide migration-status disparities arise from the main feature distinguishing internal from international migrations: the controls regulating both the flows across state boundaries and the rights of migrants after crossing into the territory of the receiving state. Since migration policies are questions of state, they are shaped by the interests of the country of immigration and its relationship to the state of emigration, with the result that some groups arrive under systematically more favorable conditions than others. Although these policies reflect the interplay of domestic interests—whether seeking enlarged migration or preferring greater restriction—they are inherently international in nature, which is why the ramifications for relationships to particular states yield profound influences on policy. Prior colonial relationships and military engagements recurrently create the conditions for facilitated legal entry, yet strategic interests can close doors as well as open them, depending on whether the regime in the source country is friend or foe. U.S. migration policy can also aim for the "soft power" that comes from training a country's elites, leading to the targeted development of international student recruitment. Finally, gates prove easier to open in times of peace than in periods of tension, which explains why international conflict leads to tightened scrutiny, with security concerns far more focused on some origins than others.[22]

Yet at the same time that migration policy can be wielded to further political or economic advantage, U.S. political actors are constrained by global forces that lie outside their control. Migration policies are embedded within a broader control structure that seeks to accommodate the far larger and ever-growing people flows produced by globalization. These movements involve the crossing of borders of tourists, intracompany transferees, students, and temporary workers, all of whom mainly arrive for sojourns of very limited duration, though sometimes they end up settling for good. Because these flows are generated by the ever-tighter economic links among states, they cannot be stopped—they can only be managed and regulated.[23] But the capacity for relatively unrestricted temporary entry varies across the globe: the residents of the world's richer countries, who are perceived as unlikely to settle elsewhere without authorization, gain access with little fuss, whereas those traveling from poorer places need visas, which are allocated only to those whom authorities deem likely to return home as planned.[24]

Consequently, country-specific flows vary in the prevalence of legal statuses, with consequences for conationals, regardless of the circumstances of their own entry. Although persons fleeing political persecution may all leave their home countries for the same reason, not all are admitted as refugees, since recognizing the political roots of their flight would embarrass the home country regime—a welcome outcome when the regime is unfriendly, but unwelcome when it is friendly. Consequently, the Vietnamese, Cubans, and former Soviet nationals arriving in the United States in search of safe haven received material and organizational assistance in getting started, while also enjoying the fruits of legal residence. Salvadorans and Guatemalans fleeing civil wars, by contrast, found their ability to get started and then to make subsequent progress impeded because the safe haven they sought was available only at the price of unauthorized presence.[25] Not only does policy produce intergroup differences at the very outset—altering population-wide standing and the availability of resources—but it leads those differences to cumulate. Thus, authorized immigrants work legally, whereas unauthorized immigrants are more likely to work "off the books"; the former are put on a path to full citizenship status right from the beginning, whereas the latter suffer long-term confinement to unauthorized status; authorized immigrants, especially after crossing the internal border of citizenship, can benefit from legal opportunities for family reunification, whereas the unauthorized can help bring relatives across the border only by hiring smugglers. For all these reasons, population-wide gaps in the rewards generated by country-specific differences in the distribution of statuses are likely to grow. And though a more-advantaged immigrant stream almost always includes some unauthorized residents and authorized residents will be found in the midst of streams primarily comprising the unauthorized, the impacts of the median status are likely to filter down to the individual level, expanding access to resources in one case and diminishing them in the other.

For illustrations of migration-control disparities and the uneven distribution of legal statuses across national-origin groups, consider the following examples from the 1980s, a decisive decade for the great majority of the immigrant-origin Angelenos and New Yorkers we study in this book, as those years provided the temporal frame for their childhood and/or adolescence. For undocumented immigrants of the 1970s and 1980s, enactment of the 1986 Immigration Reform and Control Act (IRCA) changed their status from unauthorized to legal, allowing for quick family reunification and putting citizenship within reach. Nevertheless, earlier differences in the prevalence of undocumented immigration led to greater impacts of legalization on some groups compared to others. For example, the Salvadorans who obtained legal status under IRCA's regular legalization provisions comprised 30 percent of all Salvadorans living in the United States in 1990; Mexicans and Guatemalans regularizing under the same program comprised, respectively, 29 and 23 percent of all those in their immigrant group living in the United States as of 1990, having migrated during the same period. By contrast, Chinese, Indians, and Koreans regularizing under IRCA comprised 1.6, 0.8, and 0.3 percent, respectively, of those in their immigrant group living in the United States as of 1990. Likewise, the 1980 Refugee Act, marking the official advent of U.S. refugee policy, was designed in such a way as to depoliticize the criteria used to determine eligibility for refugee status. Yet, compared to the prevalence of unauthorized status, the prevalence of refugee status varied even more widely. Thus, almost all Laotians and Cambodians who arrived in the United States during the 1980s (97 percent each) came as refugees, as did 80 percent of the Russians (ex-Soviets) and 62 percent of the Cubans. By contrast, though Nicaraguans and Salvadorans also fled violence and persecution, only 12 percent of Nicaraguans and not quite 1 percent of Salvadorans arriving in the United States during the same period were admitted as refugees. Moreover, not a single Mexican immigrant was granted refugee status during this period.

In light of these differences in status prevalence, we therefore operationalize migration-status disparities as the percentage of immigrants who fall under these two polarized statuses: the percentage undocumented as proxied by IRCA regularizations, and the percentage of new arrivals with refugee status during the formative years of the second generation's childhoods in the 1980s. Whereas individual legal status is likely to matter across all populations, group-level impacts reflect the wide national-origin variation in legal status prevalence. In particular, we hypothesize that negative impacts can be expected where undocumented immigration is widespread, as its stigma may attach, at least in part, to all group members, whether unauthorized or not. Insofar as that stigma impedes individual social mobility, it may also yield a cumulative impact, attenuating individuals' capacity to mobilize resources through ethnic social networks, whether the resources are those relevant to searching for jobs, sharing a business context, or participating in community institutions. By reinforcing exclusion from the polity, widespread undocumented status can also diminish the salience of politics in social circles, increasing overall political detachment and reducing the circulation of political information among ethnic networks that comprise both citizens and undocumented immigrants.

By contrast, refugee policy both facilitates the entry of selected groups fleeing persecution and assists their subsequent integration. Not only do refugees arrive with permanent legal residence, which gives them access to many benefits from the day of arrival, but they benefit from a variety of programs designed to facilitate their adjustment, including occupational training, English-language instruction, and support for community organizations. Of course, the *pre*-migration experience may have been traumatic, especially for refugees from war zones, such as those in Southeast Asia, Iraq, or Somalia, though probably less so for those coming from stable, if repressive, societies like Cuba and the former Soviet Union. Moreover, the initial refugee wave is particularly vulnerable; those first refugees often arrive without a base of coethnics to provide help and orientation. By contrast, the later arrivals benefit both from their own refugee status and from the advantages that this same status generated for the earlier group of newcomers. Furthermore, whereas standard modes of entry—whether as legal "non-immigrants" (tourists, students, businesspeople), legal permanent residents, or unauthorized immigrants—result from individual migrants' decisions, the decision to resettle refugees is made by the state that accepts these immigrants. Thus, among refugee groups, legal status is determined *prior* to migration and is typically applied to entire populations.

Table 3.1 The Status Prevalence Scale

Status Prevalence Scale	Percentage Legalized Under IRCA	Percentage Refugee
1 (most negative)	20% or more	None
2	1–20%	Less than 1%
3	1–20%	1–20%
4	Less than 1%	Less than 1%
5	Less than 1%	1–20%
6 (most positive)	None	20% or more

Source: IIMMLA and ISGMNY data sets; United States Immigration and Naturalization Service, 1980–1989.

To reflect both the facilitative and constraining aspects of disparities in migration status, we constructed a "status prevalence scale," which relies on secondary data on the society-wide prevalence of different legal statuses at the time of respondents' childhoods. Because the respondents sampled by ISGMNY and IIMMLA were born between 1964 and 1984 to parents who immigrated to the United States after 1964, the measurement of governmental reception needs to be temporally relevant, that is, likely to have been in place not only at an early period in the respondents' lives but also prior to the survey. The scale of status prevalence derives from two indicators: (1) the number of persons from any given country legalized under the regular amnesty program of 1986 as a fraction of the total U.S. population from that country in 1990; and (2) the number of persons admitted as refugees from a country between 1980 and 1989 as a fraction of all persons admitted to the United States from that country during the same period. We compute these proportions using data from the statistical yearbooks of the Immigration and Naturalization Service (INS) and the 1990 census.

We then distinguish six levels of prevalence. Level 1, the most negative, includes immigrant nationalities with a large proportion of undocumented individuals, for which the number of persons legalized in the 1986 amnesty programs was equal to or greater than 20 percent of the nationality's 1990 population and for which *no* persons were admitted as refugees during the 1980s. At the other extreme, level 6 includes nationalities with a large refugee component, for which the number of persons admitted as refugees during the 1980s was equal to or greater than 20 percent of the nationality's 1990 population and for which *no* persons were legalized in the 1986 program. For definitions of all levels, see table 3.1.

CROSS-BORDER TIES

In bringing the origin country into view, the international perspective adopted in this book highlights the existence of social ties that span the boundary between the sending and receiving countries. By opting for life in another country, migrants pull one society onto the territory of another state, unintentionally and unconsciously making "here," the society of destination, overlap with "there," the society of origin. This zone of intersocietal convergence—labeled the "transnational social field" by the scholars of transnationalism—arises from the migrants' own survival strategy. The newcomers turn to one another for help in solving the everyday problems of migration: how to move from the old home to the new one; how to find a job and settle down; how to pick up the skills needed to manage in their new world. Consequently, as already described, migrants extend and embed their networks across borders, creating a new community where familiar faces, tongues, and institutions reproduce the world left behind.

Yet intersocietal convergence also results from the inherent selectivity of migration. Not everyone who might want to leave can depart; nor does everyone who can leave home wish to do so. Consequently, migrations rearrange households, making them extend across space. "An unwanted and unavoidable by-product of the entire process of international migration," geographic separation often marks the relationship between immigrants and their elderly parents or extended families; given improvements in infant mortality and child welfare in many sending countries, contemporary immigrants are also now more likely to leave behind their children than did their predecessors of the last great era of migration.[26] Reunification with children often occurs when the earnings capacity of the migrating parent or couple improves, although some children left behind are separated from their parents for the entirety of their childhood. Thus, new permutations have been added to the classic pattern of young men departing, leaving wives and children behind. In some cases both parents leave together, in others emigration is more likely to involve mothers than fathers, and in still others migration may divide both couples and children. But couples then reunify more frequently than do children with their family, and sometimes one parent even returns home after the children have moved to the destination country.[27]

Familial separation also reflects the workings of the controls that exclude the many who would benefit from migration, since those who can find a way through or around systems of migration control depart first, leaving other family members with little choice but to stay behind and wait for the protracted and uncertain process of family reunification to unfold. To be sure, immigration laws do offer opportunities for later migration by kin left back home, but the very same laws facilitating family reunification also separate families. In the United States, those contrasting consequences derive from the ways in which policy discriminates in favor of citizens and against those with less-favored status: citizens have numerous legal avenues for family reunification, while permanent residents have far fewer options and the undocumented none at all.[28]

In separating households, migrations motivate both migrants and stay-at-homes to find ways of maintaining social bonds and fulfilling familial obligations across space. Consequently, the foreign-born often live social lives that span borders, sending money back home, communicating with friends and relatives who have remained behind, and traveling to their communities of origin when legal status and funds allow. International migration thus entails internationalized families, with the upshot that many second-generation members grow up in a thick web of cross-border ties. Some of those ties, such as letters and phone calls, can be maintained at relatively low cost; others—making long visits to the parental homeland, for instance, or intentionally maintaining foreign-language capacity in the parental home—may require a significant investment of family time and resources. Since these ties are present from early childhood—if not actually in place at the time immigrant offspring are born—they can act as an independent variable, shaping the lives of immigrant children both when they reside with their parents and after they leave the parental home.

We conceptualize cross-border ties as entailing two separate areas of inquiry: first, the cross-border ties of immigrant *parents* acting as an *independent* variable that influences a broad range of second-generation social and economic outcomes; and second, the cross-border ties of immigrant *offspring* functioning as a *dependent* variable relevant to debates surrounding the intergenerational transmission of transnationalism as well as its relationship to other domains of integration, such as ethnic attachment, education and labor market outcomes, and political participation.

We attempt to isolate parental behaviors and characteristics during second-generation respondents' childhood and adolescence from the cross-border connections they maintained at the time of the survey. Although both of the surveys contain relevant information on cross-border ties (see table 3.2), the IIMMLA more clearly differentiates those in childhood from those in adulthood; hence, our analyses of cross-border ties principally rely on the IIMMLA. Of these early experiences, perhaps the most important are extended visits to the parental home country. Although undergone by only a minority of second-generation members, "roots" tourism and visits to their parents' hometowns—or even longer-term stays in the home country for school or work—can have a formative impact on the

Table 3.2 Indicators of Cross-Border Activities in the IIMMLA and ISGMNY Surveys

	IIMMLA	ISGMNY
Activities during childhood		
Parents educated in the United States	x	x
Parents sent remittances (childhood)	x	
Visits during respondent's childhood	x	
Parent did not return to origin country	x	
Parent returned to origin country	x	
Parent returned to origin country and respondent joined parent	x	
Home-country language spoken in parental home	x	x
Cross-border families		
All relatives in United States / no relatives in origin country	x	
Parents in United States and relatives in origin country	x	
Parent in origin country	x	
Parents from different national origins / mixed parentage	x	x
Respondent activities		
Respondent visits	x	x
Respondent ever spent six months or more in parental home country		x
Parents send remittances (currently)		x
Ability in parental language	x	x
Respondent remits	x	x
Homeland-oriented organizations	x	
Respondent feels at home in parental home country	x	
Interest in parental home-country politics	x	
Ethnic identity	x	

Source: IIMMLA and ISGMNY data sets.

lives of these second-generation youth; as shown by other research, many of them report having had experiences of freedom and connection and a chance to deepen relationships with extended family.[29] Extended visits to the parental homeland undertaken at a young age can embed language fluency, while those undertaken in adolescence may cement interest in homeland matters, with both language competence and interest spurring deeper homeland engagements in adulthood.

A related question is whether cross-border connections can persist after immigrant offspring leave the parental household and set up on their own and, if so, how those ties are transmitted. Among the first generation, cross-border ties are ubiquitous; arising from bonds of affection and from relationships developed over the course of their childhood and adolescence in the origin country, those ties also provide the resources needed to resolve a host of practical problems in both the host and home societies. But whereas immigrants effectively create intersocietal convergence between their country of origin and the country of destination, the children of immigrants experience intersocietal *divergence* as their lives unfold in the society of reception, where their core commitments are also to be found. Consequently, immigrant offspring's homeland ties are unlikely to retain the affective importance and practical functions prized by their parents. Though generally tending toward decline, cross-border ties retain their strength for *some* second-generation members, in part because core family members remain abroad and in part as a legacy of the social learning absorbed in the parental household. Cross-border kinship ties in the first generation motivate second-generation interactions across borders while promoting an understanding that obligations and commitments to home-community relatives, even if remote, matter. Not only do children model their later behavior on the parental patterns observed at home, but parents also transmit a range of civic and political values and attachments that are retained by their children long after they have attained adulthood and independence.[30] Consequently, the cross-border ties experienced in the parental household can encourage the maintenance of home-country language and cultural competencies during adulthood; access to the cultural and linguistic toolkit produced through engagement in an internationalized family network could position immigrant offspring to participate in an ethnic economy or transnational politics.

On the other hand, maintaining close, long-distance ties requires resources, which some immigrant families can access better than others. Despite distance-shrinking technologies, cross-border engagement remains costly; thus, only a minority of immigrant parents are able to keep up a constant pattern of travel and satisfying long-distance communication. In addition to family-level resources—in the form of finances and legal status—immigrant families also differ in their incentive to maintain cross-border ties. As noted, the internationalization of kinship ties tends to diminish with time, with the result that the children of longer-settled immigrant parents are likely to find that a critical mass of relatives has gravitated to the United States. Moreover, immigrant parents who arrived at younger ages and finished their schooling in the United States are likely to be more firmly rooted there, and their longer residence will have offered them greater exposure to a more diverse set of friends and, later, potential partners. Parents of differing national origins lack the capacity to transmit home-country attachments and orientations possessed by parents who originate from the same place. Similarly, parents who differ in nativity status—one foreign-born and the other U.S.-born—produce a generation that lies somewhere in between the second and third generations, as indicated by their common designation as the "second-and-a-half" (2.5) generation; for this group, foreign influences are likely to be of less salience right from the start. Thus, we expect that the children of parents from two different nationalities and, still more, the children of one foreign-born and one U.S.-born parent will have weaker homeland attachments than those who grew up in an endogamous household.

Even those immigrant parents who are most determined to transmit their language, norms, and values to their children encounter great challenges when that next generation grows up in the United States. The process of absorbing the tastes, preferences, behaviors, and rewarded skills of the national society in which the migrants have settled—that is, what the literature calls "acculturation"—can yield further detachment in the second generation, as exemplified by changes in their linguistic practices and preferences. Although the children of two immigrant parents are likely to be exposed to the mother tongue at home, in all other domains they commonly use English, which they then come to prefer, relegating the mother tongue to kitchen-level proficiency.[31] The shift from the immigrant language to the dominant tongue reduces host-society social boundaries between the foreign-born and native-born, but simultaneously *increases* the cross-border social boundary between stay-at-homes in the country of emigration and immigrants and their foreign-born offspring residing in the country of immigration. Thus, second-generation members who lose the ability to speak the home-country language fluently are unlikely to be able to maintain close cross-border ties.

In sum, while nearly all immigrants experience intersocietal convergence at the point of migration, the type and intensity of cross-border engagement varies greatly, with implications for the second generation amplifying as their roots in the country of destination deepen. Though the children of immigrants generally have much lower rates of contact with the home country than their immigrant parents, the second-generation patterns of home-country connectedness are *not* of a piece. Most importantly, some second-generation immigrant children remain members of kin networks that are more internationalized than others; those differences, as well as differences in the specific identity of kin still living beyond U.S. boundaries, make for *intragroup* and *intragenerational* disparities in the salience of second-generation cross-border ties. Likewise, earlier parental decisions—whether or not to send remittances, to return home for extended visits, or to make the native language the dominant tongue at home—generate later second-generation differences in both the motivation and the capacity to maintain intersocietal convergence. Yet even as the parental choice to sustain homeland connections creates resources, those choices were themselves related to first-generation disparities, both in the economic resources needed to keep up with kin abroad and, most importantly, the capacity to legally travel back and forth across territorial borders. Thus, influences from a variety of channels transform the common first-generation experience of intersocietal convergence into a source of great second-generation heterogeneity—an outcome that in turn can influence immigrant children's political and ethnic attachments, as well as their socioeconomic attainments, as they reach adulthood.

CIVIC STRATIFICATION: LEGAL STATUS AND CITIZENSHIP

Measures forbidding discrimination seek to ensure that all citizens are treated equally. Yet, by its nature, citizenship metes out unequal treatment to noncitizens.[32] Only citizens can leave and reenter their home territory when they wish; only citizens enjoy the unconditional lifelong right of territorial residence; and only citizens decide when and under what conditions noncitizens can obtain membership status. Hence, exclusion from citizenship is an inherent aspect of migration control. Moreover, since gaining inclusion is not for the migrant to decide by him- or herself, the same search for the good life that impels social assimilation does not suffice for civic integration, with the result that a person who in most respects acts as a citizen may be unable, absent that status, to fully do so.[33]

Although every alien encounters the boundary of citizenship, not every alien begins in the same condition: the process of international migration creates at entry intragroup differences in legal status even among immigrants of the same national origins, with corresponding implications for their subsequent transitions to citizenship and formal equality with other nationals. The result takes the form of civic stratification—a set of formal cleavages among foreign-origin persons who may share common national or ethnic origins but differ in legal standing.[34] Hence, unlike the *formal equality* among citizens, *formal inequality* prevails among noncitizens. Some statutorily enjoy most citizenship rights, occupying the conceptual space close to the boundary delimited by citizenship status; others are conceptually located just inside the territorial boundary, where they have a far more precarious hold on any civic status at all.

Much like cross-border ties, civic stratification can be conceptualized as both an independent and a dependent variable. As an independent variable, the initial status at arrival strongly affects the family environment in which immigrant offspring grow up, whether directly, as in the case of the

1.5 generation, who arrive as children and young adults, or indirectly, as with the U.S.-born children of immigrant parents, all of whom started their lives in the United States as aliens. For undocumented or temporary aliens located at the outer edge of the conceptual territorial space, rights are few, residence is unstable, and the trajectory to citizenship is likely to involve a series of transitions across formal status boundaries—for instance, from (potentially multiple) temporary visas to permanent resident to citizen. The rights regime is more expansive for those who begin as legal permanent residents, though with no guarantee of attaining either lifelong residence or movement across the threshold of formal membership, their status is never fully certain. Traversing the boundary of citizenship is a matter of deliberate action, requiring investment and forethought, not the automatic, almost unconscious behavior that leads to language learning or the acquisition of a skill that might put a better job within reach. Given this less favorable cost-benefit ratio, naturalization rates among many immigrant groups remain low, with the result that many immigrant offspring—though far from all—are raised by parents who are excluded from formal political participation and the full set of social rights. Consequently, differences in parents' at-entry status, disparities in any subsequent opportunities to obtain full membership, and any divergent reactions to those opportunities furnish the channels by which parental variations in civic stratification yield intragroup differences among their children.

The accidents of children's birth can also directly yield intragroup heterogeneity. Since in the United States citizenship is a birthright, those immigrant offspring who start off having won the citizenship lottery begin with an advantage that their 1.5-generation counterparts have to attain. Although the accident of birth outside the United States does not inherently put members of the 1.5 generation on a different track than that followed by their second-generation peers, just when and whether the acquisition of U.S. citizenship repairs the legal consequences of foreign birth is likely to matter.

Frequently unobserved but critically important sources of intragroup difference, legal status and citizenship receive attention throughout the pages of this book. We make particular use of measures unique to the IIMMLA data that enable us to examine the impact of parental legal status at arrival on a variety of second-generation outcomes. IIMMLA data allow us to differentiate the children of immigrants with parents who arrived with temporary permits, those who arrived as permanent residents, and those in a residual category that, through the process of elimination, we assume contains primarily those who entered with undocumented status. Along with information needed to distinguish between parents who have naturalized from those who remain without U.S. citizenship, these data are used as independent variables. In addition, the foreign-born Angelenos surveyed by the IIMMLA who eventually naturalized were asked to provide the date when they acquired U.S. citizenship, information that allows us not only to analyze the determinants of both the acquisition and the timing of citizenship but also to examine the ways in which the duration of exclusion from the polity, due to alien status, affects a variety of social and political outcomes. Moreover, in analyses using both the IIMMLA and ISGMNY, we further distinguish foreign-born children of immigrants who had naturalized from those who remained outside the polity. In so doing, we can separately analyze the impact of social boundaries alongside legal boundaries—the specific result of traversing international borders.

We anticipate that the most immediate impact of civic stratification is likely to be felt by members of the 1.5 generation, who lack the birthright citizenship of their U.S.-born peers and instead are dependent on their parents' legal status and naturalization decisions. For these immigrant offspring, the cost-benefit calculus tilts strongly in the direction of naturalization. As products of receiving-society schools, they have already been socialized for citizenship; moreover, their younger age and the lower likelihood that they will ever return to the country of origin for good are factors that allow the costs of naturalization to be amortized over much, if not all, of a long lifetime. However, since the naturalization of the 1.5 generation is often a family affair, an incentive structure that provides parents with weak motivation to naturalize—and makes it impossible for unauthorized parents to do so—is likely to impinge on the naturalization even of their U.S.-raised children.

Yet formal membership is but one aspect of citizenship, and it does not perfectly align with the full practice of citizenship in either the rights, participative, or identity dimensions. It is true that all U.S.-raised children experience the many efforts designed to socialize children for national membership, whether learning to sing the National Anthem, to love the national flag, or to aspire to "good citizenship" of the type valued by schools. Yet national identity is likely to be particularly salient for those immigrant offspring who are not only de facto Americans but also de jure Americans, whose status is prized among their family members and who internalize the greater rights and sense of entitlements that status citizenship entails.[35] And even among the de jure Americans, the citizen children of parents who remain foreign nationals are less likely than their peers raised by naturalized parents to experience a household environment that reinforces identification with the people and polity of the country of immigration.

Citizenship as a formal status—and the practice of citizenship rights through political participation—may therefore significantly influence identity, ethnic attachments, and orientations. Technically, all individuals residing in the receiving country, regardless of legal standing, "have a right to have rights," the basic fundament of citizenship as famously described by Hannah Arendt.[36] But to be meaningful, the right to have rights needs to be exercised, an activity particularly difficult for aliens of undocumented status, as rights-claiming entails exposure when staying in the shadows might be the safer strategy. Thus, the influence of the formal status of one's parents and one's self is likely to be felt even in domains of civic participation where citizenship is not required, such as protesting or lobbying or meeting with a local official.

On the other hand, citizenship as eligibility for social rights and legal protections can also confer significant practical benefits. For instance, status citizens are protected by laws against discrimination based on race, religion, ethnicity, and, increasingly, sexual preference. As Alba and Nee note, it is those protections that make the choice for mobility over ethnic attachment rational, as each progressive investment yields both progress and additional opportunities to change.[37] Measures forbidding discrimination seek equality among status citizens, short-circuiting the processes that historically turned status citizens into second-class citizens. But no such concern extends to noncitizens; were the latter to be treated just like citizens, citizenship would have no meaning at all. Hence, discrimination against noncitizens, as well as discrimination that varies by precise legal status, is inevitable.

These disadvantages extend to all members of the household. Legally ineligible to work and sometimes even to drive, undocumented immigrants have limited job options; increasingly prevalent demands for proper identity documents place them under an ever-lower ceiling, leaving many in the informal sector, working only in jobs that can be accessed by foot or public transportation. Those conditions in turn constrain their housing options, producing overcrowding, which in turn yields negative consequences for children's development by depriving them of a place for study, increasing stress, and even affecting physical and mental processes by raising blood pressure and retarding cognitive development.[38]

Of course, confinement to the shadows of undocumented status rarely lasts forever; noncitizen children typically have more rights than their adult parents, and those rights, combined with longer exposure, increase their access to citizenship. Birthright citizenship ensures that no child born in the United States begins in the zone of legal liminality. Nonetheless, the disabilities associated with alienage can be transmitted from one generation to the next; to the extent that alienage either coincides with or aggravates other disadvantages, such as undocumented status, its legacy is likely to last longer. For the immigrant offspring of interest to us—those born between 1965 and 1984—these legacy effects are likely to have been modest, as their parents arrived during a period of blurrier boundaries between citizens and aliens. Furthermore, the advent of an amnesty for undocumented immigrants in 1986 limited the duration of confinement to the zone of legal liminality. Since then, however, the barriers to passage from unauthorized to authorized legal status have hardened. Subsequent efforts at legalization have repeatedly stalled, with the result that today's undocumented population of over ten million is increasingly long-settled. Simultaneously suffering from diminished rights and greater vulnerability to deportation, the children of contemporary undocumented immigrants, compared to the immigrant offspring studied in this book, are likely to experience legacy effects far deeper and more severe.

Summary

In this chapter thus far, we have sought to develop a perspective that takes into account the distinctly international elements shaping the lives of the second generation and that distinguishes between the features yielding intergroup differences and those that generate intragroup differences. Convention characterizes immigrant offspring as mainly belonging to America's minority population, yet the children of immigrants and the children of native-born minorities are separated by their backgrounds and experiences. The children of immigrants are socialized by foreign-born parents raised in a very different environment than native-born parents, bringing with them very different outlooks and orientations. In turn, this context of emigration exerts an important, and generally unobserved, influence on the household setting of the second generation. Moreover, unlike the U.S.-born, who enjoy freedom of mobility and can enter and leave the United States when they wish, immigrants arrive as foreigners who are only legally present when authorized, though the unauthorized may be tacitly accepted. Migration control policies—a constituent aspect of the state system—are used to sift entries, sort arrivals into various official categories involving unequal rights and entitlements, and put some newcomers on a path to citizenship while blocking others from ever attaining full acceptance. These migration-control disparities yield nationality-level differences in the distribution of more- or less-advantaged statuses, which in turn yield group-wide effects, regardless of an individual's own legal or citizenship status.

In addition to homeland influences that immigrant parents bring with them when moving, they also extend social ties across territorial boundaries. Growing up as part of internationalized families, the children of immigrants are raised in a zone of intersocietal convergence where ideas, finances, and social contacts flow across national borders, in contrast to the children of the native-born, whose lives generally unfold in a world circumscribed by the territorial borders of the United States. The children of immigrants, by definition, also are universally raised by parents who have spent at least some time as aliens in the receiving country, only some of whom succeeded in traversing the difficult barriers separating them from citizenship. Hence, unlike the U.S.-born children of native-born parents, the U.S.-born children of immigrants, even though status citizens at birth, were raised by parents who began outside the polity. And while the foreign-born but U.S.-raised may be de facto Americans, sharing the identity, lifestyles, and behaviors of their U.S.-born counterparts, the obstacles entailed in entering the polity make the status of de jure Americans far more elusive. Delineating these distinctively international elements — those that cross state borders (values and orientations), those that span state borders (internationalized family networks), and those that produce formal boundaries after the territorial border has been traversed (civic stratification and migration-status disparities) — and demonstrating how they shape the lives of today's second generation lies at the heart of the perspective we seek to advance in this book.

APPLYING THE INTERNATIONAL PERSPECTIVE

In elaborating a new approach, we also seek to synthesize the extensive research on which we build, assembling the many ideas generated by scholarship on the second generation so that they can be considered as a whole. That pursuit leads us to enlarge the domains of second-generation difference that we seek to explain while also providing a careful delineation of both individual- and group-level difference.

Domains of Difference

In contending that some immigrant offspring might fall downward into a rainbow underclass, the hypothesis of segmented assimilation did not simply spark the debate over second-generation trajectories; it also narrowly focused the terms of discussion around issues concerned with socioeconomic mobility. That the question of whether the children of immigrants would move beyond their parents' economic situation attracted attention is hardly a surprise. Yet as the authors of *Parents Without Papers* note, the experience of immigrants and their descendants is multidimensional, extending well beyond the limited, albeit important, sphere of socioeconomic attainment.[39]

Thus, while the first two empirical chapters of this book focus on educational and occupational attainment, later sections apply the international perspective to political and sociocultural dimensions. One such dimension entails citizenship, understood both as a status attained by the foreign-born and as an activity in which status citizens and noncitizens alike can engage (chapters 6 and 7). Unlike the social and economic attainments that garner the attention of the majority of researchers—among whom assimilation is understood as a continuous and incremental process—the formal cleavages between citizens and aliens, rooted in law, create sharply defined junctures in the path to political incorporation. Bright and unambiguous legal boundaries leave noncitizens with limited leverage over the conditions under which those boundaries can be crossed. Moreover, aliens are not of one type: some statutorily enjoy most citizenship rights, whereas the status of others is far more precarious. As most immigrants gain residency *after* migration, the trajectory taking them from alien to citizen, though likely to take myriad forms owing to the great differences in at-entry statuses, usually involves a series of transitions across formal status boundaries, each time-consuming, costly, and uncertain.

By contrast, every person, citizen or noncitizen, has the opportunity to participate in civic activity and even to engage in political activities of varying types, although voting remains off-limits to the noncitizen. Nonetheless, citizenship status—not simply the greater knowledge or more diverse contacts that may come with acculturation and socioeconomic progress—often affects the exercise of civic and political citizenship; hence, long-term effects are likely to flow from parents' initial exclusion from the polity, an experience shared by their foreign-born and U.S.-raised offspring. The individual rewards for participation are also low, which is why immigrants focusing on the search for success and the good life may see little reason to participate in public life; indeed, the "success frame" highlighted by Lee and Zhou seems to have its corollary among the Chinese immigrant offspring described in *Inheriting the City*, for whom politics is a matter of little interest. The same factor explains why citizens are not mobilized without the intervention of political parties and organizations—efforts that ignore and do little for noncitizens owing to their lack of the franchise. Last, the political domain is fundamentally different from the spheres of education and work: whereas participation in the latter requires an ability to work together in pursuit of a shared goal, politics in a democratic society is fundamentally about conflict, and immigration itself is a source of very great contention.

Similarly, continuities and changes in the broad sociocultural dimension are unlikely to stem from the same sources as those impinging on the socioeconomic dimension. We understand the sociocultural dimension as pertaining to those aspects of the immigrant and second-generation experience that entail the relationship between "them" and "us." The first, "them," evokes the receiving-country concerns on which prevailing approaches have long focused: the distinctions between people of some particular national origin and the others around them, of which ethnic identity is a standard indicator. The second, "us," evokes important symbols of difference—in particular, language use and ability—that make it easier to maintain home-country identities and meaningful cross-border ties.

To begin with, the socioeconomic dimension is relatively fixed: parents who arrive as adults largely use the education they received in the country of origin; among their offspring, relatively little additional schooling is obtained after age twenty-five. By contrast, the sociocultural dimension, whether involving the internal ("us") or external ("them") aspect, is relatively fluid: parents and their children can both decide whether to speak the mother tongue and with what frequency and whether to send money to relatives at home, and these choices can change over time. Moreover, first-generation resources, whether found at the familial or group level, are likely to have a relatively direct impact on second-generation attainment but a far more distal impact on either aspect of the sociocultural dimension. Sometimes the "them" and "us" relationships are interconnected, but they can also be independent of one another: ties to the place of origin are subject to erosion, whereas presence in an ethnically stratified society like the United States makes questions of group membership inescapable, even though the boundaries of membership are susceptible to change.

Identifying Inter- and Intragroup Differences: The Case for a Two-Level Model

As we have argued, the search for the sources of both intergroup and intragroup differences is our central quest. Immigrants from any particular country arrive with the shared experience of having grown up and been socialized in that place; this experience may not have influenced all emigrants in exactly the same way, but it is very unlikely to have left no imprint at all. Because immigration policies do not have the same impact on all sending countries but rather either provide options or impose constraints that reflect the relationship between each of these countries and the United States, legal statuses also tend to vary from one national-origin group to another. International migration is a networked phenomenon, with newcomers following and settling down where earlier arrivals put down roots, and these common experiences and attributes, as well as those that reflect a migration's selectivity—such as the average level of education among conationals—make for trajectories that vary from one national-origin group to another. On the other hand, the impact of those common features is offset by the traits that make any one immigrant differ from his or her conationals, whether legal status at entry, the amount and location of schooling obtained, the behaviors adopted after migration, the decision either to stop or continue speaking the mother tongue, or the choice to marry within or outside the cohort of conationals. Hence, locating the source of second-generation difference has to follow a strategy that can clearly distinguish the differences *between* groups from the differences *within* groups.

We emphasize that the shared features we have identified do *not* include an awareness of a common destiny or interest, such that persons of a common national origin would repeatedly mobilize around their commonalities or consistently interact with others in recurrent ways suggesting that behavior across an ethnic line follows a tacit or well-established script. Rather, we simply assume that these commonalities yield some socially significant similar behaviors, increase the likelihood of within-group interaction—and thereby both sharing of resources and exposure to deficits—and provide legible signals that allow outsiders to think that persons of the same national background may share some underlying similarities. Strictly speaking, then, we are not so much speaking about "groups"—a concept implying that persons with shared attributes understand themselves as fundamentally the same—as about categories of people.[40] Nonetheless, since the concept of "ethnic group" is so widely used and so firmly implanted in this literature, and because it so deeply influences the ways in which both scholars and the public approach the phenomenon, we fall back on this terminology as well.

In everyday as well as scholarly usage, the concept of ethnic (or nationality) group evokes a name, whether that of Mexicans, Chinese, Trinidadians, Italians, Russians, or something else. However, a name is not a variable: that is, it does not identify the salient, relevant characteristics that might make membership matter.

Under certain circumstances, names *can* be used as if they were variables, albeit only if the analyst works with great care. Joel Perlmann's classic book *Ethnic Differences*, a study of educational and occupational attainment among the children of the last age of mass migration, shows just how it can be done. Looking at a very limited number of groups— "Yankees," Irish, Jews, Italians, and African Americans—Perlmann meticulously scrutinizes each group in relation to the others, painstakingly locating each in the relevant social space and disaggregating the features that might explain the unmistakable variation in second-generation outcomes.[41] Moreover, since national origins among the earlier wave of mass migration were not quite as diverse as today's, a smaller number of groups could provide a more representative account. By contrast, contemporary flows are much more globalized: immigrants come from all corners of the earth. Even though the respondents queried by the IIMMLA and the

ISGMNY grew up in a time when migrations were less globalized than the migration streams that have arrived since 2010, national-origin diversity is a salient trait of the second-generation Angelenos and New Yorkers studied in this book.

That diversity renders the traditional group-specific approach impractical, as evidenced by the procedure followed in *Legacies*. The many regression results displayed in the tables of that book repeatedly show the results for "dummy variables" corresponding to ten different nationalities: Cambodia, Cuba, Haiti, Jamaica/West Indies, Laos, Mexico, Nicaragua, the Philippines, Vietnam, and "other." Though the authors insist that nationalities reflect different modes of incorporation, the nationalities are never compared to one another; rather, they are simply contrasted to a catchall set of nationalities that make up the omitted category in the regressions. The better procedure would have been to test each nationality against the other and thereby determine whether modes hypothesized to be more or less advantageous yield systematic differences. Yet just for the ten nationalities that *Legacies* consistently examines that task would have required tests for sixty-five pairwise comparisons.[42] That number would be unmanageable when analyzing the pooled ISGMNY and IIMMLA surveys, which include sixty-seven different nationalities.

The alternative involves moving from the names of nationalities to variables that measure the nationality attributes relevant to the outcomes of interest. That procedure in turn involves the use of multilevel modeling, a well-established technique, but one that has been extensively used only to explore ethnic difference from within the European context.[43]

To illustrate the utility of the method, we turn to an example from its most common application in the sociology of education. We can imagine a situation in which we wish to understand variation in schooling performance, for instance, scores on a standardized test. Background characteristics and familial environments—students' age, gender, parents' education, the presence of one or two parents—affect schooling performance and educational attainment. Although we can reasonably hypothesize that more-advantaged students will do better than their less-advantaged peers, we know that what happens in the classroom also affects the performance of children, regardless of whether they come from an advantaged family or not. Consequently, to properly assess the impact of social class variation on performance *within* classes, the analyst needs to control for differences in the quality of the classrooms in which students are taught. Similarly, since student performance is probably affected by the mix of more-advantaged and less-advantaged students, we want to know about the relationship between teacher qualities and children's performance, controlling for compositional differences across classes.

Naturally, each classroom can be given a unique nominal identifier—the name of the teacher. In theory, the researcher could simply compare the achievement of Renee's students to the achievement of Roger's, controlling for the individual-level characteristics of the students in each class. But that would not tell us anything about what, specifically, is advantageous or disadvantageous about Roger versus Renee. In contrast, if we had a large enough number of teachers, we could compare the achievement of students taught by teachers who vary by attributes likely to affect their performance—for example, classroom experience. We could also compare the achievement of students with teachers possessing a master's degree versus teachers with only a bachelor's degree. If we model teachers' experience and teachers' credentials together, we could even make assertions about the effect of teacher credentials *controlling* for teaching experience. Although a one-by-one comparison of Roger and Renee would not yield systematic information about differences in teacher quality, we would be able to predict how teachers possessing those attributes of Roger or Renee that are relevant to the classroom will affect student performance.

In this book, we have simply taken this logic and applied it to comparisons across the children of immigrants from different origin countries. Staying with our example, country of origin is the equivalent of the teacher, and we are interested in examining what, specifically, it is about certain countries of origin that matter for the outcomes of the second generation. Rather than comparing China to Mexico, we instead compare origin countries that vary in their value orientations, whether more rational or more traditional, or in the relative prevalence of more- or less-educated coethnics, or in the prevalence of legal statuses that are more or less favorable. Doing so, however, requires a large sample of origin countries that vary across shared features of both the context of emigration and the context of immigration. Fortunately, both the IIMMLA and the ISGMNY—and even more so the pooled IIMMLA and ISGMNY data set—provide the large number of sending countries with sufficient variation across a range of theoretically informed country-level characteristics (level 2) to test for their explanatory power while controlling for individual- and family-level compositional differences (level 1) across national-origin groups.

CONCLUSION

We now draw this lengthy chapter to a close and thank readers for their attention as we elaborated a more general model of second-generation difference, the various outcomes we believe it can explain, and the analytic strategy we will use to test it. In the chapters to follow, we will demonstrate the value of the international perspective, in particular the importance of origin-country context for socioeconomic outcomes and the influence of cross-border ties on the sociocultural and political adaptations of the children of immigrants. Using multilevel models provides new insights into the sources of differences across these varied domains: as we will show later, family- and individual-level characteristics prove to be the primary determinants: they exercise considerably more influence than characteristics linked to membership in any immigrant group. In the next chapter, however, we focus on the source of intergroup variation, offering a direct comparison of the predictions generated by our model and techniques and those that have thus far been dominant in the literature.

Part II | Transmission

Chapter 4 | The Importance of Context

WE CAN AGREE that the typical emigrant departs in search of the good life abroad, a quest that then proves transformative, as the need to get ahead as an immigrant in a new land compels a series of changes that lead the immigrant—and even more so, his or her children—to take on the traits, behaviors, and preferences of the people around them. But even though the direction of change for all immigrants may be broadly similar, neither the starting nor the ending point is the same for each and every one.

As we emphasized in the previous chapter, immigrants arrive differing greatly in the resources needed to make progress: some are advantaged by prior professional training while others have only manual skills, and some enjoy the good fortune of permanent legal status from the moment of their arrival in the United States while others linger long in the shadow of unauthorized status. Those intragenerational differences tend to produce intergenerational differences, as the inequalities in resources accessed by the parental generation are at least partially reproduced in their children. Yet we find not only a wide spectrum of differences across *individual* immigrants and their U.S.-raised and U.S.-born children, but also variation in starting and ending points across groups, with the average person originating in one country doing substantially better or worse than the average person coming from some other country. Explaining these often striking and sometimes puzzling ethnic differences provides fodder for both popular debate and scholarly disagreement.

As we saw in previous chapters, scholars have mobilized a variety of perspectives to identify the source of intergroup differences. In this chapter, we focus on hypotheses deriving from both the major works reviewed in chapter 2 and our own approach developed in chapter 3—in particular, hypotheses about intergroup differences in second-generation "structural" or socioeconomic outcomes (summarized in table 4.1).

Table 4.1 Conceptualizing and Measuring Contexts of Immigration and Emigration

Concept	O+D	LEG	ITC	AAAP	PWP	RAM	Our Measurement
Context of immigration							
Ethnic capital: socioeconomically advantaged coethnic community	x	x	x	x			Group years of education
Skin-color stratification: societal reception	x	x		x			Average group skin color
Migration-status disparities: group-level governmental reception	x	x					Status prevalence scale: group-level percentage undocumented, percentage refugee
Internally networked coethnic community		x	x	x			
Positively selected coethnic community			x	x			
Context of emigration							
More secular and rationally oriented home-country cultural background	x		x				Traditional versus secular-rational score[a]
More self-expression-oriented home-country cultural background	x		x				Survival versus self-expression score[b]

Source: O+D = *Origins and Destinations*. Portes and Rumbaut 2001 (LEG = *Legacies*); Kasinitz et al. 2008 (ITC = *Inheriting the City*); Lee and Zhou 2015 (AAAP = *Asian American Achievement Paradox*); Bean, Brown, and Bachmeier 2015 (PWP = *Parents Without Papers*); Alba and Nee 2003 (RAM = *Remaking the American Mainstream*).

[a] Positive values on the traditional versus secular-rational scale indicate greater secularism and a more rational orientation.
[b] Positive values on the survival versus self-expression scale indicate an orientation toward self-expression.

As can be seen from table 4.1, the concepts developed in each of the major works discussed in chapter 2 tend to overlap. In particular, *The Asian American Achievement Paradox*, coauthored by one of the original proponents of segmented assimilation theory, takes off from the concept of mode of incorporation advanced in *Legacies*. To explain the "exceptional" achievement of Asian Americans, Lee and Zhou point toward the very positive contexts of reception of Chinese- and Vietnamese-origin immigrants—in particular their selection as high-skilled workers, students, and refugees—as well as positive racial stereotypes about Asians at the general societal level. These authors identify supplementary education, often of an ethnically specific type, and group social norms of high achievement as drivers of success deriving from the local coethnic community. This work also shares with its predecessor a focus on social-psychological mechanisms of achievement that operate at the individual level and cannot be readily measured in the surveys we use. However, both *The Asian American Achievement Paradox* and *Legacies* use selectively chosen national-origin comparisons to argue for the importance of the three elements of the context of reception and a cohesive coethnic community.

Inheriting the City places great emphasis on the institutional advantages found in the specific metropolitan area in which the second-generation New Yorkers grew up; however, as these advantages are shared by all groups, they cannot explain variation among these same groups. *Inheriting the City* does, however, reference benefits linked to imported home-country patterns and values, such as the tendency of the Chinese-origin New Yorkers to grow up with both parents and to delay their exit from their parents' home. *Inheriting the City* never actually tests for the effects of these specific mechanisms of immigrant advantage—a task we undertake in the following chapter, which focuses on individual-level predictors of intragroup variation in achievement. Nonetheless, in our reading of *Inheriting the City*, many of the specific characteristics linked to the immigrant advantage— dual-earning families in the first generation, family-level sacrifice for children's educational needs, multigenerational households, delayed family formation—can be understood as components of a survival orientation, one of our measures of context of emigration, described in chapter 3. On the other hand, we learn from *Inheriting the City* about the ways in which Chinese parents keenly seek out information about school quality and tutoring opportunities, a behavioral pattern that seems closely linked to another one of our measures, a secular-rational orientation, which, as we demonstrated in the previous chapter, strongly predisposes those who possess it toward scholarship and educational attainment.

Despite its emphasis on the sending-country culture as a source of immigrant advantage, *Inheriting the City* neither shows that these mechanisms are group-specific nor empirically demonstrates that these specific mechanisms work as predicted. As with *Legacies* and *The Asian American Achievement Paradox*, *Inheriting the City* assumes that these mechanisms are the unique properties of particular national-origin groups. By contrast, our use of the World Values Survey provides direct measures of some of the concepts underlying the second-generation advantage hypothesis: namely, a context of emigration that values family cohesion (as indexed by a survival orientation) and a scholarly culture (as indexed by a more rational-secular orientation). By drawing on these indices, we gain the capacity to test the hypothesis that these home-country imports are a source of second-generation advantage. Moreover, subsequent analysis that exploits the excellent school quality information in the New York data (see chapter 5) further enables us to assess the intermediate individual-level manifestations of some of these advantages, namely, ethnic differences in school choice and their effect on educational attainment and occupational sorting.

The reader will see that table 4.1 leaves the columns for *Parents Without Papers* and *Remaking the American Mainstream* blank. We do so not because the authors rule out the possibility of group-level differences in educational or occupational attainment, but rather because their theoretical contributions center on individual- rather than group-level concepts. As discussed at length in chapter 2, the neo-assimilation theory developed in Alba and Nee's seminal work operates primarily at the level of individuals and individual families. *Parents Without Papers* focuses on the importance of legal *membership* in allowing other forms of integration to take place: as this work concerns Mexican-origin immigrants, it focuses necessarily only on legal status differences *within* this specific group rather than on the impact of aggregate-level differences in legal status *between* groups.

As can be seen in the international perspective column of table 4.1, the model that we develop and apply in this book yields expectations that align with those proposed by many of the other scholars we review here: we also anticipate that the context of immigration will yield significant impacts across a broad range of dimensions. But unlike the existing scholarship, the international perspective examines contextual influences stemming from both the society of immigration and the society of emigration. Moreover, whereas the scholars reviewed in the previous pages have focused on specific origin groups—Mexicans or Chinese or Cubans or Dominicans—we can draw on our objective indicators for both contexts of emigration and immigration and apply them to the analysis of differences among sixty-seven different national-origin groups.

In this chapter, we compare the results of our multidimensional approach to the conventional national-origin group comparisons used in the existing literature. We do so by focusing on two crucial variables: the years of schooling completed and the occupational status of the Angelenos and New Yorkers studied in this book. As strong indicators of "structural integration" and of access to economic and social rewards, these socioeconomic outcomes have received by far the most research attention; consequently, they are especially well suited to an assessment of the contending perspectives in question.

MEASURING CONTEXT AND HOUSEHOLD RESOURCES

Before proceeding to the analysis, we first attend to the important issue of measurement: how can we best capture the well-established concepts outlined in the previous pages? The previous chapter provided a detailed review of our own measures of the contexts of emigration and of immigration. But these need to be incorporated into a broader model that includes two sets of variables gleaned from the existing literature: (1) group-level variables related to the context of immigration, inspired by the segmented assimilation literature, and (2) the individual- and household-level variables emphasized by general population models of stratification and political engagement but adapted to the immigrant experience.

Contexts of Emigration and Immigration

Throughout this book, we examine the effects of five contextual variables. The three outlined in chapter 3—status prevalence, the survival versus self-expression orientation, and the secular-rational orientation—are meant to capture the distinctively international aspects of population movements across state boundaries. In line with our review there, we expect that having origins in countries with a strongly secular-rational, or scholarly, orientation will prove advantageous in the educational lives of immigrant offspring. Moreover, we anticipate that the children of immigrants from societies with more survival-oriented worldviews will display higher levels of educational attainment, as obedience and obligation to parents transfer well to the school environment. Finally, we predict that membership in an immigrant group with predominantly privileged legal status will prove beneficial to second-generation educational attainment.

However, a large literature argues that shared population features *within* the receiving country that are related to aspects of social structure can yield group-wide effects experienced by any range of social groups, whether of immigrant origins or not. This perspective is echoed in the hypothesis of segmented assimilation, which contends that the availability of group-level resources relevant to immigrants and their descendants vary with the class composition of their national-origin "coethnic community," and that the racial and ethnic attitudes of the native-born population, labeled "societal reaction," affect both the capacity for community-wide mobilization of resources and the utilization of individual-level human capital. In this chapter, we alter these formulations to provide the alternative concepts of "ethnic capital" and "skin-color stratification," which align better with the phenomena these ideas are meant to capture. We follow by elaborating how each concept can be operationalized and then modeled so as to be marshaled for empirical research. By developing separate indicators for each dimension of the reception context, using appropriate secondary data sources to assign each sending country a rank on each dimension, we can examine the effect of each dimension on the outcomes of interest separately, holding the other two constant. Modeling each dimension as a continuous variable at one level—the level of national origin—we can also employ multilevel models that allow us to appropriately test for both contextual and compositional explanations for group-level differences.

Ethnic Capital   The hypothesis of segmented assimilation contends that group-level resources vary with a community's class composition. In this view, working-class communities will have less to offer than more diversified professional ones. Whereas the former provides networks of mutual support that ease immigrants' efforts to find jobs, their helping capacity is constrained by the immigrants' low level of skills as well as by a "collective expectation that new arrivals should not be 'uppity' and should not try to surpass, at least at the start, the collective status of their elders." By contrast, when community members hold higher-level jobs, "the support of ethnic networks is not contingent on acceptance of a working-class lifestyle or outlook."[1] Better still are "entrepreneurial communities" in which immigrant entrepreneurs directly hire and promote their own.

As so defined, the concept of "coethnic community" conflates receiving- and sending-country effects: culture is once again introduced through the back door, since the specific cultural traits ascribed to working-class communities strongly resemble the survival orientations that immigrants are likely to import from their places of origin. Moreover, the classifications are made in ad-hoc fashion, as no text ever provides measures for determining when a coethnic community is working-class, entrepreneurial, or professional.

Given the emphasis on a group's social structure and its capacity to mobilize group resources, we maintain that the concept of "ethnic capital" provides a better fit to the underlying idea. As education is strongly associated with income, occupation, and socialization processes, we view population-wide levels of education as the key indicator of ethnic capital.

Group-level differences in educational attainment will alter the impact of individual-level differences in schooling for reasons related to the resources that schooling can access and the symbolic meaning it conveys. On average, education is likely to be correlated with other resources that are likely to affect immigrant and second-generation outcomes, whether having to do with the ways in which referral networks connect to employers and jobs, the quality and diversity of information conveyed through ethnic ties, or the degree of engagement and understanding of host-society institutions. To the extent that social circles tie immigrants and their offspring to other people of the same origin, the rewards of education or the penalties of lack of schooling may be widely shared. Effects of this type are particularly likely to redound on persons who diverge from the group average: high group-wide averages will prove beneficial to below-average members of the group as long as their social ties connect to coethnics above their level; by the same token, low group-wide averages will work against above-average members of the group to the extent that their social ties connect below their level.

Moreover, education has a reputational effect that is especially important among immigrants and immigrant offspring, given the stigma associated with foreign origins and ethnic minority status. Group-level education sends a signal to outsiders, who may focus on the obvious characteristics that a person shares with others of the same or similar background rather than that person's individual traits. Thus, instead of examining each applicant closely, an employer might engage in statistical discrimination, preferring or rejecting someone based mainly on perceptions—very possibly mistaken—of skills and capacities population-wide. Indeed, it is this tendency that discourages the migration of higher-skilled Mexican immigrants, whom employers are apt to perceive through the prism of the average Mexican immigrant, whose schooling is relatively low.[2]

To assess the impact of coethnic community resources in an objective and replicable way, we operationalize ethnic capital as a variable measuring average years of schooling by national origin for the foreign-born ages twenty-five and older in New York (for the ISGMNY) and in Los Angeles (for IIMMLA), as reported in the 1980 U.S. census.

Skin-Color Stratification   Although the average educational profile of an immigrant group may yield reputational effects, societal reception—defined by Portes and Rumbaut as "the attitudes of the native population"—matters as well.[3] Immigrants arrive as foreigners and as such are often perceived by natives as unwelcome strangers who would have done better to stay in the strange places whence they came. However, as societies of immigration are also stratified by race, ethnicity, and national origin, both natives and immigrants make further distinctions of kind. At the turn of the twentieth century, immigrants from eastern and southern Europe were seen as swarthy, but at the turn of the twenty-first century they are perceived as white and hence are indistinguishable from the dominant group.[4] Migration streams from elsewhere in the world may not share that same acceptability that comes with being perceived as white. Migrants from the Caribbean and Africa are likely to suffer from long-standing prejudices against persons of African origin. Although persons of Latin American background are often seen as occupying an intermediate position in the American racial order between blacks and whites, that characterization nevertheless implies some significant degree of rejection.[5] The prevalence of the "model minority" image may be a source of protection for immigrants from Asia, but the view that Asians are also "forever foreigners" suggests that levels of acceptability may not reach those attained by contemporary immigrants from Europe or Canada.[6]

In conceptualizing societal reception, Portes and Rumbaut highlight a core categorical distinction between the descendants of the turn-of-the-century European immigrants, who experienced diminishing discrimination as "their phenotypical similarity with members of the mainstream American population eventually asserted itself," and the "children of Asian, black, mulatto, and mestizo immigrants," who undergo "enduring physical differences from whites and the equally persistent practice of discrimination based on those differences."[7] Yet, at a time when the overwhelming majority of immigrant offspring stem from everywhere *but* Europe, this binary distinction between whites and all others provides little analytic leverage, leaving a putatively key contextual variable with virtually no variance. Moreover, the emphasis on the fundamentally structuring nature of the white-nonwhite divide elides the differences among the "children of Asian, black, mulatto, and mestizo immigrants" that almost surely affect the schemas deployed to categorize this diverse population. As Portes and Rumbaut themselves point out, the dominant categorical schema takes the form of "a racial gradient" that involves a systematic bias toward persons of darker skin, denoted in the literature as "colorism." Indeed, as demonstrated by a significant body of research, darker skin color is consistently associated with worse socioeconomic outcomes.[8]

We conceptualize this racial gradient as "skin-color stratification," an external categorization that ranks and groups people but is applied informally and thus contrasts to civic stratification, which involves differences in formal status and is rooted in law. Since skin color varies within the many national-origin groups represented in the IIMMLA and ISGMNY surveys, we note that skin-color stratification can be a source of intra- as well as intergroup differences, as indicated by recent scholarship demonstrating differences in exposure to discrimination by skin color among Mexican-origin Americans, as well as more broadly among other Latin Americans, Asians, and African-origin groups.[9] Yet if the biases associated with colorism entail systematically unequal forms of treatment, then population-wide averages in the lightness or darkness of skin color should create systematic intergroup effects, penalizing the light-skinned members of more dark-skinned groups and rewarding the darker members of predominantly lighter-skinned groups.

In moving from concept to variable, we again seek to do so in a way that avoids subjective judgments and instead relies on a standardized measure that can be replicated by subsequent research. We operationalize skin-color stratification with a measure of the mean skin color of the national-origin group as reported by interviewers from the New Immigrant Survey (NIS), a nationally representative sample of adult immigrants admitted to legal permanent residence from May to November 2003. The NIS uses an 11-point scale, ranging from the lightest (albinism) at 0 to the darkest at 10. Interviewers were provided with a chart depicting ten hands identical in form but differing in color with 1 as the lightest shade and 10 as the darkest (0 was omitted from the chart). NIS interviewers were instructed to assign each respondent a score that corresponded to the hand that most closely resembled the skin color of the respondent.[10]

In emphasizing skin-color stratification, a concept that associates differences in treatment with disparities in skin color, we recognize that skin color is but one of a number of observable phenotypical traits—including, for instance, facial features—that might systematically trigger prejudiced behavior. We also acknowledge that other embodied characteristics have powerful signaling effects regarding membership and acceptability—such as dress or even accents, which are not innate but are very difficult to lose after childhood. Our measure cannot capture these elements, nor do our data contain individual measures of respondent phenotype; nonetheless, average skin color serves as a reasonable proxy for the susceptibility to discrimination or prejudice stemming from racial beliefs or perceptions.[11]

Household Resources and Vulnerabilities

Contexts of immigration and emigration are shared, population-wide variables that yield intergroup differences; no less important are the disparities within populations that yield intragroup differences. The last age of mass migration delivered a relatively homogeneous immigrant population, primarily from rural areas in the late-developing regions of southern and eastern Europe, characterized by low levels of literacy and education and minimal urban experience. By contrast, diversity at the point of departure is one of the distinguishing features of contemporary immigrants. Perhaps most important to the structural outcomes examined here is the great socioeconomic diversity among immigrant groups, as exemplified by the gap between illiterate rural arrivals from Laos or Somalia, on the one hand, and physicians from India or Nigeria, on the other. Yet socioeconomic diversity is also an intragroup characteristic, as even the major labor migrations contain a sizable share of highly educated professionals; likewise, the streams dominated by the highly skilled include proletarians. Moreover, some highly educated immigrants may arrive having completed their schooling prior to emigration but upon arrival must run the gauntlet required for validating their credentials and, when relevant, becoming licensed to practice. By contrast, those immigrants who arrive as student migrants or who obtain additional schooling once in the United States acquire a recognized credential as well as a deeper understanding of the receiving-country system.

To control for these compositional differences within immigrant groups, we include three separate controls. First, we control for both parental education and parental occupational status. Parental education is measured in years, taking the years of education attained by the parent with the highest level of education. Similarly, parental occupational status is measured with the continuous International Socio-Economic Index (ISEI) of occupational status score for the parent with the highest occupational status.[12] An ISEI score is assigned to occupations based on their level of social prestige, mean levels of education, and mean levels of income, and thus functions as a summary measure of the quality of the job attained. The scale ranges from 19 (agricultural laborers) to 90 (physicians). Finally, we control for whether one parent, both parents, or neither parent completed any schooling in the United States.

Beyond their diverse prior experiences in school and work, immigrants arrive not just as foreigners from foreign worlds but as aliens who lack equality with citizens. Internally differentiated from one another by rights and entitlements, they vary in their capacity to pass across the internal barriers of civic stratification, both those linked to different legal categories among noncitizens and those separating aliens from citizens. This variation has its most proximate influence on second-generation schooling and occupational status through its knock-on effect on the citizenship status of the children they bring with them. As we show in chapter 6, the 1.5 generation who arrive with green cards already in place are more likely to naturalize. Thus, controls for the citizenship status of the 1.5 generation are included as an indicator of alien status, an attribute expected to diminish both schooling and occupational outcomes. We separate these two categories of foreign-born but U.S.-raised immigrant offspring from those children of immigrants who were born in the United States, further dividing the U.S.-born second generation into those with two immigrant parents and those with one U.S.-born parent.

Finally, to acknowledge additional variation in the starting points of immigrant families, we control for language spoken in the parental household. Parents who speak English at home with their children are generally more fluent in the language themselves, enabling them to engage with the U.S. educational system and to advocate on their children's behalf. Moreover, they are immediately passing on English abilities to their children from a young age, potentially facilitating their children's performance in school and the labor market.

Fortunately, both the IIMMLA and ISGMNY data sets on which we rely enable us to control for these individual-level sources of heterogeneity. Throughout the book, we generally control for generational status (separately 1.5, second, and 2.5 generation), parental language ability, and the language spoken in the respondent's childhood household.[13] Having defined our key individual-level variables, we now turn to the assessment of contextual effects.

COMPARING CONCEPTUALIZATIONS OF CONTEXT

National Origin

We start with the common mode of measurement, namely, national-origin proxies. To examine the range of variation that can be captured with the national-origin groups available in the combined New York and Los Angeles data sets, we focus on the national-origin groups represented by a minimum of fifty observations in those data: China, Colombia, the Dominican Republic, Ecuador, El Salvador, Guatemala, Jamaica, Korea, Mexico, the Philippines, Russia, and Vietnam.[14]

To systematically select the appropriate country-of-origin groups for comparison, we apply the *Legacies* framework, as well as the conceptual variables used in that book, to create a three-way table that fully reflects the criteria enunciated in *Immigrant America, Legacies*, and other publications. We display the possible combinations of the three variables of policy reception, societal reception, and coethnic community in table 4.2. Then we populate each cell with the origin groups found in the IIMMLA and ISGMNY, drawing on data from the U.S. census of population and the Immigration and Naturalization Service (now U.S. Citizenship and

Table 4.2 Context of Immigration for Immigrant Groups in the IIMMLA and ISGMNY: Immigration Policy, Societal Reception, and Coethnic Community

Coethnic Community	Governmental Reception					
	Hostile		Neutral		Favorable	
	Societal Reception		Societal Reception		Societal Reception	
	Prejudiced	Neutral	Prejudiced	Neutral	Prejudiced	Neutral
Entrepreneurial or professional			China, Colombia, Ecuador, Peru, Philippines, West Indies		Vietnam	Former Soviet Union
Working-class	El Salvador, Guatemala, Mexico		Dominican Republic			
Poor						

Source: Adapted from Portes and Rumbaut 2001, table 3.1, 50–51.

Immigration Services, part of the Department of Homeland Security) and using the following simple assignment rules:

- *Immigration policy:* A three-category variable that is positive for groups with a large proportion of refugees (greater than 20 percent); neutral for groups with small proportions of both refugees and undocumented immigrants (less than 20 percent of each); and hostile for groups with large proportions of undocumented immigrants (greater than 20 percent)
- *Societal reception:* A two-category variable that is neutral or positive for predominantly European-origin immigrant groups and prejudiced for all others
- *Coethnic community:* A three-category variable that distinguishes between poor, working-class, and entrepreneurial or professional classes and that we determine according to the rates of self-employment and average levels of education for each group in New York and Los Angeles

Comparing countries in adjacent cells allows us to assess the effect of one dimension of the context of reception while holding the others constant. The context of reception displayed in table 4.2 provides only the rough shape of a rank, although it is fairly clear that immigrant offspring from the former Soviet Union are more advantageously placed than those from Mexico or El Salvador. Yet we also see that the great majority of the cells are empty, a pattern that similarly holds for the groups profiled in *Legacies*. As with *Legacies*, this configuration precludes a test of a key contention: that controlling for coethnic community and societal reception, policy reception decisively alters outcomes. Unfortunately, only the contrasts between Dominicans, on the one hand, and Mexicans, Guatemalans, and Salvadorans, on the other, allow us to assess that possibility. Even that contrast provides a very partial assessment, since, just as in *Legacies*, no group occupies the cell needed to compare the impact of a positive policy reception for nationalities that otherwise share a working-class coethnic community and a negative societal reception. And whereas critical cells in table 4.2 are empty, others are filled with many groups, a pattern of clustering into a single space that implies a similarity of outcomes among those groups—a logical possibility, but one that has yet to be tested.

In contrast to this rough categorization, we use the continuous measures described in this chapter and the previous chapter to measure each of the concepts underlying the context of immigration (or reception). This procedure yields two immediate benefits: we avoid empty cells, and by avoiding dummy-variable comparisons, we can use the full range of national origins to be found in our sample. We are thus able to include

Table 4.3 Descriptive Statistics of Second-Generation Immigrants, Ages Twenty-Three and Older

	Range	Mean	Standard Deviation
Context variables			
Group years of education	7.63–15.23	11.62	1.58
Status prevalence score	1.00–6.00	3.65	1.57
Skin color	1.44–7.44	3.90	1.29
Traditional versus secular-rational score	–2.06–1.74	–0.61	1.02
Survival versus self-expression score	–1.62–1.62	0.04	0.71
Dependent variables			
Years of completed education	1.00–20.00	14.82	2.31
ISEI score for main occupation (N = 2,118)	19.00–90.00	54.46	14.26

Source: IIMMLA and ISGMNY data sets.
Note: N = 2,788. All context variables reported as group-level means and standard deviations (N = 67).

all sixty-seven national-origin groups present in the pooled ISGMNY/IIMMLA sample.

Table 4.3 provides a summary view of the various contextual indicators to be used in the analysis to follow. The average years of education at the metropolitan level in 1980, our measure of ethnic capital, was 11.6 years, with an observed range of 7.6 to 15.2 years. The average status prevalence score, our measure for the governmental reception context, was 3.65, indicating that the average origin group included some IRCA legalizations (1 to 20 percent) but no refugees. The group-level average skin color ranged from 1.44 (close to the very white end of the scale) to 7.44, with an average of 3.90—close to the middle of the scale.

The World Values Survey scales are normalized such that they are centered at 0 and roughly normally distributed with a range from about –2 to 2 for all countries contained in that survey. For the traditional versus secular-rational dimension, we observe values from –2.06 (El Salvador) to 1.74 (Japan). Overall, our immigrant-origin sample is skewed toward traditionally oriented societies, with a mean index score of –0.61. In contrast, the mean score of the survival versus self-expression scale in our sample is centered on the grand mean of all of the countries in the WVS, at 0.04, and has a somewhat narrower range, from –1.62 (Russia) to 1.62 (Australia).

Table 4.3 also reports summary statistics on educational and occupational attainment for our second-generation sample. The mean for years of completed education among those age twenty-three and older is nearly a university degree—fifteen years—with most of the sample falling between twelve and seventeen years of schooling. And as with parental occupational status, we measure occupational status for those age twenty-five and older as the ISEI score of the main occupation, using the ISEI-08 coding schema.[15] The average for our sample is a midrange professional with a score of 54—which is in line with the mean education level for our young, urban sample being close to a university degree.

As a preliminary assessment of the adequacy of our measures, table 4.4 displays the correlations between each of the different contextual indicators and the years of education completed and occupational status of the New Yorkers and Angelenos in our study. A look down the first column proves revealing: the variables we have created to measure the context of immigration correlate at moderate to strong levels with second-generation educational attainment. Similarly, these variables also correlate with occupational attainment, though the sizes of the coefficients are smaller, reflecting the greater distance of occupation, in both time and socialization, from the childhood home. The context of emigration matters for both outcomes as well: higher levels on the survival versus self-expression scale (in other words, a tendency toward greater self-expression) and darker skin color go along with lower levels of schooling and occupational status; higher levels on the rational versus traditional scale and higher group-level averages in schooling correlate positively with higher levels of schooling and occupational status among our respondents. This initial cut points to the value of adding context-of-emigration variables, as they turn out to be just as strongly correlated with both of our outcomes as the variables related to the standard context of reception. We also see that the context-of-origin WVS scales are correlated, but negatively, with each other. Moreover, the groups from rationally oriented societies were generally lighter-skinned and also encountered a more positive governmental reception, whereas more negative immigration statuses prevailed among groups from societies with strong self-expression values and darker skin.

EXPLAINING VARIATION IN EDUCATIONAL AND OCCUPATIONAL ATTAINMENT

We now compare a series of models, regressing years of education and occupational status on both national-origin comparisons and our multidimensional indicators, alongside controls for individual-level factors. When modeling educational attainment, we use a combined sample of all complete observations from both the IIMMLA and ISGMNY, restricted to those ages twenty-three and older. For occupational attainment, we restrict to respondents ages twenty-five and older, a time point when only 25 percent of respondents were still in school full-time.

Table 4.4 Correlation Among Multiple Dimensions of Context, Years of Education Completed, and Occupational Status

	Years of Completed Education	ISEI Score of Occupation	Status Prevalence Scale	Group Years of Education	Average Group Skin Color	Traditional Versus Secular-Rational Score	Survival Versus Self-Expression Score
Years of completed education	1.00						
ISEI score of occupation	.48	1.00					
Status prevalence scale	.31	.23	1.00				
Average group education	.38	.23	.36	1.00			
Average group skin color	-.30	-.21	-.66	-.46	1.00		
Traditional versus secular-rational score	.35	.25	.53	.38	-.64	1.00	
Survival versus self-expression score	-.34	-.22	-.43	-.38	.29	-.74	1.00

Source: IIMMLA and ISGMNY data sets.

We enter the control variables in two steps. The first controls only for age, sex and schooling status (model 1); the second adds controls for parents' characteristics—education, country of education, occupation—and additional respondents' characteristics—place of birth, legal status, any experience of childhood separation from a parent for a year or more, childhood household structure (whether raised by both biological parents or not), and the language spoken in the household of origin (model 2). For occupational attainment, we also control for respondents' educational attainment across all models. As we are focusing on intergroup differences, these important individual-level characteristics are treated as controls. We discuss the coefficients for these variables at length in chapter 5.

When comparing the educational and occupational attainment of the children of immigrants by national origins, we follow the standard practice of inserting national-origin dummies in a single-level model. However, when examining multidimensional context indicators, we use multilevel models that take the nested structure of families within groups into account, adjusting for the correlation in individual-level characteristics within origin groups and testing for both the direct and the contextual effect of educational attainment among immigrants on the educational attainment of the second generation.[16] This procedure yields the additional benefit of allowing us to directly assess the degree to which group-level variables account for intergroup variation.

Methodologically we follow a line of inquiry that has used multilevel models to ascertain the effects of contextual variables on educational outcomes among the children of immigrants or on other socioeconomic outcomes.[17] Unlike national-origin comparisons (see table 4.5), for which the specific characteristics that influence educational attainment must be inferred from a catchall national-origin coefficient, this modeling strategy enables us to identify the specific dimension of the context of reception that is associated with second-generation educational attainment, while holding the other dimensions constant. While most of this research has examined variation across different receiving countries, here we follow other scholars in exploiting the ample variation in receiving context by national origin within the United States.[18] Table 4.6 presents a summary of these results focusing on the context measures.

National-Origin Group Comparisons

The first part of table 4.6 reexamines the standard approach to studying the context of reception. As illustrated in table 4.5, we compare the predicted

Table 4.5 Detailed View of Cells Adjacent to the Reception Contexts Under Comparison

	Societal Reception Prejudiced	
	Governmental Reception	
Coethnic Community	Hostile	Neutral
Entrepreneurial-professional Working-class Poor	Mexicans	Chinese Dominicans

	Governmental Reception Favorable	
	Societal Reception	
Coethnic Community	Prejudiced	Neutral
Entrepreneurial-professional Working-class Poor	Vietnamese	Russians

Source: IIMMLA and ISGMNY data sets.

years of educational attainment for the children of immigrants from national-origin groups in adjacent cells within the three-way context of reception (table 4.2), allowing one factor (societal reception, government reception, or coethnic community) to differ while holding the other two constant:

- *Government context of reception:* We compare Dominicans with Mexicans, Guatemalans, and Salvadorans: all faced a negative societal reception, and all are working-class, but the Dominicans enjoyed a less hostile government reception than the Guatemalans, Salvadorans, and Mexicans, among whom a large fraction of immigrants entered in unauthorized status.

- *Coethnic community:* Given the large cluster of origin groups in the entrepreneurial coethnic, neutral government, negative societal reception cell, we contrast many groups—Jamaicans, Chinese, Colombians, Koreans, Filipinos, and Ecuadorians—with the working-class Dominicans.

Table 4.6 Contextual Variables Predicting Educational and Occupational Attainment: Summary of Hierarchical Linear Regression Models

	Educational Attainment (Ages Twenty-Three and Older)				Occupational Status (Ages Twenty-Five and Older)					
	Model 1		Model 2		Demographics		Full Controls			
	Coefficient	Standard Error	Coefficient	Standard Error	Coefficient	Standard Error	Coefficient	Standard Error		
Country-by-country comparisons (N = 2,788)										
Neutral versus hostile government context										
Dominican versus Mexican	-.98	.23**	-.39	.23	-.71	1.64	.28	1.66		
Dominican versus Guatemalan	-.09	.32	.28	.31	.60	2.19	2.01	2.19		
Dominican versus Salvadoran	-.54	.28+	-.14	.27	.23	2.28	-.27	2.31		
Working-class versus entrepreneurial or professional coethnic										
Dominican versus Jamaican	.37	.30	.16	.31	1.43	2.10	1.20	2.23		
Dominican versus Chinese	1.90	.22**	1.58	.21**	4.16	1.61**	3.99	1.61*		
Dominican versus Colombian	.46	.27+	.30	.25	.75	2.03	1.01	2.02		
Dominican versus Koreans	1.78	.25**	1.35	.25**	3.46	1.76*	3.77	1.81*		
Dominican versus Filipino	1.05	.25**	.46	.25*	3.23	1.76+	3.24	1.81*		
Dominican versus Ecuadorian	.42	.26	.33	.25	.26	1.85	.38	1.84		

(Table continues on p. 106.)

Table 4.6 Continued

	Educational Attainment (Ages Twenty-Three and Older)				Occupational Status (Ages Twenty-Five and Older)			
	Model 1		Model 2		Demographics		Full Controls	
	Coefficient	Standard Error	Coefficient	Standard Error	Coefficient	Standard Error	Coefficient	Standard Error

Neutral versus hostile societal reception
Russian versus Vietnamese	−.20	.30	.38	.29	−1.58	2.14	−.18	2.17
Context of immigration (N = 2,788)								
Group years of education	.28	.06**	.14	.05**	.14	.05**	.19	.16
Average group skin color	−.19	.09*	−.17	.08*	−.17	.08*	−.59	.37
Status prevalence scale	.10	.07	.06	.06	.06	.06	.43*	.21
Intraclass correlation	.06		.05		.05		.02	
Intraclass correlation without country variables	.14				.14	.05**		
Context of emigration (N = 2,788)								
Survival versus self-expression	−.25	.16	−.16	.13	−.20	.63	−.02	.64
Traditional versus secular-rational	.44	.12**	.38	.09**	1.15	.39**	1.10	.37**
Intraclass correlation	.06		.03		.02		.01	
Intraclass correlation without country variables	.14				.07			

Multiple dimensions of context (N = 2,788)								
Group years of education	.23	.04**	.10	.04*	.31	.14*	.11	.17
Average group skin color	-.09	.08	-.06	.08	-.30	.41	-.33	.43
Status prevalence scale	.03	.05	.01	.05	.33	.21	.33	.22
Survival versus self-expression	-.32	.14*	-.19	.13	-.18	.65	-.19	.69
Traditional versus secular-rational	.27	.12*	.30	.10**	.62	.45	.62	.46
Intraclass correlation	.02		.02		.00		.00	
Intraclass correlation without country variables	.14				.07			
Individual-level controls included	Age, sex, city, and school status		All controls		Age, sex, city, school status, and years of education		All controls	

Source: IIMMLA and ISGMNY data sets.

Notes: Full results from all analyses in this chapter are found in the online appendix.

*$p < .05$; **$p < .01$

- *Societal reception:* We compare Russians and Vietnamese, as both exemplify an entrepreneurial and professional coethnic community, but the former group is the only European national-origin group in our samples, and hence the only group to which the *Legacies* framework would assign a positive societal reception.

As table 4.6 shows, comparing across countries of origin ranked at differing levels of one dimension, holding the other dimensions constant, yields few statistically significant differences. In the final model, only four of these ten origin intergroup comparisons yield coefficients that are statistically significant at the 10 percent level or higher, and only three do so at levels of statistical significance of 5 percent or higher. The *Legacies* approach tells us that the neutral governmental reception context enjoyed by Dominican-origin immigrants should translate into higher educational attainment for their children relative to the children of Central American– or Mexican-origin immigrants, among whom undocumented immigration was pervasive. However, while average levels of schooling among Dominicans did exceed the levels attained by Mexicans and Salvadorans (though not Guatemalans), that advantage disappeared with the application of controls. The analysis of occupational attainment finds no national-origin differences whatsoever. Similarly, comparing educational attainment among the working-class Dominicans to that of groups characterized by a professional coethnic community yields only inconsistent effects: net of all controls, Filipino, Chinese, and Korean immigrant offspring in our samples attained higher levels of schooling than their Dominican counterparts, but Ecuadorians, Colombians, and Jamaicans were statistically indistinguishable. The analysis of occupational attainment demonstrates that only the three Asian nationalities possessed an advantage when contrasted to the Dominicans. Finally, we isolate the effect of societal reception, comparing the children of Russian refugees to those of Vietnamese refugees: these groups prove statistically indistinguishable with respect to both educational and occupational attainment.

Context of Immigration

In the next section of table 4.6, we show the results of the same series of models, this time using separate, objectively defined indicators for each dimension of the context of immigration instead of the selectively chosen national-origin comparisons.

The multilevel models provide an additional statistic, the intraclass correlation, which displays the proportion of unexplained variation that is accounted for by differences across groups rather than within them. This statistic ranges from 0 to 1; the larger the number, the more unexplained variation can be explained by national origins; the smaller the number, the less informative are national origins. We see that in a model controlling only for age, sex, and city of residence, the intraclass correlation for educational attainment is only 0.14. In other words, in the absence of country-level controls, we already see that only about one-eighth of the unexplained variation in educational attainment derives from differences *between* national-origin groups as opposed to differences *within* them. The intraclass correlation for occupational attainment is still smaller, only 7 percent; considering that occupational attainment is further away from childhood socialization than education, this would seem to confirm that parental backgrounds exert their strongest influence on occupational attainment through their impact on educational attainment. Net of schooling, the relationship between country of origin and occupational attainment is very modest. Moreover, when we control for the context of immigration (second section of table 4.6), the unexplained group-level variation for both outcomes drops by more than half: controlling for group-level educational attainment, status prevalence, and skin color accounts for half of the correlation in educational and occupational attainment among the children of immigrants of the same origins.

When we look at the coefficients for each of these group-level variables, we see that group-level differences in the prevalence of different legal statuses do not matter for educational attainment, but they *do* matter for occupational attainment. There is a good reason to think that differences in the prevalence of status would *not* prove to be related to educational attainment: all school-age children enjoy a constitutionally protected right to primary and secondary schooling, and the school system is one domain of society where legal status should matter least, given its explicit goals of making sure that young people leave school with skills that will allow them to function as workers while also producing law-abiding, productive citizens. However, as qualitative research has shown, this variable exerts its impact later in life, particularly as the legal and social protections of the school environment fall away in young adults' transition to work.[19] Not surprisingly, then, the association between the status prevalence scale and occupational attainment proves positive and statistically significant both before and after the individual-level controls.

Turning to ethnic capital, in the first model, which applies only demographic controls, a one-year increase in average group education is associated with an increase in respondent's education of about one-quarter of a year and with a very small, but statistically significant, increase in occupational attainment as well. This coefficient declines by about half after controlling for parental education and occupation, demonstrating that family-level advantage is a primary mediator of group-level educational resources. In the final model each additional year in the average educational level of coethnics is associated with an increase of 0.14 years of completed education, though it loses significance in the regression on occupational attainment.

Finally, we turn to our measure of skin-color stratification. The first two columns show that each shade darker in the group average skin color (with a range from 1 to 8) is associated with a decrease of 0.17 years of education, an association that stays stable after individual-level controls. As seen in columns 3 and 4, darker average group skin color is also associated with a slight decrease in occupational attainment, but this association becomes insignificant after individual-level controls.

Context of Emigration

In this section, we demonstrate that our measures of context of emigration similarly yield substantial net effects on second-generation educational attainment. Turning again to the intraclass correlation, we see that origin characteristics explain a similar amount of group-level variation as context of immigration: the intraclass correlation coefficient drops again from 0.14 with no country-level controls to 0.06 after controlling for the survival versus self-expression and traditional versus secular-rational scales; for occupational attainment, the intraclass correlation coefficient falls even further, from 0.07 to only 0.02.

The association of educational attainment with the sending country's position on the traditional versus secular-rational and survival versus self-expression scales can be interpreted as the effect of a standard deviation away from the grand mean of the WVS (roughly representative of the world population) on the expected years of education of second-generation respondents from that origin country.[20] In the basic model, a one-standard-deviation change from a more traditionally oriented country toward one that is more secular is associated with a gain of nearly half a year of additional schooling; in contrast, a one-standard-deviation shift from a survival-oriented to a self-expression–oriented sending country is associated with a loss of about one-quarter of a year of schooling, although this coefficient is not statistically significant. Similarly, the children of immigrants from more secular-oriented countries have higher occupational attainment, on average, whereas there is no statistically significant relationship between survival versus self-expression orientations and occupation. This pattern aligns well with the negative association between these two variables in our sample. Both scales yield diminished effects after the application of individual-level controls. Yet even in the final model, with extensive individual-level controls, secular orientations at the country-of-origin level strongly predict second-generation educational attainment.

Multiple Dimensions of Context

Finally, we evaluate models that combine the contexts of immigration and emigration. Together, these variables account for essentially all of the group-level variation in educational attainment: the intraclass correlation coefficient here drops all the way to only 0.02; in other words, only 2 percent of the total variation in educational attainment at the group level remains unexplained. In the case of occupational attainment, the initial small amount of unexplained variation at the group level approaches 0.

As shown in the last rows of table 4.6, including the country-of-origin variables reduces the size of the coefficients of average group education and average group skin color (with statistical significance for the latter dropping out in the baseline model and not changing thereafter). By contrast, in the baseline model, both country-of-origin scales yield statistically significant effects on years of education completed, even net of their relationship to the context of reception. In this first model, a one-unit move in the direction of rational orientation is associated with a one-quarter of a year (0.27) increase in expected educational attainment, and a one-unit change toward a self-expression orientation is associated with a loss of just under one-third of a year (0.32) of expected schooling. With the full set of controls included, significance levels for the survival versus self-expression scale exceed the 10 percent level, and the size of the coefficient falls by one-third. By contrast, the coefficients for the traditional versus secular-rational scale maintain a similar size from one model to another, with statistical significance at the 1 percent level retained even after all controls.

In contrast, none of the group-level variables remain statistically significant when predicting occupational attainment, an outcome more distant from the family of origin. Given the small amount of country-level variation in this variable, it may be that five group-level variables are simply too much.

CONCLUSION: EXTENDING THE REACH AND REFINING THE OPERATIONALIZATION OF CONTEXT

This chapter engages with an enduring puzzle, one that has both preoccupied students of migration and ethnicity and caught the public imagination—namely, how to explain the sometimes striking intergroup differences among the descendants of immigrants, who have so often departed from their home country motivated by common objectives and who have repeatedly faced the obstacle of a strange environment in which their presence is neither wanted nor welcomed. Popular discourse generally points in the direction of home-country culture—though without explaining what might make one home-country culture fit better than another—and by invoking stock stereotypes that may be pertinent to a handful of origin countries but are hardly adequate when applied to the ever-growing number of places from which today's immigrants stem. These deficiencies have led scholars to take the opposite course: noting that immigrants starting out in countries that almost surely share fundamental values nonetheless fare very differently, they instead turn to features of the reception context—policies, dominant group views, shared attributes of the ethnic group—to shed light on the source of intergroup differences. Such efforts have indeed advanced the quality of scholarly debate, yet the solutions they propose, which ignore the context of emigration, are incomplete. We assess here whether our proposed remedies to these shortcomings do better, systematically contrasting our new measures of both the context of emigration and the context of immigration to those that are more commonly used.

Current empirical assessments of segmented assimilation theory rely on pairwise country-of-origin comparisons to examine the impact of differences in reception context, building on the understanding that the different components of that context come together to form a "mode of incorporation." Our systematic appraisal shows that when applied through the use of appropriately selected country-of-origin comparisons, this approach fails to consistently predict second-generation attainment after the application of the standard, individual controls. We arrive at that conclusion by systematically contrasting groups that share two dimensions of the mode of incorporation, isolating the impact of difference on the one remaining dimension. Moreover, we assess all of the potential sources of variation within our data set to provide the most comprehensive evaluation possible. We find that *none of the three dimensions said to determine modes of incorporation—the policy context, societal reception, and the coethnic community—consistently predicts second-generation educational and occupational attainment over and beyond individual-level measures*. Although nearly every group performs better than Mexican-origin youth, and many groups perform worse than the very positively received Russian-origin respondents, the finer distinctions do not hold up; indeed, differences in academic performance are often greater among groups occupying the same cell of the *Legacies* conceptual table than among those that appear in the cross-cell comparisons.

Thus, applying the framework elaborated in *Legacies* to rank national-origin groups fails to provide confirmatory evidence. Moreover, these national-origin comparisons conflate sending- and receiving-country characteristics, as the dummy national-origin variable inherently serves as a measure of both the context of emigration and the context of immigration. And as a result of the relatively small sample size of many of the origin groups in the Los Angeles and New York surveys, reliance on pairwise national-origin comparison reduces variation: only the largest national-origin groups—of which there are relatively few—can be compared.

The line of inquiry developed in this book overcomes the shortcomings of the approach adopted in *Legacies*, which fully reflects the conventions in the literature. Here we have proceeded in a different way: by disaggregating aspects of the immigration and emigration contexts into their different components, we gain the capacity to discern which dimension—migration policies (status prevalence scale), ethnic capital (mean level of education), skin-color stratification (group average skin color), or origin-country cultural orientations—exerts an impact on specific second-generation outcomes. By using multilevel modeling and distinguishing between the inter- and intragroup levels, we can assess the relative importance of the within- and between-group differences; we can also determine whether the contextual variables that distinguish one group from another yield effects that vary across outcomes. In this case, group membership accounts for a small, but non-negligible, portion of the variation in education, but there is virtually no variation in occupational attainment after controlling for education.

Our operationalization also yields individual measures of the impact of each contextual variable on second-generation attainment with the other group- and individual-level measures held constant. We can assess whether each dimension is significantly associated with each outcome, and we can also compare their relative strengths. For instance, a one-standard-deviation change (1.58 years) in group-level education in our final multiple dimensions of context model is associated with an increase of 0.16 years in predicted years of education, whereas a one-standard-deviation change toward secular-rational values within our sample is associated with an increase of 0.30 years of education. Moreover, this disaggregation of contextual effects allows a comparison of the relative importance of different dimensions across different second-generation outcomes. Although differences in the contexts of immigration and emigration directly result in differences in educational attainment, they have no direct effect on occupation; rather, contextual variables influence occupation indirectly, through their impact on education, which in turn affects the types of jobs obtained by immigrant offspring. In later chapters, we assess how these same contextual factors affect political affiliation, ethnic identity, and cross-border connections.

This methodology improves our ability to address the hypotheses outlined in the very beginning of the chapter. To begin with, the view that national-origin groups yield powerful effects—the conclusion drawn by *Legacies* and *Inheriting the City* and the core assumption from which *The Asian American Achievement Paradox* takes off—needs significant revision. Group membership does yield some effect on the socioeconomic attainment of these second-generation New Yorkers and Angelenos, but the impact is relatively slight. Far more important are the sources of intragroup variation.

As our analysis has shown, some of the specific contextual variables in question—whether proposed by other authors or developed in this study—do prove influential, whereas others do not. In particular, an imported cultural orientation—such as a secular-rational orientation—can matter, a possibility that both *Legacies* and *The Asian American Achievement Paradox* exclude. By contrast, *Inheriting the City* hints at the importance of both a secular-rational orientation and a survival orientation, but without ever transforming those speculations into clearly specified hypotheses. Yet here we see that a secular-rational orientation, which can be linked to a "scholarly culture," affects educational but not occupational attainment; by contrast, the positive association between a survival orientation and educational attainment becomes statistically insignificant once we control for compositional differences between the groups.

The value of our approach can be summarized more succinctly in the diagram in figure 4.1, which shows the changes in predicted years of education and occupational status scores for second-generation members as we vary group- and individual-level circumstances. The first set of bars depicts the difference in the occupational and educational attainment of a second-generation respondent with a high level of individual resources (born in the United States, parents with educational and occupational attainment in the seventy-fifth percentile, English spoken at home, two parents educated in the United States, raised by both parents) versus a second-generation member with a low level of individual-level resources (a noncitizen, parents' education and occupation in the twenty-fifth percentile, a foreign language spoken at home, no parent educated in the United States, not raised by both biological parents). The second set of bars shows the difference between those with an advantaged group context from a light-skinned group (twenty-fifth percentile) with high levels of average education and a prevalence of advantageous legal statuses (both seventy-fifth percentile), as well as origins in an advantageous context of origin (seventy-fifth percentile on the traditional versus secular-rational axis and likewise on the survival–self-expression axis) and a disadvantaged

Figure 4.1 Predicted Changes in Educational Attainment and Occupational Status Associated with Changes in Group- and Individual-Level Variables

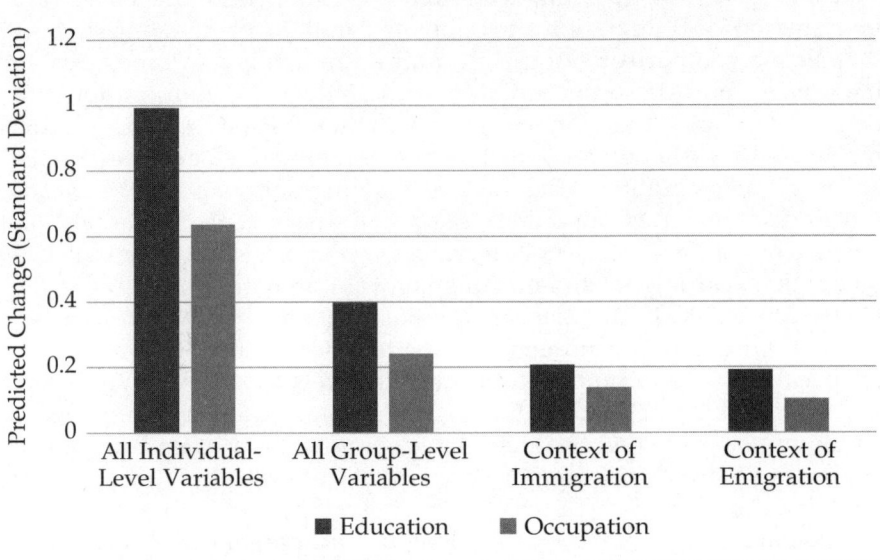

Source: IIMMLA and ISGMNY data sets.

group context (from a dark-skinned group—seventy-fifth percentile—with low levels of education and a prevalence of disadvantages statuses—twenty-fifth percentile—as well as origins in a disadvantageous context of origin—twenty-fifth percentile on the traditional versus secular-rational axis and likewise on the survival–self-expression axis). Finally, the third and fourth sets of bars show the effects of coming from a group with an advantageous context of immigration or an advantageous context of emigration.[21]

Figure 4.1 confirms a finding already noted in this chapter: individual-level factors exercise significantly more influence on educational and occupational attainment than do group-level characteristics. The figure further provides a metric for measuring the size of that difference: taken as a sum, individual-level variables are more than twice as important as group-level variables. The figure also shows that context-of-emigration effects are almost as substantial as those linked to the context of immigration. Finally, we see at a glance that both group- and family-level resources are stronger predictors of educational attainment (light gray bars) than occupational attainment (dark gray bars)—precisely what we would expect.

It is only by disaggregating the different components of the contexts of immigration and emigration and applying a multilevel modeling strategy that such a comparison is possible. Our approach is also innovative in moving beyond the preoccupation with contexts of immigration and thereby capturing the distinctively international aspects of population movements across boundaries that are likely to influence the socioeconomic and political integration of the children of immigrants: namely, the foreign influences stemming from characteristics of the context of emigration. This chapter has shown that scholarly values in the origin country translate into higher educational attainment among children of immigrants in the United States. The traditional versus secular-rational orientation scale is a strong predictor of second-generation attainment, robust to a multitude of specifications and more consistent in its effect than receiving-context characteristics. The children of immigrants from countries where science and innovation are highly valued have significantly higher educational attainment than the children of immigrants from countries where more traditional orientations prevail, even controlling for both group- and individual-level differences in legal status and parental human capital. Stronger survival orientations similarly are positively associated with educational attainment, though this relationship becomes statistically insignificant after we include individual-level controls. In later chapters, we will see that this scale is associated with a number of non-economic outcomes, such as naturalization.

We do note that some measures work better than others. Some of those shortcomings reflect the distance between the measurements we could assemble and the underlying concepts. Owing to the difficulties of measuring societal reception, we have used the position of a national-origin group in the skin-color stratification continuum as an indirect proxy for *potential* discrimination, thereby probably weakening the observed relationship between this variable and second-generation educational attainment. However, when we restrict our model to the context of immigration (omitting the context-of-emigration variables), the effect of average group skin color remains significant and in the expected direction, even in models that include all individual-level controls: therefore, it is likely to capture some aspect of societal reception.[22]

By contrast, our measure of status prevalence relies on high-quality, detailed information from official statistics at the national-origin level, and so we feel confident that this measure adequately captures the ways in which migration policies yield intergroup differences. Thus, the lack of statistical significance for this measure points to the possibility that this dimension of the reception context may not systematically affect second-generation educational attainment when we consider all immigrant groups. Given that even undocumented children of immigrants often have to "learn to be illegal" only after leaving the protection of formal schooling, educational attainment may be a second-generation outcome that is less vulnerable to group-level differences in status prevalence.[23] As we will see in the next chapter, those disparities in status prove to be strongly related to occupational attainment, and additional consequences will be demonstrated in later chapters.

Chapter 5 | Getting Ahead: Institutions, Ethnicity, and International Influences

IN CHAPTER 4, we tested hypotheses regarding interethnic variation in educational and occupational attainment, drawn from each of the major works reviewed in chapter 2 as well as from our own international perspective, elaborated in chapter 3. The assessment presented in chapter 4 demonstrated the value of our multidimensional approach for measuring the contextual influences that affect intergroup differences, as well as the importance of a multilevel modeling strategy that employs variables, rather than names, to achieve that end. We found that both sending- and receiving-country characteristics matter for the educational attainment of the children of immigrants, but not for their occupational attainment.

Just as important are the findings generated by our specific multilevel modeling strategy: although much of the second-generation literature is focused on intergroup comparisons, we find that only a fairly small proportion of the actual variation in educational and occupational attainment operates at the group level. In other words, group membership accounts for only a small proportion of overall differences in educational attainment and for almost none of the difference in occupational attainment: *intragroup* variation is responsible for the majority of total variation in socioeconomic attainment.

With this background information in place, we now turn to exploring the sources of intragroup variation in educational and occupational attainment. As in the previous chapter, we begin by deriving hypotheses from current approaches to understanding second-generation outcomes, including those from our own international perspective. In this chapter, we exclusively focus on hypotheses regarding individual- (or family-) level sources of variation in educational and occupational attainment, which we then test, mainly relying on the pooled sample of immigrant-origin New Yorkers and Angelenos, but occasionally focusing on one or the other survey for specific individual-level variables that do not appear in both. We conclude by examining possible *cross-level interactions:* as elaborated at length in chapter 2, we inquire whether specific characteristics of the immigrant context exacerbate or ameliorate family-level inequalities.

SOURCES OF INTRAGROUP DIFFERENCE: CLASS, ETHNICITY, AND INSTITUTIONS

Table 5.1 summarizes the characteristics that we anticipate will be the most important in driving intragroup difference in educational and occupational attainment. That immigrant parents' own socioeconomic resources will influence the socioeconomic achievement of their U.S.-born or U.S.-raised children represents a common point of departure for scholars of the second generation. However, both the degree to which those resources can be transmitted from the first to the second generation and the mechanisms by which transmission occurs are matters of disagreement, as shown in table 5.1 which lists those individual- or family-level characteristics deemed most important by the various approaches that we have considered thus far.

Expecting that the outcomes of the children of immigrants will eventually "regress towards the mean," the authors of *Remaking the American Mainstream* anticipate that the offspring of immigrants clustered at the bottom of the educational and occupational distributions will eventually move upwards and that those descended from parents clustered at the higher ends will eventually move downwards, with the end result entailing socioeconomic distributions for the descendants of immigrants that blend into those of the general population. Concretely, this expectation predicts that controls for family-level resources in the form of parental education and occupation will account for a large fraction of the variation in second-generation outcomes. Indeed, much research shows that once we account for initial disadvantages in parental education and other family resources, the children of immigrants frequently enjoy an advantage relative to natives, especially in educational achievement, a finding that provides the surest grounds for the optimism inherent in the neo-assimilation model.[1] If we assume that relatively high levels of *absolute* mobility continue to characterize the American stratification system, the children of immigrants should be able to progress in the labor market, entering the middle- and upper-middle-level positions now being vacated by retiring baby boomers.[2] And should that scenario prove true, today's second generation would thus follow the path of the previous children of immigrants

Table 5.1 Hypothesizing Sources of Intergroup Differences

Concept	O+D	LEG	ITC	AAAP	PWP	RAM	Our Measurement
Socioeconomic status of parent and self	x	x	x	x	x	x	Parents' education, parents' occupation, and respondent's education
Assimilation						x	Parents educated in the United States, immigrant generation
Intrafamilial cohesion in childhood		x					Childhood: intact family, foreign-language household, mixed parentage
Ethnic maintenance		x		x			Ability in parental language
Supplementary education				x			Ethnic tutoring and cram school
Hyperselectivity				x			Parent in top quintile of education (seventeen years or more)
Urban institutions			x	x			Use of city amenities, high school ranking (New York City only)
Membership exclusion	x				x		Parents' legal status, respondent's legal status (Los Angeles only)
Cross-border connections	x						Parent sends remittances, travels to home country, cross-border families (Los Angeles only)

Source: O+D = Origins and Destinations. Portes and Rumbaut 2001 (LEG = Legacies); Kasinitz et al. 2008 (ITC = Inheriting the City); Lee and Zhou 2015 (AAAP = Asian American Achievement Paradox); Bean, Brown, and Bachmeier 2015 (PWP = Parents Without Papers); Alba and Nee 2003 (RAM = Remaking the American Mainstream).

who moved up to join the burgeoning middle class that grew as a result of the great economic expansion following the Second World War.[3]

In contrast to this more general social stratification perspective, nearly all of the other approaches anticipate both intergroup and intragroup differences in the patterns of intergenerational mobility. For instance, *Legacies* situates ethnic maintenance and intrafamilial cohesion as the key individual-level variables predicting the educational and occupational success of the children of immigrants: the offspring of families that can maintain internal solidarity and ties to their coethnic community should experience better outcomes than those exposed to a less "buffered" form of acculturation. For this perspective, family structure fulfills an essential function: given the stress to which immigrant families are exposed—tensions aggravated by the likelihood that the more rapid pace of acculturation among children as opposed to parents will produce role reversal—dual-parent households are better able to preserve parental authority and monitoring. Similarly, raising children in households that maintain use of the mother tongue and transmit mother-tongue competence intergenerationally will reinforce parental authority, thereby giving parents an influence over children's behavior and school performance lost by those of their counterparts who adopt English more quickly or who fail to transmit mother-tongue competence to their children.

As we have noted before, *Inheriting the City* emphasizes not so much group resources as the institutional structure of the receiving urban center itself. In putting forth their immigrant advantage perspective, Kasinitz and his coauthors argue that the use of public goods can provide a springboard for greater upward intergenerational mobility. We will draw on the unique data collected by the ISGMNY to determine whether differences in the use of such amenities as public libraries and resources such as high-ranked public high schools yield an independent influence on occupational and educational outcomes.

As we noted in chapter 2, arguments about the sending-society culture and its orientations sneak into prevailing accounts; in particular, the literature endorses the view—either implicitly or explicitly—that family cohesion can be a home-country legacy imported by immigrants that has positive impacts on their children. In seeking to explicitly assess that possibility, the previous chapter demonstrated that a context of emigration characterized by an orientation toward survival, as opposed to self-expression, is positively associated with attainment. Even though the coefficient is generally not statistically significant and appears to be accounted for by individual-level characteristics, that result points to the possibility that origins in societies that are less individualistic than the United States provide resources conducive to second-generation success. Here we recast this hypothesis from the group level to the household level to see whether adherence to norms that might reflect a home-country survival orientation—in particular, the experience of being raised by two parents of the same ethnic origin—is independently associated with better educational or occupational attainment.[4]

The core arguments put forward in *The Asian American Achievement Paradox* concern intergroup rather than intragroup variation. In particular, *The Asian American Achievement Paradox* hypothesizes that the hyperselectivity of the Chinese and Vietnamese immigration streams—which bring populations that possess an exceptionally high level of education—serves as a major driver of the children's success. As discussed in that book, this hypothesis works at the group level: generalizing beyond the Chinese and Vietnamese studied by Lee and Zhou, it implies that the most positively selected immigrant groups will enjoy a premium in performance over and above the generally positive association between the average years of education in the group and respondents' education. Though Lee and Zhou focus exclusively on the intergroup level, logically this hypothesis should apply at the intragroup level as well: hence, if hyperselectivity matters, we should find that the children of the most positively selected parents—in our sample, the top quintile, comprising parents with seventeen or more years of education—should record levels of achievement that present a substantial increment in attainment over those whose parents are not similarly "hyperselected."

Despite its intergroup focus, *The Asian American Achievement Paradox* offers other hypotheses that should operate at the individual level as well. First, it implies that, net of other factors, immigrant offspring who avail themselves of better public schools and ethnic supplementary education should have better schooling and occupational outcomes than those who do not. For the general population, this hypothesis finds support in the sociology of education; however, we might expect the ethnic scaffolding of cram schools and foreign-language schools to be particularly important for the children of immigrants. Although we do not have any indicator of the internalization of a "success frame"—which in fact is probably impossible to measure with survey data—we can also assess whether mother-tongue competence, a component and symbol of ethnic group membership, proves to be associated with higher levels of educational or occupational attainment.

Up to this point, the concepts outlined in table 5.1 have all concerned intragroup differences arising within the receiving country. Since we contend that the distinctive characteristics of population movements across borders—namely, the civic stratification generated by systems of migration control, as well as the internationalized family networks produced by the selectivity of migration itself—impinge on second-generation trajectories, in this chapter we extend the analysis to encompass cross-border connections and legal status. Our approach partially overlaps with the membership exclusion model developed in *Parents Without Papers*, as both we and Bean and his coauthors anticipate that parents' legal status will exercise an enduring influence on their offspring. However, we take a broader view, contending that the conceptual space between the territorial border and the internal border of citizenship is itself stratified, with differences in legal status generating corresponding differences in the degree of exclusion and therefore in the ramifications for immigrant children. In particular, we expect that membership exclusion will exert a negative impact on educational and occupational attainment *independently* of group-level differences in status prevalence as well as the socioeconomic characteristics of immigrant parents.

Crossing international borders creates variation in immigrants' legal status; it also creates variation in the sources of social influences on immigrant parents and their U.S.-born or U.S.-raised children. These influences start with the border-spanning ties that migrants bring with them as they internationalize their families and extend kinship networks across states. Unlike the native-born children of native-born parents, the children of immigrants enjoy access to family support and resources found in the home country that could supplement from the resources found in the place of destination. Those home-country resources might improve their socioeconomic outcomes by providing them with entrepreneurial opportunities in ethnic markets in the United States or even in foreign markets in the origin country.[5] The children of immigrants might also visit the country of origin for extended stays—11 percent of the second-generation New Yorkers and Angelenos in our study had spent at least one period of six months abroad—which should serve as an opportunity for acquiring or reinforcing skills in another language and competency in a foreign culture. In turn, these experiences and achievements could provide an opportunity for self-development unlikely to be shared by the native-born children of native parents and might also be the source of competencies or connections that prove profitable in either the labor market or the business world.

On the other hand, those very same cross-border connections could be a source of strain or disadvantage if the family sends scarce resources home to support family members or if cross-border ties result in lengthy separations between children and parents or other important family members. In a world where time, energy, and financial resources are a zero-sum game, splitting these valuable resources between two countries may mean less investment in the future of the children of immigrants residing in the destination country, hindering their achievement while they, along with their parents, continue to invest in internationalized family ties.

Thus, we expect that the individual-level variation arising from the immigrant experience itself—the presence of cross-border ties, exposure to the context of emigration, and variation and transitions in formal legal status—will exert a main effect on the educational and occupational attainment of the children of immigrants. (The reader saw a demonstration of the direct impact of the context of emigration at the group level in chapter 4.)

Moving beyond these main effects of the immigrant experience on educational and occupational attainment, we incorporate an insight gleaned from the hypothesis of segmented assimilation, though one never formally tested by the proponents of this perspective themselves: we expect that group-level influences related to the contexts of emigration and immigration will *moderate*, or interact with, the status attainment process itself. In other words, we expect that the capacity of immigrant parents to transmit their educational achievements to their children will vary with different aspects of the context, whether encountered in the society of origin before leaving home or in the society of reception after migration. We also expect that further contextual effects will shape the ability of second-generation young adults to translate their own schooling into corresponding occupational rewards even after they have left the parental household.

Although segmented assimilation theory forefronts the interaction between the context of reception and individual-level resources, scholars advancing this perspective offer predictions that are mutually contradictory. For instance, Portes and Rumbaut maintain that when nationalities are commonly awarded refugee status, highly educated members should be particularly successful in transmitting their advantages to their children, a hypothesis that implies a *positive* relationship between the reception context and family-level resources.[6] On the other hand, they also contend that the context of reception matters most for the children of those immigrants who possess fewer resources, since access to either a "strong" or "weak" coethnic community is likely to be the crucial factor determining whether the children of less-skilled immigrants follow the path of "downward mobility" or "ethnic retention." Yet this claim points to a *negative* interaction between reception context and family-level resources: in this scenario, the reception context matters most for families with lower levels of human capital, yielding little influence on immigrant offspring whose parents possess higher skills.

Although potential moderating effects derived from segmented assimilation theory have been interpreted many different ways, these interaction effects are rarely explicitly modeled and tested. At best, the evidence of a moderating impact of "immigrant community," generally operationalized as the socioeconomic standing of the coethnic community in the local area, has provided only inconsistent support for the claims that resource advantage at the group level provides a source of resilience at the intragroup level and helps sustain achievement among those group members living in families suffering from lower resources.[7]

ASSESSING EXPLANATIONS FOR VARIATION IN EDUCATIONAL AND OCCUPATIONAL ATTAINMENT

We now turn to the results of our analyses. We first combine the IIMMLA and ISGMNY in order to maximize cases and the number of immigrant-origin groups. We start with the basic status attainment model, looking at the impact of the highest level of parental education and occupation, with controls for sex, age, and city of residence. When we analyze occupational attainment, we also control for respondent's years of education. In each model, we control group-level variation using the multidimensional contextual variables from the previous chapter: group-level mean education, group-level status prevalence, group-level skin color, and the cultural orientations of the sending country. We focus the discussion on individual-level, intragroup characteristics, which are postulated to be predictive over and above the group-level characteristics we examined earlier.

In a series of nested models, we then add indicators for the concepts outlined in the preceding pages, concluding with interactions between group context and individual-level resources. Figure 5.1 summarizes the models for both educational and occupational attainment, displaying coefficients from hierarchical linear models that adjust for individuals clustered within national-origin groups and allow for interactions between group- and individual-level indicators. Our sample includes all of the foreign-origin respondents in these two surveys, including those who were foreign-born (the 1.5 generation), those who were born in the United States to two foreign-born parents, and those who were born in the United States to one foreign-born parent and one U.S.-born parent. As in chapter 4, our educational analysis includes those ages twenty-three and older to reduce bias resulting from different school leaving rates among different ethnic groups. For our analysis of occupational attainment, we omit all respondents who were younger than age twenty-four.

Figure 5.1 Select Coefficients from Hierarchical Linear Regression Models Predicting Educational and Occupational Attainment for the Children of Immigrants

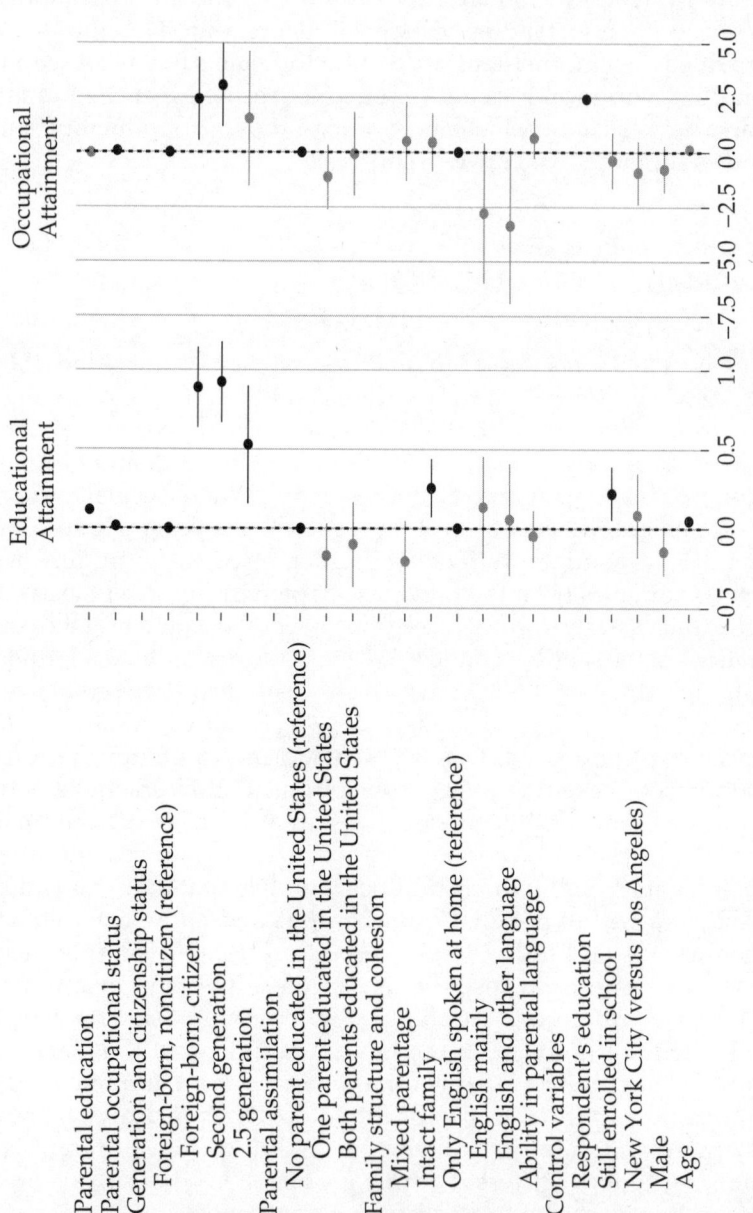

Source: IIMMLA and ISGMNY data sets.
Note: Models include a full set of country-level controls.

Assimilation: Socioeconomic Background, Place of Parental Education, and Generational Status

Figure 5.1 presents the results for these models of educational and occupational attainment.[8] We see that the well-known transmission process between parent and child socioeconomic status holds: even after controlling for all group-level characteristics as well as a range of individual-level traits, higher levels of education and occupation among immigrant parents yield higher levels of education among their offspring. In turn, higher educational attainment among these U.S.-born or U.S.-raised offspring leads to better jobs: each additional year of educational attainment is associated with 2.5 additional points on the occupational status scale.

Immediately apparent, however, is that legal status and place of birth are also very important. We start out with the core assimilation variable of generation, using two different variants to tease out possible effects. First, in a regression model not shown here, we distinguish between two categories of foreign-born respondents—those who came after the age of five and those who came at a still younger age (generation 1.5)—and two categories of U.S.-born respondents—those born to two foreign-born parents (generation 2) and those born to only one foreign-born parent (generation 2.5). When added to the regression, those with two foreign-born parents consistently performed better than both the foreign-born and those with one foreign-born and one U.S.-born parent. This result is inconsistent with the neo-assimilation view, which anticipates that improvements in attainment will come with each succeeding generation.

Next, we modify generation, keeping the two U.S.-born generations unchanged but now separating the foreign-born into two new categories: one for all foreign-born respondents possessing U.S. citizenship and the second for those who had not yet naturalized. With this new definition, as shown in figure 5.1, citizenship status proves to be the decisive factor: lower levels of schooling and occupational attainment prevailed among the foreign-born noncitizens as compared to each of the three other generational categories. However, educational attainment did not actually increase with each successive generation: foreign-born U.S. citizens had completed almost exactly the same amount of schooling as those born in the United States; U.S.-born offspring of two foreign-born parents, in turn, had completed more schooling than their 2.5-generation counterparts. Similarly, even net of schooling, naturalized citizens had better jobs than noncitizens, though there was no statistically significant difference from one generation to another. Because naturalization is facilitated by the resources that formal education provides (as we shall show in chapter 6), as well as the unobserved traits that increase educational attainment, we cannot establish a causal relationship here. Still, it is striking that the impact of generation is entirely mediated by citizenship, which, as an institution of both inclusion and exclusion, is not easily reconciled with the fundamentals of the assimilation perspective, an implication further developed and reinforced in part III of this book.

To capture the effects of exposure on parental resources, the regressions also add a variable identifying the country in which the parents obtained their highest level of schooling. Among the foreign-born respondents, fewer than 5 percent had a parent with U.S. schooling; that fraction rose to 17 percent for second-generation respondents who were born in the United States but had two foreign-born parents. By definition, virtually all of the 2.5-generation respondents had at least one parent with U.S. schooling; among half of them, both parents had received at least some of their education in the United States. We might expect that the children of immigrant parents possessing some U.S. schooling would benefit from their parents' increased familiarity with the American educational system, but this turns out not to be the case: the only significant difference between those with zero, one, or two parents with U.S. education was that those born to one parent with U.S. education who attained slightly less education than those born to two parents who had obtained their entire education abroad.

Family Cohesion

To these standard assimilation variables, we then add a series of individual-level variables meant to capture the claims regarding familial cohesion and ethnic maintenance advanced by the theory of segmented assimilation. As a two-level approach, segmented assimilation emphasizes the direct effects both of shared context and of household strategies and features, in particular those that increase parental influence and generate the familial cohesion needed to guard against "dissonant acculturation" and its presumably deleterious effects. Consequently, we add an indicator variable to capture whether the respondent lived with both parents (biological or adoptive) during childhood (ages six to eighteen) and a further indicator for mixed parentage, which includes the children of two foreign-born parents from different national origins. In addition, we include two language variables: one identifying the language spoken in the respondent's childhood household (English only, mainly English, or mainly another language) and the second capturing the respondent's facility with this language (a summary of scores from 1 to 4 on speaking, reading, writing, and understanding the foreign language spoken in the home). We note that the latter not only is an outcome (analyzed separately in chapter 9) but also was measured at the time of the survey and thus after respondents' completion of schooling. We nonetheless include this variable in the regression because the theory of segmented assimilation contends that bilingualism works to increase familial cohesion and also benefits children's schooling.

Three-quarters of the respondents grew up in two-parent households, and of these, nearly 90 percent had parents from the same origin country. As figure 5.1 shows, the children of intact families had higher attainment (with a coefficient equivalent to one-quarter of a year of additional schooling), and those of mixed parentage had lower attainment (with a coefficient equivalent to one-fifth of a year of schooling, though statistical significance is only at the 10 percent level). Neither variable has any effect on children's occupation, indicating that family structure primarily yields effects via its influence on educational attainment, an intuitively plausible channel, as education is the outcome more temporally proximate to the home family environment.[9] To assess the segmented assimilation claim that a two-parent, ethnically cohesive family is a source of protection against the liabilities associated with a negative context of reception, we interact these variables with both of the statistically significant group-level variables: group education and the traditional versus secular-rational scale. Neither of the interactions is statistically significant, indicating that, regardless of context, a two-parent household has a positive effect on children's educational attainment, whereas birth to parents of mixed nationality has no effect at the 5 percent level.

Although most immigrant offspring (58 percent) were raised in an environment where a foreign language prevailed, language use in the parental home is not associated with years of schooling; however, those who spoke mainly English or English only in the parental household did report a higher level of occupational attainment (significant at the 10 percent level). By contrast, differences in mother-tongue fluency—a little over one-quarter of the sample reported bilingual competency—prove to be unrelated to both educational and occupational attainment, a pattern also evident in the more focused analyses presented later in this chapter.

Explaining "Exceptional" Achievement

As conceptualized by Lee and Zhou, hyperselectivity refers to the parental condition of being significantly more highly educated than both the average sending-country compatriot and the average national of the receiving country. Lee and Zhou hypothesize that parental hyperselectivity results in a second-generation mobility pattern that is qualitatively different from that experienced by immigrant offspring whose parents' educational attainments are more typical for either the sending or receiving country.

Figure 5.2 Expected Years of Education, by Parental and Group Educational Quintiles

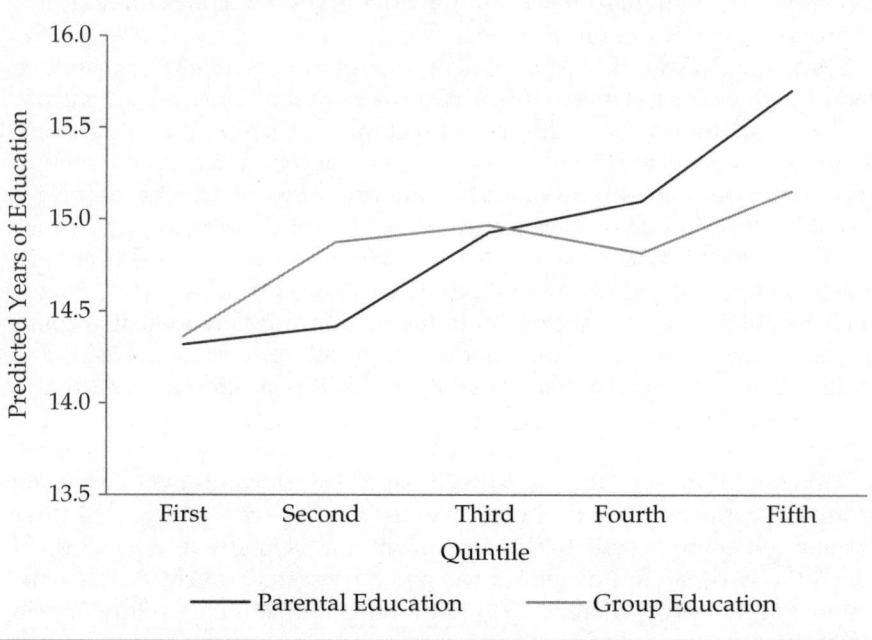

Source: IIMMLA and ISGMNY data sets.

At the group level, we interpret hyperselectivity to denote origins in an immigrant group characterized by levels of schooling substantially above the average; concretely, this puts the top quintile for the groups represented in the pooled sample at an average of thirteen years of schooling. At the individual level, we similarly create quintiles of parental educational attainment and isolate those in the highest quintile—seventeen years of education or more. Entering these categories into the model fails to yield a disproportional increment in achievement at the higher ends of either measure.[10]

For parental years of education, the largest increases appear from the second to the third quintile, as well as from the fourth to the fifth (see figure 5.2). For group years of education, the largest increase by far is from the lowest quintile to the second. Net of other group- and individual-level factors, the children of immigrants from groups in the lowest education quintile had a half-year less education than those in the second quintile; in contrast, those in the fifth quintile had only one-third of a year more education than those in the fourth. Similarly, at the individual level, while those children of parents with some postgraduate education (upper quintile) had about a half-year more education than those whose parents only completed college (fourth quintile), that disparity is matched by the leap between those whose parents completed only high school (second quintile) and those with some college (third quintile).

Echoing earlier writings on the benefits of growing up in an ethnic enclave, a central tenet of *The Asian American Achievement Paradox* is that the children of immigrants benefit from increased access to and use of supplementary education, whether in the form of schools that principally prepare children for competitive tests, such as the SAT, or schools that simply seek to transmit the parents' mother tongue and national identity. Both the New York and Los Angeles surveys gathered information on supplementary schooling, but the indicators are not wholly comparable. Whereas the Los Angeles survey asked specifically about language schools ("Did you ever attend a weekend school or after-school program to learn a specific language other than English?"), the New York survey question was more general: "I am going to read you a list of programs that are sometimes offered in high school. Just answer YES or NO if you have ever participated in them." The six options that followed were either in-class options (honors or Advanced Placement [AP] classes) or remedial in nature (special education, English as a Second Language [ESL]), with the one exception of "cram school/private tutoring," which we use as our indicator of supplementary education in New York. Participation in supplementary schooling was a minority occurrence among all nationalities, involving only one in eight respondents in Los Angeles and one in ten in New York. This pattern did vary from one group to another, though even among those who attended cram schools or language schools the most, such as Koreans and Taiwanese, the great majority—three out of four—did not. Rates among other groups were still lower: only one in six of the Vietnamese-origin youth and only one in twenty Mexican-immigrant offspring reported having received supplementary education.

We next examine the association between supplementary education and educational and occupational attainment, taking the model just summarized and adding to it an indicator interacted by city to allow for the difference in measures across survey instruments. As Lee and Zhou anticipate in *The Asian American Achievement Paradox*, attending a language or cram school is significantly associated with years of education completed: those who attended such a school obtained, net of the other factors, an additional one-third of a year of schooling. However, the interaction between this variable and residence in New York City is negative, indicating that only the Los Angeles respondents benefited from prior attendance in a cram or ethnic school. The disparity separating the New Yorkers from the

Angelenos may reflect some underlying difference rooted in these two different places, but we suspect that the source of the difference lies in the distinctive wording used by each of the two surveys: whereas cram schools and tutoring are not intrinsically or specifically ethnic enterprises, schools that offer instruction in the parents' tongue are quintessentially ethnic organizations.

Consequently, we drill down further into the Los Angeles data set to fully assess the possibility that access to supplemental schooling accounts for some of the paradox of high education among the children of low-educated Asian immigrants, as contended by Lee and Zhou. If this is the case, we would expect that the children of low-educated parents from groups enjoying favorable contexts of origin and reception to be the ones reaping the greatest educational rewards from attendance at language schools.

Restricting our analysis to Los Angeles respondents only, we interact parental education, supplementary education, and the most important group-level variable affecting educational attainment: the traditional versus secular-rational score of the immigrant country of origin. Figure 5.3 displays the results of this three-way interaction. As can be seen by the first set of bars, those respondents raised by parents who had higher levels of education and came from rationally oriented societies were expected to obtain a university degree, regardless of prior participation in supplemental schooling or not. Among respondents lacking this double advantage—those whose immigrant origins were in a rationally oriented society but who were raised by parents with lower levels of education, or those who came from a traditional society but were raised by well-educated parents—supplementary schooling generated only a very slight (and statistically insignificant) increase in expected years of education. By contrast, and as the last set of bars shows, supplemental schools were associated with significantly higher levels of schooling among those relatively few children who were raised by less-educated parents *and* who also came from a traditionally oriented country. Thus, it is the children of poorly educated parents from traditional societies—Filipinos, Salvadorans, Mexicans, and others—*not* the East Asian second-generation groups on whom Lee and Zhou focus, who benefit from supplementary language and ethnic schools.

Interactions Between Family Resources and Context

Having established an important interaction between group- and individual-level sources in understanding supplementary education in

Figure 5.3   The Interaction of Supplementary Education, Parental Education, and Traditional Versus Secular-Rational Scores

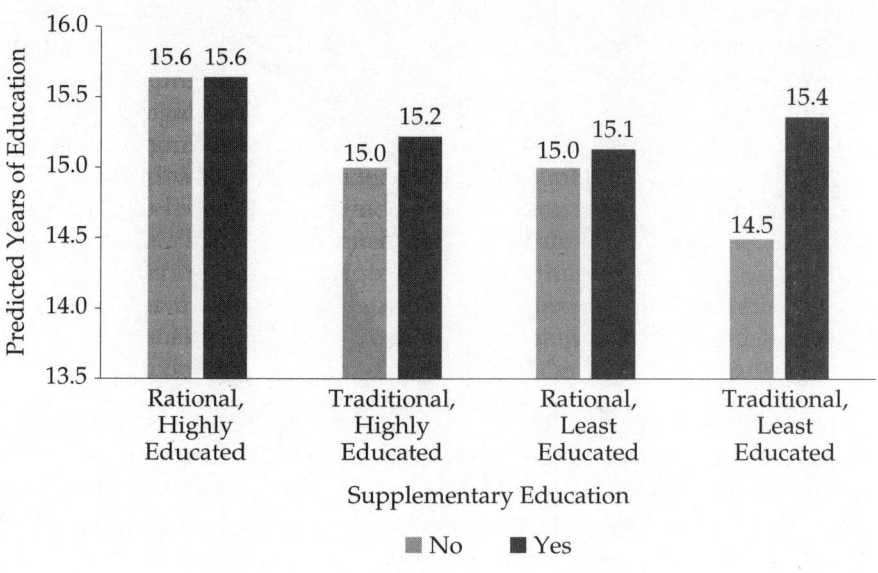

Source: IIMMLA and ISGMNY data sets.

Los Angeles, we now more systematically explore how group-level effects interact with specifically family-level resources. A central tenet of segmented assimilation theory holds that group-level effects should alter the very process of status transmission itself, such that parental and individual-level resources should matter more or less depending on the context of reception of the immigrant group. Members of more privileged immigrant groups—those with a more positive legal status or a more educated coethnic community—should be better able to transmit their attainment to their children than those in a less-privileged group, where the differences in attainment between parents are reduced by group-level disadvantages that affect the mobility of all group members.

We begin by assessing interactions between the context-of-immigration variables—skin color, status prevalence, and group education level—and individual-level resources, as measured by highest parental education and highest parental occupational status. We test each potential interaction individually for both outcomes—educational as well as occupational

Table 5.2 Interaction Effects Between Highest Parental Educational and Occupational Attainment and Context Characteristics When Predicting Educational and Occupational Attainment of the Second Generation

	Parental Resource	Direction of Interaction	Statistical Significance	Outcome of Interest
Context of immigration				
Status prevalence scale	Both	0	None	Both education and occupation
Group years of education	Education	+	.05 level	Education only
Average group skin color	Both	0	None	Both education and occupation
Context of emigration				
Survival versus self-expression scale	Both	0	None	Both education and occupation
Traditional versus secular-rational scale	Both	0	None	Both education and occupation

Source: IIMMLA and ISGMNY data sets.

attainment. We also interact the context-of-emigration variables with both parental education and parental occupational status in turn.

The results of testing for these interaction effects are summarized in table 5.2. The first column shows the context variable, the second the parental resource (occupational or educational attainment) with which it is interacted, the third column the direction of the interaction, the fourth whether it was statistically significant, and the fifth the outcome of interest—educational attainment, occupational attainment, or both. As the table shows, there is only one statistically significant interaction among all of the possible interactions between parental resources and contextual characteristics.

For instance, while the full model shows that origins in secularly oriented societies is positively associated with second-generation educational attainment (as we saw in chapter 4), it does not *moderate* the relationship between parental resources and educational attainment. In other words, the difference in attainment between children with highly educated parents and those with low-educated parents is the same regardless of whether the child's national origins are more or less secularly oriented.

However, the same pattern does *not* hold true for group-level education. Although group-level education helps elevate the educational attainment of all group members, its impact is felt most strongly among the most highly educated members of the group, as evidenced by a positive interaction between group years of education and parental education. Thus, the more-advantaged group members benefit the most from being part of a more highly educated group. Interpreted another way, it is only within more highly educated coethnic group contexts that immigrant parents are able to impart their educational advantages to their children, contradicting the expectations of neo-assimilation theory, which anticipates that parents' schooling will affect children's educational attainment in like ways across groups, regardless of whether contexts are favorable or not.

To sum up, then, the expected interaction between context of immigration and family-level resources in shaping second-generation attainment is lacking: out of twelve potential interactions, only one proves to be statistically significant. Even in the absence of any underlying statistical associations at all, given the number of tests we have implemented, the probability of generating at least one statistically significant coefficient simply on the basis of random chance is .46.

If there is little evidence that context moderates the association between parent and child, what of the relationship between second-generation members' *own* resources and their occupational attainment? In other words, does the context of emigration or immigration shape the trajectories of the second generation as they make their transition from school to work? Such an interaction effect would be more in line with expectations proposed by the hypothesis of segmented assimilation, namely, that a positive reception context increases returns to human capital.

Whereas we found that there was only one statistically significant interaction between the contextual variables and parental resources, nearly every single contextual variable interacted with respondents' education in determining their occupational attainment, as summarized in table 5.3. As it happens, the one exception involves group-level education, the only variable that significantly interacted with parental resources to influence educational attainment. Just as higher group status, in the form of higher group education, amplifies the impact of parental education so too does higher group status, in the form of greater percentage refugee or documented and lighter skin color, result in better returns on respondents' own educational attainment.

A positive context of immigration thus helps to ensure that second-generation effort—here the acquisition of education—yields labor market rewards. This is manifested in a *more positive* relationship between respondents' own education and their occupational attainment when they are from more positively received groups, in terms of both governmental reception and societal reception. Whereas there were no significant interactions between values at origin and parental resources, we see that values at origin do influence the impact of a respondent's own educational attainment. Membership in groups from societies that are more oriented toward survival, as opposed to those that more strongly value self-expression, increases the benefits that these second-generation New

Table 5.3 Interaction Effects Between Second-Generation Educational Attainment and Context Characteristics When Predicting Second-Generation Occupational Attainment

	Direction of Interaction	Significance
Context of immigration		
Status prevalence scale	+	.05
Group years of education	0	None
Average group skin color	−	.10
Context of emigration		
Survival versus self-expression scale	−	.10
Traditional versus secular-rational scale	+	.05

Source: IIMMLA and ISGMNY data sets.

Yorkers and Angelenos glean from their own schooling. (We remind the reader that societies characterized by orientations toward self-expression receive positive values.) At the same time, respondents with immigrant parents from societies characterized by a secular-rational orientation experience a stronger relationship between their educational and occupational attainment than do those from more traditional societies.

REFINEMENTS

At this point, we shift from focusing on both New York and Los Angeles to zero in on the New Yorkers and then the Angelenos separately, to take advantage of the unique qualities of each data set. In these area-specific portions of the chapter, we begin by examining issues related to the use of urban institutions—highlighted in *Inheriting the City* and *The Asian American Achievement Paradox*—by making use of unique data on high school characteristics and amenity use collected by the ISGMNY. We then switch to the impact of citizenship and legal status as well as cross-border connections—matters underscored in *Parents Without Papers* and central to the international perspective developed in this book—by utilizing detailed information collected uniquely in the IIMMLA.

High School Quality in New York

First, we expand our New York sample to include all respondents ages eighteen and older, and we also examine predictors of high school quality, using detailed information on high school type. For this analysis, we focus on those who attend or attended New York City public schools, a segment that includes 75 percent of all the ISGMNY respondents (the other 25 percent were raised outside of New York City, attended private schools, or are missing information), to allow us to take advantage of the ranking data on public school performance in New York City. The team that prepared the New York data set first matched the high school that survey respondents reported attending with information on high school performance in the city; these high schools were then anonymized and ranked into quintiles in terms of performance, based on a variety of indicators collected by the Division of Assessment and Accountability of the New York City Board of Education.[11] Once having assessed the determinants of high school quality among all the New York City respondents surveyed by the ISGMNY, we then go on to examine the relationship between high school quality and private school attendance on the eventual educational and occupational attainment of all respondents age twenty-three or older in our New York sample. For this analysis, we collapse the middle three quintiles together and separate out the highest- and lowest-performing quintile schools.

The results reported in figure 5.4 show the main predictors of high school quality in the New York sample. We see that both group- and individual-level characteristics, whether stemming from contexts of immigration or emigration, matter in determining school quality. Each of the two value orientations in the context of emigration matters; however, whereas stemming from a country leaning toward more secular-rational values had a positive influence on overall years of schooling attained, the more powerful connection linked attendance at higher-quality schools with origins in a society more oriented toward survival and hence one that emphasized family cohesion. (We again remind the reader that societies characterized

Figure 5.4 Hierarchical Linear Regression Model Predicting High School Quality for the Children of Immigrants in Public Schools in New York City

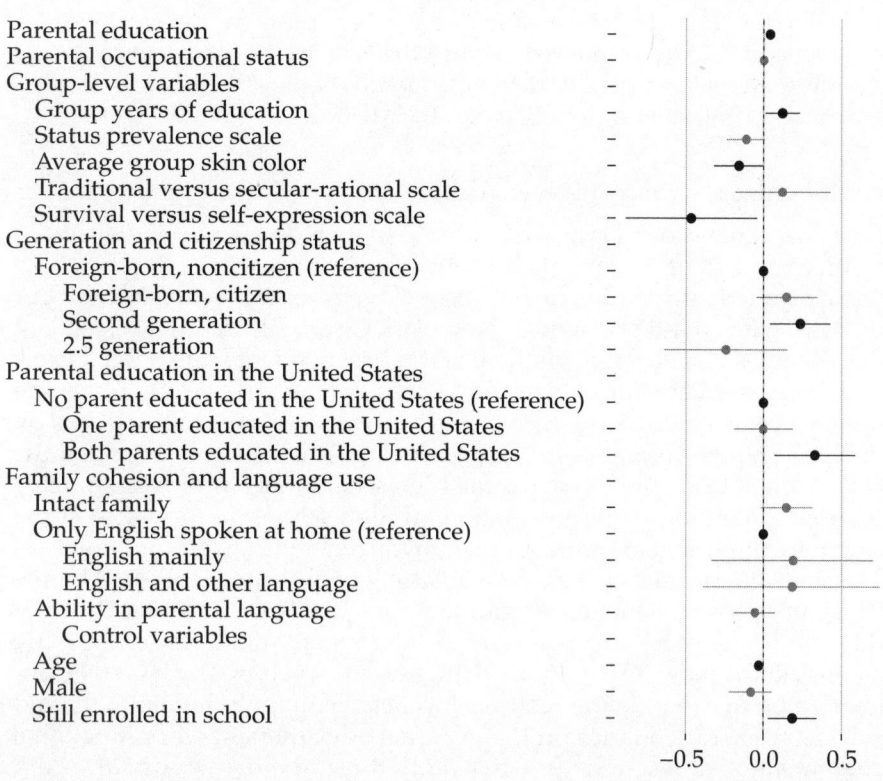

Source: ISGMNY data set.

by orientations toward self-expression receive positive values; hence, the negative coefficient indicates that immigrant offspring from countries oriented toward self-expression were less likely to attend high-quality high schools.) On the context-of-immigration side, group years of education increased the likelihood of attending a higher-quality high school, just as it influenced overall years of schooling attained. Yet, unlike overall educational attainment, this outcome was also associated with skin color, indicating that, at the 10 percent level, lighter-skinned students were more likely to attend better high schools. By contrast, students belonging to groups among whom more favorable statuses prevailed were more likely to attend high schools of lower quality, contrary to our expectations.

Yet the regressions show that even *within* these relatively more- or less-advantaged groups, variation occurs at the individual level as well. As we would expect, the children of parents with higher levels of education were more likely to attend better schools, even after controlling for average group levels of education. Though in the pooled sample parental schooling acquired in the United States appears to have had no effect on educational attainment, it did influence access to higher-quality high schools: immigrant offspring with two parents who completed schooling in the United States were more likely to attend higher-performing schools. Naturalized 1.5-generation respondents not only attained higher overall levels of schooling but also were more likely, along with the U.S.-born, to attend a higher-quality high school than those who remained foreign nationals. By contrast, children raised in a two-parent household achieved higher levels of education overall but were no more likely to attend better-quality schools than their counterparts raised by one parent. The language spoken in the parental home and respondents' own mother-tongue language ability, variables with no impact on educational attainment, similarly had no association with high school quality.

Thus, in contrast to overall educational attainment, ethnic influences on high school quality most strongly connect to intergroup variables rather than to those operating at the family level. But as suggested by *Inheriting the City* and *The Asian American Achievement Paradox*, ethnic influences, whether at the group or household level, should have an impact above and beyond their association with attendance at higher-quality high schools. To assess this hypothesis, we restrict the sample to those New Yorkers who were age twenty-three or older, though doing so diminishes the number of cases to 670 and substantially reduces statistical power. Figure 5.5 presents the results of regressions of years of education and occupational status using the same predictors as before, but supplemented with an indicator for school quality: lowest-performing public high school quintile, middle three public high school quintiles, highest-performing public school

Figure 5.5 School Quality and Educational and Occupational Attainment of Immigrant Offspring in New York City

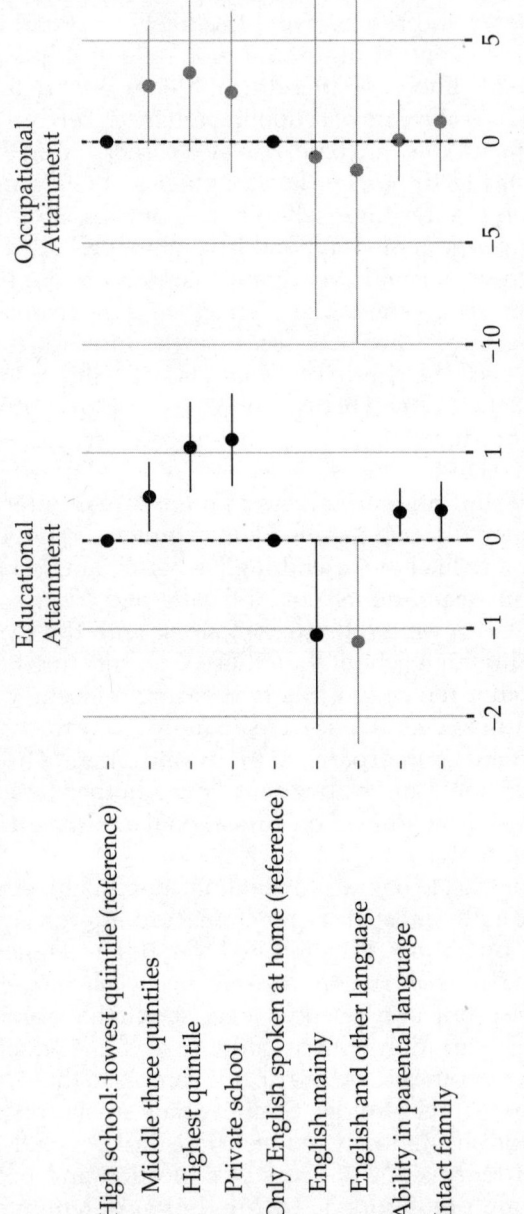

Source: ISGMNY data set.

quintile, and private high school. We examine the change in coefficient size as we move from the model with and without high school quality.

Starting with educational attainment, New Yorkers who attended a middle-performing high school obtained, on average, half a year more education than those in a low-performing high school; those attending a high school in the highest-performing quintile or a private school obtained an entire year more, net of the other individual- and group-level characteristics. By contrast, ethnic effects operated mainly via their impact on high school quality: the coefficient size for group education drops by half once we control for school quality, indicating that much of the association between group-level education and educational attainment is explained by attendance at high schools of greater quality. At the individual level, a childhood spent in an intact family (raised by both parents) positively affected overall educational attainment, even when controlling for high school quality. Likewise, despite controls for high school quality, childhood years spent in a household where English was not spoken exclusively had a negative effect on educational attainment, while foreign-language competence made for higher levels of schooling. Since, as we will see in a later chapter, foreign-language competence is strongly affected by the childhood linguistic environment, in this regression it may simply serve as another indicator of academic performance or ability.

For occupational attainment, the reduced sample size and very young age of the New York sample renders these results particularly tentative. We note that none of the contextual variables proved statistically significant. However, we see that even net of respondents' own schooling, those who attended a higher-performing public school or a private high school had jobs of superior quality, as compared to those whose secondary education took place in a lower-quality high school (results statistically significant at the 10 percent level).

Finally, in addition to the in-depth analysis of school quality with ISGMNY data, we also examined whether one additional variable only found in the ISGMNY, the use of public amenities, mediated the relationship between positive contextual variables and educational attainment. We measured the use of public amenities as a combination of reports of using libraries and museums during childhood. Respondents could answer that they used libraries or museums "a lot," "sometimes," or "never." We grouped together those who used both amenities "a lot" (8 percent) and those who used at least one "a lot" (41 percent), and we combined those who used libraries or museums only "sometimes" (49 percent) with the remaining 2 percent who never did. These differential levels of use of public amenities were not associated with educational or occupational attainment, nor did they mediate any of the contextual variables.

Cross-Border Ties in Los Angeles

Having examined the intragroup sources of variation related to ethnic maintenance, parental assimilation, and school choice, we now turn our focus to Los Angeles to assess the international perspective put forward in this book and determine whether international influences operating at the household or individual level—as opposed to the group level, as treated in chapter 4—affect educational and occupational attainment. The perspective we advance emphasizes two sources of intragroup variation in attainment, both of which can be examined with the data from the IIMMLA: cross-border ties and legal status.

We start with cross-border ties. Using the IIMMLA, we can identify three measures of parental cross-border ties: (1) whether a parent returned to the country of origin during the respondent's childhood, with or without the respondent; (2) whether parents sent remittances to the country of origin; and (3) whether the respondent belonged to a transnational family, differentiating second-generation respondents with no close family members abroad, those with close family members abroad but no parent abroad, and those with a parent abroad.

As with the New York analysis, but restricting our sample to the Los Angeles data, we display the results of adding each cross-border indicator into a regression model that includes all the basic stratification- and immigration-related variables we explored in the joint New York City–Los Angeles model. The results appear in figure 5.6.

Looking at cross-border ties, we see that they primarily exert their effect via second-generation educational attainment. The children of immigrant parents who sent remittances back to the home country had higher educational attainment, all else being equal, than the children of immigrants who did not. In contrast, parental visits to the home country—whether with or without the second-generation respondent—had no net association with second-generation achievement. Although parental visits to the country of origin did not seem to matter, long-term parental separation did: the children of immigrants with a parent still in the origin country had lower educational attainment than those whose parents were both in the United States.

Parental Legal Status in Los Angeles

As a final potential source of intragroup difference—and one central to both our international perspective and the membership exclusion model reviewed in chapter 2—we turn to parental legal status as a predictor of second-generation variation in educational and occupational attainment. Although we did not find an association between group-level status

Figure 5.6 Cross-Border Ties and Educational and Occupational Attainment of Los Angeles Immigrant Offspring

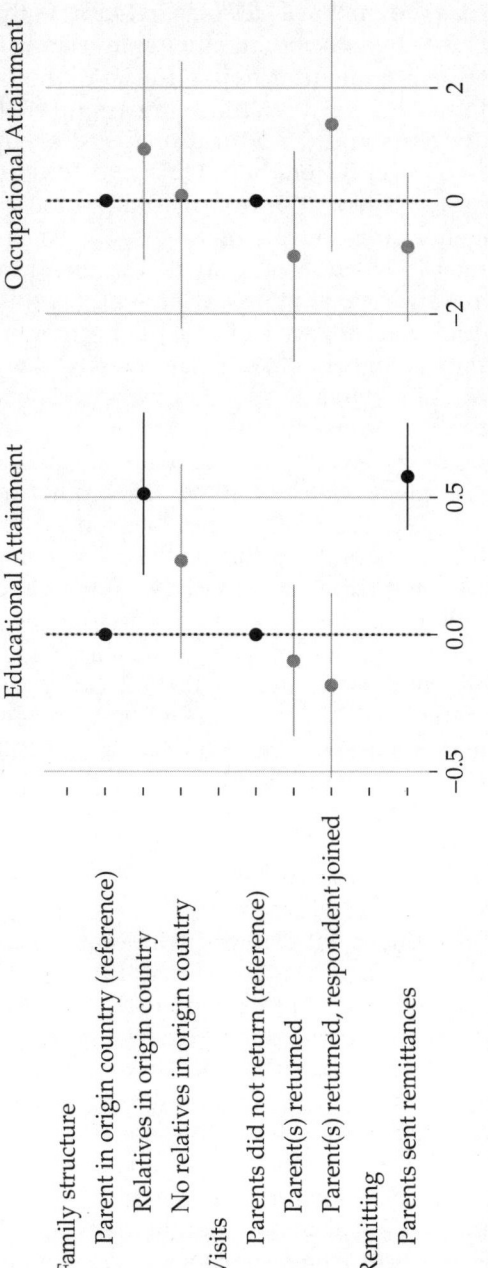

Source: IIMMLA data set.

prevalence and second-generation educational attainment (see chapter 4), other research has shown that a lack of legal status at the family or individual level affects life chances and mobility in myriad ways. We explore this possibility here, using the information found in the Los Angeles sample to test for a relationship between the membership exclusion experienced by immigrant parents and the educational and occupational outcomes experienced by their children, both U.S.- and foreign-born. We do this with two separate models: the first uses a pooled sample of the U.S.-born and 1.5-generation sample members; the second model excludes birthright citizens and focuses only on the 1.5 generation. We identify four categories of parental legal status at arrival: (1) one parent U.S.-born or citizen, (2) both parents arrived as legal permanent residents (LPRs) (omitted reference category), (3) one parent arrived with LPR status, and (4) no parent with LPR status. Respondents who did not know their parent's documentation status at arrival were omitted from the analysis.

We first examine whether parental legal status has a direct effect on educational attainment over and above the group- and individual-level controls in our baseline model. As can be seen in figure 5.7, the effects of parental legal status on both the U.S.-born and foreign-born children of immigrants diverge from our expectations: the children of immigrants who arrived without legal permanent residence status had *higher* educational attainment than those with parents who arrived with the greatest set of rights—that is, either two parents who both possessed green cards upon arrival or one parent with U.S. citizenship (the 2.5 generation). Although these results fly in the face of our theoretical expectations, we believe that they can be straightforwardly explained. First, this analysis shows the impact of parental legal status, *controlling for respondent's citizenship status,* yet it is precisely at the point of gaining U.S. citizenship that parental legal status exercises a powerful effect. As the next chapter shows, when compared to respondents who arrived as LPRs, immigrant offspring who came to the United States with either a temporary visa or in unauthorized status obtained U.S. citizenship at a slower rate. As the next chapter will also demonstrate, beyond these family-level characteristics, the prevalence of more favorable statuses increases the speed at which citizenship is acquired; hence, we suspect that the direct link between parents' legal status upon entry and children's attainment is weakened by the influence of both household- and group-level differences in naturalization rates.[12]

Furthermore, legal status at the time of parents' arrival is temporally quite distal from the years of schooling attained by respondents in their twenties and thirties; a massive legalization program in the mid-1980s allowed many of these initially undocumented parents and children to adjust their status and obtain legal permanent residence; and the unauthorized parents and

Figure 5.7 Legal Status of Los Angeles Immigrant Parents at Arrival and Socioeconomic Outcomes for Their Children

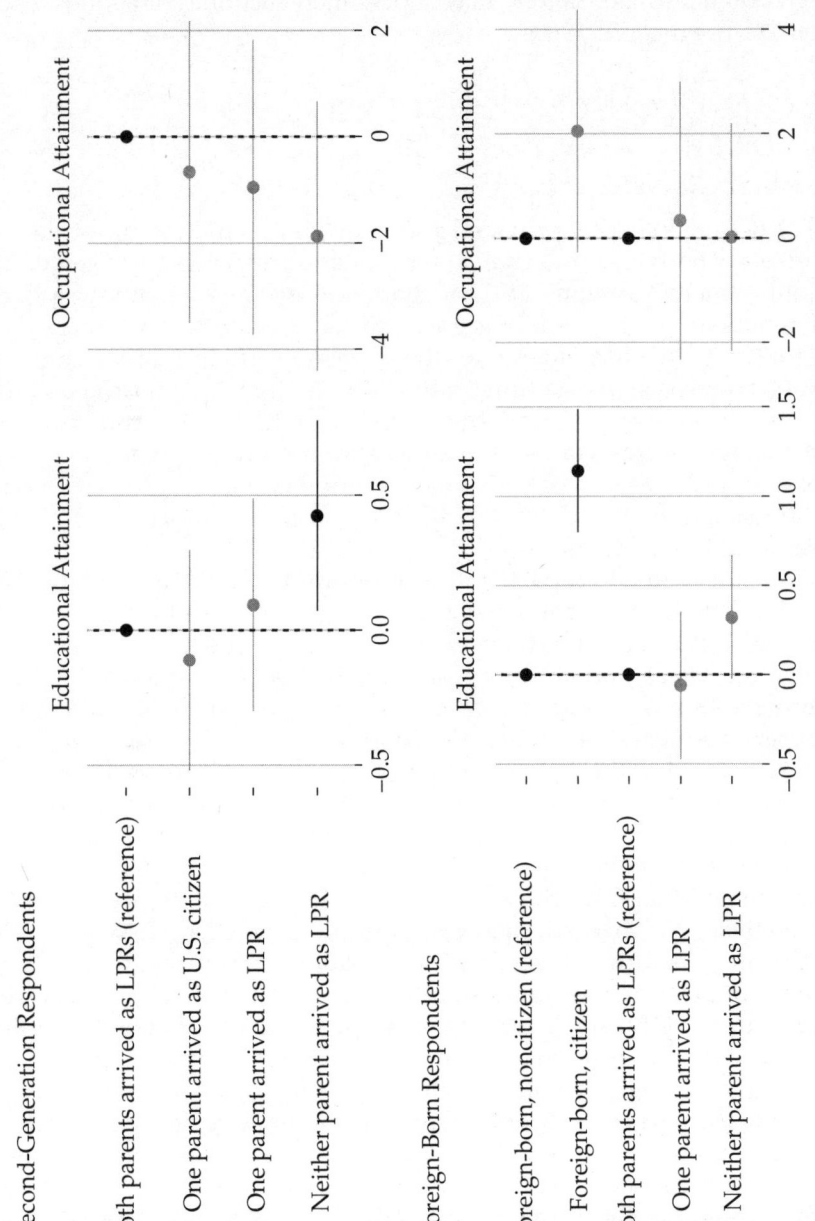

Source: IIMMLA data set.

children who arrived during the 1970s and 1980s experienced a far less harsh environment than the one that undocumented immigrants have encountered since the mid-1990s.

CONCLUSION: CROSSING BORDERS AND STATUS ATTAINMENT OF THE SECOND GENERATION

The previous chapter provided a strategy for identifying contextual effects linked to both place of origin and destination and demonstrated that both contexts affect attainment. That chapter also showed that intragroup differences are larger than intergroup differences, setting the stage for this chapter, which has focused on the sources of intragroup variation. Here we have proceeded systematically, deriving hypotheses from each of the prevailing perspectives discussed in chapters 2 and 3 and then testing those hypotheses against data drawn from both the pooled Los Angeles and New York samples and, when appropriate information could only be found in either the ISGMNY or IIMMLA, each survey separately. Table 5.4 sums up our findings.

In one crucial respect, these immigrant offspring resembled their native-born counterparts: their attainments—the levels of schooling they completed and the jobs they obtained—were influenced by their parents' own resources, and most importantly, by their education. Yet individual and parental household characteristics bound up with the immigrant experience also shaped their destinies.

Assimilation theory, in both its classical and revised versions, underlines the importance of generation because, with each successive generation further removed from the place of origin, exposures shift from the home country to the host country. Although all of the New Yorkers and Angelenos queried in these surveys were immigrant offspring, they could nonetheless be divided, following prevailing practices, into a set of intermediate generations based on age of arrival in the United States (among the foreign-born) and parentage (among the U.S.-born). Applying this procedure, only one generation—the "true" second-generation children of two foreign-born parents—appeared to do any better than the others. Similarly, though assimilation theory would suggest that greater parental exposure to host-country education should benefit their host society–raised children, we see only partial support for this claim: the offspring of two parents with at least some U.S. education did not obtain more schooling than their counterparts raised by parents who never received any schooling in the United States, though they were more likely to attend better-performing high schools.

Table 5.4 Summary of Findings on Educational and Occupational Attainment Among Immigrant Children

Concept and Measurement	Educational Attainment	Occupational Attainment	Source
Socioeconomic status of parents			All
Parents' education	Positive	None	
Parents' occupation	Positive	Positive	
Respondents' education		Positive	
Assimilation			RAM
Generation, parents educated in the United States	None	None	
Childhood intrafamilial cohesion			LEG, ITC
Intact family	Positive	None	
Foreign language spoken in the home	None	None	
Parents of same national origin	None	None	
Ethnic maintenance: Respondents' foreign-language competence	None	None	LEG, AAAP
Supplementary education	Positive	None	AAAP
Hyperselectivity: nonlinearity at top of parental and group education	None	None	AAAP
Urban institutions			
Attended specialized high schools	Positive	Positive	ITC, AAAP
Used urban amenities	None	None	ITC
Membership exclusion			
Citizenship	Positive	Positive	O+D
Parents' legal status	None	None	PWP, O+D
Cross-border ties			
Parents sent remittances	Positive	None	O+D
Parent in origin country	Negative	None	O+D
Return visits of parents and children	None	None	O+D

Source: O+D = Origins and Destinations. Portes and Rumbaut 2001 (*LEG = Legacies*); Kasinitz et al. 2008 (*ITC = Inheriting the City*); Lee and Zhou 2015 (*AAAP = Asian American Achievement Paradox*); Bean, Brown, and Bachmeier 2015 (*PWP = Parents Without Papers*); Alba and Nee 2003 (*RAM = Remaking the American Mainstream*).

Other perspectives, including our own, offer a variety of challenges to assimilation theory: one set emphasizes the importance of variables that fall outside the core assimilation framework; another contends that differences in context, whether of immigration (as maintained by the proponents of segmented assimilation) or of emigration or both immigration *and* emigration (as we have suggested), can amplify or diminish the impact of individual resources. One potential source of advantage, proposed by Lee and Zhou, is hyperselectivity: membership in a group with levels of education significantly higher than the level of education possessed by both sending-country compatriots and the average person in the receiving country. Yet our test of this hypothesis failed to provide confirmatory evidence: whether at the inter- or intragroup level, the offspring of the most highly educated did not achieve at distinctively higher levels. Instead, the significant differences were found at the low end of the distribution: the children of the least well educated, whether measured at the group or individual level, did significantly worse than those one or two steps above.

The authors of both *Legacies* and *The Asian American Achievement Paradox* also propose that parental efforts to retain ethnic attachments and practices should improve second-generation progress. However, our regressions provide only very modest support for these claims as well. In the pooled sample, immigrant offspring raised in parental households where a foreign language prevailed neither achieved more schooling nor held better jobs than their counterparts raised in English-language households. Likewise, the products of those households where a foreign language prevailed—namely, respondents retaining a high level of mother-tongue competency—did no better than their counterparts who had abandoned the mother tongue for English. The results for mixed parentage—a condition that would presumably weaken the transmission of a national or ethnic identity from parents to children—provide a partial exception, as this background depressed educational attainment, albeit slightly, with a coefficient statistically significant at the 10 percent level; it had no effect, however, on occupational attainment. Additional hints that distinctively ethnic practices might spur higher attainment come from the positive impacts associated with supplementary education. However, we note that no more than three out of every ten respondents were engaged in this activity, regardless of national origin; furthermore, detailed analysis showed that supplementary education benefited only those few respondents raised by less-educated parents who came from countries oriented toward traditional values.

Ethnic strategies and practices need not be confined to the household: as the authors of *Inheriting the City* and *The Asian American Achievement*

Paradox suggest, those strategies may also take the form of parallel efforts to increase access to higher-quality public goods, whether by moving into suburbs with high-quality public schools or, in New York City, gaining information about, and later entry into, the city's competitive specialized high schools. The unique data found in the ISGMNY do reveal the importance of ethnic influences, but only those operating at the intergroup, not the intragroup, level. Most importantly, respondents whose families came from countries oriented toward survival as opposed to self-expression—and who thus likely placed greater emphasis on family cohesion—as well as those from groups with higher levels of education were more likely to gain entrance to these highly desirable New York City schools. By contrast, no effects could be attributed to linguistic practices in the childhood home and mother-tongue competency. As we might expect, attendance at more competitive high schools had a positive impact on overall levels of educational and occupational attainment.

We have focused, by contrast, on those factors related to the distinctively international aspects of migration across state boundaries. Systems of migration control can produce membership exclusion, as argued by the authors of *Parents Without Papers*, who focus on the impact of unauthorized residents; more generally, as we have contended, those systems yield civic stratification, which generates differences in legal status and citizenship that then spill over into outcomes of varying sorts. Our analysis provides mixed support for this point of view. On the one hand, noncitizen, foreign-born, but U.S.-raised immigrant offspring are outperformed by their naturalized citizen counterparts, a pattern in both the educational and occupational dimensions. On the other hand, analysis of the Los Angeles data fails to uncover any effects that could be linked to parents' legal status upon entry.

Again, relying on the IIMMLA only, our analysis shows that respondents' attainments were related to cross-border engagements, though in complicated ways. To begin with, those homeland connections influenced educational outcomes only, not occupational attainment—a predictable pattern given the greater distance between these childhood experiences and adult experiences in the labor market. Moreover, different modes of homeland connectedness yielded different outcomes, evidence of its multidimensional nature: parental sending of remittances is positively associated with educational attainment, and schooling levels tended to be lower when a parent resided abroad, but a childhood experience of return travel had no effect at all.

Beyond these main effects lies the prospect that group-level influences related to the contexts of emigration and immigration will moderate or interact with other variables impinging on the status attainment process.

As noted earlier, the hypothesis of segmented assimilation advances precisely this possibility; thus, Portes and Rumbaut contend in *Legacies* that "the experiences of a national group do not affect its economic performance directly so much as facilitate or constrain the influence of individual-level predictors."[13] However, aside from an effort to compare immigrant *parents* from groups that are more or less advantaged and to determine whether they are equally rewarded for their skills, Portes and Rumbaut never explore the very proposition that they advance, nor do they consider the likelihood that group-level effects stem from the context of emigration as well as the context of immigration.

In this chapter, we have seen that group level of education interacts with parents' education in ways that generate further advantages for the children of higher-skilled immigrants; otherwise, neither contexts of emigration nor contexts of immigration interact with parents' resources in ways that affect children's attainment. However, origin and reception characteristics do influence the ability of members of the second generation to capitalize on their own human capital investments by obtaining higher-status jobs, and in remarkably consistent ways. The children of immigrants from a negative context of immigration, whether one characterized by darker skin color, lower legal status prevalence, or lower levels of education, gained lower returns to their education than did the children of immigrants from more-advantaged groups. Moreover, we find that immigrant offspring from societies characterized by stronger orientations toward self-expression received lower returns to their educational attainment. A privileged group status appears to strengthen *intergenerational* ties between parent and child as well as the *intragenerational* relationship between second-generation members' own education and the status of their jobs. Membership in more-advantaged immigrant-origin groups appears to provide real benefits in transforming educational attainment into better jobs—for oneself and for one's children. For those who belong to an immigrant group more oriented toward survival, the cohesiveness of such groups seems to offer benefits that elude the grasp of persons who come from more individualistic societies.

And thus we end this part of the book by concluding that context matters, both directly and indirectly, for the process of status attainment among today's second generation. Whether that pattern holds in other domains is the question we take up next.

Part III | Transformations

Chapter 6 | Acquiring Citizenship

THIS BOOK FOCUSES on the ways in which the distinctively international aspects of population movements across borders affect the experience of the children of immigrants, both those born abroad and raised in the United States and those born in the United States. The international impinges directly on the acquisition and exercise of citizenship, the topics treated in the next two chapters. On the one hand, every emigrant departs as a home-country citizen to arrive as a destination-country alien, a status less tractable to individual initiative than was the initial decision to seek a better life in a new land. For those who enjoy the possibility of acquiring a new citizenship and who successfully exercise that option, the acquisition of citizenship marks the transition from the old nationality to the new. On the other hand, all immigrants in a democratic society can exercise citizenship, as mere territorial presence confers the right to engage in a broad, though not full, panoply of civic and political activities. Yet to access these different options for involvement, immigrants need the resources required for understanding a strange, new environment and for engaging with civic and political matters at least one step removed from the demands of everyday survival.

Acquiring and exercising citizenship, though related, are nonetheless distinct. Formal U.S. citizenship—holding a U.S. passport—is a status from which every foreign newcomer is automatically excluded. By contrast, the exercise of citizenship—engaging in civic or public life as a concerned member of the public—is a possibility of which all new immigrants, whether permanent or temporary, authorized or undocumented, can avail themselves. However, enjoying this option does not imply that possession of citizenship is irrelevant to its exercise. Even though many forms of political participation do not formally require citizenship, political parties, lobbying groups, and rights activists generally target potential voters in their campaigns, thereby omitting noncitizens from organizing efforts. Considering that many citizens—and sometimes most of them—do not cast a ballot when they could, the right to vote may not meaningfully distinguish those who have crossed into the polity from those who remain outside it. Yet it is precisely because the individual incentives to go to the polls are so weak that political organizations, parties, and candidates expend extraordinary resources in the effort to cajole voters to do so. Hence, those lacking the potential to vote may find themselves not just excluded from the exercise of the privileges that come with formal citizenship but cut off from the processes that produce the exercise of citizenship itself.

Acquiring citizenship is a challenge for only some of the adult immigrant offspring with whom this book is concerned: specifically, those born abroad but raised in the United States. Yet, as at least one parent—usually both—arrived as an alien and that status often proved enduring, noncitizen status is a background condition for everyone in the families of these adult immigrant offspring. Indeed, for each and every one of the New Yorkers and Angelenos we studied, the strangeness of the civic and political environment was part of their familial setting, albeit to varying degrees. In this chapter, we seek to understand the processes affecting the acquisition of citizenship as a status; we then segue in the next chapter into an exploration of the exercise of citizenship, understood as engagement with civic and political life.

Citizenship, whether viewed as status or exercise, is an essential component of full membership in a democratic society. Yet, with the exception of *Inheriting the City*, how citizenship is acquired and practiced is a topic that the key books on the second generation have ignored. This gap in coverage stems in large part from an unspoken assumption that the relatively liberal U.S. regime—in which the barriers to naturalization are limited and every person born on American soil automatically gains U.S. citizenship—makes alien status unproblematic for later political participation. But as we have already seen, alien status *does* matter, depressing both educational and occupational attainment, even though the people in question, 1.5-generation New Yorkers and Angelenos, were raised in the United States and therefore de facto Americans, even if they lacked de jure status. Moreover, the barriers to naturalization and the link between legal status and second-generation civic engagement are far from trivial, as we explain in the next chapter.

While none of the books discussed in chapter 2 inquire into the determinants of naturalization, we can utilize our two-level model to straightforwardly develop hypotheses regarding the intra- and interethnic sources of differences in naturalization rates and patterns. As we have argued, systems of migration control inherently produce civic stratification, generating a proliferation of legal statuses that inhibit full membership in all its dimensions—political, social, and economic. Whereas adaptation can help generate the resources that allow immigrants to meet the conditions of entry into citizenship, it is politics that determines those conditions. Those conditions have changed significantly over the course of U.S. history; recently, exclusion based on race and ethnicity has diminished, but exclusion based on class characteristics—most notably, knowledge, information, and financial capacity—has increased. Consequently, this chapter begins with a short history of the social and legal context affecting naturalization in the United States, followed by a discussion, from the international perspective developed in this book, of potential inter- and intra-group sources of variation in the decision to naturalize.

OUT OF ALIENAGE: THE POSSIBILITIES AND PROBLEMS OF CITIZENSHIP ACQUISITION

Right from the beginning of its history as an independent country, the United States has offered immigrants easy access to citizenship while promising their U.S.-born children citizenship upon birth. Though not often noticed, these practices amounted to a de facto immigration incentive program that reflected the new republic's need to attract a population that could fill up its land mass and help wrest territory from the indigenous population. Indeed, for the signers of the Declaration of Independence, "obstructing the Laws for the Naturalization of Foreigners" was one of the many grievances that led the American colonists to break with Britain. The Constitution, approved in 1788, granted Congress the right to determine a "uniform rule of naturalization"; Congress acted two years later, making citizenship available to any "free white person" who had resided in the United States for two years. Nonetheless, naturalization proved an early flashpoint as well: the minimum waiting period was increased to fourteen years in 1798, and then lowered back to five years in 1802, the level at which it has remained ever since.

From their outset through the early twentieth century, naturalization procedures took an ad-hoc form, varying from one locality to another, with approval heavily influenced by the degree to which local political regimes perceived immigrants as likely friends or foes. However, as opposition to immigration grew, so too did efforts to impede the route to naturalization. In the mid-nineteenth century, the anti-immigrant Know-Nothing Party agitated for a twenty-one-year waiting period before immigrants could apply for citizenship. Although that bid failed, at the turn of the twentieth century the rising tide of nativism eventuated in a significant change. The Naturalization Act of 1906 shifted responsibility to the national level, imposed requirements for rudimentary knowledge of English and American civics, and mandated payment of a $6 filing fee—the equivalent of $120 in 2016 currency. The contours of naturalization practices have since then remained roughly stable, though standardizing the naturalization test took protracted form and fees have fluctuated, most recently increasing from $60 in 1989 to $680 as of this writing—or 1.32 percent of median family income.[1] As of this writing, the United States extracts a higher fee from prospective citizens than do Australia, Canada, and New Zealand—the other Anglophone settler states that have historically facilitated access to citizenship as part of their effort to encourage immigration.[2]

By contrast, birthright citizenship, at the outset an inheritance of English common law, took deeper hold during Reconstruction, when passage of the Fourteenth Amendment, extending citizenship to blacks as well as whites, gave it constitutional status. Another piece of Reconstruction legislation, the Naturalization Act of 1870, made foreign-born blacks eligible for naturalization but was deliberately written to keep Asian immigrants barred from citizenship. Although a few decades later the Supreme Court ruled that all persons born on U.S. soil possessed citizenship from birth, regardless of race and ethnicity, persons born in Asia continued to be deprived of the right to acquire U.S. citizenship until 1952.[3] Hence, unlike many countries in Europe, where the children and sometimes grandchildren of immigrants have been compelled to remain citizens of the country of emigration even when born and raised in the country of immigration, the U.S.-born children of immigrants have always begun life as status citizens—an often taken-for-granted and unacknowledged precondition of the multigenerational assimilation process.

Nonetheless, a large and growing population of children, often described as the 1.5 generation, now accompany their parents as immigrants, thus arriving without the benefit of birthright citizenship. For these parents and children, the route to citizenship often involves a trajectory quite unlike the course followed by the immigrants of the last age of mass migration. Until the advent of migration controls in the 1920s, the naturalization clock started ticking virtually upon arrival in the United States. But once imposed, those restrictions inherently put foreign arrivals into different classes: some disembarked with long-term, though ultimately provisional, status, others came for visits of strictly limited duration, and still others arrived without any authorization at all. Over time, the contradictory pressures that have led the United States to open access to its territory but in ways that inhibit long-term settlement have caused a multiplication of noncitizen statuses, varying in rights and entitlement, and the liminal zone between the territorial border and the internal boundary of citizenship has become stratified. As a result, even legally present foreigners often spend

Figure 6.1 Cumulative Probability of Naturalizing for 1.5-Generation Los Angeles Respondents by Status of Entry

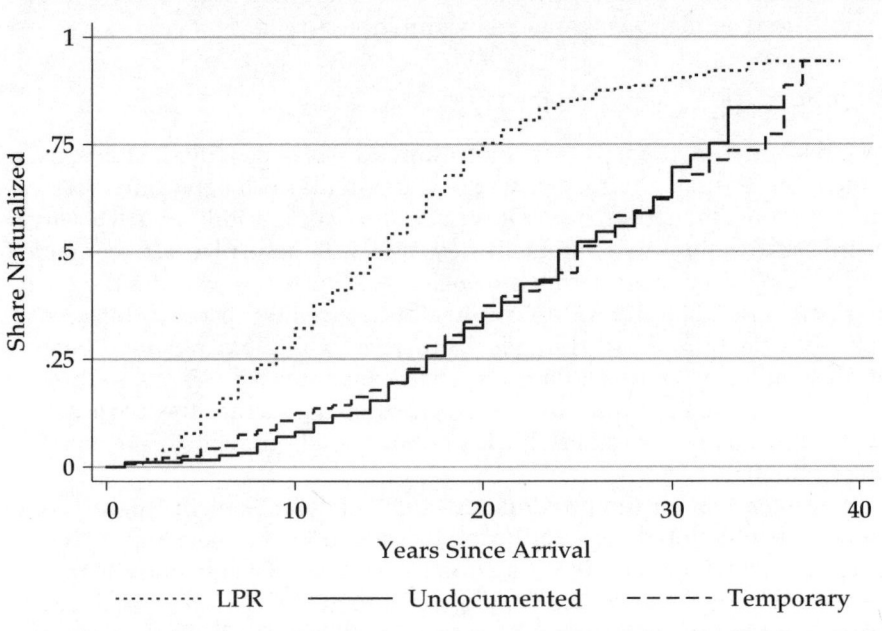

Source: IIMMLA data set.

time in a temporary status before gaining legal permanent residency, and the moment at which the naturalization clock starts ticking is delayed. Yet even among those immigrants who do become eligible to gain U.S. citizenship, relatively few actually naturalize. In 2010, for example, roughly eight million of an estimated twelve million legal permanent residents living in the United States were eligible to naturalize, yet not quite 620,000 of them, or 5 percent, opted to acquire citizenship.[4]

Unfortunately, we lack information on the timing of status transitions in the New York City data, and the Los Angeles data, though they provide the timing of naturalization, lack information on the date when permanent residency was acquired and the citizenship clock began to tick. Nonetheless, since the IIMMLA allows us to control for respondents' legal status upon arrival, we can see that the naturalization trajectories of those who arrived without LPR status diverged strongly from those of newcomers who arrived without any legal status at all, as shown in figure 6.1. Whereas roughly half of the respondents who arrived in the United States as LPRs naturalized after fifteen years of residence, it took roughly twenty-five years of residence for the fraction of respondents arriving without lawful permanent residence to reach that same 50 percent mark. Those who entered the United States lawfully but as temporary "non-immigrants" experienced similarly slow naturalization trajectories.

PERSPECTIVES ON NATURALIZATION

Neo-assimilation theory posits that adaptation is driven by the rewards it yields. But the assimilatory power of the pursuit of the good life derives from its constant action, invisible effects, and compatibility with a range of migrant plans. Investment in new skills or helpful social contacts, by bringing greater material well-being within reach, change the costs and benefits of staying in the country of destination or returning to the country of origin; these changes, in turn, help explain why settlement and assimilation so often happen whether wanted or not. As we noted in chapter 2, neo-assimilation theory further posits that these proximal mechanisms rest on an underlying institutional environment, which impedes discrimination.

However, neither the proximal nor the distal mechanisms highlighted by neo-assimilation theory apply to the acquisition of citizenship, a binary outcome for which a deliberate effort is required. Unlike mastering the dominant tongue—or at least enough of it to get by—citizenship is not a quotidian concern, as it cannot be reliably read from the everyday encounter. Indeed, to the dismay of the naturalized citizen whose accent gives away his or her foreign origin, citizenship is often *mis*read. Yet precisely because, in the near to medium term, citizenship provides little help and its absence poses little hindrance, its acquisition is likely to be postponed. Thus, while the proximal mechanisms are short-circuited, the distal mechanisms prove of little importance: regardless of labor market conditions, the institution of citizenship is inherently exclusionary, as neither successful adaptation nor societal commitment suffices for gaining formal membership. On the contrary, citizenship policy, by making naturalization an option only for the legally eligible, discriminates against undocumented or temporary immigrants regardless of how many years they may have lived in the United States or how extensively they may have adopted "American ways." And even the legally eligible find themselves on an uneven field, as differences in finances, information, and comfort with bureaucratic procedures put citizenship within range for some and out of reach for others.

In popular opinion, immigrants are expected to gain citizenship as soon as they have the chance; judging by the official rhetoric that prevails in naturalization ceremonies, governments similarly view citizenship as a status every eligible immigrant should seize the opportunity to acquire.[5] And yet the stickiness of noncitizen status is not an anomaly but stems from the very nature of the institution itself. Encompassing more than a status and an activity, citizenship is also an identity—the symbol linking the individual to the nation or people to whom he or she belongs. While home-country citizenship may not prove of much use, its emotional valence often makes it hard to discard. Hence, immigrants' reluctance to give up the citizenship of their native country may deter them from taking on the citizenship of a previously foreign people, although the passage of dual-nationality laws diminishes the conflict by making new and old allegiances compatible.[6]

As status, citizenship is simultaneously a mechanism of inclusion and exclusion, both an instrument and an object of citizens' social closure, to borrow the concepts formulated by Rogers Brubaker.[7] Providing status citizens with a monopoly on the vote, indefinite residence, and a handful of other benefits, citizenship no longer serves as the potent instrument of internal closure against resident noncitizens that it did during the mid-twentieth-century era of low immigration. Yet if for nothing else than its symbolic importance, status citizenship remains a powerful object of closure. Even the United States, a country with a comparatively liberal citizenship regime, compels would-be citizens to vault over an increasingly high wall. Needless to say, resources increase the likelihood of leaping over the wall with success and diminish the relative costs of the effort. However, since citizenship is for the "deserving" only, its acquisition entails a level of scrutiny that some potential citizens might prefer to avoid.[8] Consequently, aspirants have to ask themselves whether the quest for citizenship is worth the gamble, a question that has no clear answer. While prospective citizens ponder the question, their residence within the territory but outside the polity persists.

As institution, citizenship is inherently political; hence, we anticipate that the distinctively political aspects of migration across state boundaries—which lie at the heart of the perspective we develop throughout this book—will heavily impinge on the process whereby immigrants gain formal membership in the state where they have come to live.

As the reader by now knows, the approach elaborated in this book seeks to unravel both the intergroup and intragroup sources of differences in naturalization rates. In general, we anticipate that disparities in status prevalence will be closely associated with intergroup differences in the acquisition of citizenship, though the mechanisms linking policy context to naturalization decisions probably vary. Prevalence may yield a direct effect: the greater the density of persons with more-advantageous status, and thus the higher the fraction of them who are eligible to naturalize, the higher the likelihood is that more of them will take advantage of the opportunity, in turn providing examples for others and thereby diminishing the informational costs and uncertainties entailed in naturalization. Since peer judgments typically matter, independent but parallel decisions to opt for citizenship might indicate a community-wide consensus, thereby diminishing the symbolic dilemmas of acquiring a new nationality. Prevalence could also yield influence through its communicative effect: more commonly found advantageous statuses might signal that membership in the new nation would be welcomed, and more commonly found disadvantageous statuses might portend rejection.

Aggregate differences in the circumstances of migration might also affect intergroup propensities to acquire citizenship. In particular, groups primarily made up of refugees—persons who emigrated for fear of persecution and who may feel rejected by their home country and thankful for the haven found in the host country—might be particularly likely to take up citizenship when possible. Yet, as we pointed out earlier, conferring refugee status is a political act bearing little relationship to the actual circumstances of migration; thus, refugee status almost always eluded Salvadorans fleeing civil war, but was almost always granted to the Vietnamese escaping communism after the fall of South Vietnam. Consequently, the crucial influence on intergroup differences is likely to stem from differences in the prevalence of statuses, *not* the circumstances of migration. When advantaged statuses are overwhelmingly prevalent, as in the case of the ex-Soviets or Vietnamese among whom the great majority arrived as refugees, we anticipate that the indirect effects of advantaged status will be especially strong.

Yet differences in home-country value orientations may also affect group-level disparities in citizenship take-up rates. As we will discuss, the individual costs of naturalization may outweigh its near-term individual benefits; consequently, persons originating in survival-oriented societies may more keenly feel the tug of homeland loyalties than those whose homeland is inclined toward higher levels of self-expression. However, insofar as a survival orientation predisposes emigrants and their descendants toward reducing risk and uncertainty, it may instead produce the strategy that Greta Gilbertson and Audrey Singer have described as "protective naturalization": acquiring U.S. citizenship as insurance against adverse changes in the social and political context and a guarantee of continued residence in the United States.[9] In yet another possibility, the survival orientation may influence outcomes through its impact on familial cohesion: families from more solidaristic societies may be more likely to naturalize as a unit.

Among persons eligible to become U.S. citizens, the politically determined demands imposed by the naturalization process itself ensure that intragroup resource disparities powerfully influence intragroup differences in citizenship take-up rates. On the most practical level, applying for citizenship requires navigating a long bureaucratic process that, as famously summarized in the title of David North's report *The Long Grey Welcome*, may repel as much as it appeals.[10] As Irene Bloemraad argues in her comparative study of citizenship acquisition in the United States and Canada, as an agency, the Immigration and Naturalization Service prioritized its enforcement over its integrative functions, with an organizational culture stamped by the preoccupation with control.[11] Although border and interior enforcement have since been spun off to a new entity, the U.S. Citizenship and Immigration Services, the ethos prevailing in this INS successor agency is unlikely to have changed greatly. Among migrants, the INS/USCIS suffers from its image as an organization to be avoided whenever possible, and stories about negative treatment by its agents abound.[12] Since naturalization also entails a thorough review of an applicant's immigration history and record, which could uncover a previously invisible problem that threatens even permanent residence status, concerns over the negative consequences of close scrutiny clearly lead some potential citizens to stay clear of the entire process. Those willing to put themselves under a microscope need to undergo an exam testing their English ability and knowledge of basic facts about the United States. Although the vast majority of applicants pass—about 91 percent in 2016—the ordeal may discourage some potential citizens, especially those with less education and little or no prior test-taking history.[13] This factor probably weighs less heavily on the 1.5 generation—who are more likely to be fluent in English and familiar with the basic subjects covered by the test—than on immigrants who arrived as adults. Costs are a further deterrent, one of ever greater weight since the late 1980s, when INS, and then USCIS, were transformed into agencies funded not by the U.S. Treasury but by user fees; between 1988 and 2015, fees rose fivefold in constant terms, with barely 3 percent of applicants granted waivers.[14]

Consequently, naturalization confronts potential citizens with significant material and informational barriers, making it imperative that they process the resources to leap over those obstacles. To begin with, not all immigrants travel the same route to eligibility. Those who arrived without authorization but subsequently acquired LPR status may be particularly inhibited from later pursuing a citizenship application, as indicated by the experience of the Mexican beneficiaries of the 1986 Immigration Reform and Control Act, who were significantly less likely to naturalize than their non-IRCA conationals, who had lived in the United States for a comparable number of years.[15] Their reluctance may have been related to the trajectory leading up to legal permanent residence, which involves a series of potentially costly transitions across formal status boundaries that may deplete the material capacity needed to undertake naturalization. The formerly undocumented might also be the most reluctant to expose themselves to the scrutiny involved in citizenship acquisition. The key point is that status upon entry is likely to matter at the intragroup, as well as intergroup, level.

As we have emphasized, citizenship is a clearly defined, unambiguous boundary crossed only by taking a discrete step that requires deliberate action; by contrast, social boundaries are gradually weakened through a continuing iteration of lower-cost investments and transactions. Nonetheless, the competencies that immigrants and their offspring acquire in the pursuit of socioeconomic mobility are almost surely relevant for the take-up of citizenship as well. Proficiency in English ranks especially high among those competencies, not simply because the citizenship exam tests for familiarity with English, but because that skill makes the U.S. political and institutional environment accessible. By the time of adulthood, English is unlikely to be an obstacle of any sort for the foreign-born New Yorkers and Angelenos with whom we are concerned. However, minor children gain citizenship as derivatives of their parents—as happened with roughly 28 percent of our 1.5-generation respondents. Consequently, parental English-language competency and levels of education can directly affect the probability of naturalization: immigrant parents who are more proficient in English will find the hurdles in applying for naturalization less daunting, and those with more formal education may be less hesitant to engage the bureaucratic process involved in citizenship acquisition and will on average have more experience with host-country political life. For the immigrant offspring who gain citizenship as adults, the channel from parental resources to naturalization is more likely to be indirect, operating via the impact of parents' behavior and skills on children's own education, which in turn will facilitate the transition out of permanent resident status.

The costs of naturalization are beyond dispute; the benefits are more uncertain and less concrete. Naturalization provides the ticket of entry to the polity, an outcome that could have a significant effect if large numbers of naturalized citizens voted, and an even greater effect if naturalization numbers were to grow. Yet if some new citizens clearly prize voting—as suggested by Sofya Aptekar's interviews with applicants waiting for their naturalization interviews—others seem indifferent; Asian immigrants, for instance, naturalize at high levels but then only occasionally go to the polls.[16] Beyond the vote, new citizens gain few opportunities in addition to those they already possess as legal permanent residents: unlike the situation a half century ago, citizenship rarely serves as a prerequisite for employment, with the exception of a few branches of the government and selected grant programs.[17]

By contrast, a U.S. passport may offer both greater security when traveling and greater freedom of international movement, a question of importance to immigrants from countries whose passport holders need visas to enter the developed world. On this count, the U.S. passport is not the most powerful—it lags behind German and U.K. passports—but it still opens significantly more international doors than Mexican, Taiwanese, Salvadoran, or Dominican passports (the last being close to the very bottom of the list).[18] Moreover, legal permanent residents wishing to spend time with family members in the home country—where the costs of living are often lower—need to return to the United States every six months. By contrast, U.S. citizens can remain abroad indefinitely without risking loss of residence; this consideration was likely to matter in the eyes of the 1.5-generation respondents we studied, as many of them had parents and relatives abroad and had themselves undertaken much foreign travel. A more powerful motivation to become a U.S. citizen may be that citizenship substantially facilitates the immigration of close relatives still abroad because there is no numerical limitation on the number of spouses, minor children, and parents who can be sponsored by U.S. citizens.

Yet the most compelling of citizenship's concrete benefits may be its function as an insurance policy against the risk of deportation. In contrast to citizenship, legal permanent residency is a conditional status, revocable by the state without much legal recourse, especially since the 1996 Illegal Immigration Reform and Immigrant Responsibility Act (IIRIRA), in conjunction with the 1996 Antiterrorism and Effective Death Penalty Act (AEDPA), which greatly increased the number of violations that can trigger deportation. Indeed, the absolute number of permanent residents experiencing deportation has soared in the years following these acts, climbing from 15,539 in 1994 to 24,702 ten years later, in 2004.[19] Yet, for the individual legal permanent resident, the risk of deportation remains very low. Given an estimated LPR population of 11.5 million in 2003, this translates into a probability of just 0.2 percent per year.[20]

PATTERNS AND PATHWAYS TO CITIZENSHIP

The 1.5 generation is socially similar to the second generation, as the great majority entered the United States at a very young age: in our samples of immigrant-origin New Yorkers and Angelenos, for example, half of the foreign-born respondents arrived in the United States before the age of seven and 90 percent before reaching the age of thirteen. Yet from the beginning, the social similarity produced by exposure to a common environment coexisted with a fundamental categorical difference in their legal status. Some began statutorily with most citizenship rights, occupying the conceptual space close to the boundary that citizenship as status demarks; others are in a far more precarious position, conceptually located just inside the territorial boundary.

By contrast, the U.S.-born children of immigrants all share U.S. citizenship and hence begin life as formal equals. Yet, as the offspring of parents who entered the United States as aliens, they tend to grow up in environments where other family members lack U.S. citizenship. To capture differences in the immediate presence or absence of citizenship, we have created a simple measure of familial citizenship density by counting the number of citizens included in a parent-child trio, with the range varying from 0 to 3. In both New York and Los Angeles, an all-citizen parent-child trio accounted for the majority of cases, though in the New York sample the fraction barely exceeded the 50 percent level. And though the children in question were all adults, parent and child statuses seemed intertwined: only 40 percent of those without citizenship had a parent who had naturalized, whereas over half of those New Yorkers and Angelenos who successfully went through the naturalization process had two parents who had also acquired U.S. citizenship.

Looking across national-origin groups reveals significant intergroup differences. The contrasts reach their height among those Angelenos born abroad but raised in the United States: among Mexicans, the average citizenship density barely exceeded 1, whereas among Vietnamese, almost all (90 percent) parent-child trios had already gained citizenship. Citizenship density rose among second- and 2.5-generation Guatemalans, Salvadorans, and Mexicans; nonetheless, Asian-origin nationalities showed higher levels of citizenship density in every generational grouping. Among the 2.5-generation Angelenos—that is to say, those U.S.-born respondents with one U.S.-born parent, every Korean and Chinese parent-child trio was an all-citizen trio; among Mexican 2.5-generation Angelenos, by contrast, one out of every four still had a parent who had not naturalized.

These intergroup disparities are likely to have roots in different sources. To begin with, they may reflect differences in the longevity of the various migration streams. Since naturalization is generally possible only after five years of legal residence, the nationalities among which new arrivals are particularly prevalent will be prone to lower naturalization rates. However, the sampling universe in both the New York and Los Angeles samples included only the adult children of immigrants who arrived during adolescence, so only thirteen cases in our entire sample (all thirteen of these respondents are from the former Soviet Union in the New York sample) would have been ineligible to apply for citizenship at the time of the survey because they had not lived long enough in the United States. To be sure, time spent in the host society increases exposure and thereby directly facilitates language acquisition and socioeconomic mobility, and thus indirectly eases the path to citizenship; however, time's impact on the acquisition of citizenship is far more conditional, as the clock only starts ticking with the acquisition of legal permanent residency. Most new LPRs are not new immigrants—in the sense of persons freshly arrived—but rather persons who previously came to the United States with some other status— whether as legal "non-immigrant" tourists, students, temporary workers, or intercompany transferees or as unauthorized entrants—and thus the cross-group divergence in citizenship take-up rates that we see in our data is likely to be linked to differences in the policy context and the disparate distributions of status prevalence that it generates.[21] And indeed, as shown in the first set of graphs in figure 6.2, more than 65 percent of national-origin groups that faced the most favorable context of reception had the highest citizenship density (3), while that share was just over 50 percent of those whose context of reception was the least favorable. Similarly, groups with more group-level resources showed higher levels of citizenship density. Finally, we see greater citizenship density in national-origin groups from survival-oriented societies; by contrast, those from societies characterized by greater self-expression had lower citizenship densities.

Narrowing the scope to the foreign-born Angelenos—for whom alone we have information about both date of arrival and, for those who became citizens, date of naturalization—provides further evidence of the extent of intergroup differences (see figure 6.3). Naturalization trajectories proceed more slowly among those groups characterized by a prevalence of disadvantaged statuses, lower group-level schooling, and origins in societies more oriented toward self-expression, as evidenced by substantial differences in naturalization rates. For example, among groups with the most positive status prevalence score, 50 percent of the 1.5-generation respondents had naturalized after roughly fifteen years, whereas it took more than twenty years for those with the least favorable group-level context to reach that same level of naturalization. Differences in group-level schooling yielded even greater disparities. Although there was no appreciable gap between the groups with the highest level of education and those in the middle range, among groups with the least resources, it took almost thirty years before 50 percent of the respondents had naturalized. These gaps are almost as large when we stratify along the survival versus self-expression dimension: the most survival-oriented groups reached the 50 percent naturalization threshold about ten years earlier than those from the most self-expression-oriented groups.

In the next step, we examine the extent to which these differences hold up once we control for individual characteristics and other group-level variables.

Figure 6.2 Citizenship Density (Number of Citizens in Child-Parent Groupings) by Select Group-Level Characteristics

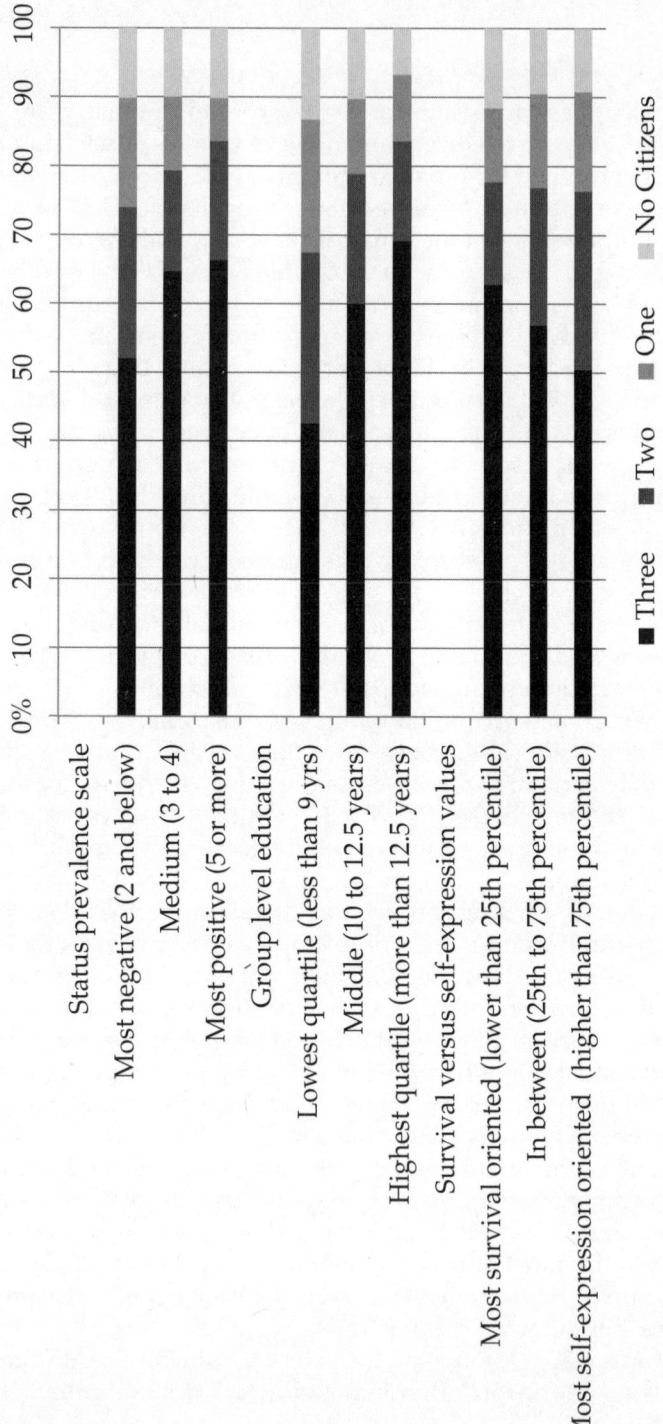

Source: IIMMLA and ISGMNY data sets.

Multivariate Analysis: Citizenship Density and Time to Naturalization

Our multivariate analysis proceeds in two steps. First, to probe in greater detail the differences in citizenship density in the families shown in figure 6.2, we estimate a mixed-effects poisson regression predicting the number of family members (respondent plus parents) possessing U.S. citizenship at the time of interview. This analysis combines both the New York City and Los Angeles data and considers all respondents, including those born abroad as well as born in the United States.

Second, because the ISGMNY data do not provide information on when respondents or their parents naturalized, we turn to the IIMMLA data and employ an event history model to analyze the timing of the naturalization decisions of the 1.5-generation respondents. Unlike the U.S. census and most other data sources used in the analysis of citizenship acquisition, the IIMMLA asked respondents both *whether* they had naturalized and, if so, *when* they acquired U.S. citizenship. We draw on this information, as well as responses to questions about the year of immigration to the United States, to generate a variable for the number of years separating arrival in the United States from acquisition of U.S. citizenship. We then use a discrete time proportional hazard analysis to model the naturalization trajectories of 1.5-generation respondents.

The first five rows in figure 6.4 summarize the results of the group-level variables that characterize the contexts of immigration and emigration, which are the focus of our discussion.[22] The left panel shows the coefficients from the mixed-effects poisson model predicting the number of citizens in a family, and the right panel summarizes the results of the event history regression of the speed of naturalization of 1.5-generation respondents.

Contexts of Immigration

As Irene Bloemraad has shown, the decision to naturalize is conditioned by the larger social and political context. Her comparison of the United States with Canada, where naturalization rates are very high—close to 90 percent of newcomers naturalize within ten years—shows that this context clearly varies across countries.[23] We see here that the social and political context can also vary within a country. Although our data sets, as surveys of two places, are ill suited to assess the importance of geographic context, they contain immigrant offspring from a myriad of countries and thereby provide traction on the ways in which national-level differences in the context of immigration affect the naturalization decision. For the acquisition of citizenship, the policy context—which we define as the prevalence

Figure 6.3 Naturalization Trajectories for 1.5-Generation Los Angeles Respondents by Select Group-Level Variables

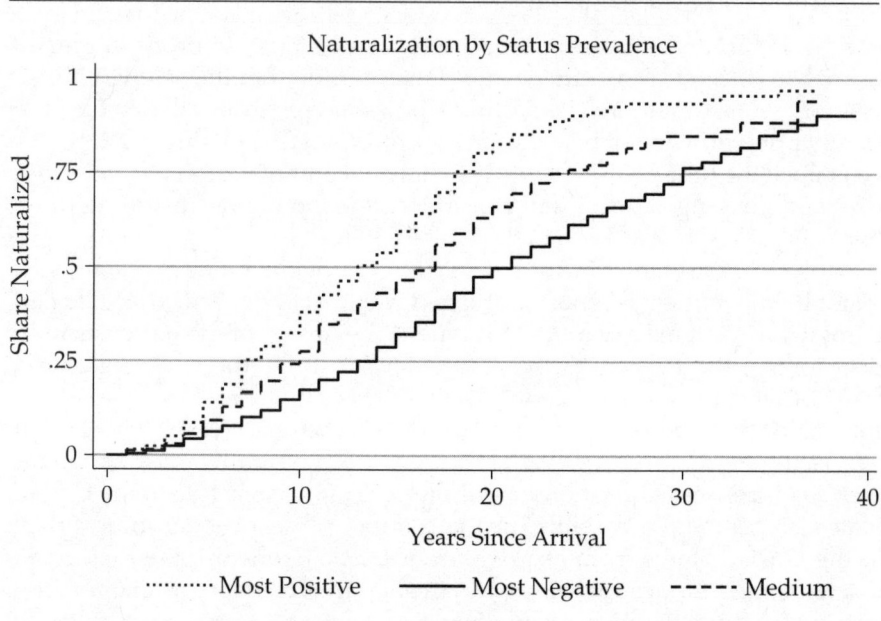
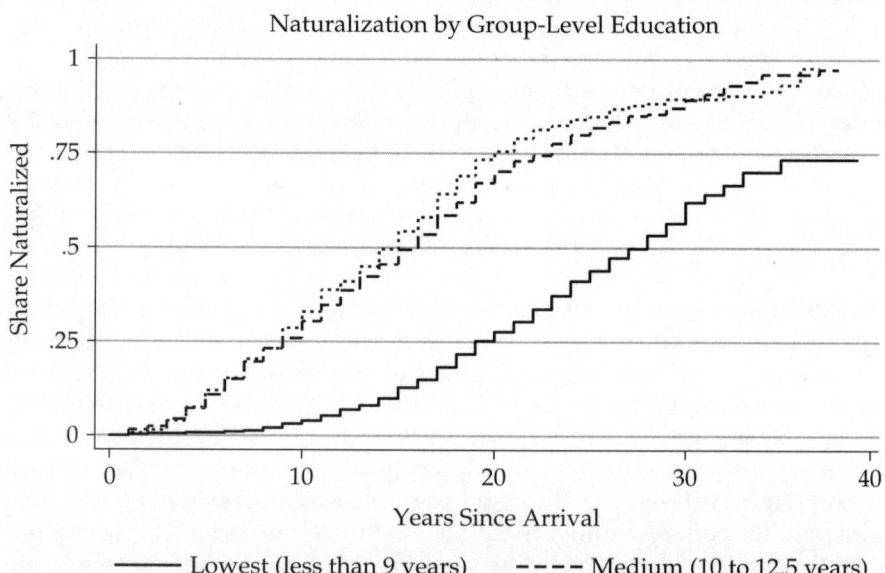

Figure 6.3 Continued

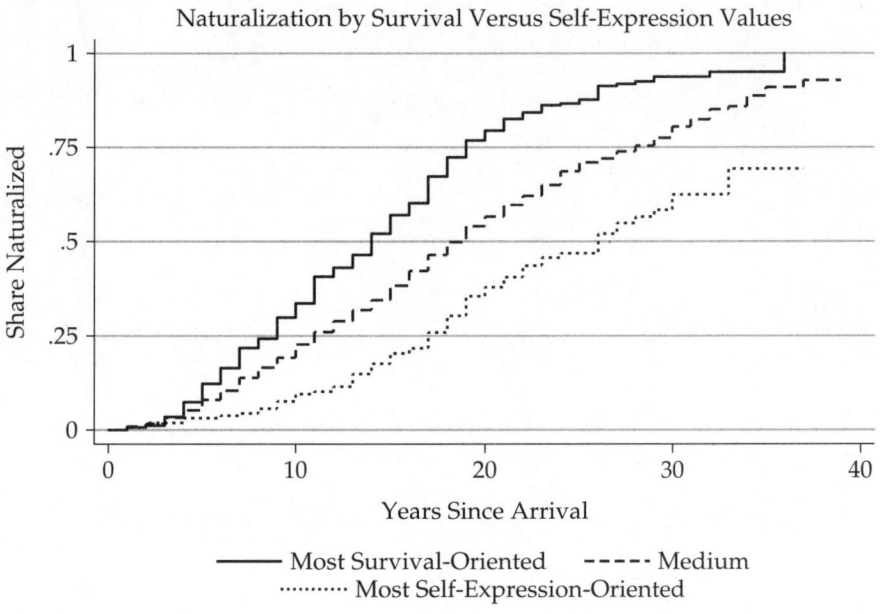

Source: IIMMLA data set.

of more-advantaged (refugee) or less-advantaged (undocumented) status—is likely to be a factor of particular importance.

Although our data do not allow us to identify the precise mechanisms by which status prevalence exercises influence on naturalization outcomes, the regressions nonetheless point to the impact of our legal-context-of-immigration measure. Controlling for all other variables, the analysis predicts citizen density rates of 2.5 (out of a family of three) for nationalities with the most favorable legal context, as opposed to 2.1 for those with the most negative legal context rating. In the event history analysis of naturalization among the foreign-born, U.S.-raised Angelenos, the coefficient for the legal context variable is similarly positive, but does not reach statistical significance.

In contrast, once we control for individual-level factors, neither skin-color stratification (average skin color of the national-origin group) nor the variable indexing the resources stemming from ethnic capital (as indicated by average level of education) yields significant effects.

Figure 6.4 Effects of Select Individual-Level Variables and Measures of Context of Immigration and Emigration

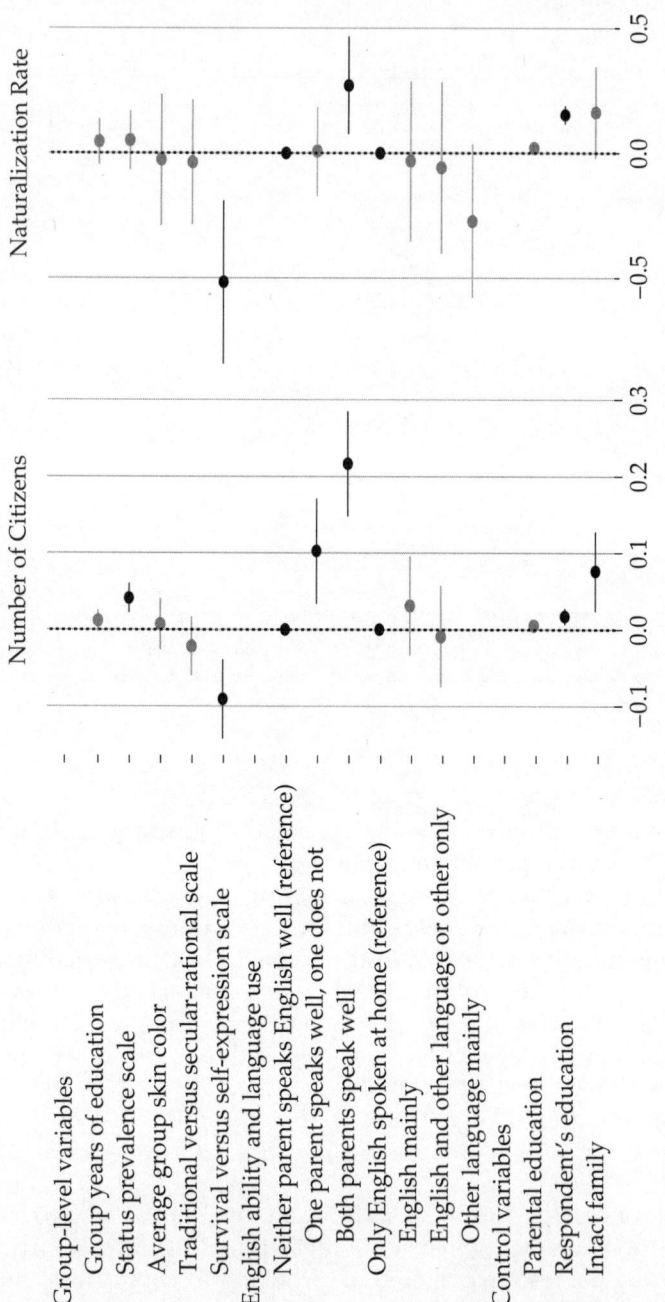

Source: IIMMLA and ISGMNY data sets; results for naturalization are from the IIMMLA only.
Note: Results of mixed-effects logistic event history model for time to naturalization are shown in right panel; results of mixed-effects poisson model predicting number of citizens in the family are shown in left panel. Full regression results and methodological details are available in the online appendix. Higher scores on the survival versus self-expression scale indicate an orientation toward self-expression, which is associated with a slower naturalization; higher scores on the traditional versus secular-rational scale indicate a greater orientation toward rational and secular values.

Contexts of Emigration

The decision to naturalize is shaped by engagement with the polity "here" (the host country), but the imprint of socialization "there" (the society of origin) is likely to matter as well. Because our analysis focuses on persons born abroad but raised in the United States, we anticipate that any sending-country influences will mainly be indirect, through socialization in the parental household and exposure via other coethnics, though visits to the country of origin may be an additional source of direct influence.

As we have argued in this chapter, the migrant generation may find the identity dimension of citizenship a particular hurdle to naturalization. To the extent that a higher self-expression orientation will privilege identity concerns, those from societies with lower levels of self-expression and a greater orientation toward survival values will be quicker to naturalize.

In fact, our analyses do point to the influence cast by the survival versus self-expression axis. Even after controlling for individual-level characteristics and other group-level variables, citizenship densities were higher among families who originated in societies more inclined toward survival values. Everything else being equal, families (that is, the trio comprising the respondent and both parents) from countries that are approximately one standard deviation more survival-oriented than the average (−1 on the scale) had 2.4 citizens, while those from countries one standard deviation above average in terms of self-expression (+1) had 2.0. Likewise, 1.5-generation respondents from survival-oriented societies showed significantly steeper naturalization trajectories, seeking citizenship at an average rate of 3.7 percent, as compared to those from societies where self-expression is more highly valued, who naturalized at a rate of 1.3 percent per year.

Settlement and Adaptation: Time in the United States

At the most basic level, greater time spent in the United States yields greater opportunities for naturalization. In the family-level model predicting the number of citizens in families and drawing on the pooled sample, we measure time by including the number of years the parents had stayed in the United States, taking the maximum of both parents. For our individual-level analysis of naturalization of 1.5-generation respondents, drawing on the IIMMLA only, we include information on the age at which they arrived (expecting that those who arrived at older ages will be less likely to have naturalized by the time of interview) as well as their age at the time of the survey. In this individual-level analysis, each respondent is considered at "risk" of naturalizing every year since entry to the United States. The data have one case for each person-year until the respondent is naturalized. Once naturalized, the respondent is removed from the data (the "risk set") and no longer figures in the analysis. The model includes a third-order polynomial for time to control for the fact that those who had lived longer in the United States would have had more opportunity to naturalize (the baseline hazard).

The family-level analysis shows that, other things being equal, the model predicts that there will be just one citizen (on average 0.8) in families in which the first parent arrived less than five years before the survey, but predicts 1.5 citizens in families with parents who had spent five to ten years in the United States. Even after this early period of acclimatization, time in the United States increases naturalization: our model predicts a significant increase in citizenship density—2.2 (out of a possible 3)—for those with eleven to twenty years of parental residency. However, we see no statistically significant increase in citizenship density for further increases (twenty-one years or more) in U.S. residence.

Conditions of Arrival: Place of Birth and Legal Status

As outlined in the preceding sections, the status with which family members arrive is a central determinant of naturalization. By default, citizenship densities will be higher among families in which one parent was born in the United States (in the 2.5 generation) or in which the respondent (the second generation) was born in the United States. In the family-level model, we enter this information with one indicator variable identifying the place of birth of the respondent (the United States or abroad) and another identifying a parent born in the United States. When looking specifically at naturalization with the IIMMLA data, we further enter controls for respondent's legal status on arrival.

The analysis of family-level citizenship density shows that respondents born in the United States were much more likely to live in families of higher citizenship density. Some of this association is surely accounted for by the citizenship status of these birthright citizen respondents themselves, yet even among the foreign-born, those who arrived in the United States as very young children—before the age of six—lived in families with higher citizen prevalence than those who arrived later in their childhood.

We remind the reader that only legal permanent residents enjoy eligibility for naturalization (after a five-year waiting period). Unfortunately, we lack information on status at arrival for parents in the New York City data and thus cannot consider the impact of parents' on-arrival status in the family-level analysis. Although that information is found in the Los Angeles data, the IIMMLA lacks information on the date when permanent residency was acquired and the citizenship clock began to tick. Nonetheless, since the IIMMLA allows us to control for respondents' legal status upon arrival, we find that even after controlling for other characteristics, the basic descriptive pattern shown in figure 6.1 still holds: the naturalization trajectories of those who arrived in an undocumented or temporary legal status diverge strongly from the trajectories of those who arrived as legal permanent residents. Whereas roughly half of the respondents who arrived in the United States as LPRs naturalized after fifteen years of residence, it took roughly twenty-five years of residence for those respondents who arrived without LPR status to reach that same 50 percent mark.

Competencies and Skills

As we have argued in this chapter, competencies and resources—whether those of parents or of adult children—provide crucial capacities for leaping over the naturalization hurdle, as borne out by our analysis. As shown in figure 6.4, parental knowledge of the English language is important at the family level. With other factors held equal, our model predicts that a significantly higher share of families with two English-speaking parents (2.4 out of 3) will be naturalized than in families with no English-speaking parent (1.9 out of 3). Whereas parental proficiency in English clearly matters, parental educational attainment yields a more modest effect: although the coefficient is statistically significant, substantively the association is small. The difference in the expected number of citizens in a family between those with the lowest levels of English ability and those with the highest would translate into a difference of more than twenty-eight years of education—a nearly impossible gap, and one certainly not found in our data, the highly unequal levels of education among immigrants to the United States notwithstanding. The association with respondent's education is somewhat stronger. But we should emphasize here that this is strictly an association, as time order or causality cannot be inferred from the data we have.

The event history model of naturalization timing in the 1.5 generation confirms these results and sheds further light into these processes. The coefficient for parental education is not significant when modeling naturalization of the 1.5 generation, a result suggesting that parental education exercises little direct effect on the citizenship trajectories of the 1.5 generation but rather influences those trajectories *indirectly*, whether via parental naturalization (which affects mainly minor children) or via the impact of parents' schooling on their children's educational attainment. Since naturalization rates are higher only when both parents speak English well, it appears that households in which both parents lack full competence in English may constrain the family's engagement with U.S. politics and institutions and thereby delay children's naturalization. Yet once controlling for parents' English-language competency, *language practices* at home do not make much difference, as those practices may reflect an effort to transmit home-country language to the next generation and have little to do with engaging in host-country politics.[24] Indeed, the analyses show that only those who did not speak any English in the childhood home differ from those who spoke English only, and then merely at the 10 percent significance level.

CONCLUSION: FROM ALIEN TO CITIZEN, CROSSING THE INTERNAL BOUNDARY

In global perspective, the internal boundary of citizenship in the United States proves relatively easy to cross. As the history of U.S. citizenship shows, the permeability of that boundary is a by-product of U.S. history, as the relatively low barriers to naturalization—most importantly, the five-year eligibility term—are best understood as a policy designed to attract the population needed to seize land from the indigenous inhabitants of North America and then control and settle that territory. Of course, the early American republic was ready to accept only some newcomers, not all; that pattern would last until the early 1950s, when racial prerequisites for citizenship were finally abandoned. Although the reaction against the explicit use of racial and ethnic criteria in both access to entry and eligibility for citizenship has in some ways led to increased permeability, a countertrend involving the imposition of racially neutral but resource-demanding, and hence class-biased, criteria for eligibility has had an offsetting effect in the past century. Dating from the Naturalization Act of 1906, this countertrend has seen a combination of fees, examinations, and increasingly careful scrutiny of prospective citizens' backgrounds. Indeed, the 1988 decision to convert the Immigration and Naturalization Service (and later Citizenship and Immigration Services) into an agency funded entirely by user fees ensured that naturalization would become ever more financially taxing. And though there are tentative efforts to ease up on some of these financial demands—for example, by allowing applicants to pay with credit cards rather than in cash—conflict over access to what remains a privileged status has thus far constrained efforts at encouraging immigrants to become Americans.[25]

Hence, the barriers to naturalization, which discriminate against potential Americans who lack the material and informational resources to surmount them, confronted the immigrant offspring studied in this book with a significant challenge. Although the U.S.-born among them enjoyed citizenship by birthright, many grew up in households where one or even both parents remained noncitizens. That pattern was all the more prevalent among the 1.5 generation, those born abroad but raised in the United States, for whom the acquisition of citizenship was often a protracted process. As shown in the family-level analysis, net of controls, a respondent's foreign birth was associated with a lower level of family-level citizenship density, indicating that the 1.5-generation respondents continued to live in households with few citizens.

Although citizenship densities rise with years of settlement, the coefficients for parents' and respondents' years of education point to the importance of material resources in conditioning the capacity to clear the impediments to citizenship; likewise, the impact of parents' acquisition of English-language skills underlines the centrality of informational resources.

In a sense, the influence of these individual-level variables is in keeping with the predictions of neo-assimilation theory. Yet, as we have seen, even among those arriving with the legal status that starts the naturalization clock, given the long interval separating arrival in the United States from the acquisition of citizenship, it seems reasonable to think that these foreign-born but U.S.-raised Angelenos and New Yorkers were de facto Americans long before they could gain that de jure status. In turn, that long time span suggests that the proximal mechanisms producing assimilation or integration are impeded by the discriminatory mechanisms built into the institution of citizenship itself.

Moreover, neo-assimilation theory operates at only one level: that of the individual or household. However, the empirical analysis demonstrates that citizenship acquisition is affected by factors found at both levels—the individual and the group—a finding made possible by the multilevel modeling strategy pursued throughout this book. As this chapter has shown, tendencies toward naturalization vary greatly *across* groups, with some almost uniformly acquiring citizenship and others traveling a different trajectory as they either never acquire citizenship or do so only after significant delay. Consequently, contexts—whether of emigration or immigration—weigh heavily on the decision to take up a new citizenship. At the individual (and therefore intragroup) level, status clearly matters: among the 1.5-generation respondents surveyed by the IIMMLA, those who began their U.S. sojourn without legal permanent resident status took significantly longer to gain citizenship than those who began their

American lives with a green card in hand. And yet we see that group-level difference in status prevalence can still exercise a strong effect, dampening family-level citizenship densities among members of groups where less favorable statuses prevail and increasing densities among groups where statuses are more advantageous. Similarly, although there are more citizens in two-parent families at the intragroup level, intergroup differences in citizenship density and naturalization decisions are also explained by survival orientations at the group level, with immigrant parents and 1.5-generation respondents from more survival-oriented groups naturalizing sooner and more frequently.

Thus, alongside the usual factors that contribute to social stratification and garner the attention of migration scholarship, the civic stratification by status produced by policies intended to control movement across the external boundary of the state has subsequent effects on mobility across the internal boundary of state membership. But citizenship can be exercised even in the absence of status citizenship. In the next chapter, we take up the question of how these prior experiences of inclusion and exclusion combine with the conditions associated with international migration to affect immigrants' engagement in and with the polity.

Chapter 7 | Exercising Citizenship

RESEARCH ON POLITICAL participation often begins and ends with status citizens. To be sure, not all status citizens are of the same class: informal barriers to participation and lack of rights can effectively create a second-class citizenry whose collective engagements under the banner of equality—whether on the ground of race, ethnicity, religion, gender, or sexual preference—involve citizenship struggles. But states that accept the arrival of foreigners from abroad simultaneously accede to the growth of a population that lives on the territory but lacks status citizenship. As chapter 6 just showed, exclusion from the polity via one's parents—both present and past, both direct and indirect—is one of the central lines of variation among the immigrant offspring analyzed in this book. Having highlighted these varied experiences of exclusion from and inclusion in citizenship understood as a status, we now seek to understand how these experiences affect the capacity of these immigrant offspring, whether status citizens or not, to exercise citizenship as de facto, if not de jure, members of a democratic polity.

In a democratic society, exclusion from the polity does not imply exclusion from politics. Noncitizens enjoy the core civil rights of freedom of expression and assembly: they can engage in a variety of non-electoral political and civic activities, whether in their capacity as parents, neighbors, or political actors demonstrating in the street or even directly pressuring politicians. And though politicians may not be interested in reaching out to persons who cannot vote, noncitizens are nonetheless affected by politicians' decisions, news of which is broadcast to anyone who cares to pay attention, their legal status or citizenship notwithstanding.[1] In short, while the electorate is clearly bounded, the boundary between society and the polity is fuzzier, with many aspects of political life accessible to all.

As we conceptualize it here, the exercise of citizenship can take two forms, one broad and one more narrow. In its broadest form, the exercise of citizenship entails participation in one's community, whether that community is understood in national, local, or even transnational terms. With the exception of voting and its prerequisite, registration, these forms of participation do *not* require citizenship status: being civic-minded—that is, being sufficiently concerned about the community to do something, whether writing a letter, attending a meeting, or just belonging to a civic organization—is good enough. Hence, most forms of participation are open to those who want to exercise citizenship, whether status citizens or not, though only status citizens can avail themselves of the full gamut of participative possibilities. In its more narrow form, the exercise of citizenship involves an orientation toward organized politics that denotes political integration.

As we noted in chapter 6, citizenship—both its acquisition and its exercise—has been a neglected theme in the literature on the second generation. Of the major works to which we have referred throughout this text, only *Inheriting the City* devotes attention to civic and political engagement. Kasinitz and his coauthors argue that participation and alienation constitute the central axes of group variation: Chinese and Russians experience little political alienation but generally abstain from participation, West Indians experience a high level of alienation and yet participate at high levels, and Latin American groups are alienated and also disengaged. Thus, as in the rest of the book, *Inheriting the City* uniquely focuses here on the intergroup contrasts, to the exclusion of the intragroup differences—in education, citizenship status, and English-language competence—that, as the reader will soon see, turn out to be more influential. Moreover, since the shared characteristic of second-generation advantage cannot explain second-generation differences, these authors offer a diffuse explanation that emphasizes the effects of history, exposure to discrimination, and, revealingly, home-country experiences.

By contrast, politics goes virtually unmentioned in *Remaking the Mainstream:* the longest treatment is barely a paragraph long. Moreover, in emphasizing that the European immigrants of the nineteenth and early twentieth centuries "inserted themselves qua groups into political processes . . . in ways that created tangible rewards for ethnic membership," Alba and Nee again suggest that group membership, as opposed to individual characteristics, can matter, but neither follow up to identify the *specific* immigrant groups for which this might be the case nor explain in what ways group membership might matter.[2] Moreover, their perspective lacks an account of individual-level variation in political participation; neo-assimilation theory argues that adaptation is driven by the rewards it yields, yet civic and political participation contribute to public goods and hence yield few individual benefits, whether for citizens or foreigners. Consequently, these activities are unlikely to advance the core immigrant goal of searching for the good life. Moreover, the costs of attending to politics may be particularly high when the system, the parties, the politicians, and the policies all appear strange and foreign.

As noted in the previous chapter, there are costs and benefits to acquiring citizenship, and the balance between them is not easy to determine. However, we do anticipate a positive link between adaptation and social mobility, on the one hand, and political participation and interest, on the other. Political engagement and knowledge are both likely to increase as immigrants acquire the capacity to understand the world around them, gain the resources needed to attend to and engage with civic and political matters that do not produce immediate benefit, and develop proximity and ties to a more diverse network of established persons who are more likely to transmit political signals and stimuli. This process will be shaped by those differences at the individual and familial level that can make the new environment more or less strange or more or less easy to learn: immigrants arriving with higher levels of education, and especially those who receive some of their education in the United States, are likely to find the environment both less unfamiliar and easier to learn, advantages that should be transmissible to their U.S.-born or U.S.-raised children. Similarly, differences in the pace of parental adaptations—the speed with which they master the dominant tongue and the degree to which it replaces the mother tongue both outside and inside the home—should facilitate or hinder the political and civic engagement of their children.

Thus, building on neo-assimilation theory, we can forecast that social assimilation might straightforwardly lower the costs of civic participation, possibly transforming a nonpartisan activity into a source of nonmaterial benefits. Yet social assimilation is but one of the influences affecting citizenship acquisition—which, in turn, provides the key unlocking the door to electoral participation. Moreover, social assimilation cannot furnish the means of political integration, as there is no politically undifferentiated mainstream to be found. Rather, since politics is explicitly structured around conflict, political integration entails finding one's place in the political landscape, a terrain that has become increasingly polarized in recent decades and in which group membership often comes to define the key political divides, precisely because membership in an immigrant-origin group is meaningful to some large segment of the native population.

Though *Legacies* and other, related works bypass the analysis of civic and political participation completely, one might think that the hypothesis of segmented assimilation would provide useful insights, given the inherent segmentation of the political landscape itself. However, extrapolating from the socioeconomic to the political sphere is not straightforward. The hierarchically ordered segments of society that are the referents in the standard segmented assimilation approach have no clear relationship to the cleavages of U.S. politics. As to the context of reception, it is not clear which of the three dimensions should matter and in what ways. Although the approach contends that different groups trigger migration policy responses that vary from positive to hostile, it simultaneously contends that all non-European immigrant groups encounter a hostile societal reception, which leaves one wondering which of these two contextual factors will affect political and civic engagement and why.

By contrast, the political lies at the heart of the international perspective developed throughout this book; we argue that systems of migration control inherently lead to exclusion from the polity, endowing only citizens with the full array of political rights and, as we have seen, impeding access to citizenship for others. As emphasized in *Parents Without Papers*, the burden of exclusion falls most heavily on the undocumented, whose status is itself the by-product of immigration restriction. Yet, as we have maintained, migration control entails a multiplicity of statuses that vary in rights and entitlements and hence in the degree of exclusion they represent. Living on the *wrong* side of the bright line of citizenship is a core aspect of the immigrant experience, and we expect that noncitizen status will influence both forms of participation—narrow as well as broad—and depress political and civic engagement independent of time spent in the United States or other resources that might encourage political involvement.

We also anticipate that civic and political engagements will reflect other influences stemming from the distinctively international nature of migration across state boundaries. As we have emphasized, immigrant offspring typically belong to internationalized family networks, and these relationships could have both positive and negative consequences for civic and political engagement. If relatives abroad serve as a family's focal point, whether via the sending of remittances or travel for visits, their influence could be negative, thus detracting from familial resources that could spur political engagement. Similarly, visits might strengthen homeland loyalties, thus diminishing interest in host-country politics. On the other hand, those same relatives abroad could have a positive influence by stimulating civic and political engagement, whether with the aim of lobbying to help the homeland or facilitating visits or immigration by those relatives. Other international influences may stem from the value orientations that prevail in the society of origin. These orientations may endow immigrant parents with distinctive political preferences, whether favorable or averse to political and civic participation, or whether leaning toward one or the other set of partisan or ideological leanings that prevail in the country of destination; in turn, these parents may transmit these orientations to their children, a tendency made all the more likely if matters related to legal or citizenship status keep parents from being drawn into the polity.

WHO EXERCISES CITIZENSHIP? SOCIAL ASSIMILATION AND POLITICAL EXCLUSION

In the area of political engagement, as in the many other domains covered in this book, we contend that initial formal exclusion has deep and long-lasting effects. This chapter principally seeks to assess this hypothesis, comparing how social assimilation affects political participation as opposed to at-entry formal exclusion. As in the preceding chapters, the logic of the analysis builds on our knowledge of time order: we want to see how the conditions under which our respondents grew up influenced their later behavior as adults. Because only the IIMMLA provides information on respondents' and parents' legal status at time of arrival, as well as the timing of naturalization, we confine this portion of the analysis to the Los Angeles respondents.

If political incorporation is an extension of social assimilation, then the same rational choice processes emphasized by neo-assimilation theory should lie behind second-generation engagement with politics. Competence in the dominant language develops just as the conventional approach insists: language learning grows with time and exposure as immigrants are impelled by the need to acquire competencies that are rewarded and valued by the destination society. In turn, a greater capacity to comprehend and make sense of the world around them should facilitate immigrant parents' exposure to political signals and increase their ability to make sense of political matters. Similarly, parents who received at least part of their education in the United States will be more familiar with the institutions and political landscape and be able to transfer this knowledge to their offspring.

By contrast, the more a foreign language dominates in the household, the more foreign the political environment will appear. For that reason, we take language in the parental household as a window through which we can examine how social assimilation could yield political impacts, since differences in parents' ability to speak English should affect their capacity to first absorb political information and then transmit it to their children. Following a similar logic, we could argue that foreign-language use is *negatively* related to political and civic engagement, which rises instead with greater parental English-language capacity. But using the home-country language does not have to come at the cost of English, especially for the children of immigrants. And holding parental English *ability* constant, home-country language use may in fact reflect parental investment in cross-border engagements, which may not only be compatible with but actually foster host-country participation.

Regardless of how social assimilation influences political participation, we expect that the experience of living on the *wrong* side of the bright line of citizenship will have an effect of its own, depressing political engagement independent of exposure or other resources that might encourage political involvement. We hypothesize that past and present formal exclusion from the polity, net of all other factors, including language use, will yield negative effects on a broad range of political and civic involvements, including those for which citizenship is not required. We measure past and present political exclusion with a five-category variable distinguishing the two-thirds of the sample who were birthright citizens—all with at least one foreign-born parent—from the foreign-born respondents, who are in turn classified into four categories: those who became citizens between ages zero and sixteen, those who became citizens between ages seventeen and twenty, those who became citizens between the ages of twenty-one and thirty-eight, and those who had not acquired citizenship by the time of the survey. A little over 7 percent of the respondents had become U.S. citizens by age sixteen; those who acquired citizenship between ages seventeen and twenty and between ages twenty-one and thirty-eight each comprised roughly 8 percent of the sample; those who never naturalized accounted for 10 percent of the sample. Recalculating these percentages using the foreign-born as the denominator tells us that fully 30 percent of those Los Angeles respondents born outside the United States had not yet obtained citizenship as of the time of the survey, compared to just under 20 percent who had naturalized in childhood or early adolescence.

In our view, naturalization represents the activation of the political self in the country of reception. Consequently, we seek to draw further insight from theories of political socialization, a literature that has long focused on the role of age in the socialization process. Some scholars in this field have argued that one's political perceptions crystallize and mature during the period from preteens to early adulthood.[3] Several studies demonstrate that behavior during the formative years has a strong effect on political involvement during adulthood and that, after these formative years, individuals' political attitudes (and presumably behaviors) remain highly stable throughout their lifetimes.[4]

In this light, not just if but *when* naturalization occurs is likely to yield a long-term effect. When the citizen self is activated prior to the age at which most youth begin to form their own adult political identities, greater engagement should ensue. By contrast, individuals who approach the formative period of early adulthood while remaining outside of the polity are less likely to engage and to create a U.S.-centered political self.

Furthermore, for the 1.5 generation, the circumstances under which naturalization occurs varies with biographical time. Among our foreign-born respondents, naturalization prior to the age of sixteen was closely synchronized with the naturalization of their parents (occurring at the same time or shortly thereafter). Therefore, these early naturalizers grew up in households with parents who had recently undergone the civic and political education needed to gain citizenship status, who possessed the resources to acquire citizenship for themselves and their children, *and* who saw value in doing so. Hence, as young citizens, these second-generation youth were likely to have been primed for political socialization: knowing that the polity was open and that civic participation was expected, they would have been more receptive to appeals to protest, petition, vote, and contact local and national elected officials.

By contrast, later naturalization may yield a weaker causal impact than an earlier, family-centered naturalization process. Acquisition of citizenship as an adult is much more likely to be the individual's own decision, not one directly resulting from or related to the decisions of his or her parents. Moreover, an individual's decision to naturalize later in life is more likely to be the *consequence,* rather than the *cause,* of socioeconomic integration and political and civic engagement. Individuals with higher levels of education, an interest in U.S. politics, and friendship and familial networks that encourage political and civic participation might choose to naturalize as adults in order to participate more completely. Thus, for these individuals, naturalization is more likely to be endogenous to political and civic outcomes, as suggested by the likely future of the undocumented immigrant rights activists who have been mobilized through informal channels outside the mainstream political process and have gained political awareness well before they are even eligible for citizenship.[5]

EXERCISING CITIZENSHIP: PARTICIPATION IN FORMAL AND INFORMAL POLITICS

Our analysis of participation includes a study of both civic engagement and participation in formal politics and integration into the party system. Although non-electoral participation in politics is, in principle, open to all, relatively few participate. Only one-third of the Los Angeles respondents reported participation in any of the three forms of civic participation mentioned by the interviewers—attending a protest, attending a rally, or contacting a politician. Moreover, the different types of participation significantly overlapped—in other words, the group of engaged second-generation men and women who belonged to organizations were also more likely to participate in non-electoral politics. That correspondence between organizational membership and civic engagement reflects the fundamentally social core at the heart of political and civic activity: participation proves deeply responsive to the level and intensity of political involvement in an individual's social circles, through which political information also flows.[6]

This social core is reflected in a variety of associations between civic engagement and individual- and group-level characteristics. As mentioned, the life-course phase in which naturalization occurs may determine reception to the social triggers of political engagement. For the population as a whole, young adulthood is a prime age for political engagement, and if 1.5-generation youths and young adults remain outside the electorate during this crucial period, they may be isolated from the social pressures that ignite political participation. Context is also likely to matter: if noncitizen immigrant offspring mainly live among other aliens, then foreign-born but U.S.-raised persons are likely to find themselves in an environment that reinforces detachment because politics is of low, if any salience. Indeed, as Jennifer Hochschild and John Mollenkopf point out, mobilizers play an especially important role in triggering activity among newcomers to the political system.[7] Consequently exposure to messages directed at voters may not be enough to stimulate their participation; instead, some voters may need to be prodded into action through the mobilization efforts of neighbors, friends, and institutions that are already active.

To be sure, the children of immigrants are exposed to political ideas. But the relevant information and ideas about politics, political parties, and government may stem from the parental place of origin rather than from the place of their own current residence; whether any such exposure encourages or discourages political participation will vary greatly depending on the state and polity of origin. Furthermore, the informational component of that package is likely to be of limited use, given the particularities of each country's political structure.

Of course, even in the absence of family political socialization, the barriers to participation faced by immigrant parents may be overcome by the broader socialization process in U.S. schools and U.S. society. But since many immigrants' children are themselves immigrants, the obstacle of noncitizen status may inhibit participation in a similar fashion. And as we argued, whether native-born or not, whether citizens or not, immigrants' immediate descendants are unlikely to receive the same political socialization as their peers who are both native-born and children of the native-born. Most importantly, the political signals received from parents may differ in quantity and quality, as parental disengagement—and even more so, exclusion from the polity—is likely to transmit messages of both an explicit and implicit kind.

Drawing on a set of regression models, we now ask whether these concepts of social assimilation and political exclusion will matter over and above standard socioeconomic and demographic predictors of political participation. We insert indicators for each of the concepts outlined, controlling for demographic characteristics, parental language use and English ability, home-country ties, legal status at arrival, and our context-of-emigration and context-of-immigration measures. The first block of dependent variables examines non-electoral forms of participation: belonging to an organization; contacting a government official, whether by telephone, by email, or in person; attending any political meetings, rallies, speeches, or dinners in support of a political candidate; and taking part in any form of protest, such as picketing or a march, demonstration, or boycott. We then look at electoral participation among current citizens, such as being registered to vote and voting in the past election (these models omit the not-yet-naturalized). Table 7.1 provides a summary of the different measures.

Figures 7.1 to 7.3 concisely summarize these many regression models by plotting summaries of key regression coefficients.[8] To increase legibility, we plot those coefficients that are statistically significant at the 5 percent level or higher in black, those significant at the 10 percent level in dark gray, and all others in light gray. Figure 7.1 shows results for participation in civic or non-electoral political activity; figure 7.2 shows results for two measures that aggregate several activities in a scale; and figure 7.3 summarizes results for regressions on engagement in electoral politics.

Social Assimilation: Parental Language Ability and Education in the United States

Because social assimilation is driven by a continuous process of adaptation, we expect that greater levels of parental linguistic adaptation and experiences—such as receiving at least some education in the United States—would increase parental exposure to the American political system and thus provide the channel linking parental assimilation to children's civic and political behavior. Indeed, greater parental English-language ability was positively associated with a range of outcomes related to both civic engagement and political participation. Somewhat similarly, respondents raised in households where at least one parent had received some schooling in the United States were more likely to engage in at least some

Table 7.1 Dependent Variables, Labels, and a Summary of Survey Items

Label	Item/Definition
Member of an organization	Do you belong to any community organizations, work-related organizations, sports teams, or other nonreligious organizations?
Attended a protest	In the past twelve months, have you taken part in any form of protest, such as picketing or a march, demonstration, or boycott?
Attended a meeting	In the past twelve months, have you attended any political meetings, rallies, speeches, or dinners in support of a political candidate?
Contacted a public official	In the past twelve months, have you contacted a government office about a problem or to get help or information, either by telephone, by email, or in person?
Any civic activity	Sum of the three above
Any civic or political engagement	Engaged in any civic activity, member of any organization/club, or member of a home country–oriented organization
Has a party ID	Identifies with a party
Registered to vote	Is registered to vote
Voted	Did you happen to vote in the October 7 California recall election last year [2003] or not?
Was reached out to	In the past twelve months, has anyone you know encouraged you to support a specific candidate or political party in the United States?

Source: IIMMLA data set.

civic activity, but they were no more likely to participate in electoral politics than their peers whose parents were entirely schooled abroad. By contrast, language use when growing up shows no consistent association with our measures of engagement in formal politics and only one statistically significant association with engagement in civic activity: we see a higher likelihood of attending protests among those who grew up in households in which a language other than English was mainly spoken.

Exclusion and Time Spent Outside the Polity

Participation in civic life and non-electoral political activity is open to all residents of the United States, regardless of citizenship or legal status;

Figure 7.1 Predicting Participation of Los Angeles Respondents in Civic or Non-electoral Political Activities: Summary of Key Regression Results

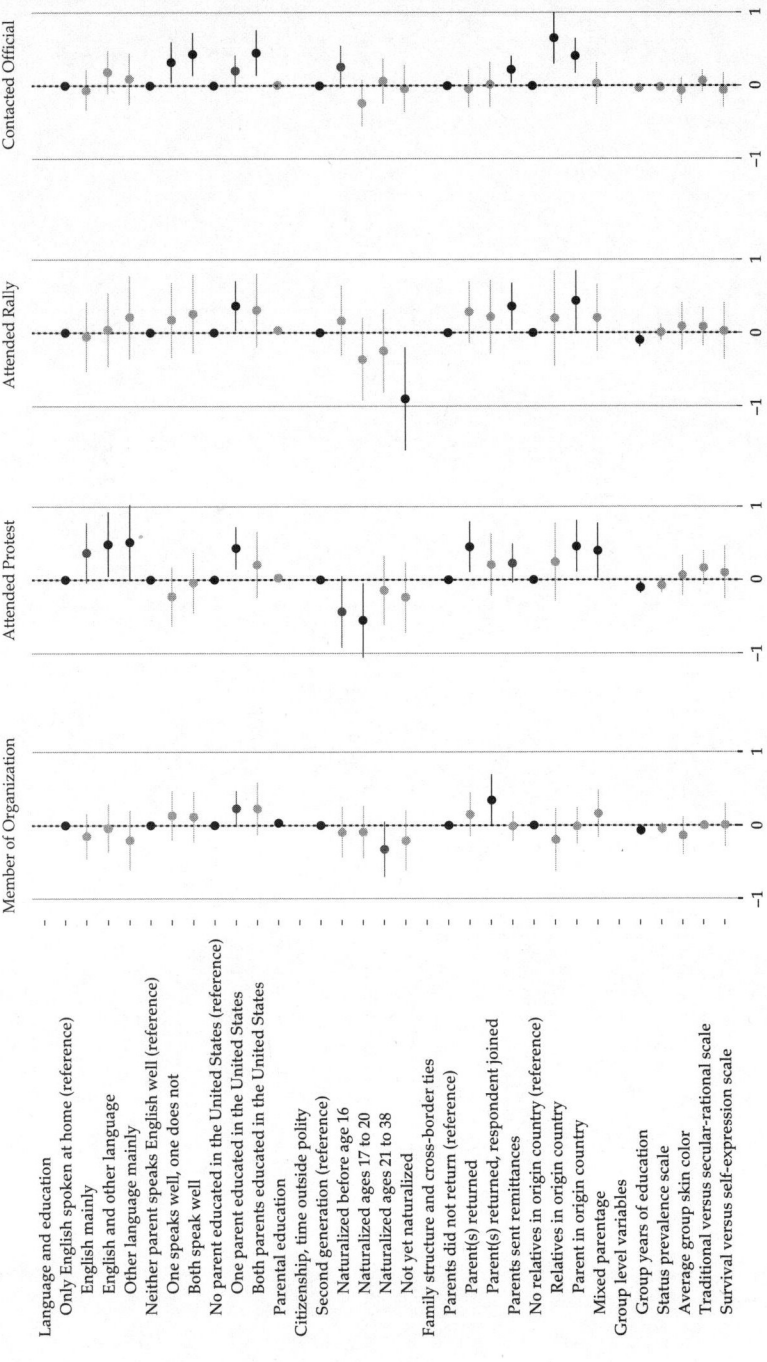

Source: IIMMLA data set.

Figure 7.2 Predicting Aggregate Measures of Los Angeles Respondents' Civic and Political Engagement: Summary of Key Regression Results

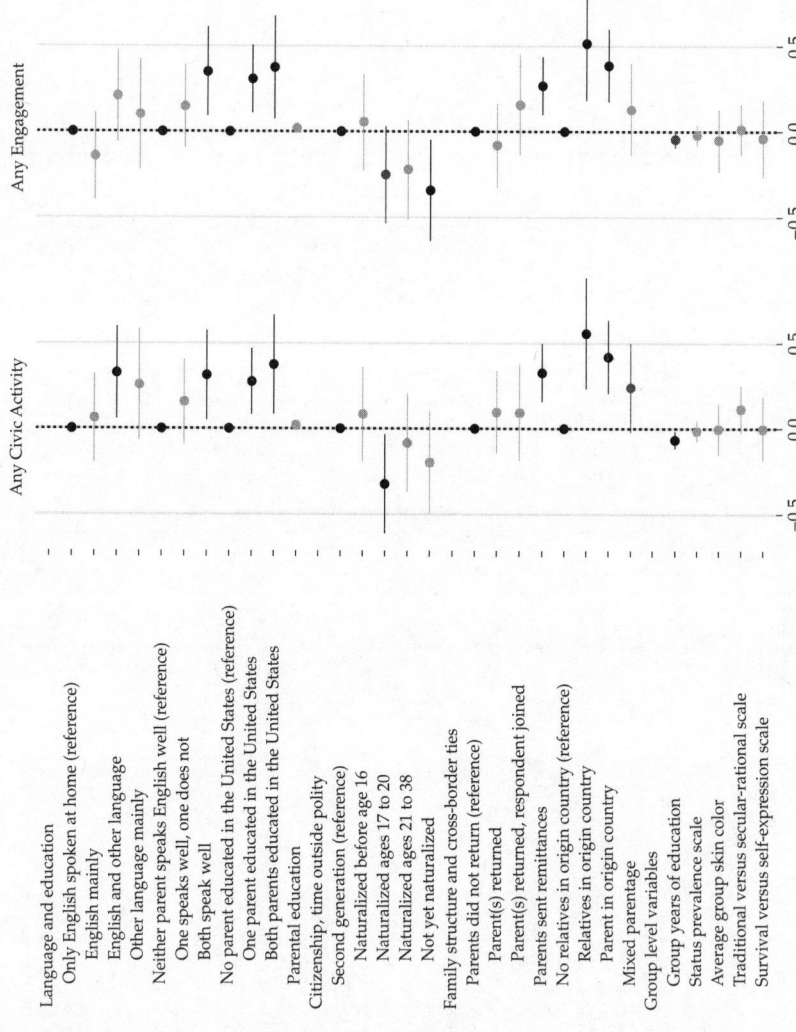

Source: IIMMLA data set.

Figure 7.3 Predicting Engagement of Los Angeles Respondents in Electoral Politics: Summary of Key Regression Results

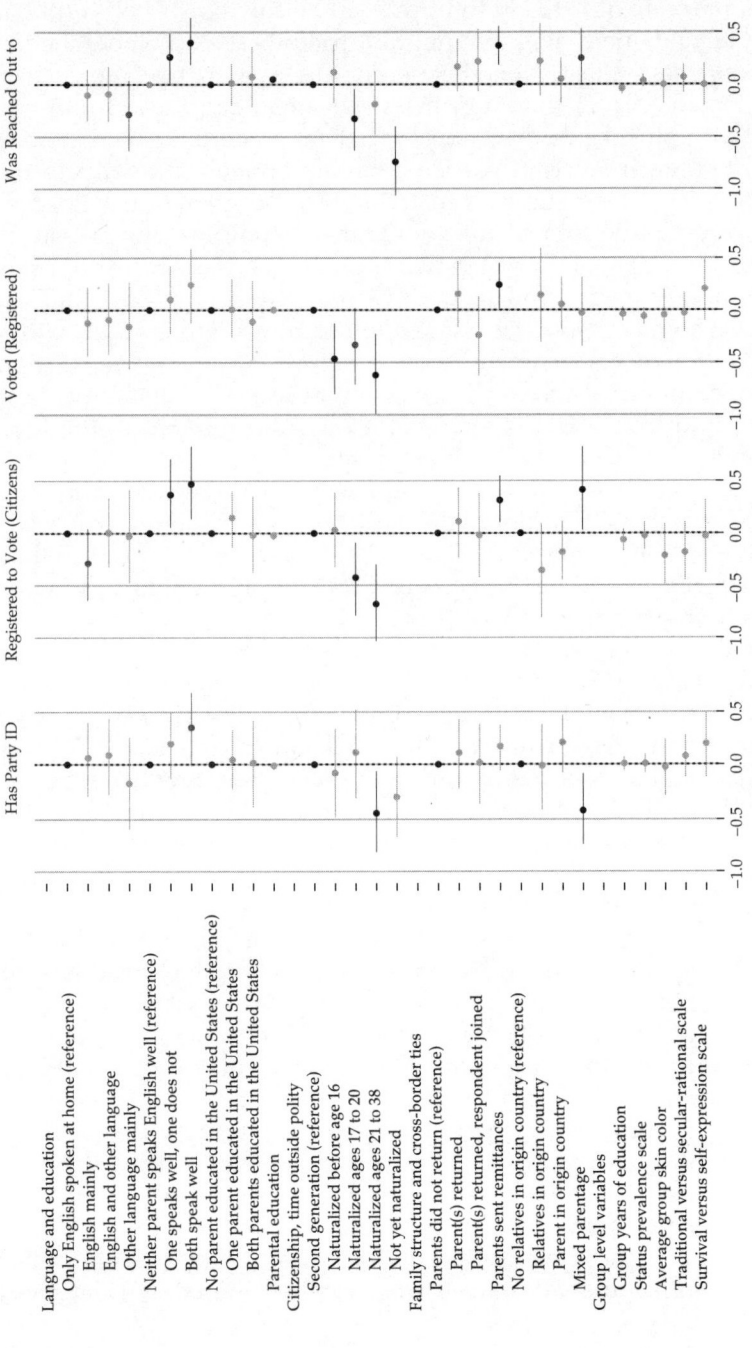

Source: IIMMLA data set.

the environment is likely to have been all the more open in the increasingly liberal, increasingly immigrant-friendly region where the IIMMLA respondents resided. Nonetheless, civic life is more likely to elicit engagement from citizens than noncitizens; even among the naturalized, those who naturalized after the critical socialization period of early adolescence reported lower levels of participation in non-electoral political and civic matters. Thus, as figures 7.1 to 7.3 show, time spent outside of the polity is strongly associated with a broad range of political and civic outcomes. Regardless of whether or not the outcomes require formal membership, nearly every kind of political participation is less likely among those who naturalized as a late adolescent or young adult, with coefficients that are consistently below 0 (signifying a negative relationship); although not all reach the 5 percent significance level, many are statistically significant at the 10 percent level. As compared to the U.S.-born, and net of controls, the analysis of specific forms of civic participation shows that only the adolescent naturalizers were significantly less likely to attend a protest and only the noncitizens were significantly were less likely to attend a meeting. Overall, however, the later naturalizers and the noncitizens had distinctively and statistically significantly lower levels of civic engagement.

Unlike learning the dominant language—the rewards of which are sufficiently large for individual immigrants do so on their own, without urging or support—the individual rewards of political involvement are too scanty to provide much motivation, which is why mobilization by parties, interest groups, neighbors, or friends proves so crucial; the latter two especially may provide both reinforcement and moral example. Answers from IIMMLA respondents indicate that only a minority (barely over one-third) received encouragement of this sort from people whom they knew. Encouragement from the politically active turned out to be significantly less common among *all foreign-born* respondents, whether they had naturalized or not. Not surprisingly, noncitizens were the least likely to have had any contacts with the politically active: they reported a rate of just over 60 percent of the native-born level (25 percent versus 41 percent), after controls.

Not only are the once excluded and the formally excluded less likely to engage in activities with no formal citizenship bar; the once excluded, notwithstanding their own prior success in clearing the citizenship hurdle, are less likely to engage in political activities for which citizenship is a prerequisite. The late naturalizers and the young adult naturalizers were less likely to report having registered to vote than either the birthright citizens or the early naturalizers, a statistically significant difference that even increased after all controls were applied. Similarly, the application of controls shows that among those who naturalized as adults, significantly fewer turned out to vote (50 percent) compared to their second-generation counterparts (63 percent).

Cross-Border Connections

As we noted earlier, cross-border ties and home-country engagements could exercise both negative and positive effects on civic engagement and political participation. The analysis shows that the effects of visits to the parental home country on civic participation as contrasted to engagement in electoral politics are inconsistent, although the coefficient for the specific measures of civic engagement is generally positive. By contrast, membership in internationalized family networks is generally associated with deeper engagement in American civic life, as respondents with a parent and/or relatives abroad were much more likely to engage in at least some civic activity compared to their counterparts whose kin networks had relocated to the United States. Interestingly, respondents whose parents earlier sent home remittances reported *higher* levels of current political participation and civic engagement on virtually all of the indicators reviewed in this chapter. As we shall see in the next chapter, remitting is transmitted from parents to children as the children of remitters are much more likely to remit themselves. The giving of scarce resources is both a moral action and an indicator of one's embeddedness in social relations; the intergenerational transmission of remitting may therefore suggest that parents are teaching their children a lesson about the significance of the action and the importance of the relationship. If we further assume that remitting is an aspect of not just familial but societal cohesion, we may then understand why parental remitting is also linked to children's later political engagement.

Intragroup—but Not Intergroup—Differences: Group-Level Variables

Although we see significant variation on the individual level, our variables measuring the context of immigration come up empty. The one exception is average group-level education, though here, rather than increasing participation, resources seem to depress political involvement. On the individual level, resources—in this case, parents' and respondents' education—facilitate civic and political engagement, but at the group level it appears as if a lack of resources stimulates a need to engage; this possibility is in line with the pattern of defensive naturalization detected in the previous chapter. To be sure, and as shown in chapter 5, more schooling at the group level has a positive effect on respondents' own education and thereby exercises an indirect effect on civic and political engagement. But if we think that civic and political participation provides a means of compensating for the lack of resources, then at the group level education may be an indicator of available collective resources that can be mobilized without the need to engage in mainstream political activities.

Similarly, our measures of origin-society context do not yield direct effects on any of the different aspects of civic and political engagement that we have examined here. For the international perspective we advance in this book, this points to an interesting contrast: as the differences between the 1.5 and second generations and the effects of time to naturalization show, the individual-level experience of crossing a territorial and political boundary clearly matter for the degree of involvement in host-country politics, yet the group-level characteristics of the sending society, as measured in the World Values Survey, do not.

However, as we show in the next section of this chapter, both the receiving and sending contexts exert considerable influence on the location of immigrant offspring in the political landscape.

FINDING A PLACE IN THE POLITICAL LANDSCAPE

Whether proceeding from the viewpoint of neo-assimilation or segmented assimilation theory, sociologists focus on the boundary between minorities and the mainstream, a place where ethnic origins are supposedly of little or no importance. In politics, however, there is no mainstream to be found. Rather, democratic politics is inherently a domain of conflict in which participants, whether citizens or not, have to take sides.[9] From the perspective of the receiving polity, the political alignment of newcomers can play out in two different ways. One path would involve a political counterpart to social assimilation, entailing "the replacement of ethnic division over time by cleavages based on class, gender, generation, or other categories that cut across ethnic lines," as suggested by Kathryn Pearson and Jack Citrin.[10] Another trajectory, better captured by the term "political incorporation," would see ethnic categories and political cleavages continuing to overlap to a significant degree. From this perspective, an association of ethnic identity with party identity would be a persistent feature of immigrant political incorporation in the short as well as the medium term. Either way, participation in politics must first entail becoming oriented to the cleavages dividing the polity and then deciding on the faction with which to throw one's lot. But what are the factors that shape the political orientations of the second generation?

At least some of the features impeding political participation are also likely to stand in the way of understanding partisan divides and developing partisan loyalties. As political scientists have argued, partisan loyalties are transmitted from parents to children, but this is unlikely to happen in immigrant families, where parents often lack detailed knowledge of the political system, participate at much lower rates, and rarely possess, even when knowledgeable, the intense partisan loyalties that would breed similar attachments among their children. Entering without knowledge, immigrants have a significant informational threshold to surpass. Thus, even though immigrant offspring will almost certainly absorb information about the political system as part of everyday socialization, they are likely to enter the polity with a lower stock of knowledge and weaker political convictions than their peers born to citizen parents. Hence, as Zoltan Hajnal and Taeku Lee have argued, immigrants and their offspring may lean toward independence, experiencing difficulty in making meaningful differentiations between the parties and determining the relevance of ideological differences to their own concerns.[11]

Alternatively, loyalties may be the result of a process of ongoing information collection, in which voters identify with one party or the other based on their evaluation of a party's cumulative performance. Existing political cleavages, specifically on immigration policy, may give immigrant and immigrant-origin persons all the information they need to decide on their partisan and ideological loyalties. On this issue, the Democratic Party seems poised to attract the large majority of votes from naturalized Americans and their children. The repelling effect of anti-immigrant sentiment within the Republican Party is likely to be most salient among those who feel that their "group" faces discrimination from the national majority population. In this way, for some immigrants and their children at least, the development of immigrant partisan loyalties may be endogenous to the politics and process of immigration itself. On the other hand, those immigrants who fled repressive left-wing regimes and were greeted by welcoming, possibly supportive policies may find that their natural home lies in the Republican Party, especially considering that, in the past, Republican leaders proved repeatedly willing to open doors for immigrants in flight from Communist regimes. The Cuban refugees who arrived in waves in the years between the Cuban revolution and the early 1970s and the immigrants from the former Soviet Union who began entering the United States in the 1970s exemplify this alternative pattern.

In moving into the American polity, immigrants encounter a system structured around lines of race and ethnicity; these divides, in turn, are likely to influence their partisan preferences and ideological loyalties. The ethnic social ties that migrants rely on in the migration and settlement process can be translated into political loyalties, as the social ties that help migrants find jobs, housing, or social services can extend into the electoral process. The urban political machines of the nineteenth and twentieth centuries were masters at the game of building political loyalties by easing the pains of settlement. Political entrepreneurs provided material assistance and access to government services and jobs as well as symbolic recognition, and new Americans in turn delivered a dependable bloc of votes. Although these urban political machines may have lost much of their influence since their heyday a century ago, local party organizations still exercise considerable influence when they overlap with ethnic networks. Some community-based organizations (CBOs) that deliver social services in immigrant neighborhoods also engage in electoral politics, thereby effectively re-creating the patron-type exchange relationship that characterized urban machine politics in the past.[12]

The district-based election system in the United States, in combination with patterns of residential concentration by ethnicity or national origin, provides further opportunities for ethnic politics, especially at the state and local levels, where the many electoral districts that closely track "ethnic neighborhoods" and ethnic segregation are effectively majority-minority districts. Districts that align with immigrant neighborhoods include citizens as well as noncitizens and thereby "reinforce the linkages of interests in these populations" and offer newcomers "the opportunity to develop an awareness of U.S. politics that is shaped in an ethnic context."[13] On the other hand, elected representatives from these districts also represent populations in which a relatively high share are ineligible to vote because they are under the age of eighteen or they lack citizenship status.[14] Depending on the competitiveness of elections, incumbents may be better served simply mobilizing their core supporters rather than mobilizing the entry of new voters whose loyalties and behaviors are hard to predict.

Apart from shaping the electoral mobilization of immigrants, these features of the political system also influence how immigrants and their children align with party politics. For example, as political parties become less active in mobilizing new voting constituencies and nonparty institutions such as labor unions and civic associations become relatively more important, partisanship among new voters may decline and the share of those choosing not to align with a party but to identify as independents instead may increase. Political geography may similarly matter less where larger political districts, which make narrowly targeted ethnic mobilization less useful, dampen partisan alignments.

Political Identity

Before examining predictors of partisan loyalties, we follow Hajnal and Lee in insisting on a logically prior question: namely, individuals' capacity to orient themselves to the prevailing political divides.[15] One indicator comes from a response to questions about partisan loyalty, from which we create a variable distinguishing those who answered either Democrat, Republican, or independent from those respondents who said "don't know," refused to answer, or responded that they didn't think of themselves in partisan terms. The first column in figure 7.3 ("Has Party ID") summarizes results from a regression of this variable on our set of predictors.

On this measure, the U.S.-born children look much like their third-generation counterparts born in the United States and socialized by U.S.-born parents: in both cases, a large majority identified with at least one of the conventional U.S. partisan categories of Democrat, Republican, or independent. Finding a place along the partisan spectrum proved harder for the foreign-born respondents, however: one-quarter of the non-naturalizers and one-sixth of the late naturalizers did not connect with any of the conventional partisan identities. When we include the set of control variables used in models on political participation, differences for the non-naturalized fall just outside of the 10 percent level of significance, but late naturalizers remain statistically less likely to claim a party label.

A related question about ideology provides yet another clue about the capacity of immigrant offspring to orient themselves to the relevant divides in a political system that either they or their parents encountered as foreign. Results from an analysis not shown indicate that respondents found it easier to categorize themselves on the liberal-conservative spectrum than to claim affiliation with a particular political party. In contrast to the sizable proportion of those who did not connect with any political party, a full 91 percent of the sample identified as conservative, liberal, or moderate, with no significant differences related to generation, citizenship status, or experiences. However, as is the case with party identification, late naturalizers were less able to situate themselves ideologically.

As a last effort to capture respondents' capacity to make sense of the political system, we combine responses from the questions about partisan loyalties and placement on the left-to-right spectrum to create a three-category variable: one category includes the very few respondents (4 percent) who could make no sense of the prevailing political divisions and were unable to identify a partisan identity or an ideological placement; a second category comprises the nearly one-fifth of respondents who selected either a partisan or an ideological placement but not both; and the great majority who provided a politically appropriate answer to both questions make up the third category. Whereas almost all respondents were able to get their bearings somewhere in the political system, lack of citizenship nonetheless made for greater uncertainty: only 69 percent of the noncitizens were able to identify both an ideological placement and a partisan identity, as opposed to 78 percent among the citizens. In an analysis not shown, the proportion of noncitizens (76 percent) as well as late naturalizers (70 percent) fell short of the 80 percent of birthright citizens who could clearly situate themselves on the political spectrum, net of all controls.

Partisanship

Having examined the factors that affected their capacity to situate themselves in the partisan landscape, we now ask how and why our respondents did so. For this analysis, we narrow the focus to include only those respondents who both possessed citizenship and reported having registered to vote, while simultaneously expanding the focus on the Angelenos to include the New Yorkers, thereby increasing sample size and variance on country-of-origin characteristics. To facilitate interpretation we use ternary plots (figure 7.4), which position respondents according to their three-party registration in a triangle whereby the position in the space represents the probability of a particular respondent (or share of a demographic) being registered in each party.[16] New York City and Los Angeles are, of course, far from the U.S. average in terms of party politics, leaning heavily Democratic (New York even more so than Los Angeles) among native-born as well as foreign-born registered voters. Consequently, as shown in the first panel of figure 7.4, most of the variation we document happens within the "Democratic corner" of the ternary diagram.

The most striking finding from the regression results is the absence of any robust associations between party registration, on the one hand, and any of the individual-level measures of language competency, arrival status, and generation, on the other. Once we restrict the analysis to citizens only, the 1.5 and second generations hold very similar positions in the party space, a pattern that remains unchanged after applications of controls. By contrast, only the demographic controls of age, gender, and parental education prove consistently significant. We also find a relationship between parental English ability and children's political alignments (significant at the 10 percent level): having two parents who do not speak English is associated with a five-point increase in Democratic registration, relative to having two parents with English-language skills.

Figure 7.4 Predicted Marginal Probability of Party Registration Varying Average National-Origin Group Skin Color and Sending-Country Traditionalism

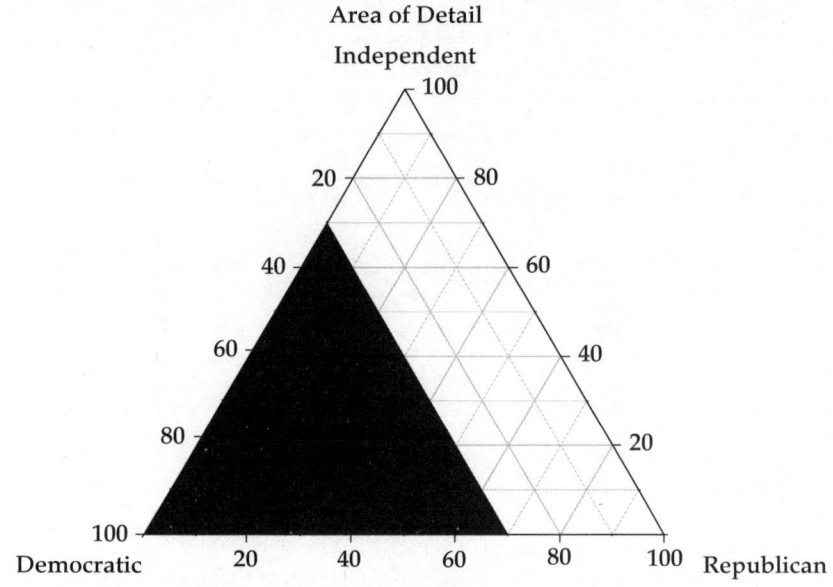

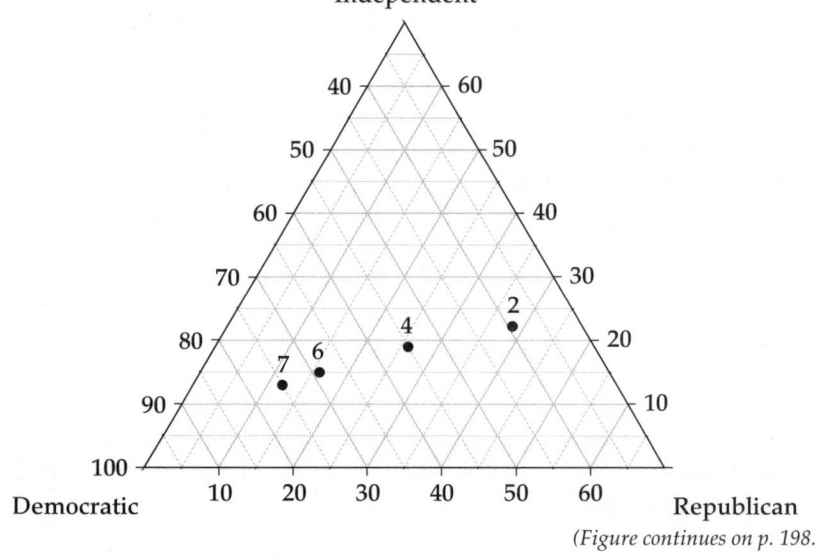

(Figure continues on p. 198.)

Figure 7.4   Continued

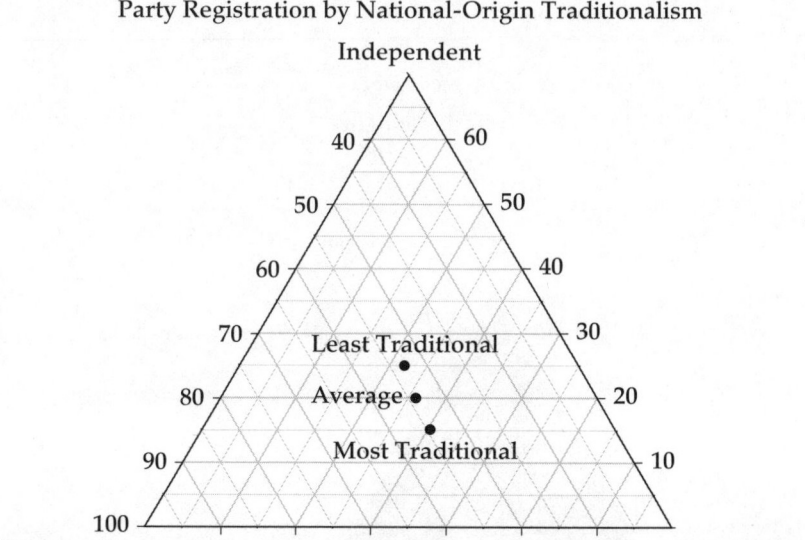

Party Registration by National-Origin Traditionalism

Source: IIMMLA and ISGMNY data sets.
Note: Average group skin color scale ranges from 0 (lightest) to 10 (darkest). The range found in our data is 1.4 to 7.4.

More importantly, these individual-level differences are overshadowed by the gaps in partisan loyalties separating national-origin groups. A regression model that includes both individual-level variables and our group-level variables lets us explore some of this variation. We see that respondents from darker-skinned national-origin groups are much more heavily Democratic ($p < .05$), while those from more traditionally oriented origin societies are more heavily Republican ($p < .10$). As the ternary plots in figure 7.4 show, the differences are not trivial: a move from 2 on the 10-point scale (the lighter end of the skin-color distribution; the minimum observed was 1.4) to 7 (the darker end; the maximum observed was a 7.4) is associated with an almost 40-point increase in Democratic registration (from 39 to 75 percent), a significant decrease in Republican registration, and a small decrease in the probability of registering as independent. Though differences on the traditional versus secular-rational axis yield somewhat smaller effects, a move from the most secular end of the scale as measured in the World Values Survey (2) to the most traditional end (–2) translates into about a 10-point decrease in registration as independent and an almost corresponding increase in the share registered as Republican.

CONCLUSION

The immigrant offspring with whom we are concerned have had the good fortune of growing up in a democratic society where civic and political participation is open to all comers, both nationals who can trace their presence on U.S. soil back for centuries and the newest arrivals who just walked off the plane with foreign passports still in hand. Although the majority of the second-generation New Yorkers and Angelenos studied here were U.S. citizens by birth, nine out of twenty had been born abroad; at the time of the surveys, three out of twenty remained foreign nationals, lacking citizenship in the country where they actually lived. And though the noncitizens, like their citizen counterparts, often abstained from participation in civic and political life, they also frequently engaged with it — evidence that passage across the *external* boundary at the territorial line can suffice for partaking in the communal affairs of the people among whom one lives, even if one stands outside the formal *internal* boundary of that community.

But understanding the sources of that engagement, as well as the factors that constrain it, is quite another matter. Extending assimilation theory from the sphere of social life to civic and political life provides but limited illumination. To be sure, certain by-products of the quest for a better life can foster engagement with political and civic life, as when the acquisition of dominant-language skills increases an individual's ability to understand an initially foreign political environment. As we have seen, one channel from the social to the political aspects of assimilation does indeed seem to flow from those parents with higher levels of capacity in English to their adult children's greater involvement in civic or political affairs of varying types. And yet the lessons likely to be learned from enhanced comprehension of the political environment are unlikely to be compatible with the assimilation framework, since that environment lacks an established, consensual mainstream. Rather, because the political world is characterized by conflict, with opposing groups and parties contending over how the mainstream is to be divided and by whom, enhanced learning takes the form of gaining orientation to the relevant divides and positioning oneself appropriately.

Segmented assimilation, the most influential alternative approach, is limited as well. When it comes to the exercise of citizenship, results are contradictory. Higher levels of education at the group level have statistically significant but *negative* effects on civic participation and organizational membership, pointing to the possibility that greater resources at the group level, independent of individual resources, reduce the need to pursue common solutions through collective action. Turning to the within-family variables, it is not clear how home-country language use in the parental household—an indicator of ethnic retention and therefore selective acculturation—should increase or decrease civic or political engagement and, if so, what might account for any such effect. Our results do show that speaking the mother tongue positively increases the probability of engaging in at least one of the three forms of civic participation. Yet a standard assimilation variable—parents' understanding of English—generated far more consistent and powerful effects.

Our analysis provides mixed support for the factors on which segmented assimilation places greatest weight. Group differences in skin color, for instance, yielded no effects whatsoever on civic engagement, as the coefficient for this variable failed to reach statistical significance across all of the civic and political outcomes reviewed in this chapter. Yet, when we look at orientations toward partisan divides, it had a considerable association with identification with the Democratic Party. The indicator of policy reception, however, had no effect on any outcome.

By contrast, the analysis developed in this chapter demonstrates how a cross-border perspective can illuminate the ways in which the distinctive features of migration across state boundaries yield long-term impacts on political and civic engagement. Although international migration brings strangers into a strange environment, that strangeness diminishes with time and social learning, facilitating movement across the internal boundary of citizenship as well as greater involvement in civic and social life. Yet, as we have emphasized, migrants arrive not just as strangers but as citizens of the foreign polity that they left, and also as aliens in the society that they have joined. Moreover, whereas citizens are formal equals, the policies that govern migration controls produce formal inequality among noncitizens, who vary in status and corresponding entitlements.

As we saw in chapter 6, those differences matter for transitioning across the internal boundary of citizenship. They further serve as impediments to the exercise of citizenship, even though noncitizens and citizens share the very same rights to many forms of civic and political citizenship. The widespread effects of current and prior noncitizenship status are all the more striking in light of the fact that in its overwhelming majority, the 1.5-generation respondents grew up as de facto Americans: 50 percent reported coming to the United States at age two or under, a fraction only marginally lower among those respondents who still lacked citizenship as of adulthood. Yet among those who had not yet naturalized, even an entire childhood spent in the United States frequently failed to produce the level of political and civic involvement found among those with citizenship status, though some of this difference was explained by variation in socioeconomic and linguistic use between the two groups. Thus, for many of the de facto Americans, simply understanding the basic contours of the U.S. political system proved challenging: the late naturalizers were less likely to select any conventional partisan loyalty and were least likely to be able to both place themselves on an ideological spectrum and select a partisan identification. Although the competencies generated by social assimilation unquestionably contribute to the capacity for understanding the political environment, the signals provided in one's immediate environment also help. However, those signals are precisely what many of the de facto Americans in our study lacked. Those who had not naturalized were significantly less likely to be encouraged to support a candidate or political party—a result possibly related to their higher tendency toward civic detachment. Moreover, these noncitizens, like the adolescent and later adult naturalizers, showed the least propensity to engage in civic or associational activities open to all comers, citizenship status notwithstanding.

Thus, migration controls have a long reach, constraining civic and political participation well after both external and even internal boundaries have been crossed. Nonetheless, the path-dependent results of America's early development remain deeply influential, which is why the great majority of the adult immigrant offspring studied in this book found that the door to engagement with public issues remained open. Yet their options for political engagement were shaped by prior histories of political development and conflict: the political preferences of these New Yorkers and Angelenos overwhelmingly tilted toward the Democratic Party. Yet even within the Democratic Party space, contexts of both immigration and emigration mattered. On the one hand, respondents from more secular sending countries were more likely to lean independent and those from more traditional societies were more likely to lean Republican. On the other hand, the strength of the preference for Democrats proved to be related to skin color: though all groups were inclined toward the Democrats, the darker the group-level skin color, the stronger the preference for Democrats. Of course, we are presenting this picture in hindsight; the political developments that have transpired since the turn of the millennium, when these two surveys were conducted, have probably somewhat altered levels of engagement and changed affiliations. We suspect that any such changes are less affected by the factors highlighted in this book—those related to origins, context, and strategies of adaptation—and instead are driven by the conflicts over the presence of the very immigrants and immigrants' offspring we have studied and the increasingly deep cleavages riven by these conflicts.

Chapter 8 | Cross-Border Connections

ONCE DESCRIBED AS the "uprooted," then the "transplanted," migrants are now often described as "the transnationals." That label almost surely goes too far, but it is certainly true that many, perhaps most, migrants remain connected to the place from which they departed and the people who stayed there.

Cross-state connections are often part and parcel of the familial survival strategies that propel migration in the first place. That pattern holds best for labor migrants—exemplified by the Italians of the last era of mass migration and the Mexicans of the current era—among whom movement from poor to wealthy societies is a way to generate resources at the point of destination to be used at the point of origin.[1] Migrations of this sort send one household member to a place where wages are high, who in turn transmits savings to be spent on consumption or investment in a place where the cost of living is low. Hence, connectivity is integral to the migration experience itself: the things that flow across borders—information, resources, support—provide the glue needed to bind family members now separated in space.

Of course, the migration of low-skilled laborers, usually of peasant background, is only one of many migration types. High-skilled labor is far more likely to be welcomed as well as wanted, yet these streams often involve temporary and sometimes circular movement, as exemplified by the foreign graduate students enrolled in American universities or the foreign engineers working on short-term contracts in high-technology companies. In both cases, U.S. law classifies these sojourners as "non-immigrant" residents, a seeming contradiction in terms. Many of these non-immigrants reemigrate home; others transition from "non-immigrant" to legal "immigrant" status; in the intervening interval, many are uncertain about their ultimate destination. By definition, refugees and asylum-seekers cannot go back, at least not as long as the homeland conditions that expelled them persist. Although for some the breach is definitive, for others the ties to the places and, more importantly, the people left behind remain compelling.

Regardless of the motivations that lead people to leave home and the circumstances under which they do so, international migration involves at best a partial displacement of a migrant's key social network. To varying degrees, parents, spouses, children, siblings, and more distant relatives may remain at the point of origin, or migrants themselves may return there after a sojourn in the destination country; either way, the migrant's inner circle is likely to extend across territorial boundaries. And the connections are not simply a matter of people but of things. Migrants depart without necessarily abandoning the properties they own at home: while those are often the objects of the migrants' investment plans, they also comprise commitments that can reinforce the dependency on relatives or friends at home looking after the migrants' assets.

Thus, population movements across national boundaries do not necessarily involve "immigration" as defined by the dictionary and as understood by most social scientists: namely, relocation for the purposes of settlement. Moreover, cross-border connections are not simply vestigial, but an ongoing component of migrants' lives. Thus, to put it colloquially, being out of sight does *not* mean being out of mind. And it is not simply that migrants move while many of their most important social relations, as well as significant assets, stay put, though that is certainly the case. Something else is involved: namely, the interdependencies between migrants "here" and their connections "there," the former often furnishing material resources, the latter often providing care, whether of dependents (the young and the old) or of material assets. And even if self-interest no longer provides the motivations for immigrants to connect with the stay-at-homes, obligations to maintain long-standing social ties remain a powerful, reinforcing force.

Though cross-border ties are an inherent aspect of the immigrant experience, their causes and consequences have only recently gained attention from migration scholars, with the impetus coming from the now-extensive literature on transnationalism. Of the books reviewed in chapter 2, only *Inheriting the City* and *Remaking the Mainstream* ask about the connections that might link immigrant offspring to the people and places their parents left behind. The two books address this question in similar ways, contending that while evidence of persistent connections to parental origins can certainly be found among today's second generation, the homeland is at best a residual presence, with its importance steadily declining.

This response ignores the fundamental lesson to be gleaned from the literature on transnationalism: namely, that migration researchers need to adopt a different standpoint, one that enlarges the boundaries of inquiry to include both sending and receiving places. The conventional wisdom directs scholars to put their backs to the border, restricting the focus to those postmigration changes that uniquely unfurl on receiving-society soil. Like any way of seeing, this conventional approach is also a way of not seeing: in this case, it neglects the continuing back-and-forth of people, ideas, information, resources, and political and communal engagements that international migrations inevitably trigger. By contrast, the transnational literature has provided a new and better optic. However, that literature has also gone perhaps a step too far, leaping from a transnational *perspective* on migration to transnational*ism*—a claim about the persistent nature of the phenomena extending across borders and the ties between places of origin and destination. But the possibility that homeland ties may endure is just that—a possibility, and one that can only be determined through empirical analysis. Moreover, in highlighting a recurring element and one so often threaded through the migration experience, the scholars who underlined the importance of transnationalism stopped short of asking how we might explain variation in homeland connectedness—whether between groups, among households and individuals starting from the same point of origin, or between immigrant parents born and socialized in the country of *emigration* and immigrant children raised in the country of *immigration,* with at best partial direct exposure to their parents' place of birth—and frequently no exposure at all.

The international perspective elaborated in this book points us in a different direction. The political and social logic of international migration ensures that immigrant offspring typically grow up in internationalized families, with kinship networks stretched between "here" and "there." Moreover, childhood is a time when parents and other adults decide how those networks should be configured—whether or not to bring everyone together in a single place—and how, if at all, connections to relatives still abroad will be maintained. Thus, cross-border connections, as an aspect of childhood experience that, by definition, precedes adulthood, can be conceptualized as an *independent* variable that yields later influence on immigrant offspring once they become adults.

Indeed, earlier chapters have demonstrated just how those homeland ties might matter. As we saw in chapter 5, the Angelenos who grew up in households in which one parent lived abroad attained significantly fewer years of schooling than did their counterparts with immediate kinship networks entirely transplanted to the United States. By contrast, parental remitting increased educational attainment, an initially counterintuitive finding. Yet as chapter 7 demonstrated, parental remitting also had a strongly positive effect on civic and political participation among their offspring, suggesting that remitting is an aspect of familial cohesion and hence yields effects on outcomes seemingly unrelated to homeland ties.

In asking about the determinants of homeland ties among the immigrant offspring New Yorkers and Angelenos, this chapter principally focuses on those connections as *dependent* variables influenced by the homeland engagements and orientations of their parents, as well as by the broad range of contextual and individual- or household-level variables treated in previous chapters. In particular, we spotlight five outcomes of interest, three of which relate to behavior—remitting, visiting, and participating in homeland-oriented organizations—and two of which pertain to attitudes—interest in homeland politics and the place where respondents "feel at home." In the pages to follow, we show that homeland connectedness does indeed decline from one generation to the next, just as argued in *Inheriting the City* and *Remaking the Mainstream*. And yet, as this decline neither proceeds in uniform fashion nor affects each dimension of homeland connectedness in quite the same manner, this chapter seeks to identify the sources of variation, whether within or across the various groups of second-generation New Yorkers and Angelenos.

THE HOMELAND AND THE IMMIGRANT HOUSEHOLD

In moving across borders, migrants find themselves in what we have called the "zone of intersocietal convergence," a liminal space in which physical presence is "here," in the society of destination, but key social and emotional attachments, as well as identities, remain rooted "there," in the society of origin. For those who move as adults, personal experience magnifies the strength of the homeland connection, which is why nostalgia— better understood as "homesickness" in light of the word's roots in the Greek *nostos* for "place" and *algia* for "pain"—is so common an immigrant condition. But for the U.S.-raised immigrant offspring with whom we are concerned, that sense of dislocation or being out of place is unlikely to fuel their attachment to a place where they never, or only briefly (if themselves foreign-born), resided. These adult children of immigrants nevertheless were apt to grow up in households that were not fully separable from the place of origin, in part because parents and other relevant adults often used the home tongue. More importantly, they came of age in contexts in which the familial circle included members in both the country of emigration and the country of immigration. Among the immigrant offspring surveyed in Los Angeles, almost 6 percent reported that at least one parent *never* came to the United States, a proportion that jumped to 13 percent among those who came to the United State after the age of five (but before the age of fifteen). A much larger fraction—80 percent—had relatives still living in the country of origin; even among those with one U.S.-born parent, over 60 percent had kin in the foreign-born parent's home country. Moreover, those connections were the fulcrum around which familial activities, often involving the use of scarce resources, were organized. Sixty percent of the 1.5- to 2.5-generation respondents grew up in households where parents sent home remittances. Twelve percent reported that their parents had returned to the home country at least once during childhood, and another almost 8 percent reported returning with parents for a stay lasting at least six months.

Both the New York data and other sources tell us that the pattern found in southern California extends more widely. For instance, among the New York 1.5 to 2.5 generations, 57 percent reported that their parent sent remittances, 70 percent had visited their parents' home country at least once, and, of these, nearly one in five had visited for at least six months at a time. Turning to other data sources, we see that 20 percent of interviewees queried in a nationally representative 2006 survey of Latin American immigrants in the United States had a child still living in the country of origin; among respondents with children, that fraction rose to just over one-quarter. Almost 70 percent of all respondents were also sending remittances to support relatives still at home. While those with children abroad were the most likely to do so, they accounted for only one-fifth of remittance-senders. Parents were actually more likely than children to be remittance-receivers: 40 percent of the sample sent money to their fathers or mothers. Another 7 percent were transmitting funds to siblings. Piecing together the information on children's location and remittance recipients tells us that almost 60 percent of these respondents still had a close relative living outside the United States. The data on Asian immigrants in the United States do not allow for the same degree of detail; nonetheless, a large-scale, 2012 nationally representative survey of Asian Americans found that over two-thirds of the foreign-born respondents reported having immediate family members (spouse, parents, or sibling) still living in their home country.[2]

Thus, immigrants' offspring share the liminal space defined by the zone of intersocietal convergence. For most respondents, the home country is not an abstraction, but rather a reality that they themselves have encountered. Reflecting those experiences, most immigrant offspring agreed with the statement "I am interested in the politics of my/my parent's home country," with as many as one-fifth stating that they strongly agreed with it. On the other hand, symbolic commitments seemed a good deal stronger than the material engagements requiring respondents to use their own resources to help out relatives abroad: only 30 percent of the second generation reported having ever sent remittances, of whom fewer than half did so more than once a year. Overall, relatively few proved completely detached from home-country connections: barely 6 percent fell into a category that we have elsewhere called "the bordered"—those who had not visited the home country, sent remittances, or displayed any level of interest in home-country politics.[3] But even fewer conformed to the transnational ideal of persons "living lives across borders": barely 1 percent had not only sent remittances but also traveled to the home country six times or more and maintained a high level of interest. Rather, the overwhelming majority of respondents in both New York and Los Angeles maintained some type of homeland orientation—possibly remitting, or visiting, or just retaining an interest—but not all of them.

Foreign Detachment?

Ties across national borders clearly persist among the second generation. Yet those connections are subject to the corrosive effects of host-country experiences, which is why the tissue of second-generation home-country linkages is unlikely to match the web maintained by the parental generation. Unfortunately, data limitations complicate the task of getting a precise handle on the extent of the falloff from one generation to the next. Information on second-generation cross-border ties is amply supplied by our two surveys; however, only the IIMMLA tells us about the homeland connections that parents maintained during our respondents' youth, and even this otherwise excellent source only allows for a direct intergenerational comparison of remitting behavior.

Not surprisingly, our Los Angeles respondents remitted at far lower rates than did their parents while the respondents were growing up: whereas 60 percent of the parents had sent money to kin living in the home country, only one-third of the respondents were doing so at the time of the survey. In contrast to this now-versus-then comparison, the New York survey provides a contemporaneous, but nonetheless confirmatory, picture. Remitting behavior was more than twice as prevalent among the parents as among the respondents themselves (68 percent versus 28 percent). More revealingly, parents were a good deal more willing than their offspring to put their hands regularly into their pockets in order to fulfill obligations to kin still at home: thus, whereas almost one-third of the parents sent remittances several times a year, only 14 percent of the children did the same and were still less likely to remit on a more frequent basis.

Remitting is just one of the activities spanning home and host countries, however, and perhaps one in which the second generation is particularly less likely to participate than the first, so we turn to other sources to shed further light on the intergenerational comparisons. Before going any further, we note some caveats: the necessary contrasts are made at the aggregate level and therefore do not compare immigrant parents with their own children. Furthermore, the data about the first generation are at a national level, whereas the data on the second generation come from our two metropolitan surveys.

Nonetheless, the comparison proves illuminating. The best information on first-generation home-country ties comes from the 2006 Latino National Survey, which limits the comparison to three of the groups that also appear in the IIMMLA and ISGMNY—Mexicans, Salvadorans, and Dominicans. To capture a population comparable to the likely parents of our respondents, we restricted the sample to persons ages thirty-five to sixty, who are in turn contrasted to New Yorkers and Angelenos ages twenty to thirty-two. As table 8.1 shows, some adult immigrants, just like the immigrant offspring at the center of our study, fell entirely out of the cross-border sphere. Yet for most of them, home-country ties were sufficiently strong to motivate their expenditure of scarce resources, whether for in-person visits or the transmission of cash. Only a small minority of adult immigrants returned for long-term sojourns, however, and in this way, not surprisingly, they paralleled the immigrant offspring, who generally visited the home country only when taken abroad by their parents. By contrast, home-country politics seemed to elicit a good deal more interest from the immigrant offspring than from the adult immigrants, though, as noted previously, this form of engagement is essentially costless.

TRANSMITTING THE CONNECTION

Thus, home-country connections are less pervasive and less intense among the second generation than among the first. Nonetheless, they are far from absent: for some, the ties are minimal, but not trivial, and for a number of immigrant offspring those ties remain intense. Why, then, do some immigrant offspring detach while others stay connected?

As already discussed, part of the answer lies in the incomplete and transitional nature of the migration process itself, in that some significant others almost always stay behind. Where cross-border kinship ties persist, so too will connections; moreover, the closer the kinship connection, the more intense the cross-border involvement. But as familial cross-border connections are very common, their existence alone cannot explain the variations in second-generation connectedness. Something else may be at work; the multilevel perspective put forward in this book suggests that this something else is to be found at both the familial and group levels, and

Table 8.1 Comparative Cross-Border Behavior: Immigrants Ages Thirty-Five to Sixty (Latino National Survey) Versus Immigrant Offspring Ages Twenty to Thirty-Two (IIMMLA and ISGMNY)

	Mexicans		Salvadorans		Dominicans	
	First Generation (LNS)	Second Generation	First Generation (LNS)	Second Generation	First Generation (LNS)	Second Generation
Sends remittances						
Never	40%	61%	19%	56%	32%	63%
Several times yearly	48	22	72	26	58	22
Never visits	21	30	28	39	13	11
Pays no attention to home-country politics	25		41		28	
Not interested in home-country politics		13		15		
Has returned for six months	11	9	11	5	15	28

Source: Latino National Survey 2006; IIMMLA and ISGMNY data sets.

that it involves the ways in which parents may impart or neglect homeland connections, as well as the group-level factors bearing down on those of a common origin country.

Intragroup Variation in Cross-Border Ties: Parental Socialization

In part, transmission of home-country ties is a matter of socialization and social learning. As in the previous chapter, we make use of the literature on political socialization, applying it here to understand variation in cross-border ties. This body of scholarship has long emphasized the ways in which experiences within the parental household during childhood and youth affect civic and political values, attachments, and activities undergone later in adulthood.[4] These perspectives generally take citizenship for granted, applying social learning processes to explain civic engagement and political loyalties in the country of birth. Indeed, as Virginia Sapiro notes, "political socialization research has focused primarily on the development of citizenship in the United States," assuming away the possibility of nested nationalities, memberships, or citizenships.[5] While nested affiliations of these sorts are precisely the phenomena of interest here, the underlying issue asks the same question posed by the students of political socialization, transformed to ask how parents' attachments linked *to their country of emigration* are transmitted to children raised in the parents' *country of immigration*. As we have seen, homeland ties are often an integral part of immigrant households. Parents' engagements with the homeland and the people still living there are likely to influence their children, serving both as examples for the children to later follow while also providing a critical pathway by which the native-born second generation can acquire the competencies and loyalties that both motivate and enable homeland engagement.

For some types of cross-border ties, such as political interest in the home country, predictions from the (narrower) political socialization literature can be extended straightforwardly. Research on political transmission has shown that children growing up in highly political families are more likely to be politically engaged as adults themselves and have more stable political orientations.[6] In much the same fashion, we can expect that children of migrants who are actively involved in home-country affairs will be more likely to be engaged or interested in homeland politics during their adulthood.

However, the literature on social learning and social cognition provides insights that are likely to apply to other cross-border connections, such as home-country visits or the sending of remittances, for which the data set supplies information. These theories suggest that observational learning through actual and symbolic modeling is a key feature in the acquisition of competencies, attitudes, values, and loyalties—and furthermore that the process by which children absorb parental social practices and customs from parental models is central to the reproduction of cultural patterns over generations.[7] An example of how parental models might be absorbed in the cross-border context comes from an ethnographic study of migrants in Finland: "although phoning and staying in touch were mostly parental practices," and children often just exchanged a few words or just listened, they were nonetheless "incorporated in the transnational communication patterns and knew who called who, how often, and how much it cost."[8] Thus, since parents provide the key models, their own engagement in cross-border activities will strongly influence the extent and intensity of those ties among their children.

However, the impact of the parental example also depends on the degree to which parents have both retained relevant homeland traits or practices and transmitted them to their children. In this respect, second-generation competence and comfort in the home-country language is likely to be key. Yet, as we have already noted, and as we explore at greater length in the next chapter, transmitting that capacity runs into a slew of obstacles. America, after all, is a great destroyer of languages, as sooner or later English almost always reigns supreme. Only one space is somewhat sheltered from these linguistically corrosive forces, namely, the parental household; this is the one place where the mother tongue can consistently prevail. Clearly, comfort and familiarity lead parents to prefer the mother tongue; any desire they have to impart bilingualism, let alone to convey home-country attachments, is probably of much lesser importance. But even if unintended, persistent home-country connectedness is almost surely a consequence of the linguistic environment in the parental household, as engaging with the homeland is difficult for those who cannot function in the home society with the competencies approximating those of natives.

Although the environment in the parental household is crucial for the transmission of cross-border ties, we should remember that cross-border connections take myriad forms, whether involving communication, travel, the sending of remittances, political engagement, profit-making ventures, philanthropy, or simply the attention paid to homeland events. These different activities are *qualitatively* distinct, as argued by Thomas Faist: some entail particularistic connections between specific families or kinship groups; others work at a higher level of aggregation, involving identification and engagement with a homeland community, at either a national or local scale; some involve a resource-consuming activity; in other cases, the engagement is purely symbolic. As Faist argues, each type of cross-border tie possesses its own social logic, based on a distinct "mechanism of integration" and a set of resources and norms, all of which undergird connectivity.[9]

Many scholars have also underscored the *quantitative* differences in the range and consistency of cross-border activities. High-intensity, across-the-board activities involving physical movement are what characterize the "transmigrants"—a rare breed even among the foreign-born.[10] More commonly, migrants engage more selectively, as we have shown elsewhere. Looking at a nationally representative sample of Latino immigrants in the United States, we found that the great majority maintained some type of cross-border connection, but that remitting, travel, and regular cross-border communication rarely came together in a single package. Instead, migrants were picking and choosing among the relevant possibilities, generally tending *not* to combine the costlier activities of travel and remittance-sending. Furthermore, each option was associated with a distinct set of specific migrant characteristics.[11]

For these reasons, rather than trying to ask how "transnationalism" might be passed from parents to children, we focus here instead on the various aspects of cross-border connections, with the expectation that no single factor explains the persistence of these linkages, but rather that each tie is likely to be pursued for a different reason and with a different set of resources than the next. Parents typically choose among a range of activities that entail or facilitate cross-border involvement, and each choice is likely to yield a certain effect on later second-generation cross-border engagement. For example, sending remittances demands a sense of loyalty and responsibility to a family member that is not necessary for maintaining an emotional attachment to the parental home country. Likewise, feelings of connection to a parental homeland may not entail the skills or interest needed to participate in a homeland-oriented organization. Similarly, one can display an interest in homeland politics without possessing the linguistic fluency needed for easy interaction in the homeland context.

Focusing more specifically, we expect that parental remittance-sending will have a behavioral modeling effect. Although the parents' remitting and the associated conversation in the parental household may be part of a learning process that transmits filial obligations to the second generation, remittance-sending is also a very targeted activity, one aimed at a limited kinship circle and no one else. Therefore, parental remitting may not transmit the set of loyalties linked to other realms, such as emotional connections to the parental homeland, political interest, or visiting.

Though costly, sending remittances is relatively simple. Visits are costlier; as the ethnographic evidence shows, they are also complex to manage, as they can "emphasize difference as much as generate shared understandings."[12] Hence, while parents making return visits may send children a signal about the importance of loyalty to the people and places left behind, more may be needed if the children are to sustain those visits during adulthood. By contrast, childhood visits undertaken *with* parents are likely to impart both the competencies needed to fit in during a visit and the skills and dispositions required for managing and negotiating long-distance relationships that only occasionally involve copresence. Moreover, if the experience during childhood is positive, the relationships generated and the memories attached to them may fuel further cross-border attachments in adulthood.[13]

Similarly, the use of the parental language in the household will have two kinds of effects. As we have argued, facility in the parental native language is a competency key to maintaining numerous cross-border activities, most notably those in which language ability is integral to the experience, such as visiting. As use of the mother tongue in the household when growing up is probably the central transmission mechanism for parental language fluency, we expect that those respondents who grew up in households with a strong home-country language presence will be more likely to visit these places as adults, net of other factors.

But language is not simply a tool for communication; it also has powerful emotional connotations. Home, as Alfred Schuetz noted decades ago, is where shared meanings and understandings can be taken for granted, which is why he understood "to feel at home" as "an expression of the highest degree of familiarity and intimacy."[14] Precisely for that reason, as noted far more recently by Rogers Brubaker and his colleagues, "the experience of speaking 'one's own' language is often associated with a feeling of phenomenological comfort, a sense of being at home in the world."[15] Following these authors, we expect that the presence of the parental home-country language will predict emotional attachments such as the likelihood of feeling at home in the country of origin. In contrast, we expect that, other things being equal, language should matter little, if at all, for homeland-oriented activities in the host country for which linguistic facility is not required, such as political interest in homeland matters or membership in organizations oriented toward the parental homeland.

Intergroup Variation in Cross-Border Ties: Context

Thus, parents provide children with the motivation and tools specifically suited for maintaining cross-border connections. But as we have seen throughout this book, context generally matters as well, and we expect that group-level characteristics, whether related to resources, circumstances of migration, or home-country background, will again yield an effect above and beyond those available at the individual level. In chapters 2 and 3, we noted that as refugee policy both facilitates the entry of selected groups fleeing persecution and assists their subsequent integration, the prevalence of refugee admissions should be associated with positive outcomes. In this case, however, the opposite outcome is more likely: people who flee a country for fear of persecution are less likely to keep up homeland ties—especially those involving personal contact or homeland political matters. In most cases, by contrast, flows with a large unauthorized component are generally economically, not politically, driven migrations. With many migrants also motivated by the goal of securing destination-country resources in order to reinforce survival strategies undertaken in the country of origin, these are migrations that inherently generate cross-border connections in the form of remittances and visits to kin left behind. On the other hand, insofar as the density of unauthorized migrants weakens community-level resources and constrains host-society participation, we expect that it will depress involvement in homeland-oriented organizations and interest in homeland politics as well. Finally, because cross-border involvements entail fulfilling obligations to others rather than gratifying one's own immediate wants, we expect that these activities are more likely to be associated with backgrounds in societies characterized by traditional and especially survival values.

To assess the impact of contextual effects, we use both the New York and Los Angeles surveys. In addition to our contextual variables, we control for a set of individual-level variables standardized across the two data sets, including age, gender, years of education for the parent with the highest level of attainment, respondent's education, and indicators indexing whether one or more parent never moved to the United States, the level of parental English-language facility, the language used in the parental household when the respondent was a child, and the respondent's citizenship and legal status (whether birthright citizen, naturalized citizen, green-card-holder, or other). Since cross-border connections are facilitated by parental legal status as well, we also control for the number of parents holding U.S. citizenship (neither, one, or two).

Not surprisingly, and as shown in figure 8.1, respondents emanating from migration flows with high levels of refugee admissions (high on our status prevalence scale) were less likely to engage in home-country visits than those from flows that included few refugee admissions.[16] Thus, persecution seems to exercise a long-term deterrent effect, keeping immigrant offspring away even after the initial conflict that sparked the outflow has passed into history.

Figure 8.1 Regression Results: Effects of Group-Level Variables on Remitting and Visits to the Parental Home Country

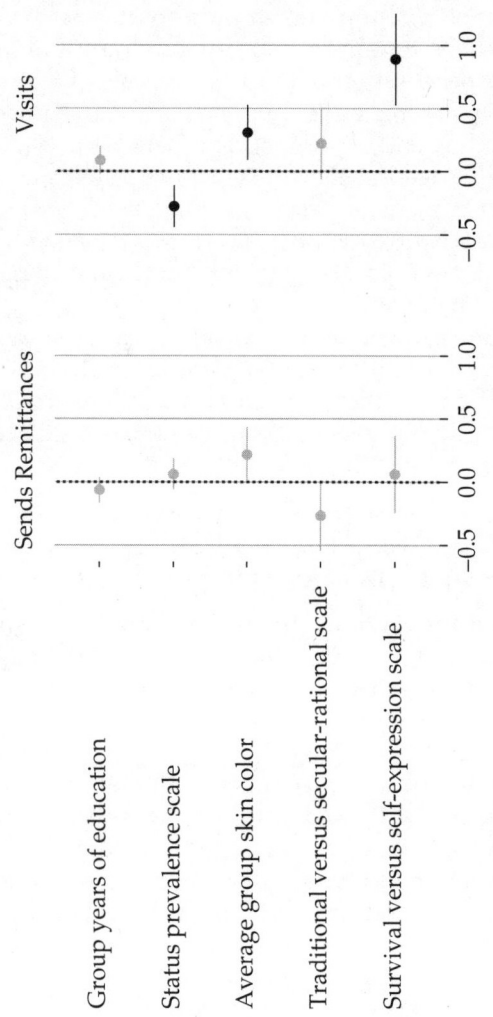

Source: IIMMLA and ISGMNY data sets.
Note: Higher scores on the survival versus self-expression scale indicate an orientation toward self-expression, which is associated with more frequent visits in this case; higher scores on the traditional versus secular-rational scale indicate greater orientation toward rational and secular values, which are associated with less remitting in this case.

As we have emphasized, keeping up the home connection through visiting and remitting entails significant material demands; hence, we would expect home-country value systems that are supportive of familial cohesion and reinforce intrafamilial obligations to be associated with higher levels of cross-border activity. But as already discussed in the previous chapter, remitting and visiting are very different cross-border activities. The former is first and foremost about maintaining family obligations. Surely visits to the parental place of origin can also be driven by family obligations, but they are just as likely to be part of an ego-centered quest, oriented toward finding and expressing an aspect of one's identity. Indeed, we find very clear indication that those from societies characterized by higher levels of self-expression (and thus higher levels of individualism) were more likely to visit frequently. In contrast, those with roots in more traditional societies were more likely (significant at the 10 percent level) to maintain remittance behavior across generations.

Higher values on the average group skin-color scale were associated with higher reports of remitting (significant at the 10 percent level) and long-term visits abroad. Other contextual factors exercised few, no, or inconsistent effects. Group years of education had no discernible effects on levels of visiting or remitting.

BOTH HERE AND THERE: THE IMPACT OF INTERSOCIETAL CONVERGENCE

As we have argued throughout this book, most immigration scholars adopting the traditional approach assume that social relations are bounded by the territorial frontier. But as demonstrated by the vast literature on emigration, as emphasized by theories espousing the "new economics of labor migration," and also as seen from the pervasive nature of the cross-border ties maintained by our respondents, that assumption fundamentally diverges from reality. By and large, immigrants *and* their immediate descendants remain in a zone of intersocietal convergence, with both feet in the society of reception but hands extended to close relatives still living in the society of origin. In the remainder of this chapter, we seek to understand which immigrant offspring find themselves in that social space and why, focusing on the Los Angeles sample only.

As we have noted, most Los Angeles respondents had parents or other relatives still living in the country of origin and thus stood in the zone of intersocietal convergence. In most cases, their parents were living in the United States, but just over 16 percent of all the foreign-origin respondents had a parent still living in the country of origin. Figure 8.2, which summarizes a set of regression models drawing on the IIMMLA

Figure 8.2 Regression Results: Effects of Parental Location and Family Structure on Cross-Border Ties in the Los Angeles Second Generation

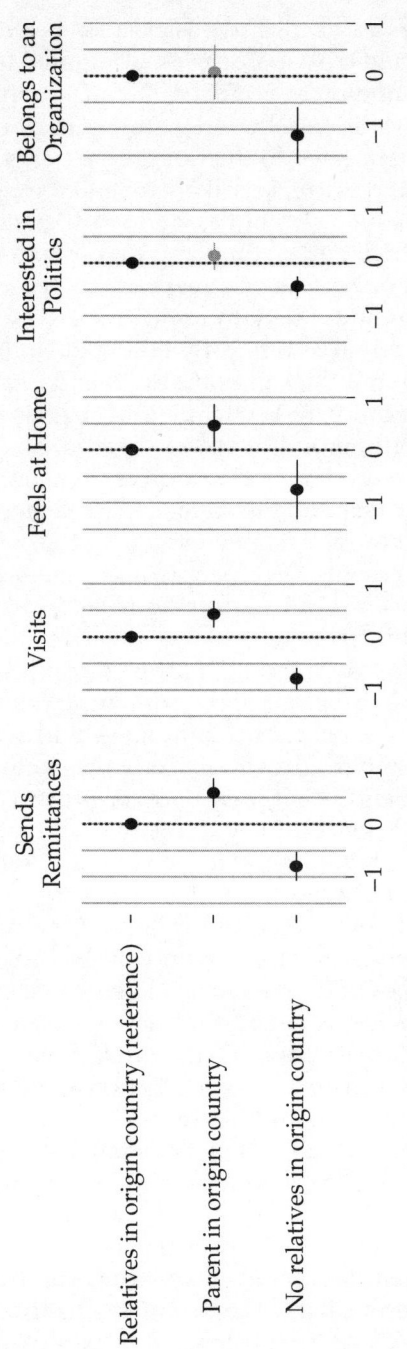

Source: IIMMLA data set.

data, demonstrates a clear positive association between the share of family members abroad and cross-border ties. Compared to those with parents in the United States and other relatives abroad, respondents whose kinship networks were entirely U.S.-bound were significantly less likely to belong to organizations connected to their or their parents' homeland, less likely to have visited that country, less likely to send remittances, less likely to be interested in that country's politics, and less likely to think of the country of origin as home. Similarly, compared to respondents with parents in the United States and only other relatives abroad, those with a parent abroad were significantly more likely to remit and visit frequently and to think of the country of origin as home. By taking the international perspective, which considers family ties in both origin and destination countries, we observe that the location of key family members is a main driver of cross-border engagement among the second generation, over and above any other individual- or group-level resources or inclinations.

But since most respondents remained attached to cross-border kinship networks, other factors inevitably activated or undermined second-generation engagements with people and places abroad; a particularly important influence was a legacy of homeland involvements transmitted from parents to children. Figure 8.3 summarizes the effect of the relevant independent variables. Parental remitting during childhood left an unambiguous impact on these immigrant offspring after their own entry into adulthood: those who grew up in a household where parents remitted were themselves significantly more likely to belong to transnational organizations, to frequently visit their parents' (or their own) homeland, and to frequently send home money to relatives in that homeland. Likewise, respondents who, as children, returned to their homeland for a six-month stay were significantly more likely as adults to frequently visit, to have higher levels of interest in that country's politics, and to think of that country as their home. In contrast, when only the parents returned for extended periods of time, the children were less likely to visit the country of origin.

As we have previously suggested, these parental cross-border activities provide a model for children to later emulate. As we have seen, parental remitting also has unanticipated positive consequences in other domains, such as civic engagement and interest in parental home-country politics; consequently, we infer that it captures some unobserved qualities related to familial and societal cohesion, which suggests that the legacy of parental remitting entails more than simple modeling. Visiting, especially for extended stays, can yield a variety of effects, making the parents' "foreign" home feel and seem less strange, sparking children's interest in home-country politics, and establishing connections that could lead to further visits in adulthood. Although long-term parental absence could spark

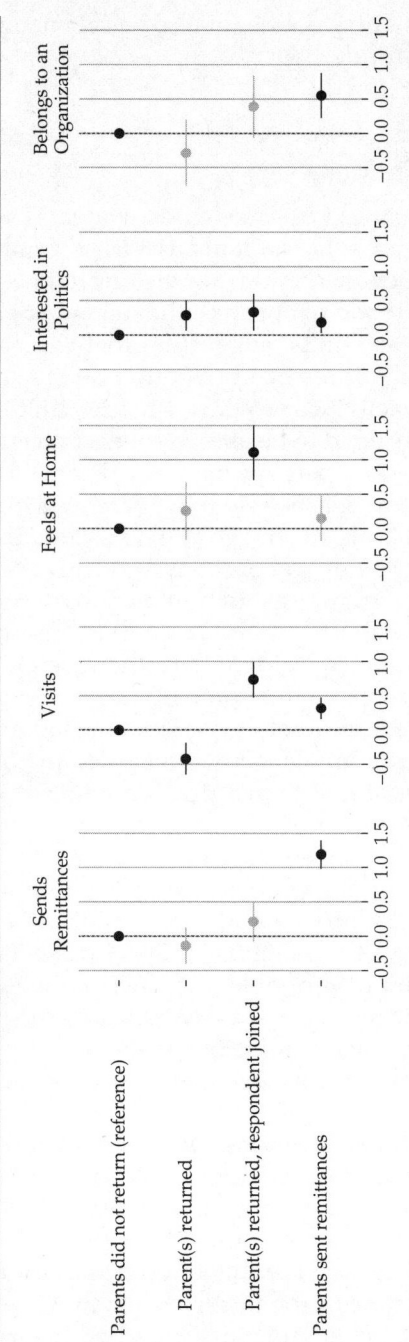

Figure 8.3 Regression Results: Effects of Parental Cross-Border Activities on Cross-Border Ties in the Los Angeles Second Generation

Source: IIMMLA data set.

interest in origin-country politics, it also has alienating effects, depressing the likelihood of future visits.

Making the Connection: Resources and Capacity

The great majority of our Los Angeles respondents (two-thirds) grew up in households where parents maintained at least some type of cross-border engagement, whether via remitting or visiting. Nonetheless, many respondents with no childhood exposure to homeland engagement maintained some engagement as adults, suggesting that exposure was a sufficient, but not necessary, condition of cross-border involvement. Although direct parental homeland activities provided a model, children growing up in the United States also needed to be able to connect meaningfully with a place that was no longer—and perhaps had never been—fully familiar; our data suggest that the language spoken in the parental household provided the key unlocking the ability to engage abroad as adults. Net of other factors, respondents who grew up in households where only English was spoken had the lowest level of interest in home-country politics and were least likely to remit and visit frequently. By contrast, respondents whose childhood was spent in households where the foreign language was used (as opposed to English only or some mixture of English and the foreign language) were the least likely to be so detached and the most likely to report high levels of homeland involvement. The only activity not predicted by parental language practice is membership in home-country-oriented organizations.

Thus, preexisting cross-border ties and parental example provide a continuing motivation for these second-generation immigrant Angelenos to maintain a home-country tie; consistent childhood exposure to the homeland language provides the linguistic capacity needed to make those connections familiar and comfortable. But since daily life is experienced *here*, not *there*, cross-border engagements are unlikely to engage the same imperatives as everyday survival. Calling homeland involvement a luxury may be a stretch too far, but it does involve some degree of discretion, which is why resources are likely to matter.

The relevant resources can take a variety of forms, from disposable income needed for sending remittances to some level of cognitive capacity required for taking an interest in homeland matters or participating in a homeland-oriented organization. Focused as we are on causal influences, we are less concerned with the resources that were available to our respondents at the time of the interviews than we are with the resources transmitted to them by their parents. Standard theory would suggest that parental education ranks among the most important of those resources, via the channels of respondents' own educational and occupational attainment, as we have seen in chapters 4 and 5. Although we anticipate that levels of schooling will influence all the ties of interest, we expect to find the strongest impact on the activity for which cognitive resources are the most important—namely, participation in homeland organizations and interest in homeland politics.

However, the survey finds limited evidence of such impacts (see figure 8.4). As predicted, parental education is associated with significantly higher levels of engagement in homeland-oriented organizations and interest in politics, activities that rely on cognitive resources, and also with higher levels of visiting, which is dependent on material resources. Parental education, however, though significant in statistical terms, yields effects that are substantively negligible compared to other associations. For example, the disparity in visiting propensities between respondents who grew up in English-only families versus mother-tongue-only families corresponded to the difference produced between those with parents who had twenty years of schooling and those whose parents had no schooling at all. Similarly, an eight-year difference in parental education had roughly the same effect on membership in a homeland-oriented organization as did childhood residence in a household where parents sent remittances.

Respondents' own education yields similarly limited impacts: as we would expect, years of education have a significantly positive effect on organizational membership, and results are similar for interest in homeland matters and visits after controlling for contextual measures. By contrast, respondents with higher levels of education were less likely to send remittances ($p < .1$). Ironically, a standard indicator of assimilation—namely, parental familiarity with English (net of the language actually used in the household during childhood)—had a more consistently *positive* effect, influencing organizational membership interest and even visiting. As this variable had a similar effect on many of our measures of civic and political participation, we conclude that the channel is similar: parents' greater English-language ability helps convey to their children the cognitive resources needed for organizational participation or to motivate them to become interested in an ultimately foreign place.

Sometimes it is possible to engage "there" while remaining "here": whether participating in an organization, taking an interest in homeland politics, or even sending remittances, there is often no need to actually cross the border. Visiting, of course, is the great exception. When understood as "transnationalism," cross-border involvement requires engagement in both places to the extent that motivation and resources allow. But something more is involved in traversing the border: the right to cross

Figure 8.4 Regression Results: Effects of Language Spoken at Home, Generation, Citizenship Status, and Parental Education on Cross-Border Activity in the Los Angeles Second Generation

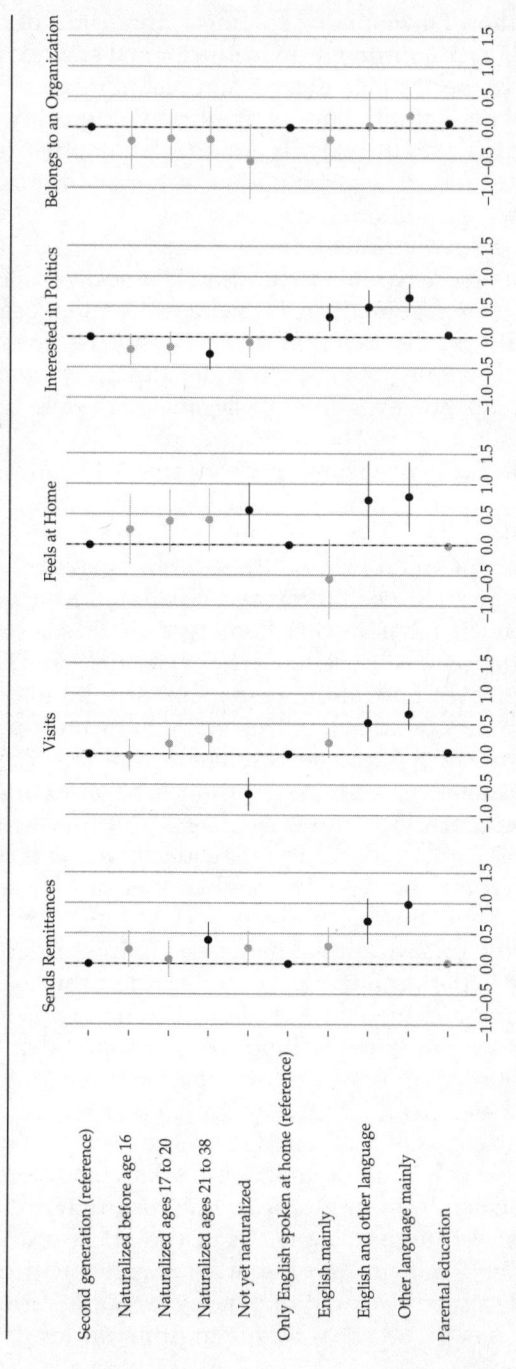

Source: IIMMLA data set.

back and forth at will. In our Los Angeles sample, as we have seen, only a relatively small proportion of the respondents lacked legal status at the time of the interview. The New York survey did not collect this information, but the relevant migrations were all dominated by persons who had arrived legally, and thus we suspect that even fewer of the New Yorkers were in an irregular status at the time of the survey. Even though legal permanent residents have the right to travel internationally at will, they are far more constrained than citizens, as they cannot stay abroad for more than six months. Because citizenship influences a range of civic and political activities for which it is required, we expect that its effects on cross-border connectedness will prove similar.

Not surprisingly, those respondents lacking U.S. citizenship as of the time of the interview were the *least* likely to visit the homeland, a pattern that held both before and after controls. As these same respondents were also the *most* likely to experience the key factors stimulating home-country engagement—relatives abroad, parents who remitted, use of the foreign language at home, and so on—their low level of homeland visiting underscores the specific constraints on movement produced by exclusion from the citizenry.

CONCLUSION

The people opting for life in another country are not just *immigrants* but also *emigrants*. Before the migrants depart, the ties linking them to those who have already settled in the strange land facilitate their movement to that land, reducing the costs and risks associated with long-distance displacement. As migration is selective—those most likely to gain from it go first, others follow slowly, if at all, and the elderly often stay behind—the process internationalizes families over the long term, linking them across borders through chains of mutual help and the continuing exchange of information and ideas. Although the social and economic logic of migration encourages families to internationalize, the ever-greater focus of receiving states on migration control has the same effect. Under these circumstances, those leaving home are the people most likely to succeed in crossing the border, whether or not they are legally authorized to do so; those lacking that capacity stay behind.

Consequently, the children of immigrants—whether born abroad and raised in the country of destination or born and raised there—grow up in what we have called a zone of intersocietal convergence, with familial networks typically stretching across borders. The prevalence of those networks and the importance of the connections often provide the motivation to keep up those ties, even if doing so requires the expenditure of scarce resources.

Looking inwards, assimilation theory necessarily loses sight of the attachments that extend beyond the boundaries of the destination state. Looking outwards, by contrast, the transnational perspective productively enlarges the boundaries of inquiry beyond the sociology of immigration alone. However, it loses purchase when it insists that cross-border ties necessarily produce transnationalism, without ever providing an account of why and how those linkages might persist, let alone which types of migrations or migrants would be most likely to retain homeland connections. The matter is all the more critical for the subjects of this book, for whom the sending society is no longer the native environment and for whom the social center of gravity is found, not in the place of origin, but where they reside. Hence, the second generation is unlikely to match their parents in possessing both the tools and the incentives required for continued cross-border activity.

Nonetheless, we have found ample evidence of homeland ties among the second generation, albeit at diminished and diminishing levels. As this chapter has shown, the stimuli for continued connectedness stem from varying sources. Contexts of both immigration and emigration matter. Thus, group-level status prevalence can simultaneously hinder and facilitate continued cross-border attachments: departures caused by persecution discourage later visiting but encourage later remitting, probably because refugees are the migrants most likely to have left families sundered between the countries of origin and destination. The values imported from points of origin also seem to exercise long-lasting effects: respondents from societies characterized by more traditional orientations were more likely to keep up attachments that tied them to kin abroad.

But this chapter makes its central contribution by showing that cross-border ties should be understood as both independent and dependent variables. At the individual level, the crucial influences on the homeland ties maintained by the young adult Angelenos studied in this book stem from the location of key kinship ties and childhood exposures. Migration is a transitional process, and one that was still quite incomplete as of the time our respondents were surveyed; the majority of them retained close contacts abroad, which in turn influenced their propensity to keep up those ties. Cross-border connections and activities were far more prevalent among those with relatives abroad than among those whose kinship networks were entirely U.S.-bound. Among the former group, those with a parent still abroad were the most attached, on several counts, and more so than those who had kin abroad but whose parents resided in the United States. Although the geographic spread of kin mattered, so too did earlier childhood exposures. Parental example was a powerful influence on our respondents' behavior as adults: those raised by parents who remitted were themselves more likely to evince a homeland attachment. Growing up in a household where a foreign language was mainly used similarly prompted activities oriented toward the home country during young adulthood.

Despite the persistence of connections and activities beyond U.S. borders, the long-term trend involved capture. Foreign kinship ties had a powerful inertial effect. In particular, respondents who still had a parent living abroad were the least likely to abandon homeland ties, yet the overwhelming majority of respondents reported that their parents were residing in the United States. As we will see in the next chapter, language, the tool most needed for meaningful cross-border interactions, was subject to corrosion, even among the minority who grew up in households where the parents' mother tongue dominated. Thus, in the end, the social boundaries of these immigrant offspring in America's most heavily immigrant cities converges with U.S. territorial boundaries. Foreign detachment prevails over foreign connections.

Chapter 9 | Ethnicity: Crossing Blurry Boundaries

THE IMMIGRANT OFFSPRING at the center of this book are the children of people who crossed territorial boundaries only to find themselves confronted with the inner, less visible, but no less real boundaries that distinguish citizens from aliens while simultaneously generating differences among aliens of different types. Yet, since international migration internationalizes kinship networks, these immigrant offspring were raised in families that retained cross-border ties. Those ties connect them to family members still residing in their countries of origin and often enable them to engage with people and places in the country that their parents left behind.

Yet the second generation also encounters informal boundaries in the form of those that separate them from others of different ethnic backgrounds, both those who belong to majority or minority segments of the native population and other foreign persons like themselves who have origins in some other place. Tracing back to the work of the Norwegian anthropologist Fredrik Barth, the concept of boundaries has gained growing favor in the analysis of ethnicity, as it lacks the assumption that populations of any given ethnic or national origin inherently constitute a group—a group being bounded, having a sense of solidarity, and being capable of concerted action—and instead emphasizes the relational, contrastive, mutable nature of the phenomenon in question.[1] As Andreas Wimmer has suggested, the concept of a social boundary has both a categorical and a behavioral dimension, the first establishing distinctions between one population and the next ("we" and "they") and the second pointing to the interactive implications of that distinction.[2]

For immigrant parents, the ambit between "we" and "they" is frequently a by-product of the life-course sequencing that led to migration: since the decision to depart home for life in another country is usually made after adulthood has been reached, immigrant parents typically leave after the process of socialization has been completed. Consequently, they import the nationally prevailing orientations, scripts, and values transmitted to them by their own parents, as well as by the relatives, peers, and institutions who also took part in their socialization. Since the migrants of the contemporary world generally come from established nation-states, their socialization also includes *nationalization,* or the implantation of values and orientations toward their home state, one crucial element of which is identification with the nation to which they putatively belong. National identity, like ethnic identity, is relational, and so it evokes both the capacity to distinguish the national "we" from all others and a set of dispositions favoring other nationals of the same kind, as against foreign people from foreign lands, whose worthiness is likely to be in question. Indeed, as shown in table 9.1, a high level of national pride flourishes in the countries from which the immigrant offspring studied in this book came. Considering that pride in the national self also coexists with a sense of distance from—if not suspicion toward—non-nationals (as also displayed in table 9.1), we think it reasonable to assume that first-generation parents arrived with both the capacity to distinguish fellow nationals from the many other peoples to be encountered in their new world and a preference (of varying intensities) for nationals of their own kind. Hence, this chapter asks whether those nationality-defined social boundaries and related preferences—most notably, those for the parental native tongue—were maintained through the second generation or whether, instead, the immigrant offspring crossed the ethnic boundaries that separated their parents from immigrants of other nationalities and the native-born.

CATEGORIES AND BOUNDARIES

The categorical dimensions of an ethnic boundary include both external and internal referents. One corresponds to the formal borders of territory and citizenship, which contrast the national "we," located "here," to the foreign "them," usually located "there."[3] Worldwide, that schema aligning people and territory is correct: as the globe is entirely split up into non-overlapping states, the great bulk of humanity is born and dies in the state of their birth, and only a small minority opt for long-term or permanent moves across borders. In the United States, however, globalization renders that schema less accurate, because migration leads an ever-growing number of foreign people who start out in foreign places "there" to subsequently come "here"; in so doing, migration changes America from a society of Americans native to the United States to a society that the Americans share with foreigners. Consequently, immigration triggers questions of membership, making the national divide a salient categorical principle. Regardless of the reaction

Table 9.1 Level of National Pride and Suspicions of Foreigners in Select Sending Countries

Country	How Proud of Country?		Confidence in Foreigners	
	Very Proud	Not at All Proud	Little	None
Laos	99%	0%		
Thailand	91	0		
Trinidad & Tobago	89	0		
Vietnam	84	0		
Philippines	83	1		
Cambodia	82	0		
Honduras	78	2	30%	43%
Colombia	76	1	36	31
Dominican Republic	74	1	36	36
El Salvador	72	2	37	36
Ecuador	71	1	44	37
Canada	66	1		
Mexico	65	2	32	46
Paraguay	64	2	32	29
Guatemala	64	2	36	32
Peru	62	2	34	40
China	35	3		
Russia	35	6		
Taiwan	30	6		
South Korea	27	2		
Germany	21	9		

Source: World Values Survey; Latinobarómetro 2007.

produced by migration, American identity is at once an unspoken component of the fabric of everyday life and a way of understanding oneself, the value and importance of which is instilled in immigrants' children from their earliest days in school and elsewhere repeatedly reaffirmed. And just like the people of the countries from which the immigrants come, Americans have a great deal of national pride, and they often prove reluctant to confer on foreigners the same level of trust they give to fellow Americans.

Yet the relevant categorical referents impinging on immigrants and their descendants are not just external, deriving from the organization of the world. They are also internal, emerging from the processes of migration and settlement while also shaped by internal fractures within the country of destination. Movement to a new society is lubricated by existing contacts with friends and kin; no sooner do migrants arrive in the new place than they connect with friends, relatives, hometowners, and others seemingly like themselves. But social circles in the new world are never like those in the old: the diversity of contacts is always much greater. Even the largest of migrant groups comprise quantitative minorities, which is why the range of possible connections extends beyond the universe imaginable back home, leading the circle of the "we" to inevitably expand. Moreover, identities are further shaped by the attribution errors of outsiders, who impose labels that are inconsistent with the old ways of thinking and yet are so pervasively held as to organize experiences. If, back home, sensitivities to regional or linguistic differences rank high, they diminish or even collapse in the new context, thanks to the lumping efforts of the unknowing members of the native population and the unexpected commonalities discovered among other newcomers with whom the migrants would have never associated had they remained on home soil.[4] Consequently, the systems of categorizations and related scripts that define ethnic boundaries are not imported from the society of origin but rather made in the United States. The foreign-born may retain attachments to smaller-scale places like their hometown or region, but those affiliations lose meaning among their children brought up in the United States, who may, depending on the circumstance, understand themselves as Mexican, Chinese, or Italian but who rarely, if ever, think of themselves in terms of the narrower, specific identities that made sense to Mom and Dad.

The internally fractured nature of the American national community provides still more alternative options for identification. In theory, adherence to the "American Creed" of hard work and individual reliance, as identified by Gunnar Myrdal more than a half century ago, should suffice for full membership as an "American."[5] Yet the United States is also characterized by an intractable conflict between the fundamentally liberal principles of the Creed and a contradictory, no less deeply held view that legal or functional membership should be restricted to persons of visibly European descent.[6] Consequently, the American people are themselves divided, with the notion of an "ethno-racial pentagon" providing one widely held schema for sorting the different types of Americans. In principle, the ethno-racial pentagon pushes aside Old World, exclusionary national affiliations and home-country animosities and replaces them with panethnic identities, each of which encompasses a broad population characterized by national and cultural variation. Practice may sharply contrast with principle, yet the categories defined by the ethno-racial pentagon provide the basis for classification, whether by state or nonstate institutions, and thus are part of the classificational universe that immigrants and their offspring inevitably encounter.

Thus, the immigrant New Yorkers and Angelenos studied in this book grew up in a context offering myriad options for ethnic categorization and affiliation. Not only are the possibilities multiple, but the situations in which ethnic or national background becomes relevant are equally variable, with the result that an identification embraced in one setting may be dropped in favor of some different attachment when the environment changes or when the set of potential interactions shrinks or expands. But if the migrants and their offspring enjoy new choices, they are also constrained by the range of available categories recognized as meaningful and relevant by both the individuals with whom they interact and the institutions that they encounter. The distinction between the individual and the institutional level matters: nationality may be a meaningful signifier in everyday interactions, but the broader categories of America's ethno-racial pentagon, which lump together persons who would never have seen themselves as the same prior to emigration, enjoy institutional recognition. The recurring encounter with those categories and the demand to place oneself within the institutionally recognized classification system may undermine the relevance of the categories imported from abroad or transmitted from parents to children. Although the new national identity of American offers another option for self-definition, it lacks the relevance and utility of the narrower alternatives. On the one hand, it does not provide an adequate way of positioning oneself relative to the everyday, more sharply defined contrasts, and on the other hand, it gets pushed into the background by the institutionalization of the ethno-racial pentagon, which is precisely designed to highlight differences among Americans, that is, persons who share the same nationality.[7]

Weber famously linked ethnicity to a belief in a common descent.[8] But for our purposes, descent is more important as a biographical fact, as all of our respondents had either arrived with a foreign nationality or had it as part of their immediate inheritance. Migration typically foregrounds aspects of descent that previously lay deep in the background, foremost among them nationality: migrants become more self-conscious about their nationality than they might have been before they moved from a context where the predominance of conationals reduced the salience of nationality to one where the confluence of peoples from all over the globe adds to preexisting ethnic diversity, bringing differences in nationality to sharp relief. Consequently, the degree to which members of the second generation can either detach nationality from their self-definition, or instead largely find themselves defined by precisely that attribute, says much about the permeability of the social boundaries encountered after crossing territorial borders.

In addressing the question of boundary change, this section applies the perspectives that the reader will now surely find familiar. Neo-assimilation theory predicts that ethnic attachments among our second-generation New Yorkers and Angelenos will prove highly sensitive to *intraethnic* differences in parental resources and levels of acculturation: the children who were raised by more highly educated parents or who grew up in environments where English was exclusively or mainly used will be least likely both to identify with the country of origin and to rate ethnic identity as important; they will also be most likely to self-describe in terms of multiple ethnicities. However, this approach lacks an explanation for any intergroup differences that we might find. The hypothesis of segmented assimilation, of course, addresses that issue head on, contending that intergroup differences stem from disparities in the mode of incorporation. Yet tracing the path linking the mode of incorporation to any one of the ethnic options available proves difficult, an impediment that may explain why the analysis of identity presented in *Legacies* emphasizes the impact of *intraethnic* differences in nativity, citizenship status, family composition, and the early school environment, but not the mode of incorporation. By contrast, the international perspective advanced in this book seeks to shed light on both intra- and interethnic differences. We anticipate that a foreign national identity will retain its greatest hold among those children of immigrants who, by virtue of their context of immigration, occupy the position furthest away from status citizenship and closest to the territorial border. Members of groups characterized by the prevalence of unfavorable legal statuses should be least likely to adopt U.S.-centered forms of identification; moreover, those with a context of emigration predominantly oriented toward the values of tradition and survival should also be most likely to maintain the home-country national identities passed down by their parents. At the within-group level, we expect that nationally-defined identities will prevail among those respondents still connected to the homeland, through either childhood exposures or persistent internationalized kinship networks; likewise, we anticipate that lack of authorization at the time of entry as well as persistent noncitizen status will slow the adoption of a U.S. nationally defined ethnic identity.

Traversing Ethnic Boundaries

Categorization and identity are inextricably intertwined: one can experience a sense of belonging to some broader collectivity only if one's self-categorization coincides with the classifications made by the relevant others, whether those inside or outside the self-assigned category. Yet since recognition—whether wanted or not—does not inherently yield importance, the salience of any ethnic category is subject to flux, gaining or losing centrality depending on the occasion, the characteristics of the actors encountered, and the actions that the category stimulates or the meanings with which actors invest it. And as ethnicity is only one of the many lines of social division, it may fall into the background, its significance overshadowed by some other categorical difference unrelated to ancestry and a linked sense of belonging.

Consequently, the analysis to follow distinguishes between the labels respondents use to place themselves in a social category and the importance or centrality that they attribute to that category.[9] To do so, we rely on a battery of related items from the IIMMLA, beginning with the question: "When thinking about your own ethnicity or ancestry, how do you identify, that is, what do you call yourself?" Questions like this run the danger of reifying ethnic boundaries, attributing a degree of stability and consistency belied by the mutability of everyday life, a problem compounded when questions related to origins alert the interviewee to the issues that the interviewer deems important. Nonetheless, since the IIMMLA allowed for open-ended responses, following this initial question with two prompts querying respondents about their use of other labels, then requesting that respondents indicate their preferred label, and last, asking about the importance of that preferred label, it provides an adequate basis for assessing the malleability of ethnic categories and identities.

Thus, while the IIMMLA respondents originated in fifty-five different countries, they chose to describe themselves with a dizzying number of terms, which we subsequently simplified for analytic purposes. A small though nontrivial minority (almost 4 percent) simply refused to answer, though they shortly thereafter reported willingly on the language used in their childhood home, indicating that they had grown up mainly in households where a foreign language prevailed. A still smaller minority (1 percent) rejected the exercise altogether, whether playfully—as with the respondents who answered "dude" or "a human being"—or seriously—as with the interviewee who insisted, "I don't go by labels, I'm a person." Others (just under 2 percent) emphasized the mixture of their origins ("I'm a mutt," "Heinz 57," "a half-breed"), making pigeonholing impossible. Respondents also offered different labels to refer to a like category—for instance, with such discrepant answers as "latin," "latino," "latina," "Hispanic," "Hispanic American," and "Latino and American"—suggesting a good deal of fuzziness as to the ways in which the category is comprehended, perceived, and contrasted from others. Similarly, some answered in English and others in the native tongue. Since the decision to answer in Spanish, for example, required distinguishing between *mexicano* and *mexicana*—versus English, in which case the corresponding response, "Mexican," encompasses both genders—differences in how a seemingly identical label was expressed probably pointed to subtle differences in how the label was understood. The descriptors offered up by respondents rarely coincided with the labels preferred by ethnic activists: fewer than 3 percent of the Mexican-origin respondents described themselves as "chicano," and though many of the Angelenos with roots in Mexico or Central and South America mentioned a panethnic label, the great majority of those who did so used the term "Hispanic," not the term "Latino" (or one of its variants). Nor did respondents hew to a single ethnic label when asked to describe themselves: of those who provided at least one label, almost 30 percent claimed to use two terms, and another 9 percent reported using three terms when describing themselves ethnically. Twelve percent of those who mentioned more than one label lacked a preference for one over the other, suggesting that as the options for ethnic labeling grow, the particular salience of any one label may decline or become more situationally specific.

To make the open-ended responses tractable to quantitative analyses, we first reduced them to nineteen different categories; we placed references to a single country of origin in a nationality category, did likewise for all hyphenated labels, listed all specific racial or panethnic terms mentioned, and then aggregated a few less commonly used terms into appropriate categories. Adapting the procedure developed in *Legacies*, we then implemented a second classification, sorting all labels into six different categories, which we labeled "national," "panethnic," "hyphenated," "American," "mixed," and "other." A residual category captures those who refused to answer. As shown in figure 9.1, almost all respondents (94 percent) in their first mention provided a label that fit into one of the four conventional categories of "national," "panethnic," "hyphenated," or "American," with the labels ranked in precisely that order; "national" led the pack at 34 percent and "American" lagged far behind at 6 percent. Though those same categories still captured the great majority of preferred labels, a somewhat larger minority (11 percent) claimed no preference, refused to answer, or offered a discrepant response that we categorized as "mixed" or "other." The majority of respondents (54 percent) rated their preferred ethnic label as "very important" to them, with only 17 percent answering, "not too important." Yet importance varied by the specific label that respondents preferred: 60 percent of those preferring a national-origin label rated it as "very important," as opposed to 49 percent of those who opted for a panethnic label. Those who mentioned three labels when queried were somewhat less likely than those who mentioned only one

Figure 9.1 Mentions of Ethnic Labels and Importance of Ethnic Labels Among Los Angeles Respondents

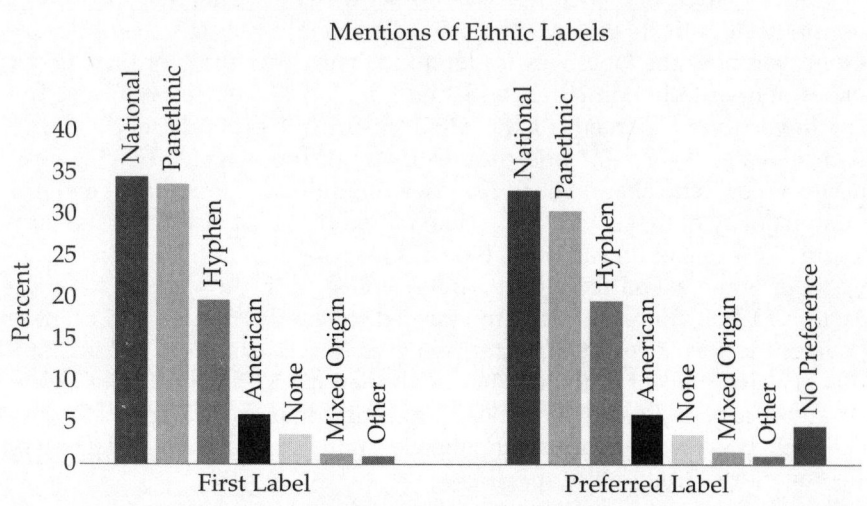

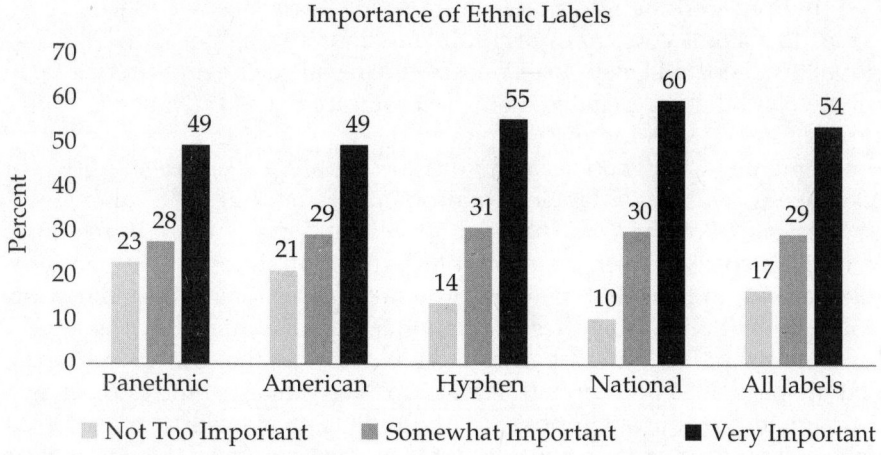

Source: IIMMLA data set.

label to say that the preferred label (49 percent versus 56 percent) was "very important."

Having described the basic response patterns, we now analyze the choice of label and the importance ascribed to that choice. We use mixed-effects logistic regressions to analyze choice and mixed-effects ordered logistic regression to model importance.

Figure 9.2 summarizes the key coefficients of a subset of these models.[10] Family configuration strongly conditions the choice of ethnic label. Respondents whose parents came from different countries were consistently less likely to identify with either a single national label or a hyphenated label than were those whose parents were of the same national origins. Other things being equal, those with same-origin parents were two and a half times as likely as respondents with mixed-origin parents to prefer a hyphenated label (10 percent versus 25 percent) and 50 percent more likely (35 percent versus 23 percent) to prefer a national-origin label. By contrast, mixed-parentage respondents were much more likely to prefer a panethnic label (43 percent as compared to 26 percent of interviewees with same-origin parents, holding other variables constant).

Although the facts of parental ancestry clearly condition label choice, so too do respondents' biography and political membership. Not surprisingly, a clear divide separates the foreign-born from the U.S.-born: the latter were much more likely than the former to choose labels with an explicitly American component, whether a hyphenated American label or the "American" label pure and simple. Yet the factors influencing the choice of ethnic label went beyond place of birth, reflecting the importance of status as well. As shown in figure 9.3, current and prior noncitizenship status matters: while the late naturalizers were de jure and de facto Americans and the non-naturalizers were de facto Americans, they all proved significantly less likely than their U.S.-born counterparts to self-categorize as Americans of either the hyphenated or plain sort; noncitizen respondents were particularly more likely than the U.S.-born to prefer a national-origin identity.

Looking beyond the legal status of the respondents to the at-entry status of their parents, in figure 9.4 we see a lasting effect of arriving without a visa: those children who chose not to provide information on their parents' legal status at arrival were the most likely to choose a panethnic identity, and the least likely to choose an American identity.

Taken together, these results illustrate some of the constraints that origin and political membership impose when the second generation chooses from the menu of available options. Labels with a national-origin component did not fit those respondents who lacked a single, unambiguous national origin, and a lack of political membership or a U.S. citizen parent made for an uneasy fit with labels that invoked "American."

Although these results highlight the interplay of parental origins, place of birth, and legal status in identity choice, the picture that emerges from the variables measuring parental acculturation and the linguistic environment is much less consistent. As we will show, parents' language competence and their decisions about which language to speak at home are associated with second-generation linguistic competencies and preferences, as well as

Figure 9.2 Select Regression Coefficients for the Ethnic Categorization Preferences of Los Angeles Respondents: Parental Origin Status at Arrival, Respondents' Generational and Citizenship Status, and Language Practices in the Household

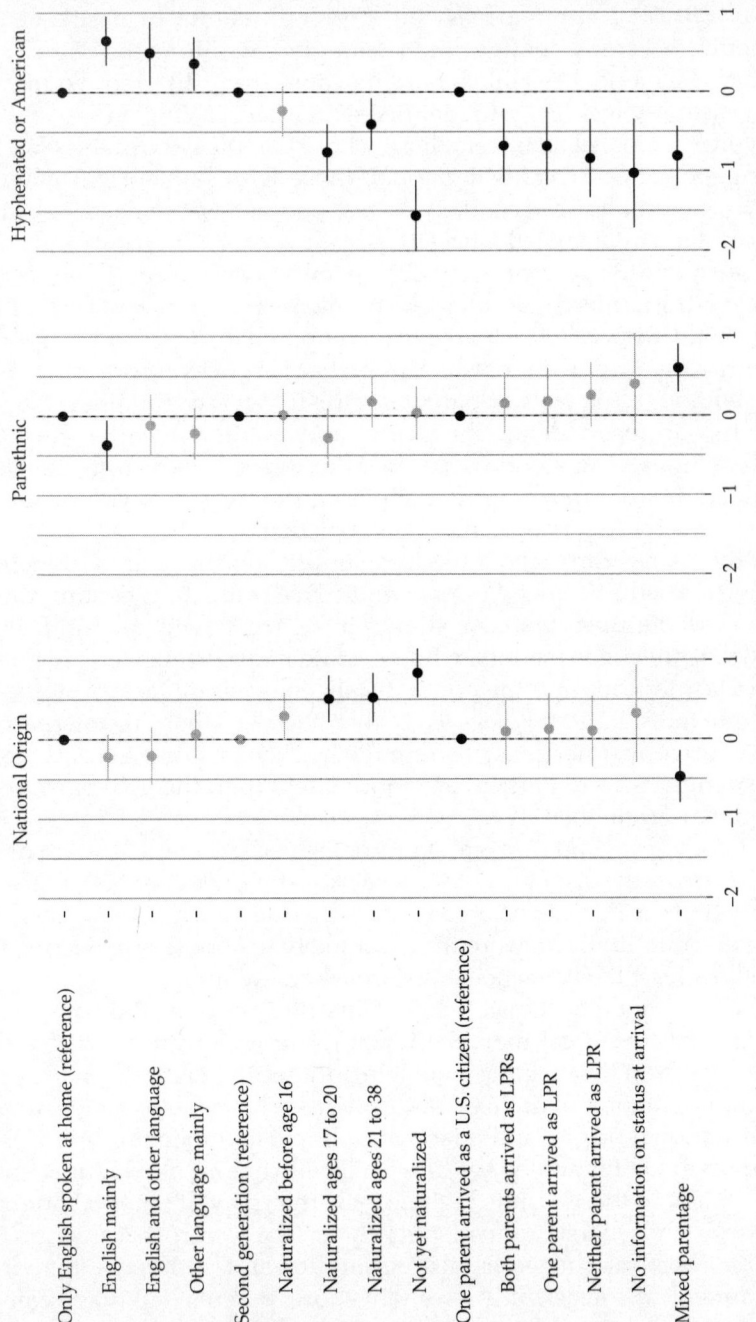

Source: IIMMLA data set.

Figure 9.3 Los Angeles Respondents' Preferred Ethnic Label by Generation and Naturalization (Regression-Adjusted Predicted Probability)

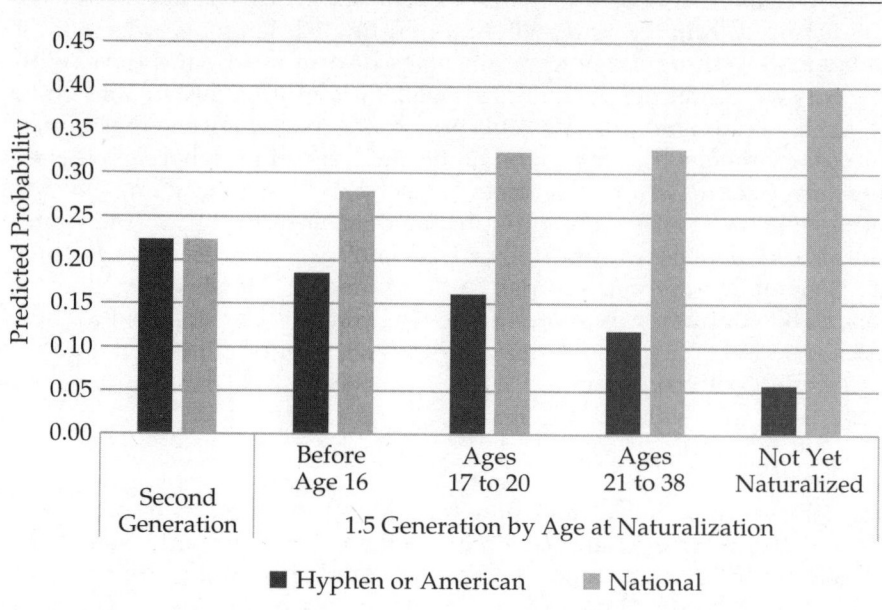

Source: IIMMLA data set.

Figure 9.4 Predicted Probability of Los Angeles Respondents' Preferred Ethnic Label by Parental Legal Status at Arrival

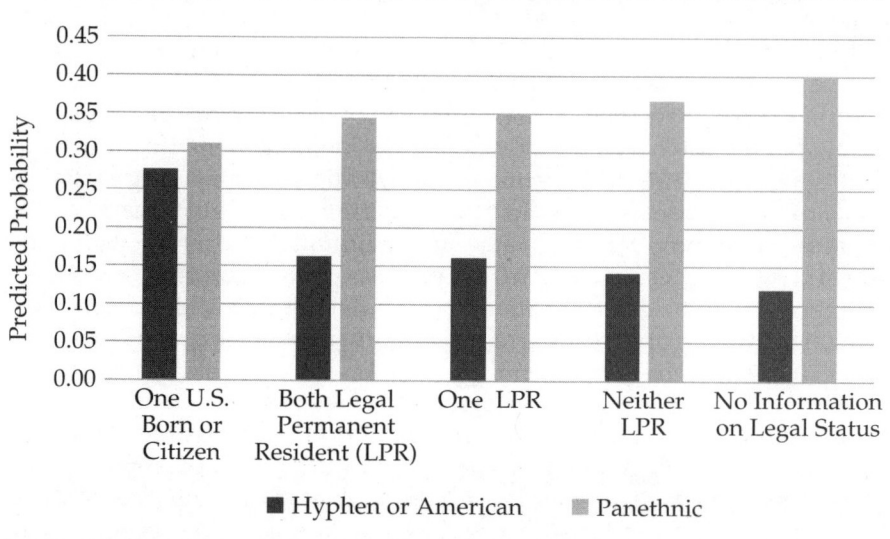

Source: IIMMLA data set.

with the salience of the home-country connection (see chapter 8): respondents raised in households where a non-English language was mainly spoken were more likely to retain place-of-origin ties, and those with parents who did not speak English well were more likely to hold on to their foreign tongue. We also find some connections between the linguistic environment of the childhood home and later ethnic labels and identities: respondents who grew up in households where only English was used were less likely to prefer hyphenated labels or the term "American" than respondents who grew up in mixed-language environments. We find no systematic differences in preference, however, for the other types of labels. By contrast, parents' competence in English, as opposed to their decision to use English at home during respondents' childhood, had no association with label choice.

LANGUAGE: RETENTION AND LOSS

Of the various practices and preferences that immigrants import from the country of origin, language may be the most important of all. After all, language serves as more than a mere marker of group difference; it constitutes a fundamental human quality and as such possesses an emotional valence that other cultural imports, such as clothing or food, may not enjoy. Second-generation retention of the home-country culture is conventionally viewed as a source of disadvantage, which is why immigrant parents' mother tongue is thought to inevitably give way before the dominant tongue in the adopted country. Indeed, when arguing that assimilation results from "the unintended consequences of practical strategies and actions undertaken in pursuit of familiar goals," Alba and Nee mention language loss first among the examples they provide to illustrate their point.[11] In turn, that contention explains why these authors see the past as prelude to the future, with the language loss demonstrated by the grandchildren of the turn-of-the-twentieth-century migrants providing a reliable guide to the experience of the children and grandchildren of those joining the mass migrations of today. To be sure, gravitation into an English-only world does not imply that all traces of the ancestral culture are fated to disappear; nonetheless, as language so centrally defines the self, any old-country cultural remnants persisting in the absence of language ability are likely to be symbolic in nature.[12]

While Alba and Nee lightly pass over the mechanisms impelling acculturation, their views are deeply informed by the influential model of language change developed by the sociolinguist Joshua Fishman, who advances a perspective completely compatible with the tenets of neo-assimilation theory. In broad brush, Fishman's story of intergenerational change reads like this: The first generation retains the mother tongue for most purposes, switching to the dominant language to get by or get ahead, but using it only in those domains where its use is required. Immigrants' children may be exposed to the mother tongue at home; however, usage lapses as the dominant tongue rules in all other domains—at school and work, even in the neighborhood—leaving the parental home as the one place where the mother tongue is regularly heard, though even there it is used with diminishing frequency. Once heading up their own households, immigrants' children make limited use of their parents' language, perhaps using it as a shield that allows them to talk about private, difficult matters within their own children's earshot without worrying that the children will understand. Hence, immigrants' grandchildren are at best passive bilinguals, retaining a scattering of mother-tongue expressions for use on special occasions, but otherwise conversing exclusively in English. At the end of the chain, the fourth generation grows up as dominant-language monolinguals.[13]

One takeaway message of *Inheriting the City* mainly supports the Fishman model and neo-assimilation theory: English is used on a near-universal basis by the 1.5- and second-generation New Yorkers surveyed by the ISGMNY. Yet the book's confirmatory tale comes with a twist: the authors also contend that "the real story is about second language retention, and the group differences here are strong," most notably, the rapid attenuation of foreign-language competencies among the Russian Jews and the Chinese and the relatively strong retention of Spanish among Dominicans and other Latin Americans.[14] That emphasis on intergroup differences runs against the grain of the Fishman model, which instead emphasizes the importance of processes operating at the individual level—namely, the linguistic shifts that emerge with successive generations as exposure steadily grows to contexts where English prevails—at work, in school, and in the street. And the factors adduced to account for Spanish's great resilience—the greater density of same-language speakers, a vibrant ethnic media, proximity to the home community—are orthogonal to the overarching claim of cultural hybridity creating "second-generation advantage" given that those in the most-advantaged second-generation groups are the ones who most quickly become English monolinguals.

The hypothesis of segmented assimilation broke with the conventional wisdom, insisting that, under certain circumstances, better outcomes could be assured if assimilation could proceed at a slower pace. As noted in chapter 2, the proponents of segmented assimilation advance a two-level model, one emphasizing the group-level effects associated with the context of reception, the second emphasizing the interaction between those group-level effects and household strategies that might mediate their impacts.

Those strategies matter most for groups facing an unfavorable context of reception, which exposes families to deprived environments and leaves parents short of the material and informational resources best suited for retaining influence over their children. Consequently, familial cohesion is put at risk, a danger aggravated by the children's exposure to the hedonistic, individualistic orientation of the society around them. For these reasons, segmented assimilation contends that successful transmission of key elements of the home-country culture can maintain familial solidarity, reducing the gap between parents and children, diminishing conflict, and increasing parents' capacity to give their children useful help.

Thus, in *Legacies*, Portes and Rumbaut propose a threefold typology, identifying consonant, selective, and dissonant acculturation as the key variants. Where acculturation takes a consonant form, parents and children absorb elements of the so-called mainstream culture at roughly equal rates, a pattern purportedly "most common when immigrant parents possess enough human capital to accompany the cultural evolution of their children and monitor it."[15] In the dissonant variant, children's adaptation greatly outpaces that of their parents, exacerbating the role reversal that often afflicts immigrant parents and striking at parents' capacity for exercising influence over their brood. Last, in selective acculturation, immigrant children acquire the key cultural competencies valued by the society of reception while simultaneously maintaining core elements of the origin culture—most notably, continued competence in the parents' native language.

For the proponents of segmented assimilation, language loss presents a particularly potent threat to familial cohesion, increasing the likelihood of dissonant acculturation. The analysis of language loss and retention developed in *Legacies* contends that the "dimensions of parental national background, family socioeconomic status, and household values and norms play key roles," setting aside mode of incorporation to instead emphasize nationality.[16] Though the children of Spanish-speaking parents prove the most likely to retain mother-tongue competency, the book's findings showed that on average no group could be considered fluent in the parents' home language. Consequently, the authors conclude that "lack of knowledge of parental languages coupled with the wide parent-child gap in English among many Asian and Latin American nationalities, points to the likelihood of dissonant acculturation."[17]

Unlike the approaches reviewed in the previous pages, the international perspective advanced in this book underscores the continuing influence of the home country. Differences in the cultural orientations imported from abroad will affect *intergroup* disparities in foreign-language competency and preferences for English; in particular, we expect that loss of the origin language will be greatest if the context of emigration tends toward self-expression and secularism. Though the influence is somewhat distal, we also anticipate that groups among whom undocumented migration has been more prevalent will be more likely to retain mother-tongue competence than those for whom refugee status—which reduces the likelihood of return travel or migration—is relatively common.

But because language is a more private dimension of social life, we expect that the most important differences will be found at the *intragroup* level. In particular, we anticipate that differences in cross-border ties will be a driving factor: mother-tongue retention will be strongest among immigrant offspring who remain part of internationalized family relationships and/or who grew up in households that sought to maintain and fortify the tie to the place of origin. We also anticipate individual-level effects analogous to those at the group level: the offspring of more-advantaged immigrants will be the most likely to shift to English monolingualism, exemplifying the pattern that Portes and Rumbaut describe as consonant acculturation. However, we recognize that language transmission can be both a choice and a constraint. For less-advantaged immigrants, there may be no element of choice in the decision to pass on the native tongue: if the parents do not speak English, then there is simply no other option. On the other hand, for the privileged, putatively hyperselected immigrants studied by Lee and Zhou, settled in privileged ethnic enclaves with ethnic institutions designed to impart sending-country culture, passing on the home-country language may be a conscious effort and a choice. In more privileged groups, then, we might expect that it is the more-advantaged immigrants who can afford to practice selective acculturation.

Mother-Tongue Competence and Language Preference

We begin by focusing on the transmission of language competence and language preference. For this analysis, we use the combined Los Angeles and New York sample, but omit those respondents whose parents came from countries where English was an official language: thus, we exclude the children of West Indian parents from the New York sample. In so doing, we can safely make the assumption that the mother tongue was retained (or abandoned) as part of the acculturation process rather than as a function of the language prevalent in the sending country.

Following convention, both the New York and Los Angeles surveys proceeded in multistep fashion, first asking whether a language other than English was spoken in the childhood home. When respondents answered yes, they were then asked to identify the language spoken and subsequently to answer questions about the frequency of its use, their competence in that language across a series of domains, and their own language preferences. The questions about language competency focused on four domains—speaking, understanding, reading, and writing—to which respondents had the option of answering "very well," "well," "not well," or "not at all." Summing the answers and dividing by four generated a scale of mother-tongue competence from 0 to 4, with all respondents raised in English-language households ranked as 0 and ranks for all other respondents starting at 1 and then progressing by one-quarter intervals. As the questions concerning mother-tongue competence were asked only of those respondents who grew up in households where a language other than English was at least occasionally used, the data, by their nature, produce a pattern in which *no* respondent who grew up in an English-only household can possess foreign-language facility—a pattern that in all likelihood closely corresponds to reality but undoubtedly misses exceptional cases. Overall, 90 percent of the children of immigrants whose native language was not English grew up in households where their parents' native language was spoken; among those respondents, scores on the mother-tongue competency scale averaged 3.2, with a median of 3.5, a score that could not be obtained without responding "very well" on at least two of the four domains queried.

Generation strongly influenced the use of any non-English tongue in the parental home. Hence, whereas 98 percent of the children of two foreign-born parents (from non-English-speaking origin countries) grew up in a household where a language other than English was spoken, and thus were questioned about their mother-tongue competence, this latter question was posed to only 60 percent of the 2.5-generation respondents.

To further assess the determinants of foreign-language ability among the children of immigrants, we next turn to our multilevel framework to examine the main group- and individual-level predictors of competence. Key results of this model appear in figure 9.5.

Even within this full model, which includes many individual- and group-level controls, we see how time extinguishes foreign-language ability. Whereas the predicted foreign-language competence score for "average" 1.5-generation respondents who arrived in later childhood is 3.5—that is, they would have answered "well" or "very well" on all four domains—the 2.5-generation respondents had a predicted score of 2.05, well under the median for the entire sample. For the purposes of understanding the transmission of language competence, generation is a measure of exposure as produced by biography—one's own prior direct exposure to a linguistic environment entirely different from that in which one currently lives (the 1.5 generation) or one's exposure to parents

Figure 9.5 Coefficients from Linear Regression Predicting Mother-Tongue Proficiency (Scale) and Preference for English

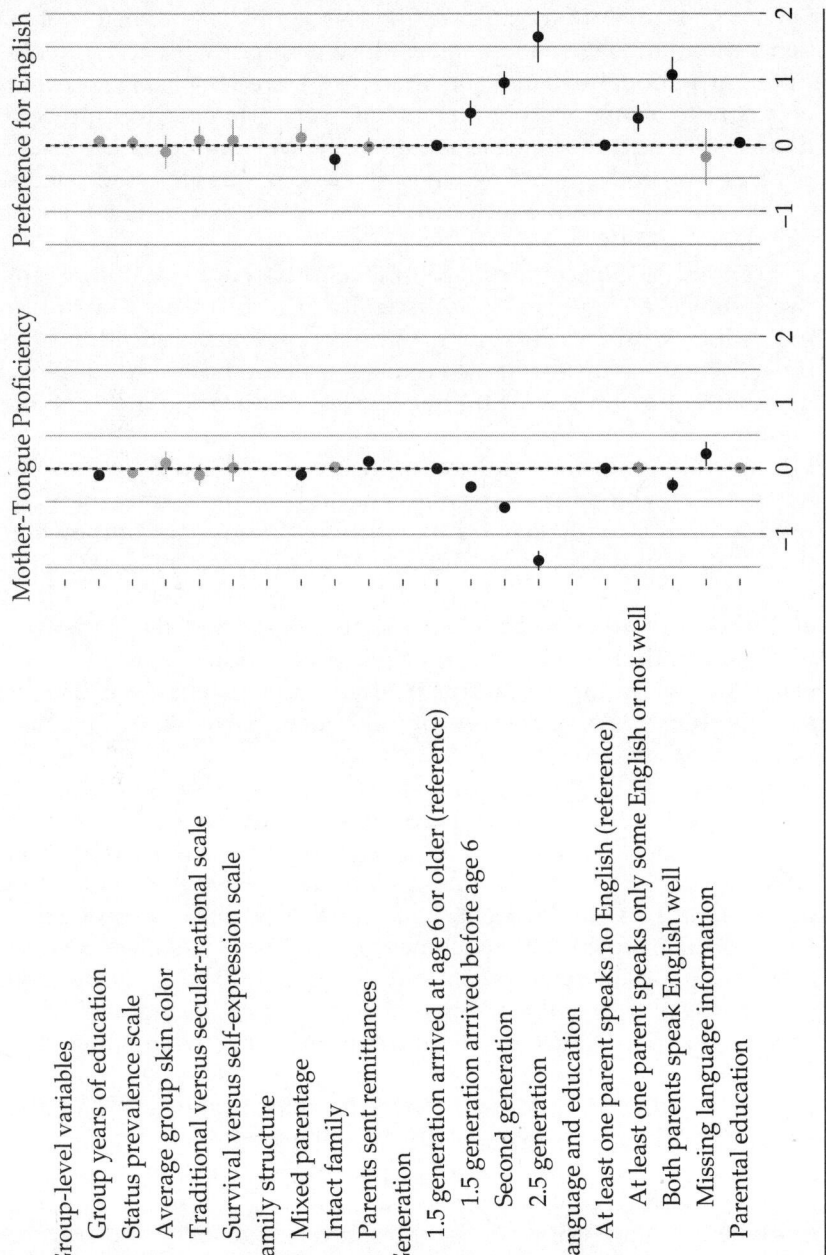

Source: IIMMLA and ISGMNY data sets.

who grew up in such an environment (the second and 2.5 generations). Similar measures of exposure are likewise significant predictors of second-generation language competence: those children who had parents from different national origins, and therefore were less likely to experience exposure to a single foreign language, were also less likely to be fluent; mother-tongue competence was similarly lower among the children of two parents who both spoke English well. Gender was also associated with a statistically significant effect: men scored lower than women (about one-eighth of a point).

Contrary to expectations, group-level differences in foreign-language competence are generally statistically insignificant. Controlling for individual-level factors, only group-level average education proves to be associated with foreign-language competence: second-generation members of groups with higher levels of education are less likely to maintain their foreign-language ability. On the other hand, we do see initial evidence of the importance of the cross-border ties emphasized by the international perspective: children of immigrant parents who remitted are more likely to report foreign-language competence than the children of parents who did not. Moreover, we can detect a channel linking civic stratification to the relatively private domain of language ability: in a regression model (not shown here) that keeps the two U.S.-born generations unchanged but separates the foreign-born into two categories according to citizenship status, noncitizens were likely to possess significantly higher levels of mother-tongue competence than their naturalized-citizen peers.

Capacity is one thing; desire to use that capacity is another. For the second generation after they leave their parental household, that desire may count more than competence. Because the broader environment not only disapproves of public foreign-language use but also offers limited occasions for its deployment, it may be only those second-generation adults with an emotional attachment to the home language who work to maintain their language capabilities and transmit them to the next generation. In contrast, if the children of immigrants feel stigmatized by their parents' foreign origins, the demeaning, difficult jobs in which they may be employed, and the foreign tongue they speak, they may allow a competence acquired in childhood to wither, absent some offsetting, positive emotional resonance evoked by the parental tongue.

Both the IIMMLA and ISGMNY provide information on the language preferences of those respondents who grew up in homes where a non-English language was spoken, though the two surveys do so through somewhat different approaches. The Angelenos were asked to respond to the question, "Which language do you prefer in your home, English or [language mentioned]?" with the option to respond, "English," "other language," or "both about the same." By contrast, the New Yorkers were asked, "Which language do you prefer to speak in your home most of the time now?" with only one response category offered. We harmonize these two variables by examining preference for English as compared to both languages (chosen by 8 percent of the IIMMLA sample) or foreign-language preference. In our combined sample, 55 percent of the respondents who grew up in homes where a non-English language was spoken reported that they preferred to speak English. Not surprisingly, those second-generation children of parents from non-English-speaking countries who preferred English reported a lower level of foreign-language competence (mean = 2.5) than those who preferred their parents' native tongue (mean = 3.5). However, as indicated by the fact that 37 percent of those reporting the highest level of competence across all four domains still preferred English, competence was only one of the sources fostering attachment.

Moving from bivariate statistics to the regression summarized in figure 9.5 reveals that, as with foreign-language competence, preference is mainly a reflection of individual-level rather than group-level differences. Receiving-country exposure, as measured by generation, affects both competence and preference: whereas only 45 percent of the respondents who arrived after the age of five preferred English, a full two-thirds of those born in the United States did, and among those with a U.S.-born parent, only 22 percent did not prefer English. The offspring of more-educated parents were somewhat more likely to prefer English than those raised by parents with lower levels of schooling; however, these differences were modest. By contrast, preferences for English sharply rose with age. Net of controls, 54 percent of twenty-year-old respondents preferred English as opposed to 64 percent of their thirty-year-old counterparts, a disparity likely to be related to rising age at departure from the parental home, a hypothesis that we explore further with IIMMLA data in the following pages.

Chapter 5 found few associations between parental practices reflecting or promoting ethnic retention and socioeconomic outcomes, contrary to the claims made in *Legacies* and *The Asian American Achievement Paradox*. By contrast, the analysis of language competence in this chapter has revealed the powerful impact of the home environment, most notably in its different impacts on capacity and valence. Net of controls, parents' own English-language ability had only a minor effect on respondents' foreign-language competence (one-quarter of a point), but it strongly shaped the latter's preference for English. Thus, 72 percent of respondents with two parents who spoke English well preferred English, a level that dropped to

49 percent when neither parent spoke English well; this disparity points to the ways in which parents affect children through modeling.[18] Similarly, respondents raised in two-parent households were no more fluent than their counterparts raised by single parents, but they were significantly less likely to prefer English. By contrast, mixed parentage was associated with both lower levels of mother-tongue competence and a higher preference for English.

For deeper insight, we now focus exclusively on the Los Angeles respondents so as to exploit information uniquely available in the IIMMLA. To a large extent, as shown in figure 9.6, the variables discussed show similar and statistically significant effects when analysis is restricted to the Angelenos: a preference for English proves to be positively related to parents' English-language capacity as well as negatively related to exposure measured via generational status. At the group level, those from more highly educated origin groups were more likely to prefer English.

The IIMMLA allows us to separate respondents who still live with extended family from those who have struck out on their own, so we can see that age and independence both matter, though they yield distinctive effects. As in the pooled sample, older respondents were more likely than their younger peers to prefer English, but once we control for household residence, the discrepancy is slight. By contrast, only 56 percent of the respondents still residing with their parents or extended family members preferred English, a fraction that jumped to 71 percent among those living on their own. Again demonstrating that capacity and valence capture distinct aspects of the relationship between ethnicity and language, respondents living on their own were more likely to prefer English at every level of foreign-language competence, including those who reported the highest level of fluency across all four domains of speaking, understanding reading, and writing.

Of course, the interviewees who had already struck out on their own had effectively crossed the social boundary separating the parental household from the rest of the world. Since that social boundary also often coincided with the social boundary demarcating the limits of the ethnic "we," setting up their own households seems to have freed these respondents to also detach from the mother tongue. But as we have emphasized throughout this volume, for many immigrant offspring the relevant social boundaries extend beyond territorial borders, which is why engagements with parents and communities in the place of origin may in turn reinforce ethnic attachments in the place of destination. Some prior engagements are likely to matter more than others, precisely because of the skills or dispositions they impart. Thus, the regression shows that preferences for English were significantly lower among respondents who had spent a six-month period

Figure 9.6 Predicting Los Angeles Respondents' Preference for English

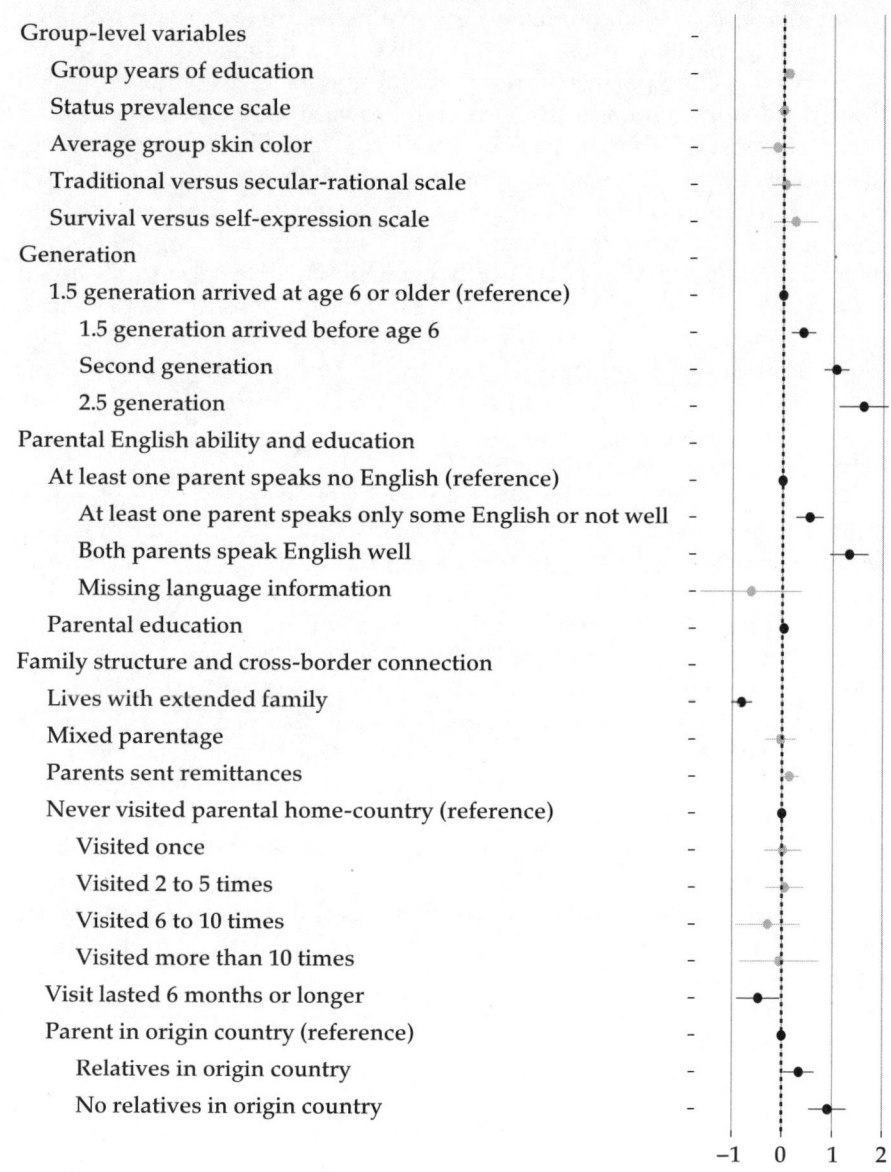

Source: IIMMLA data set.

in the country of origin (54 percent preferring English) than among those with no such experience (63 percent preferring English).

Yet as we have seen, homeland involvements are not simply vestigial but ongoing, partly because kinship networks continue to extend across territorial lines, and partly because parental activities—both those oriented toward the homeland and those oriented toward maintaining homeland practices, most notably, language—predispose children to keep up long-distance contacts. As we have emphasized, though the persistent tendencies toward intersocietal convergence are deep-seated, they nonetheless are undermined by the opposing forces of intersocietal *divergence,* as evidenced by the fact that, net of controls, even those with a parent still abroad preferred English to their parents' native tongue (55 percent). Nonetheless, mother-tongue attachment is still feebler among those whose kinship network has been entirely consolidated in the United States: respondents without kinship ties abroad were more likely to prefer English (72 percent); among those with relatives abroad but with both parents in the United States, 62 percent preferred English.

Though pertaining to the strictly social dimension of everyday life, language preferences and the boundaries that they denote nonetheless bear the trace of civic stratification. When we include a measure of citizenship in the pooled (IIMMLA and ISGMNY) regression (results not shown), the respondents born in the United States are much more likely to prefer English than those born abroad, but no difference in English-language preference separates the foreign-born but naturalized respondents from their foreign-born peers who never obtained U.S. citizenship. Using the IIMMLA allows us to look more finely at the impact of prior and current exclusion of citizenship on language preference, separating early from later naturalizers. After controlling for group- and individual-level factors, those Angelenos born in the United States were much more likely to prefer English than those who naturalized, whether as adults or as children; moreover, those who naturalized as children were significantly more likely to prefer English than those who naturalized after the age of twenty or not at all.

Thus, while we find a good deal of variation in the retention of mother-tongue competency and preferences for English, the overall pattern is a shift toward the dominant tongue. Even if some degree of mother-tongue competency remains, language change can be the mechanism by which the relationship between parents and children is overlain with the social boundary of native versus foreign. After all, parents and children do not always communicate with ease, but the discomfort is unquestionably heightened if they do not share the same vocabulary, cannot express their thoughts or feelings in language that the other can readily understand, or

Table 9.2 Generational Language Knowledge and Types of Acculturation

Parental English Proficiency	Child's Foreign-Language Ability		
	Score Less than 2	Score 2 to 3.5	Score More than 3.5
One or more parents speaks no English	Dissonant 0.6%	Partially dissonant 5.5%	Selective 6.2%
One or more parents speaks some English or does not speak English well	Partially dissonant 5.9%	Partially consonant 30.7%	Selective 22.4%
Both parents speak English well	Consonant 7.3%	Consonant 11.3%	Selective 7.4%
Missing language information			Selective 2.9%

Source: IIMMLA and ISGMNY data sets.
Note: Children's language score is the sum of answers to questions about speaking, understanding, reading, and writing English.

find that the simple act of communication has become a burden. Hence, we now move to the analysis of acculturation patterns.

UNDERSTANDING ACCULTURATION OUTCOMES

As originally conceptualized, the Portes-Rumbaut threefold acculturation typology—distinguishing among consonant, selective, and dissonant types of acculturation—served to identify a moderator of reception context, important for its hypothesized effect on socioeconomic attainment. Here, however, we ask a different question: namely, how do our second-generation New Yorkers and Angelenos fall out among these acculturation types, and why?

We begin by sorting our respondents according to the definitions of acculturation type that appear in *Legacies*. Table 9.2 is a two-way table that cross-tabulates parental English capacity by the second-generation child's foreign-language capacity and is designed to "present the theoretical relationship between language ability and types of acculturation across generations."[19] The rows present three different parental language abilities as reported at the time of the surveys: at least one parent with no English-language ability; at least one parent with some or only a little

Table 9.3 Distribution of Acculturation Types

Dissonant	0.58%
Partially dissonant	11.37
Partially consonant	30.66
Consonant	18.60
Selective	38.79

Source: IIMMLA and ISGMNY data sets.

English ability; and finally, families where both parents speak English well. Even in young adulthood, a sizable minority of the sample (12 percent) reported a parent with no English ability. The columns present respondents' mother-tongue language competency, broken down into three categories. These categories, in turn, come from the questions about language competency in the four domains of speaking, understanding, reading, and writing. Table 9.2 shows that over 80 percent of respondents possessed at least some competence in their parents' native tongue, and 39 percent reported a high level of proficiency, having answered "very well" to questions about language competence on at least three of the four domains queried.

Notwithstanding the emphasis that Portes and Rumbaut place on extreme cases in which parent-child communication completely breaks down because neither can understand the other, dissonant acculturation is an extremely rare occurrence: of the 4,628 cases of children of immigrants from non-English-speaking countries, exactly 27, or 0.6 percent, fell into the dissonant acculturation cell. The pattern we find among our Angelenos and New Yorkers actually holds for the immigrant offspring analyzed in *Legacies:* calculating an identical cross-tabulation to table 9.2 using the Children of Immigrants Longitudinal Study data, on which *Legacies* is based, similarly reveals that only 4 percent of all respondents lack foreign-language ability and have at least one parent with no proficiency in English.

Dissonant acculturation affects only a very few families, but partially dissonant acculturation—both parent and child lacking true fluency in each other's primary language—is more common; 11 percent of the second-generation sample fell into this category (table 9.3). Still, the great majority (88 percent) of the IIMMLA and ISGMNY respondents did not display the linguistic grounds for intergenerational conflict and role reversal—the ingredients, according to Portes and Rumbaut, of reduced self-esteem, poor school performance, and possible slippage into delinquency. Roughly 20 percent of the sample fell into the consonant acculturation category,

Figure 9.7 Acculturation Type by Generation

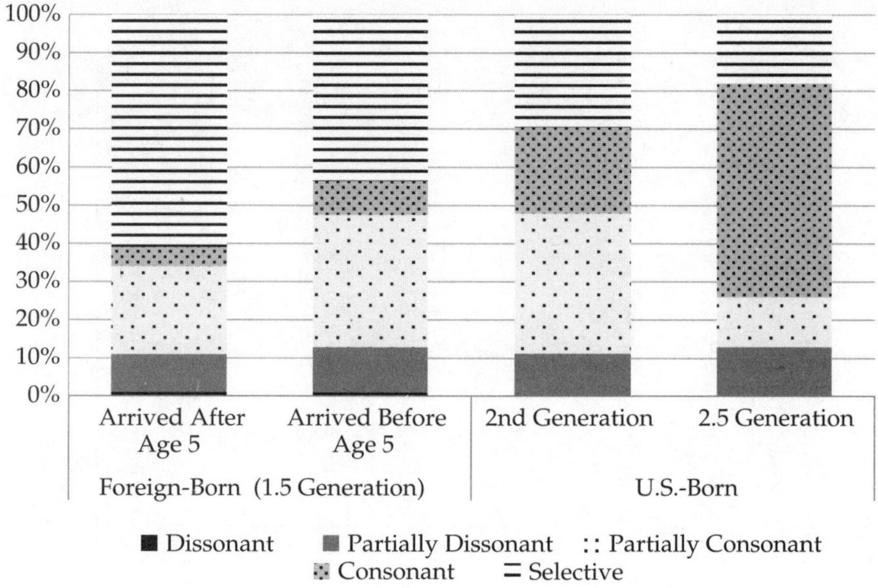

[Stacked bar chart showing acculturation types (Dissonant, Partially Dissonant, Partially Consonant, Consonant, Selective) across four generation categories: Arrived After Age 5 and Arrived Before Age 5 (Foreign-Born, 1.5 Generation), and 2nd Generation and 2.5 Generation (U.S.-Born).]

■ Dissonant   ■ Partially Dissonant   :: Partially Consonant
※ Consonant   = Selective

Source: IIMMLA and ISGMNY data sets.

a fairly high percentage given that respondents from English-speaking countries were excluded. Another 30 percent of the sample fell into the partial consonant acculturation cells; the remaining 39 percent were practicing selective acculturation: both parent and child maintained fluency in a foreign language.

But what accounts for the distribution of respondents among the different acculturation types? Figures 9.7 and 9.8 show key predictions for the distribution of acculturation types from our multivariate model. As shown in figure 9.7, a powerful association links the standard assimilation variable of generation to the sorting of immigrant offspring among acculturation types. Among our first-generation respondents—defined here as persons who arrived in the United States after the age of five—selective acculturation prevailed: net of other controls, 61 percent of those who moved in later childhood retained native-tongue fluency. By contrast, among respondents with one U.S.-born parent—the 2.5 generation—the great majority (56 percent) fell into the consonant acculturation category, with only 18 percent retaining fluency in the language of their foreign-born

Figure 9.8 Difference in Predicted Probability of Acculturation Type by Remittance Behavior of Parents, Parental Education, and Group-Level Variables

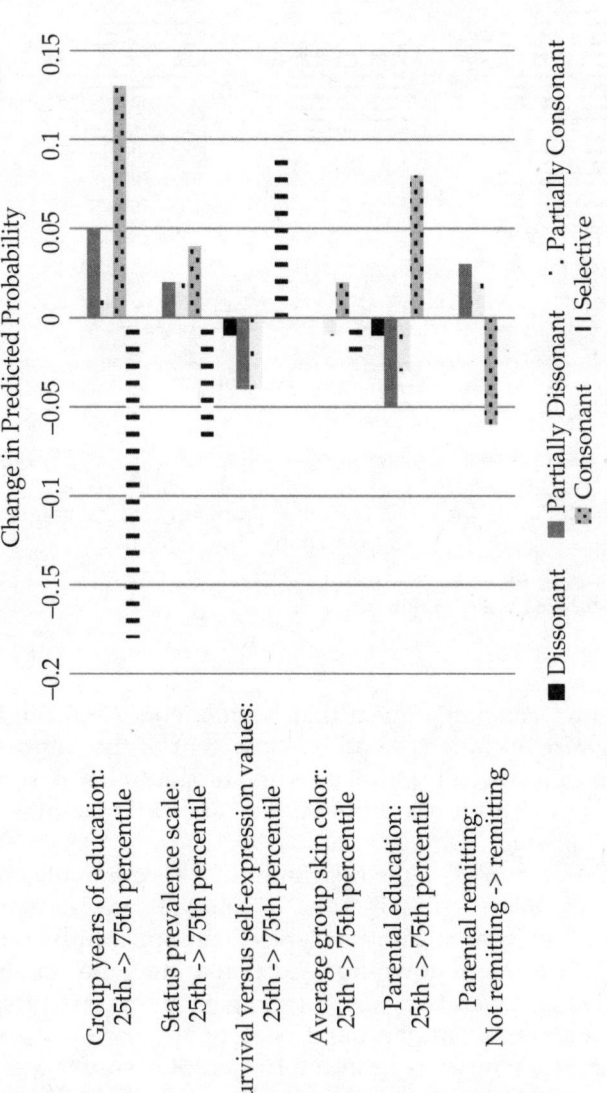

Source: IIMMLA and ISGMNY data sets.

parent. Turning to figure 9.8, we see that higher levels of parental education had a modestly positive association with consonant acculturation, whereas the association with parental remitting proved negative.

If at the individual level, we find a weak link between differences in resources, on the one hand, and acculturation type, on the other, a different pattern emerges when we look at the impact of group-level variables. As we have seen, native-tongue fluency proves more likely to persist when average ethnic capital is low. Net of controls, a member of an immigrant group with a lower average level of education (the twenty-fifth percentile, or nine years) was eighteen percentage points more likely to practice selective acculturation than a member of a group with a high average level of education (thirteen years). Similarly, respondents were more likely to retain mother-tongue competence when the policy context was negative, with the result that, net of controls, those immigrant families from countries with a negative policy context were seven percentage points more likely to practice selective acculturation than those from a more positive policy context. Put somewhat differently, parents and children were most likely to jointly retain the capacity to communicate in the mother tongue when the context of immigration was unfavorable—thus exactly contradicting the predictions set forth in *Legacies*. Turning to the context of emigration, we see that, further contrary to expectations, those with origins in more self-expression-oriented societies were more likely to grow up in families that practiced selective acculturation strategies.

The hypothesis of segmented assimilation casts acculturation as a moderating variable: resulting from a complex set of interdependent choices, acculturation type can speed up assimilation or slow it down. However, parental options are also conditioned by resources available in the coethnic community: a stronger coethnic community—understood as one in which group-level resources rank high—should enable families to decelerate the pace of acculturation. These community-wide resources should be most important when they offset the threats to familial-level solidarity generated by socioeconomic disadvantage. To assess this possibility, we examine how the relationship between parental education and acculturation types varies with differences in coethnic community structures, testing the impact of an interaction between parental education and group-level averages in education on acculturation patterns.

These interactions were collectively significant at the 1 percent level, meaning that parental schooling and group-level education do not affect acculturation type independently of one another; rather, the effect of one depends on the value of the other. Figure 9.9 illustrates this interaction, showing the probability of both consonant and selective acculturation as a function of parental and group levels of education. The y axis reports the

Figure 9.9 Predicted Probability of Selective and Consonant Acculturation by Parental and Group-Level Education

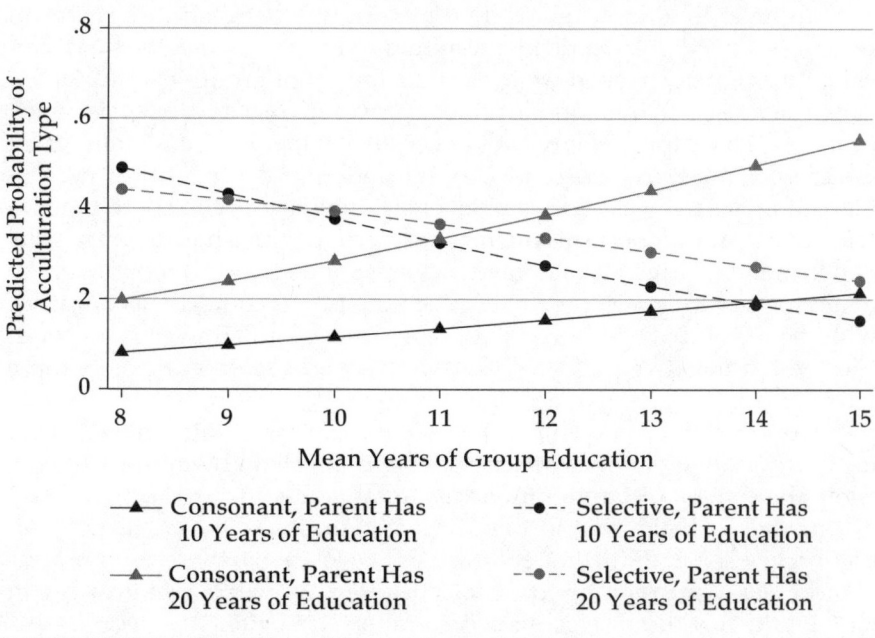

—▲— Consonant, Parent Has 10 Years of Education
--●-- Selective, Parent Has 10 Years of Education
—▲— Consonant, Parent Has 20 Years of Education
--●-- Selective, Parent Has 20 Years of Education

Source: IIMMLA and ISGMNY data sets.

predicted probability of the two acculturation types at varying levels of parental education (represented here as those with parental education of ten and twenty years) and levels of group education (the *x* axis).

The two solid lines represent the probability of consonant acculturation, and the dashed lines refer to the probability of selective acculturation; black lines display the pattern for a respondent with a parent with ten years of education and the grey lines for a respondent with a parent with twenty years of education. The black lines start off relatively close together at the bottom left corner and rise with increasing group-level resources. They do so, however, at different rates. While consonant acculturation became more frequent as group-level education rose, it did so much more among the best-educated parents in these groups.

Highly educated parents were more likely to pursue consonant acculturation in all groups, and they were twice as likely to practice consonant acculturation in the least-educated groups (20 percent versus 10 percent). The gap grows dramatically, however, in more-educated *groups,* both in relative and absolute terms. In the most highly educated groups, highly educated parents were almost three times as likely to practice consonant acculturation (58 percent versus 20 percent).

Overall, the propensity for selective acculturation (dashed lines) decreases with increasing group-level education. Given group-level education, the differences by parental education are relatively small. At low levels of group education, respondents whose parents had little schooling were somewhat more likely to grow up in households characterized by selective acculturation. By contrast, in groups with high levels of education, that pattern was somewhat more likely to be found in households where parents had high levels of schooling.

The hypothesis of segmented assimilation suggests that the families headed by low-skilled immigrants will be best able to slow down acculturation where group resources are higher. Yet the patterns found among these second-generation New Yorkers and Angelenos point in the exact opposite direction: it was precisely among these most-at-risk families that selective acculturation was most common.

CONCLUSION

The trajectories followed by the second generation profiled in this book show evidence of both continuity with parental patterns as well as rupture. The parents traversed territorial boundaries only to discover that their lives in the new foreign place often unfolded behind invisible social boundaries connecting them to people of like background and separating them from immigrant others who were somehow distinct. Ironically, those social boundaries delineating one population from another are a by-product of the migration process itself, as immigrants tend to look to one another to solve the everyday problems associated with movement to a strange place and then settlement. In turn, immigrants take up residence in towns, cities, and neighborhoods where prior migrants from home have already settled; as immigrant densities grow, so too do the commercial, religious, political, and sports institutions that serve them, providing the newest arrivals with yet further sources of attraction.

While building their own small worlds, the immigrants who move to global cities like New York or Los Angeles encounter people from across the planet who have undergone a similar experience of displacement and strangeness. Because immigrants are quantitative as well as sociological minorities, they cannot live in communities that are completely self-enclosed. Consequently, they end up sharing neighborhoods and workplaces with persons of varying ethnic backgrounds, and these overlaps often lead to closer connections. Moreover, the need to adapt to the exigencies of life in a new place compels the newcomers to learn how to manage that environment and make the most of it; the lessons they learn make them more likely, in turn, to have contact and interaction with insiders. If and when those lessons also yield increased rewards, the need for coethnic help declines, loosening ties to others of the same background.

The process takes accelerated form among immigrants' children, for whom language is rarely an obstacle to interaction with others: they rapidly pick up English when it is not already learned in the household, are plunged into schools where English is the language of instruction, and find themselves absorbed by a dizzying array of English-language media. Growing up in an environment where patterns of cultural consumption at once reflect homegrown diversity while simultaneously absorbing influences from around the globe, immigrant offspring find the divides between them and others shrinking, abetted by the cultural distance from their foreign-born and foreign-raised parents that so many experience.

Consequently, the particular ethnic boundaries that may have separated the first generation—whether from other ethnic outsiders or from native-born ethnic insiders—lose salience; those boundaries grow blurry, and their crossing becomes ever more common and ever less worthy of note. Thus, the contemporary second generation follows in the footsteps of their predecessors from the last age of mass migration: they abandon their parents' mother tongue for the lingua franca of the society in which they have grown up. Even when they remain competent in the mother tongue, these adult immigrant offspring often prefer English. Although many still categorize themselves in national-origin terms, the majority do not; as labels shift away from a connection to the country of origin, the importance with which these labels are invested also shrinks. Moreover, earlier boundary crossing and blurring in the parental generation facilitates more of the same, leading to changes that go even further among the second generation. Thus, adults who grew up in families where a foreign language was used but English was dominant have weaker command of their parents' mother tongue and show a clear preference for English. Likewise, those respondents raised by parents of differing national origins—marriages that are by-products of the out-group contacts arising in an environment where immigrants are both sociological and quantitative minorities—are more likely to prefer panethnic over national-origin labels. And when travel along the life course leads children to cross the social boundary of the parental household and set up on their own, independence is associated with a greater preference for English—even among respondents who remain bilingual and who were raised in households where the mother tongue prevailed.

Nonetheless, the standard assimilation approach does not accurately capture the trajectory of change, as the story emerging from this chapter tells a tale, not of the decline of ethnic distinction as such, but rather of the decline of one type of distinction and its replacement by another. Although the boundaries that mattered to the parental generation do seem to diminish, boundedness does not necessarily disappear. Rather, immigrant offspring find themselves in a world where origins still retain significance, albeit configured in ways that are shaped by the circumstances and history of the country their parents decided to join. Indeed, "made in America" was an essential ingredient of the labels that the second-generation Angelenos offered up on their own. To be sure, only a minority of immigrant offspring understood themselves to be Americans, presented as an ethnic descriptor requiring no modification. However, nothing is more American than a panethnic label, which makes friends out of persons who might have seen each other as enemies had their parents never left home. On the other hand, contrary to the claims of the transnational literature, the small-scale identities so relevant to many immigrant parents seem to have slipped off their children's radar screens, as *none* of the almost 3,200 respondents who provided an ethnic label categorized themselves by reference to some subnational place in the homeland, whether hometown, region, or state. (Though one respondent did answer, "Californian"!)

We also find that the possibility of an impending dissonant acculturation—immigrant children finding themselves cut off from their roots yet bereft of the competencies they need to make a place in the world in which they have grown up—lacks any substance: for all practical purposes, *almost none* of the 5,000 or so New Yorkers and Angelenos whom we studied grew up in households where parents and children could not understand one another because the parents spoke no English and the children had no command of the parents' tongue. More modest language gaps did affect a small minority: 11 percent of the immigrant offspring whom we studied fit the definition of partially dissonant acculturation. But while the great majority of immigrant parents and their adult children could communicate, their communication took different forms: some households were characterized by consonant acculturation—with both parents and children shifting to English—and others by selective acculturation—with parents possibly commanding English or not, but children retaining competence in their parents' tongue. That discrepancy highlights a further weakness of the standard assimilation approach: it fails to shed light on the broad spectrum of second-generation variation that we repeatedly find, with some immigrant offspring very much still connected to their parents' origins and others much less so.

The topics explored in this chapter relate to the more intimate dimensions of our subjects' lives, including the languages they commanded and preferred and the categories they used to distinguish themselves from others around them. Not surprisingly, then, significant intergroup differences were few; unlike the other aspects of the second-generation experience examined in previous chapters, with the exception of ethnic capital, contextual factors exercised limited influence on ethnic affiliations and language choices.

Rather than *intergroup* differences linked to a specific place of origin, *intragroup* differences involving attributes located at the proximate individual or household level provided the more important international influences. Ties that spanned *international* boundaries typically constrained the crossing of the *within-country* social boundaries on which this chapter has focused. Thus, compared to immigrant offspring with kin networks that had relocated to the United States, those with relatives abroad had higher levels of mother-tongue competency and were less likely to prefer speaking English. Holding cross-border ties constant, we see that homeland-oriented activities can also matter: adult immigrant offspring who, as children, visited the homeland for six months or more preferred the mother tongue over English. Likewise, the internal boundaries associated with formal differences in citizenship and legal status affect the potential for the crossing of social boundaries, which are purely informal. All of our respondents could be considered de facto Americans. Nonetheless, the foreign-born were more likely to prefer a national-origin label and less likely to prefer an American or hyphenated label; even so, the noncitizens stood out from their naturalized counterparts for their distinctively stronger endorsement of a national-origin label. Though for the most part the parents of our respondents were longtime residents of the United States at the time of the survey, we find a lingering negative effect of the parents' legal status on the propensity to prefer an American or hyphenated label. Hence, this chapter demonstrates the value of a different way of seeing: by looking across borders, the perspective we have developed in this book demonstrates how the distinctively international features of population movements across state boundaries influence second-generation experiences in ways that extend beyond careers or politics and reach into the private dimensions of their lives.

Part IV | Conclusion

Chapter 10 | Conclusion: The Making of the Second Generation

WHETHER IN CLASSICAL or updated form, assimilation theory presents a perspective appropriate to the short, albeit terrible, twentieth century, when the nation-states of what we now call the developed world largely kept the rest of the world at bay. At the time, society and state seemed to naturally converge, which is why it was reasonable to think that the process of assimilation could be uniquely driven by the mix of costs and benefits found within the country of destination, with the dynamics internal to that country determining the pace and direction of change.

But now that the social has burst through the societal, that perspective provides a far less accurate guide. In today's age of mass migration, the people crossing borders actively shape their own destinies, doing what neither home nor host state wants, improving their lives through movement and making effective use of the resource that they almost all possess—one another. Yet even the help of kin and friends and the support structure found in migrant communities cannot make displacement to a strange, new world any less difficult and arduous, which is why it is best undertaken by those ready to run risks and to then struggle to make it under adverse circumstances. For that reason, it is often the young who migrate, typically leaving home as adults but doing so at that stage in the life course when they are either bearing or bringing up young children. Consequently, the arrival of immigrants—some of whom do not yet know whether they will stay or return—yields a second, even more fateful result: the emergence of the "second generation," a population made up of the children of foreign-born parents, both those born in the United States and those born abroad but brought here at a very young age.

This book seeks to provide a new way of understanding the sociology of the second generation by breaking with the conventional perspective, which focuses only on the trajectories of the second generation as they unfold in the destination country, and instead bringing both *origins* and *destinations* into view. In so doing, we have sought to highlight the persistent influences stemming from the distinctively international nature of migration across borders. This perspective brings into focus the doubly international nature of migration as both movement across nations, understood as meaningful social units, and movement across states, understood as territorial units. Immigrant offspring are raised "here" by parents who grew up "there"; though they certainly do not remain the same people they were at the moment of departure, those parents can never fully free themselves from the grip of the values and orientations implanted in them in childhood. Hence, the *context of emigration* creates an origin-society legacy that is transmitted from parents raised abroad to children raised in the United States. Moreover, as the U.S.-bound migration streams have diversified, so too have the sources of cultural influences from abroad.

For migrants, movement from the developing to the developed world is transformative: the environment encountered in the societies of immigration extends far beyond its pocketbook effects, as the immigrants and their children benefit from the investment in public goods and the societal security and political stability that undergird economic growth in the countries on which the newcomers converge. Although migration can benefit the many, in reality it works to the advantage of a relatively small number, thanks to the migration controls that developed countries use to keep the rest of the world at bay. Those controls cannot keep everyone out; indeed, they are not designed to do so, but rather to sort and select the desirable few from the unwanted many. But since the popular preference for reducing migration stands in tension with the people flows produced by a globalized economy, the persons who move through the system of migration control are sifted in ways that stratify the foreign-born population by legal status. Ranging from the most favorable (admission as a refugee) to the least advantageous (crossing the border without authorization), legal statuses vary in prevalence from one origin group to another. The incidence of more protected or more vulnerable statuses affects societal perception, the overall level of resources on which coethnics can draw if and when they turn to one another for support, and the facility and speed with which full membership can be obtained. Thus, regardless of individual attributes, the *contexts of emigration* and the *contexts of immigration*—both reflecting the distinctively international aspects of population movements across state borders—have long-lasting effects on the experiences of the foreign-born as well as their descendants, producing interethnic differences.

Yet, as we have emphasized throughout this book, diversity in second-generation experiences does not simply fall out along the lines of national origin; rather, trajectories vary among immigrant offspring whose parents stem from the very same place. These intraethnic differences arise from a variety of bases; in seeking to develop a perspective sensitive to the distinctively international nature of population flows across borders, we have spotlighted two sources: cross-border connections and civic stratification.

Cross-border connections are common among international migrants; as we have shown, four in five second-generation youth have family members still abroad. However, those connections are not fully ubiquitous, as family reunification is more desirable or feasible for some rather than others; nor are cross-border links uniformly resistant to the tie-eroding pressures associated with settlement. Hence, disparities in the extent, intensity, and type of cross-border connections constitute an important source of second-generation difference—in this case, not so much between different immigrant-origin populations as within them.

Thus, the geographical range of the immigrant families building new lives in the destination country varies greatly. Yet at the outset, all immigrants—both parents and their foreign-born but U.S.-raised children—share one common connection, namely, their legal status. *Every* would-be new American begins as a foreigner standing outside the circle of citizenship and the full package of rights and entitlements that citizenship status confers. That circle can be penetrated, but access is inherently restricted. Consequently, the process leading to full membership takes fundamentally different form than the trajectory traced by conventional theories of assimilation, which explain how an initially strange environment becomes utterly familiar and strange people from a strange place eventually come to think of themselves, and to be treated, as natives. Moreover, in entering the country of immigration, the new arrivals find themselves in a conceptual space between the territorial border and the invisible but no less real border of citizenship; that is the space where immigrant offspring are sorted by a system of *civic stratification*, either directly if foreign-born or indirectly, via their parents, if U.S.-born. These individual-level disparities in status—both those encountered at the moment of entry and those that evolve over time—shape second-generation trajectories, producing variation among people who originated in the same place and hence were socialized by parents who probably shared common value orientations at the time of departure from home.

ASSESSING THE INTERNATIONAL PERSPECTIVE

In introducing this new approach, we acknowledge our debt to the researchers who have come before us and the lessons to be found in the scholarship that they have bequeathed us. Building on the knowledge from this vast relevant literature, this book seeks to incorporate the insights gained from existing approaches into a new framework that treats both group-level and individual-level sources of differences and does so while attending to the distinctively international features of cross-border migration.

Throughout this book, we have been in dialogue with the authors and the influential books that have preceded us; table 10.1 provides a summary of the approaches developed in these books, the key concepts they contribute, and the level (within or across groups) at which they operate. In the next sections, we ask whether, in advancing a new perspective, we have now shed new light on the second-generation experience and, if so, what might be the distinctive lessons learned from our book.

Contextual Variables and Intergroup Variation

Contexts of Emigration: Value Orientations   In the standard approaches, the people opting for life in a new land appear only as immigrants, yet those same persons are also emigrants, and collectively they bear the traces of their origins in an ever-growing myriad of countries, each with its own specific features and distinctive historical trajectories. This theoretical blind spot—no attention to the ways in which the place of origin leaves its imprint on immigrant parents—leaves the field wide open for ad-hoc "culturalist" explanations. In pop-sociology, such accounts take the form of simple cultural essentialism—hailing the purportedly superior traits of a seemingly successful group or ascribing a pattern of less achievement to supposedly inferior cultural traits. To be sure, the literature does furnish more sophisticated perspectives, such as those that posit an "immigrant advantage" associated with norms about family structure imported from abroad, or those that reframe the issue around cultural toolkits.[1] Yet these formulations have yet to be systematically applied to a wide range of immigrant groups, across a diverse range of outcomes.

We offer an alternative: a thoroughgoing account of origin effects on a wide variety of second-generation outcomes, using standardized information on a large number of sending countries supplied by the World Values Survey. The two dimensions identified by researchers working with the World Values Survey—the survival versus self-expression axis and the traditional versus secular-rational axis—do not represent hermetically sealed, categorically distinctive cultures but rather *value orientations*. Cross-nationally, these orientations vary along a gradient ranging from more to less, and it is difficult to precisely determine where one shades into another; they also differ among the people residing in any one state, though the variation across countries typically exceeds the variation within them.

Table 10.1 Summary of Key Theoretical Approaches and Their Empirical Treatment in This Book

Theoretical Approach	Level of Variation	Concept	Measures Used in This Book
International perspective	Between groups		
	Context of emigration	Home-country cultural background	WVS value orientation measures: survival versus self-expression and traditional versus secular-rational
	Context of immigration	Migration status disparities	Status prevalence scale
		Ethnic capital	Average group years of education
		Skin color stratification	Average group skin color
	Individual and within groups	Civic stratification	Legal status at arrival; time to citizenship
		Cross-border connection	Remitting, home-country travel, relatives abroad, language use when growing up
Neo-assimilation	Within-group: individual	Acculturation	Parental English ability, immigrant generation
		Parental assimilation	Mixed parentage
			Parental education, education received in the United States
Minority mobility model	Between groups	Hyperselectivity	Parental quintiles of education
		Ethnic group resources	Supplementary education

(Table continues on p. 266.)

Table 10.1 Continued

Theoretical Approach	Level of Variation	Concept	Measures Used in This Book
Second-generation advantage	Between groups	Urban institutions Ethnic cohesion	High school quality; use of urban amenities WVS value orientation measures: survival versus self-expression and traditional versus secular-rational
Membership exclusion	Within-group: individual	Legal status	Parents' and respondent's status at arrival; respondent's current citizenship status
Segmented assimilation	Between groups Modes of incorporation	Socioeconomically advantaged coethnic community Governmental reception Societal reception	Average group years of education Status prevalence scale Average group skin color
	Individual and within-group differences	Family relations	Parental mother-tongue use; two-parent family; parents of same national origin; acculturation type

These orientations also combine in distinctive ways, such that a secular-rational orientation may accompany a survival orientation in one place, but not necessarily in another.

Just as importantly, the value orientations identified by the WVS are not fixed in stone but rather are products of specific historical, social, and economic circumstances and, as such, are inherently susceptible to change. Hence, the position in the two-dimensional WVS space along which immigrants from any one country fall out is a legacy effect. Although influencing the behavior of immigrant parents socialized in an environment different from the one in which they opted to reside, the origin-country value orientations that immigrant parents transmit to their children in no way preclude adaptation to the very different orientations found in the United States (and other developed, immigrant-receiving states).

Our analysis of educational attainment amply demonstrates the gains to be made from our approach. We show that immigrant offspring originating in countries where the population more strongly espouses "scholarly" values achieve higher levels of schooling and are more likely to attend better-performing high schools than the children of immigrants from more traditionally oriented societies; moreover, that relationship holds true even when we hold constant the parental and group levels of educational attainment. We also demonstrate that although secular-rational values matter for education, they exert only a minimal direct impact on occupational attainment. Instead, the children of immigrants from countries where secular-rational orientations tend to prevail enjoy superior returns to their own investments in education compared to their peers from more traditionally oriented sending societies. Moreover, although survival versus self-expression values are not significantly associated with educational attainment, we show that the children of immigrants from more cohesive groups similarly gain better returns on educational investments.

These findings lend support to the often implicit, and never before systematically tested, expectations that parental sending countries will exercise a lasting cultural influence on the economic lives of the children of immigrants. These impacts stem from experiences shared by immigrant parents who departed from a common point of origin; in turn, the lessons imported from abroad yield interethnic differences among immigrant offspring. However, when we zoom in on ethnic strategies that individual immigrant parents might deploy, we generally fail to find evidence indicating that a specifically "ethnic" toolkit creates second-generation success. For instance, though many immigrant offspring grew up in households where the parents' mother tongue was used—an experience that in turn fostered widespread adult mother-tongue competence—this distinctively ethnic practice proved unrelated to occupational or educational attainment. Unlike mother-tongue use, commonly found among immigrant households, only a small minority of the second-generation New Yorkers and Angelenos we studied attended after-school cram or language programs that might be considered part of an ethnic toolkit. However, when immigrant parents did use strategies such as language schools, most of the affected respondents did not experience any positive effects. Rather, ethnically specific language schools only helped a very small group: the children of less-educated parents who came from traditionally oriented societies.

Thus, we find that the imported home-country culture matters, albeit at a group level, not an individual level. Moreover, the home-country culture yields effects in ways that vary across different domains of life. When we evaluate second-generation "success" as indexed by socioeconomic outcomes, we find that origins in societies characterized by a secular-rational orientation directly and positively influence educational attainment and also increase the return to respondents' own schooling. However, when we examine another important form of "integration," namely, political participation, we find that, contrary to the commonsense anticipation that immigration will always swell the ranks of the Democratic Party, the children of immigrants from societies with more traditional values are more likely to lean Republican. By contrast, the greater cohesion found in more survival-oriented societies proves positively associated with educational attainment, but not at statistically significant levels. However, this cohesion does translate well in the U.S. labor market, helping second-generation youth find jobs more commensurate with their training. Likewise, the cohesion imported from the homeland facilitates naturalization, yielding higher rates of citizenship density among immigrant families and accelerating the pace at which 1.5-generation respondents naturalize.

Context of Immigration: Migration Status Disparities   For the neo-assimilation approach, the immigrant search for the good life can prove successful because the advent of antidiscrimination policies *within* U.S. boundaries systematically diminished racial and ethnic barriers to achievement, producing the virtuous circle between adaptation and reward that eventually leads to assimilation. Whatever the validity of this claim, it suffers from the blinders produced by focusing internally and ignoring the cross-border dimension. A world of nation-states inherently produces policies of migration control that discriminate *by design*, favoring citizens over aliens, and some aliens over others. In turn, migration control policies yield inter-country differences in the prevalence of different migration statuses; based on objective indicators, our status prevalence measure identifies populations on a continuum ranging from the most advantaged—those among whom refugee status was most prevalent—to the most disadvantaged—those among whom unauthorized status was most prevalent.

Whereas one of our measures of the context of emigration—a secular-rational orientation in the origin country—had a direct, positive effect on educational attainment, our measure of the context of immigration, the status prevalence scale, had no such impact. Nor did the context of immigration alter the ways in which parents' education affected the levels of schooling attained by their children. Yet differences in status prevalence did yield a significant effect on the relationship between respondents' own education and the occupations they attained: when more-advantaged statuses prevailed, the schooling acquired by second-generation New Yorkers and Angelenos had a more positive impact on their occupational status. Thus, our research confirms qualitative evidence on life-course variability in the impact of legal status. The children of immigrants from groups with a high prevalence of undocumented members are first shielded from illegality's adverse effects in childhood, but then experience an attainment-limiting shadow effect after they enter the labor market.[2]

We expected that differences in status prevalence would affect the acquisition of citizenship, if only because the greater density of persons arriving with more-advantageous status would make a greater fraction eligible to apply for citizenship once the five-year residency requirement was passed. And indeed, this is precisely what we found. After controlling for respondent's place of birth and parents' length of residence in the United States (as well as other individual-level covariates), citizenship family densities were higher for nationalities among which more-advantaged statuses prevailed. Similarly, the individual-level analysis, which included individual-level controls for status at the time of entry, found that a more favorable status prevalence score accelerated the pace of naturalization.

However, some of the associations we anticipated with status prevalence did not materialize. Differences in status prevalence seemed unrelated to the exercise of citizenship, and a higher percentage of undocumented statuses at the group level was associated with *higher*, rather than lower, levels of cross-border visits, though both phenomena were strongly and positively associated with individual-level variations in citizenship and legal status. Nonetheless, when we looked at some of the private aspects of our respondents' lives, most notably language, the reach of the disparities generated by policies of migration control could clearly be seen. Consonant acculturation was more common and selective acculturation less so when respondents belonged to a group that scored high on the status prevalence scale.

Context of Immigration: Group-Level Education and Average Skin Color   The hypothesis of segmented assimilation emphasizes the impact of disparities in the structure of coethnic communities and societal reactions on intergroup disparities. Both variables, however, are vaguely described; moreover, neither is clearly operationalized, and the levels measuring differences in these variables—for example, working-class coethnic communities versus entrepreneurial-professional ones—are assigned to national-origins groups on an ad-hoc basis. In addition, the possibility that societal reaction is negative toward all "nonwhite" groups provides little leverage when only a small and diminishing fraction of immigrants and immigrant offspring have origins in Europe and Canada. In this book, we have introduced the concept of "ethnic capital," as measured by the average level of education in a national-origin group, to capture the ways in which resources can be mobilized via the coethnic community. To assess the ways in which colorism affects a group's susceptibility to discrimination, we have invoked the concept of "skin-color stratification," which we have operationalized as group-level average skin color (on a scale ranging from 1.4 to 7.4 among the groups in our sample).

Ethnic Capital: Group-Level Average Education   The importance of ethnic capital—operationalized as group-level average education—reappears consistently throughout the book. Thus, net of other variables, second-generation educational attainment is higher in groups among whom higher average levels of education in the parental generation prevail; likewise, group-level average education interacts with parental levels of schooling in ways that lead to jobs of higher status. In the New York sample, the group level of education also increased the probability that immigrant offspring would be enrolled in high schools of higher quality. However, contrary to the minority mobility model developed in *The Asian American Achievement Paradox*, which emphasizes the advantages generated by hyperselectivity, immigrant offspring originating in the most highly educated nationalities displayed no distinctive lead. Instead, we found evidence only for the effects of *hyposelection:* New Yorkers and Angelenos from groups with the lowest levels of education did significantly worse than all others.

But if higher levels of average group education positively affected attainment, it broadly depressed civic and political participation. Respondents from groups that were more highly educated in the parental generation were less likely to belong to organizations and less likely to attend protests or civic and political meetings. Of course, the same variable that *directly* exercised these negative effects on civic and political engagement *indirectly* generated positive effects, as higher levels of average group education had a positive impact on respondent's own education, which in turn significantly enhanced political and civic participation.

By contrast, this measure of group resources appears to have more limited influence on the maintenance or pursuit of cross-border connections. We found only an indirect influence, via respondent's own education, though even here it was modest in both size and range: visits home, participation in home country–oriented organizations, and interest in home-country politics were the only outcomes amplified by higher levels of schooling. Maintaining cross-border connections is a resource-consuming endeavor, which is why the positive channel from group levels of education—whether via the direct or indirect route—is no surprise. But since resources are also likely to facilitate out-group exposures, the channel to ethnic attachments is likely to be negative, just as we find. Consonant acculturation was substantially more likely, and selective acculturation substantially less so, when group levels of education were higher; this variable also had a negative effect on levels of mother-tongue proficiency.

Skin-Color Stratification: Average Group-Level Skin Color   As a visible trait, phenotype simplifies the cognitive processes required for discrimination of a type that is patterned and recurrent but also implemented informally, thus differing from the formal differences in legal status resulting from the process of civic stratification. The pervasive, negative bias toward darker-skinned persons may increase susceptibility to unfair treatment and thereby produce skin-color stratification. As a cline, phenotype varies in continuous fashion along a range from lighter to darker, with Russians and Ukrainians at the fifth percentile in darkness, Chinese at the twenty-fifth percentile, Filipinos at the median, Mexicans at the seventy-fifth percentile, and Trinidadians at the ninety-fifth percentile. Thus, our measure of average group skin color captures real differences across the full range of second-generation national-origin groups, which is otherwise obscured by the white-nonwhite divide. Consequently, it also better reflects the more nuanced categorical schemes maintained by the dominant group— as indicated by the responses of non-Hispanic whites to a 2000 General Social Survey (GSS) question concerning which ethnic groups made "little positive contribution" to the United States: this characterization was chosen by 2 percent for the English, by 12.5 percent for Chinese, by 23.5 percent for Mexicans, by 33 percent for Vietnamese, and by 40 percent for Cubans.

Nonetheless, this group-level variable, as measured by average skin color, had only modest impacts, with no direct effect on educational attainment, occupational attainment, cross-border connections, or any of the outcomes related to ethnic attachments. However, net of other variables, darker-skinned New Yorkers were less likely to enroll in the highest-quality high schools; in the pooled sample, moreover, skin color interacted with respondents' own education in a way that lowered occupational status for respondents with higher levels of schooling but darker-colored skin. (However, the coefficient was significant only at the 10 percent level.)

By contrast, group-level skin color affected neither the acquisition of citizenship nor its exercise in aspects related to civic and political participation. Though not influencing partisan identity overall, group-level skin color did prove significantly related to the political party choice made by those immigrant offspring New Yorkers and Angelinos who were U.S. citizens and reported having registered to vote. As chapter 7 showed, net of other variables, there appears to be a clear skin-color gradient, with Democratic loyalties among the politically active growing as skin color darkens. Indeed, respondents with origins in Trinidad, Jamaica, and elsewhere in the Anglophone Caribbean had the strongest Democratic loyalties of all, with the Trinidadians still more strongly Democratic than their third-generation-plus African American counterparts.

We note that these findings pertain only to the impact of group-level differences in skin color, not to differences that may be associated with phenotypical variation at the individual level. Unfortunately, the New York survey collected no data on self-reported phenotype, and while the IIMMLA contained such a question, it was asked only of those Los Angeles respondents who identified as Latino or Hispanic in the screener.

Individual- and Household-Level Variables and Intragroup Variation

Theory provides a way of seeing . . . and of *not* seeing. The standpoint adopted by the prevailing approaches—both neo-assimilation and segmented assimilation—metaphorically places the analyst with her back to the border, uniquely focusing on trajectories undergone in the receiving country and the influences that flow solely from there. Yet as we have repeatedly emphasized, international migration inherently involves the internationalization of families; moreover, the process of crossing territorial state boundaries differs from the crossing of social borders by transforming sending-country nationals into receiving-country aliens. These two unique features of international migration require that any comprehensive account of second-generation difference consider variation in cross-border influences as well as the location of immigrants and their descendants in the receiving country's system of civic stratification.

Cross-Border Connections   In this book, cross-border connections appear as independent *and* dependent variables. Throughout these pages, we have hypothesized that internationalized family relationships and parental homeland-oriented activities undertaken when respondents were children yield direct effects on a host of outcomes, among them, the cross-border connections that immigrant offspring maintain as adults. As chapter 5 demonstrated, separation from a parent who remained in the home country strongly depresses educational attainment. Further in-depth analysis of the Los Angeles respondents showed that the children of parents who remitted while they were children had higher levels of schooling than their counterparts whose parents did not repatriate any of their earnings. The finding is counterintuitive, as we would expect the sending of remittances to deplete the parental resources available for investment in education. Yet remitting may be important not simply for its material impact but for what it signals about the nature of the household willing to sacrifice to help relatives abroad. As chapter 7 shows, among the Angelenos, those whose parents earlier sent home remittances reported *higher* levels on all of the aspects of civic and political participation analyzed in that chapter. In chapter 8, where cross-border connections function as both independent and dependent variables, we saw that parental remitting strongly influences remitting among children. Chapter 9 tells us that this same parental activity undertaken during respondents' childhood reduced their preference for English when adults. That all these results occur net of other variables, *including* the presence of parents and relatives abroad, strongly reinforces the possibility that parental remitting conveys a powerful moral message that is absorbed by immigrant offspring.

As chapter 8 notes, internationalized families represent the modal family form: though comparable data are lacking for the New Yorkers, the great majority of Angelenos—80 percent—had relatives still living in the home country at the time of the survey; even among those with only one foreign-born parent, the majority still possessed a kinship connection across borders. As that chapter shows, the cross-border engagements pursued by these second-generation Angelenos proved highly responsive to differences in the location of the kinship network, which exercised statistically significant effects on all the indicators on which this chapter focuses. But the motivation to keep up those ties emanates not simply from the obligations related to family structure; parents' own agency, whether related to remitting, visiting, or mother-tongue use, matters as well.

Although cross-border connections thus deeply affect intragroup differences across a broad range of outcomes, we also note the general trend toward reorienting activities and concerns to the country of reception. Home-country ties may be more widely found and persistent than conventional approaches previously suggested; nonetheless, these immigrant offspring, in detaching from the place of origin, are continuing a process already begun by their parents.

Civic Stratification   As with cross-border connections, civic stratification functions as both an independent and dependent variable. Chapter 5, analyzing the pooled sample, shows that noncitizens—a sub-category of the immigrant offspring born abroad but raised in the United States from childhood—attain lower levels of schooling and occupations of lesser status than their U.S. citizen counterparts, net of other variables, including the *group-level* legal-status prevalence. Given the nature of the data—the New York sample lacks the detailed information that the IIMMLA provides on respondents' and parents' legal status at the time of entry—these relationships cannot be considered causal, but rather amount to an association. Focusing on the Los Angeles sample, we see that neither respondents' nor parents' upon-arrival legal status altered the impact of citizenship status on educational attainment. Rather, for the foreign-born but U.S.-raised, the channel connecting upon-arrival status to educational and occupational attainment would seem to pass through the point at which citizenship is obtained. Migration control policies influence that outcome, as those who arrive on a temporary visa or without authorization experience a far longer trajectory to citizenship than their counterparts who possessed a green card when crossing the U.S. border. Those effects, moreover, hold net of contextual variables, most notably status prevalence, which at the group level diminishes time to naturalization for members of those nationalities with more favorable immigration statuses.

Not surprisingly, factors affecting access to citizenship influence its exercise, as demonstrated in chapter 7. As a liberal society, the United States offers opportunities for civic as well as political participation to anyone resident on U.S. soil, citizenship or legal status notwithstanding. Nevertheless, net of other variables (including the usual assimilation variables related to generation or language ability), the experience of prior or current exclusion from the polity impeded engagement in public-oriented activities for which citizenship was no prerequisite, including messages sent to political representatives, attendance at rallies or meetings, and taking part in any form of protest. Moreover, the evidence suggests that both the late naturalizers and the noncitizens were only tenuously connected to the civic fabric, as they were less likely than their citizen peers to participate in any civic activity or belong to any civic organization and also less likely to have been contacted by someone else to support a candidate or political party.

Civic stratification affects the cross-border engagements pursued by immigrant offspring in a somewhat different way, though we do note that issues of data adequacy largely limit this analysis to the Los Angeles respondents. Like writing to a public official or attending a meeting, anyone—whether citizen, green-card-holder, or unauthorized immigrant—can send remittances, take an interest in homeland matters, or belong to a homeland organization. Indeed, neither at-entry status nor prior or current experience of exclusion from the polity had any impact on the degree to which immigrant offspring took an interest in homeland matters, nor on their participation in homeland-oriented organizations. But, net of other variables, persons who arrived without authorization or on temporary visas, as well as the late naturalizers, were significantly more likely than others to frequently send remittances—a pattern that may point to the impact of migration control policies, not so much on the immigrant offspring themselves as on their close relatives still stranded in the society of origin. However, reflecting the fact that the aim of migration control policies is to discriminate between noncitizens and citizens—who can exit and enter the United States at will and live outside the country for however long they desire—the noncitizen Angelenos were the least likely to engage in homeland visiting, notwithstanding the fact that almost all of them had a relative still living in the country of origin.

The long reach of citizenship status can be perceived in the analysis of ethnic identity and attachments as well. In the pooled sample, noncitizens were significantly less likely than their U.S. citizen counterparts to prefer English—again, net of other variables. In the Los Angeles sample, a preference for English proved significantly higher among the U.S.-born than among the early or late naturalizers. The analysis of identity preferences among the Angelenos uncovered a similar pattern: noncitizens and late naturalizers were less likely than their U.S.-born counterparts to self-categorize as American, of either the hyphenated or unhyphenated sort; noncitizen respondents were also particularly more likely than the U.S.-born to prefer a national-origin identity. Despite these controls for respondents' status as of the time of the survey, those whose parents had arrived without a green card were significantly less likely than U.S. citizens to identify as hyphenated or unhyphenated Americans.

FINAL REFLECTIONS

In reaching the end of this book, the reader has gained a comprehensive review of how origins and destinations, both features of the distinctively international nature of population movements across boundaries, shape the sociology of the second generation. Like any good story, the one told in these pages can travel widely, conveying a meaning that extends beyond the place where it unfolded and the time when it transpired. Strangeness is an abiding feature of the migrant experience, as wherever they go and whenever they arrive, migrants encounter a strange environment and are treated as strangers and so must learn and adapt to the new context and change in ways they rarely anticipated at the moment of departure. Connectedness to people and places left behind is also a recurrent phenomenon: migration is always selective, and hence cross-border movements of people inherently produce cross-border family relations. Those cross-border connections are not mere products of the particular country on which this book has focused, the United States, but reappear among migrants and migrant families throughout the world. Thus, immigrant parents bequeath a mixed legacy to their children, imparting lessons learned after migration while also transmitting orientations absorbed well before they took off for life in a new land. These home-society connections—both in the cultural orientations bestowed by parents born in one country on their progeny brought up in another and in immigrant families stretched across territorial boundaries—can be thought of as immigration universals that influence, albeit in different ways and to differing degrees, immigrant offspring now and then, here and elsewhere.

Looking across geographies, the concepts and measures we have chosen to employ in this book can be used to export the international perspective to other migration systems. Civic stratification is a global issue, and one that the current refugee crisis has made particularly relevant in the Middle East and western Europe. While the United States may have one of the largest undocumented populations among rich receiving countries, the phenomenon is in no way unique to the American context, as evidenced by large-scale amnesties in the previous decade in Italy (2002) and Spain (2005) and the current climbing estimates of illegal border crossings and visa overstaying in Germany, the United Kingdom, France, and Italy. Just as in the United States, the undocumented immigrants who have migrated to Europe have children who may have been born in either Europe or the country of emigration but will be raised in Europe. Unlike in the United States, birthright citizenship is not universal throughout Europe, a fact that creates interesting scope for international comparison. The measures of undocumented prevalence and civic stratification on which we have relied in this book are becoming increasingly replicable across other contexts. One example would be the United Kingdom's Labor Force Survey, which asks the foreign-born for their original visa status at arrival. Similarly, the concept of context of emigration and the multilevel modeling framework we use have already been fruitfully applied in cross-national comparative work using standardized data sets that cover many western European destinations. This research has generally sought to test multiple indicators of sending-country context, including measures of political freedom, GDP per capita, and average educational attainment, as it seeks to understand the influence of these factors on outcomes such as the educational performance of the children of immigrants. Many of the European studies, however, have struggled to find comprehensive, cross-nationally validated measures of sending-country culture and have relied instead on summary measures such as majority religion. We believe that the World Values Survey summary measures of traditional versus secular-rational scores and survival versus self-expression scores that we use here could be very usefully exported into the European context, allowing for transatlantic as well as cross-European comparison. The recent emergence of new-immigrant oversamples of the second generation across multiple European contexts—for instance, the Children of Immigrants Longitudinal Survey in Four European Countries (CILS4EU) project—presents new opportunities to assess the relative importance of sending-country value orientations across different migration systems.[3] Such an evaluation will be particularly important in the western European receiving context, where issues of cultural and religious boundaries are more politicized and generate greater interethnic strife than in the United States.

Now looking across time instead of across geographies, we note that in the United States cross-border ties and home-society influences are recurrent aspects of the immigrant phenomenon, but that in this country we do not see other distinctively international features of systems of migration control—themselves the ever-evolving products of specific historical circumstances. As we pointed out earlier, the defining features of the U.S. citizenship regime—most notably, the relatively short residence period required of foreign-born residents and the granting of citizenship to all those born on U.S. soil—emerged from the very different reality of the late eighteenth century. The new republic required people who could conquer and maintain the lands seized from the continent's indigenous inhabitants, but who could also quickly come to see and understand themselves as members of a new nation. That process of nation-building immediately generated a backlash against the newcomers, which steadily intensified as the migrations from Europe brought populations that were increasingly different from the founding group. Yet the continuing need for people to populate expanding territories, combined with the hunger for workers driven by rapid industrialization, impeded the imposition of the migration controls for which some segments of the population called. While immigrants from China were met with exclusion as early as the 1880s, and immigrants from Japan encountered similar barriers roughly thirty years later, migration in the transatlantic sphere remained largely open until the early 1920s. At that point, the doors along the coastlines were closed, though migration from elsewhere in the Western Hemisphere escaped full control. In the process, access to citizenship also narrowed. Naturalization was barred to all immigrants from Asia; immigrants from Europe could still transition to U.S. citizenship, but starting in the early twentieth century, they were compelled to leap over significantly higher obstacles than those previously in place.

Thus, the second-generation people studied in the pages of this book differ in one profound way from their predecessors of the last age of mass migration: the immigrants of the current age of mass migration, as well as their offspring, are the products of a world of migration policies designed to control population flows across state boundaries. A common set of goals shapes those policies throughout the developed world: to discourage most potential emigrants from ever leaving home; to sift the wanted newcomers from those seen as undesirable; to expel those unwanted persons who somehow manage to slip through gates and cross over walls; and to determine the entitlements allowed to those foreigners who proceed onto national soil, including the right of eventually gaining membership in the people. That world of migration policy and control is responsible not only for the migration status disparities shared by immigrant offspring with origins in different places around the world, but also for the civic stratification that yields differences among people originating in the very same place.

And yet, while the introduction of border controls separates the children of this immigrant wave from all those who came before, in one critical aspect the children of immigrants we study here are also differentiated from those who came after them: namely, they and their parents were mainly already in residence in the United States when Congress passed the Immigration Reform and Control Act in 1986. Enactment of IRCA allowed unauthorized immigrants present as of 1982 to quickly transition to legal permanent residence, facilitated reunification with spouses and children living abroad, and provided all who legalized with eligibility for citizenship five years later. Pressure from immigrant rights advocates combined with poorly written legislation and feeble implementation led to more expansive legalization than Congress had initially anticipated. Thus, the parents of the Mexican-origin respondents surveyed by the IIMMLA arrived during a period of lax internal and border enforcement, encountered a labor market that exacted relatively modest penalties for unauthorized status, and then enjoyed the opportunity to exit from that status when their children were still relatively young. Indeed, among the Mexican-origin Angelenos with at least one parent who had entered the United States without a green card, almost half of all the parents for whom we have data had acquired U.S. citizenship as of the time of the survey, and just under 10 percent had not yet transitioned to legal permanent residence status.

Acceptance of undocumented immigration reflects the interplay of domestic interests—employers seeking greater access to labor, citizens preferring greater restriction, and political leaders wanting to satisfy the former while appeasing the latter. Yet population movements across borders are fundamentally international in nature: conflicts between and within states put people into motion, fleeing across territorial borders in search of safe haven. U.S. strategic interests accommodated massive refugee inflows from Cuba starting in the 1960s and Southeast Asia in the late 1970s and 1980s and facilitated entry for Jews from the Soviet Union in the 1970s and then again in the 1990s after the fall of communism. The Vietnamese immigrant offspring surveyed in Los Angeles and the Russian Jews surveyed in New York arrived in the United States via those side doors, mainly entering with legal permanent resident status in hand, which in turn put citizenship within reach after five years, as chapter 6 demonstrated. During the late 1970s and 1980s, by contrast, the same strategic interests sealed the fate of the Guatemalans and Salvadorans, who suffered from the bad fortune of running from political regimes that the United States supported. Hence, while the parents of the Salvadoran and Guatemalan immigrant offspring surveyed by the IIMMLA found de facto safe harbor by crossing into U.S. territory, they mainly did so at the price of unauthorized status—a condition still reflected in low levels of naturalization among Central American–origin parents as well as those of their children born abroad but raised in the United States.

Thus, in the comparison between the second generations of a past more distant (the first half of the twentieth century) and one more recent (the latter decades of the twentieth century), the salient disparity concerns the change in migration control regimes. The former were the children of immigrants who had arrived in an era when border control had yet to regulate the transatlantic zone. Those immigrant parents all arrived as foreigners, but with no further legal distinctions that would privilege some and impede others; all were legally present, and hence all were equally eligible to take up citizenship once the five-year residence period had passed. The immigrant offspring studied in this book, by contrast, were the children of parents who arrived under a policy regime that channeled newcomers through various doors: a front door that provided entry and an ample portfolio of rights to persons with needed skills or with family ties to U.S. citizens or permanent residents; a back door that recurrently granted entry to wanted workers but handed them no residence rights and few other entitlements; and a side door that opened erratically to politically selected refugee populations, who in turn were granted extensive rights and resettlement assistance.

Consequently, the second generation on which this book focuses represents the first cohort of immigrant offspring to come of age during an era that is simultaneously one of migration and one of control of migration. That distinction marks the central divide between new and old second generations, and it represents a fundamental source of continuity with the second-generation cohort that has grown up in the years since the New Yorkers and Angelenos studied in this book entered adulthood.

Like their predecessors of a century ago, the members of this "new second generation" were raised by parents who were socialized in a foreign place and grew up belonging to families whose connections stretched across state boundaries. And unlike the second generation of a century ago but just like the immigrant children profiled in this book, today's immigrant offspring are the progeny of parents who were sorted by legal status from the moment of arrival, a stratification that in turn deeply influenced their potential for crossing the internal boundary of citizenship and becoming full members in the sense conveyed by that status.

And yet current circumstances are somewhat different. The past two decades have seen steadily intensifying migration control policies and a more broadly drawn line of civic stratification between the children of unauthorized migrants and their peers raised by parents who enjoy the benefits of authorized status. Driven by America's persistent desire for labor and facilitated by the support and financing provided by migrant relatives already settled in the United States, undocumented migration resumed in the 1990s, reaching new heights after the turn of the millennium before stabilizing at around 11 million in 2009. Yet a far harsher environment greeted this wave of undocumented immigrants, starting with stepped-up enforcement at the border that made unauthorized entry more difficult and costlier for those willing to take matters into their own hands.

In focusing enforcement on the border and simultaneously abandoning internal enforcement at workplaces, the United States implicitly opted for a policy that, far from constraining undocumented migration, actually facilitates it. U.S. employers have been accommodated, but the undocumented immigrants of the new millennium have paid an especially heavy price for residing in the United States without authorization. The rights and protections available to undocumented immigrants have undergone particular contraction. Moreover, the wall between undocumented immigrants and those who are candidates to become Americans has risen higher: persons who once crossed the border without authorization can no longer transition to permanent residency without first returning to their home country for an extended stay, a risk that few are willing to take. And paradoxically, the most notable expansion in social provision since the 1960s, passage of the Affordable Health Care Act of 2010, increased the disadvantages associated with undocumented status, as only the unauthorized were barred from the benefits of expanded government-supported health care.

The last amnesty for undocumented immigrants was approved three decades before the completion of this book in 2018, and so, for many immigrants, undocumented status has increasingly become an enduring trait. At more than 7 percent, the children of the undocumented comprise a sizable and growing fraction of the school population. Although most of these children are U.S.-born, and thus citizens, roughly one in four suffers from their parents' unauthorized status. As a growing body of research has shown, whether U.S. citizens or not, the children of undocumented parents pay a heavy price for the harsh turn in U.S. policy: higher levels of parental stress, diminished resources for parenting, lower levels of children's readiness for school, and disparities in cognitive development that have already shown up in these children by the time they are two years old.

These undocumented children are just one part of a larger population of undocumented immigrants who arrived as children and then continued on in that status into adulthood. There are 750,000 such adults currently enjoying a temporarily protected status under the program known as Deferred Action for Childhood Arrivals (DACA), which seems unlikely to long survive. Legalization for the broader undocumented population, having received significant congressional support twice in the years since the millennium, now seems indefinitely postponed. Any future such action is sure to be far less generous than IRCA: under the best-case scenario, some portion of today's undocumented population may gain a multiyear transition into some type of provisional work authorization, with no guaranteed track to citizenship.

More stringent enforcement at the border has been accompanied by sharply stepped-up rates of deportation. Interior deportations rose more than sixfold after 2003 before peaking at just over 180,000 in 2011. Though the pace slowed, dropping by half as of the end of 2016, deportations at this level aggravated the family separations that migrations normally produce. Thus, Mexico records a growing number of children who were born in the United States or previously lived in the United States and who are now enrolled in Mexican schools, a transition that has often proved difficult. For the U.S. citizens among these children whose parents may be unable to maintain residence in the United States, Mexico could be only a temporary resting place; they may plan to return north of the border when they reach adulthood, although their interrupted schooling and their lack of exposure to an American curriculum are likely to impede their successful adaptation to the U.S. labor market.

American refugee policy reached its most generous heights during the years when the Russian Jews and Vietnamese studied in this book entered the United States; since the millennium, however, we have witnessed a much less accepting phase. As in the 1980s, when violence in Central America reached a crescendo in the early to mid-2010s masses of people fled north, seeking safe haven in the United States, and also as in the 1980s, the American government generally refused the migrants' request for asylum. But unlike the 1980s, these very recent arrivals have been mostly women and children, moving on their own. Once on U.S. soil, these children—often traumatized by experiences both before leaving home and on the journey—have generally been transferred to family members, who themselves are often living in an uncertain legal status, trying to cope with a policy context that has grown increasingly harsh.

Assessing the future of this newest new second generation is an inherently risky enterprise. As of now, we can only speculate about where the trends we have described will lead and how the second-generation cohorts coming of age in the next decades of the twenty-first century will progress. Moreover, immigration policies are always in flux, as are the ways in which those policies are implemented. But as we write these lines thirteen months after the inauguration of Donald Trump, in the wake of an election fueled by anti-immigrant animosity and amid continuous controversy over immigration policies, we find ample reason for worry. As we have emphasized throughout this book, the inherently international and therefore political nature of population movements across borders deeply shapes the destinies of the generation that emerges after migration in the country of destination. Indeed, differences in legal status—whether at the group or individual level—recurrently affected the immigrant-origin New Yorkers and Angelenos whose trajectories have been traced in this book. Looking forward, it may be that the cohort we studied did indeed experience a second-generation advantage, but one of a strictly temporal nature, related to the opportune time of their parents' arrival in the United States and the relative warmth of their reception. The America we observe in writing these final lines seems much chillier and, for the children of unauthorized migrants, a good deal less promising: with concern for the next second generation, we uncertainly await troubled times.

Appendix

THIS APPENDIX GIVES some more background on the operationalization of our key concepts and gives some more information on the variables used throughout the book. Full results for all analyses can be found in an online appendix available at http://www.russellsage.org/publications/origins-and-destinations.

THE WORLD VALUE SCALES

As we argue in chapter 2, hypotheses regarding the impact of sending-country culture recurrently appear in the literature on the second generation but are rarely explicitly formulated. Indeed, they are often ad hoc, in that they identify one or more home-country attributes relevant to selected populations but do not abstract from the individual cases to specify variables that can be measured and applied across cases. In this book, by contrast, we have sought to explicitly assess effects of the context of emigration. Since immigrant parents choose to migrate but do not choose their country of origin, their childhood socialization exposes them to orientations different from those prevailing in the country of destination; these parents import those orientations and, in turn, transmit them to their children. Given the diversity of national origins among the second generation as well as the cultural differences among the many countries from which the IIMMLA and ISGMNY respondents originate, we anticipate that differences rooted in the place of origin will be a source of intergroup differences in the place of destination.

To test this assumption, we have relied on data from the World Values Survey, executed in six waves between 1981 and 2013 and covering nearly one hundred countries.[1] Although the WVS has often been used to assess home-country influences among the descendants of immigrants, introducing it into the American scholarship on the second generation represents an innovation. In this appendix, we seek to provide further detail on our use of the WVS and explain why it can be successfully used to trace the impact of origin cultures.

Background

Though origin-country effects have attracted little attention from American immigration scholars, researchers from a multiplicity of disciplines have sought to understand the ways in which those influences may affect a variety of outcomes. The proximate influence comes from the work of Robert Putnam, who argues in his study of the foundations of democracy in Italy that regional differences in the distribution of social capital are both significant and rooted in long-term historical conditions.[2] The interest in social capital triggered by Putnam in turn stimulated further work on the origins of trust, since access to social capital varies depending on others' trustworthiness and their perception of one's own trustworthiness. As almost every transaction involves an element of trust, especially when the exchange takes place between parties little known to one another or involving a long period of time, the cultural sources of trust have been of particular interest to economists. A number of studies have sought to ask whether differences in trust among a population can be traced back to differences in the point of origin. For example, Luigi Guiso, Paola Sapienza, and Luigi Zingales have shown that, as measured by the General Social Survey in the United States and the World Values Survey in other countries, Americans' level of trust in others is closely associated with the national origins of their ancestors.[3] Again using the GSS and the WVS, Yann Algan and Pierre Cahuc show that current-day trust in the country of origin is strongly correlated with trust among the corresponding current-day Americans.[4] Similar relationships characterize current-day trust and the political systems of ancestors' countries, with third-generation Americans likely to be more trusting if their ancestors came from countries with more democratic political institutions. Likewise, in Europe, levels of trust in the country of origin are strongly associated with immigrants' confidence in institutions in the country of destination.[5]

Thus, our effort to search for home-country influences builds on a well-established line of research by others who have been similarly interested in home-country effects and have also used data from the World Values Survey and related surveys, though mainly focusing on outcomes different from those of interest to us. In the remainder of this appendix, we provide further detail on our use of the WVS, addressing likely questions regarding its relevance and appropriateness for the issues at hand in this book.

Choice of Variables

Because we hypothesize that parents' common socialization in the place of origin affects the legacy that they transmit to their children, we sought measurements of home-country values that identify the orientations that immigrants are likely to have absorbed during their own childhoods. Globally, the traditional versus secular-rational axis is the by-product of industrialization, which leads to rising levels of schooling and rising standards of living but also rationalization: as the external environment increasingly falls under human control, belief in the power of God and religion declines. As pointed out in chapter 3, the traditional versus secular-rational axis is associated with the average level of educational attainment of a sending society, with more-educated societies espousing more secular values, as displayed in figure A.1. As also shown in figure A.1, the traditional versus secular-rational axis links even more strongly to "scholarly culture," as measured by the number of books in the parental household, which in turn is a marker that is independently associated with educational attainment even controlling for parental education levels and holding across countries at different levels of economic development, across time, and across children of different backgrounds.[6] The scale is also correlated with GDP in 1975 and the literacy rate of adults over the age of fifteen in 1990. Thus, we hypothesize a link between origins in societies characterized by secular-rational orientations—whether because they tend toward a scholarly culture conducive to the transmission of cognitive skills or value technological change and the underlying science and formal schooling that make it possible—and a variety of outcomes, including, most importantly, educational attainment.

In contrast, as shown in figure A.2, the associations between these variables and the survival versus self-expression dimension are much weaker. Rather, a society's tendency toward greater self-expression is a consequence of the shift from industry to services, as rigidly hierarchical, massive organizations requiring discipline give way to smaller, more flexible work units that, seeking to foster innovation, value autonomy and teamwork. Combined with affluence, which allows an increasingly large share of the population to take survival for granted, these changes shift priorities from economic and physical security to self-expression. Thus, as can be seen in figure A.3, the survival versus self-expression scales are linked to indicators of individual rights and self-expression, such the UN Gender Empowerment Index, the 2003 Human Development Index scores, and democratic functioning as measured by 2003 Polity scores. In contrast, the traditional versus secular-rational index score is only weakly correlated with these measures (see figure A.4), even though it closely maps onto

Figure A.1 Correlations of Traditional Versus Secular-Rational Values with GDP, Number of Books in the Household, Average Levels of Education, and Literacy

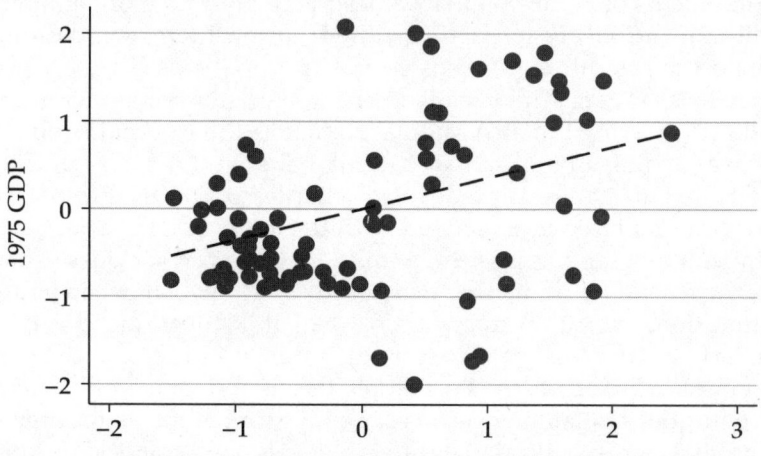

$r^2 = 0.126$

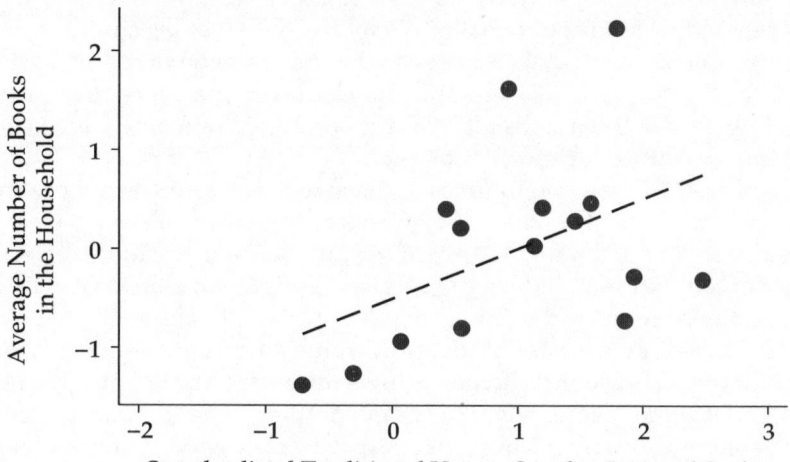

$r^2 = 0.206$

Figure A.1 Continued

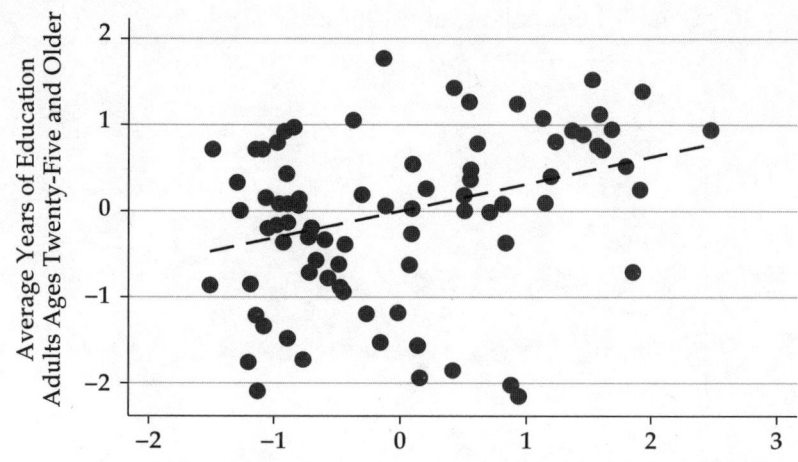

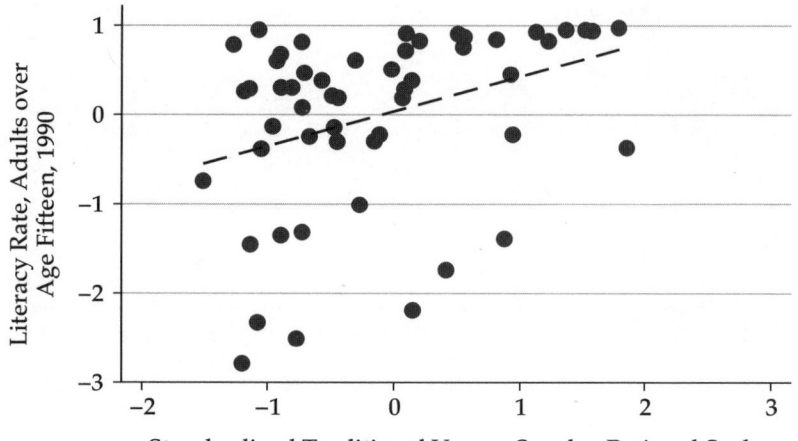

Source: Authors compiled from Barro and Lee 2013; Evans et al. 2010; Finke and Grim 2005.

Figure A.2 Correlations of Survival Versus Self-Expression Orientations with GDP, Number of Books in the Household, Average Levels of Education, and Literacy

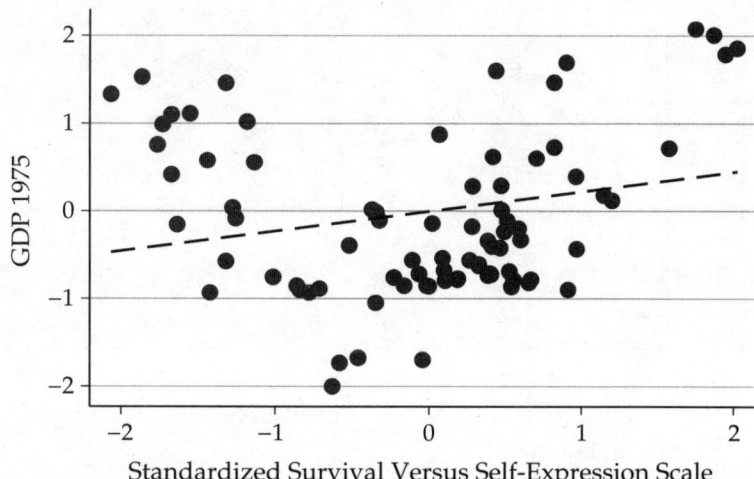

$r^2 = 0.05$

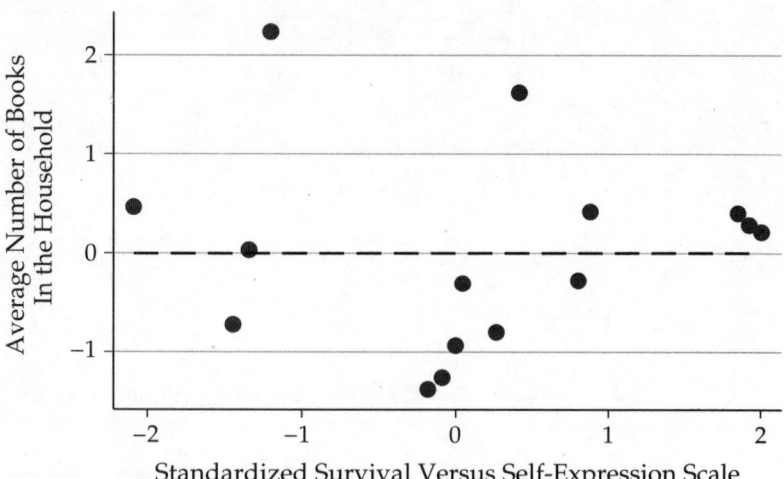

$r^2 = 0.00$

Figure A.2 *Continued*

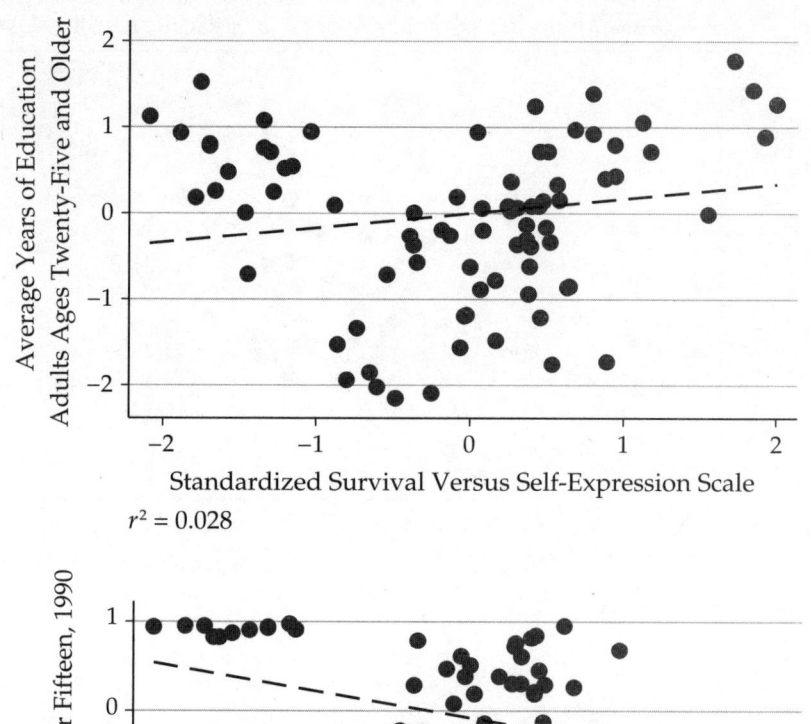

Source: Authors compiled from Barro and Lee 2013; Evans et al. 2010; Finke and Grim 2005.

Figure A.3 Correlations of Survival Versus Self-Expression Orientations with the UN Gender Empowerment Index, the Human Development Index, Polity Scores, and Contraceptive Use

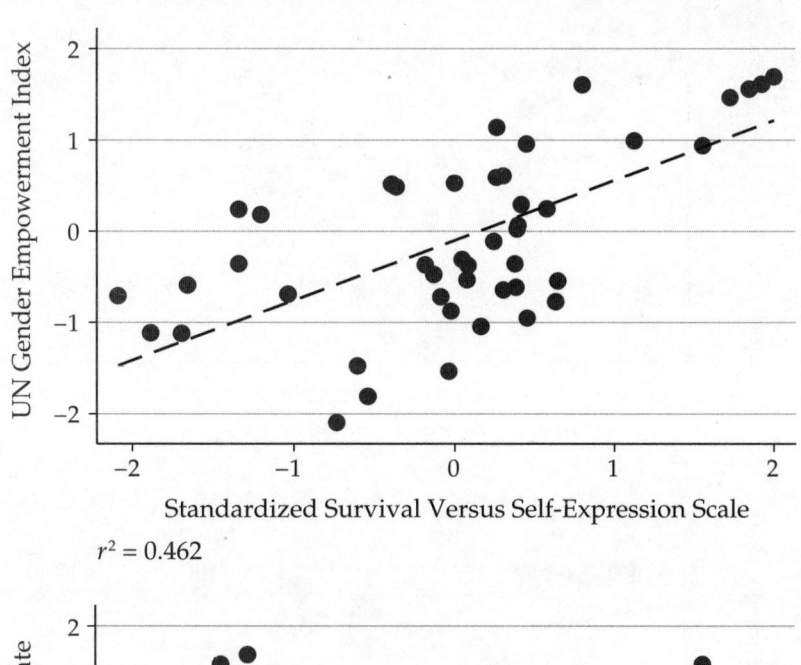

$r^2 = 0.462$

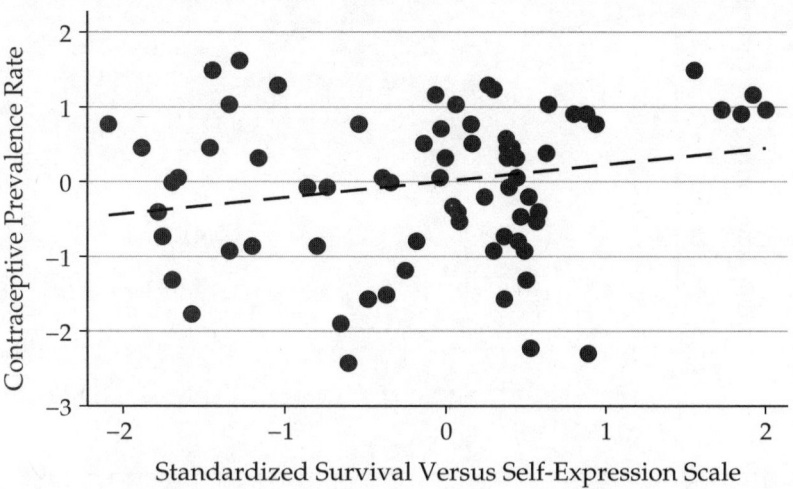

$r^2 = 0.046$

Figure A.3 Continued

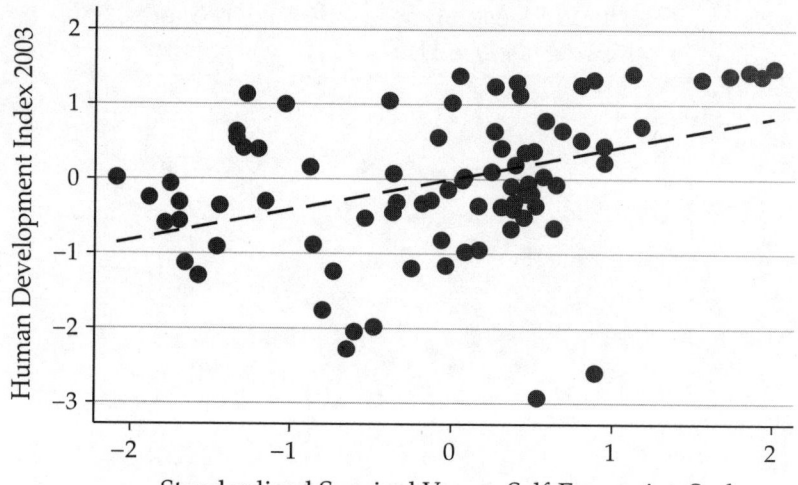

$r^2 = 0.168$

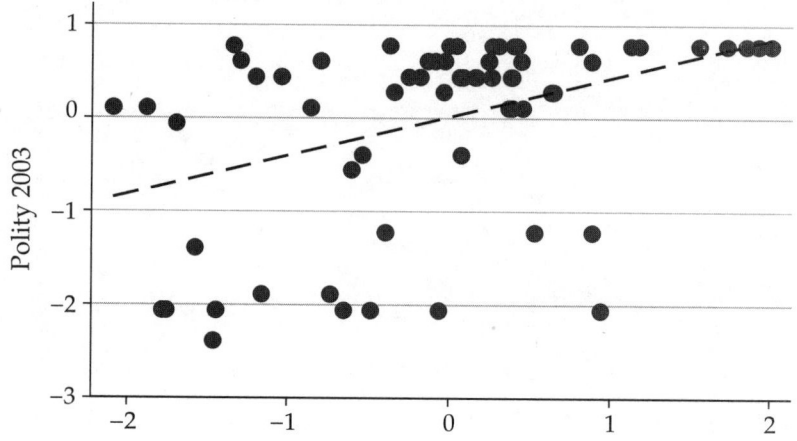

$r^2 = 0.185$

Source: Authors compiled from Finke and Grim 2005; Jaggers and Gurr 1996.

Figure A.4 Correlations of Traditional Versus Secular-Rational Value Orientations with the UN Gender Empowerment Index, the Human Development Index, Polity Scores, and Contraceptive Use

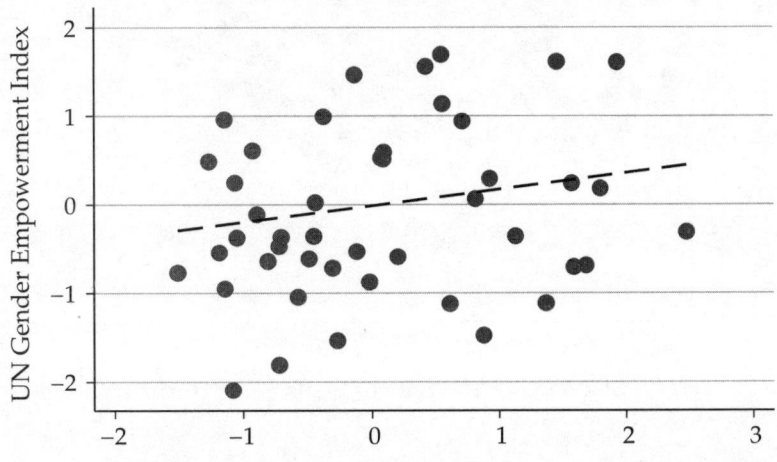

$r^2 = 0.212$

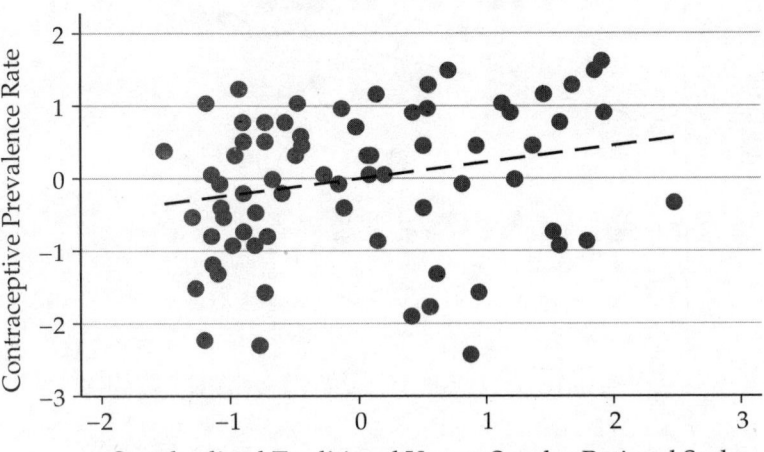

$r^2 = 0.068$

Figure A.4 Continued

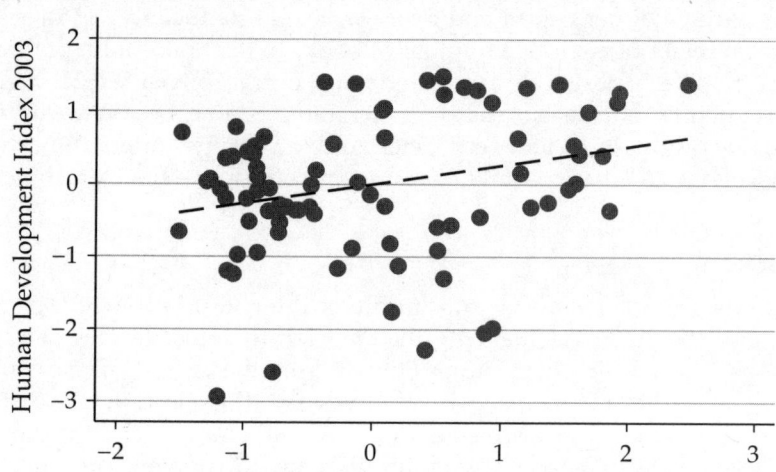

$r^2 = 0.067$

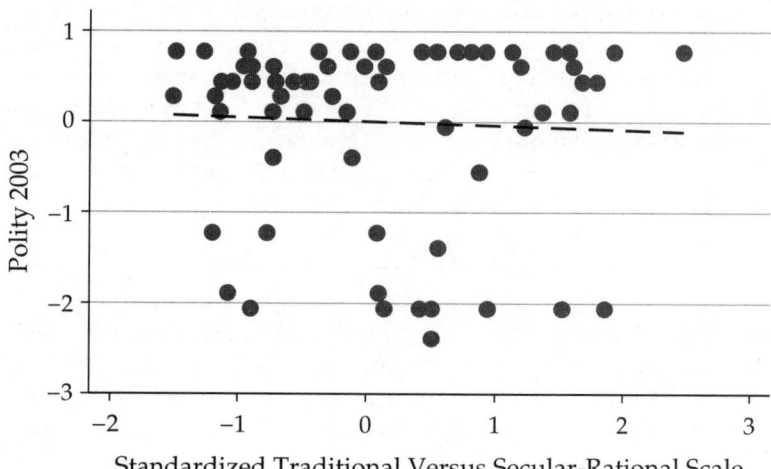

$r^2 = 0.02$

Source: Authors compiled from Finke and Grim 2005; Jaggers and Gurr 1996.

educational attainment, which is correlated with all of the above. Likewise, the survival versus self-expression scale is positively, but weakly, correlated with GDP per capita and average years of education. However, it bears no relationship to the number of books in the household. Both measures are weakly positively associated with contraceptive prevalence rates. Consequently, as a measure of the cultural sources of cohesion, we hypothesize that origins in societies characterized by a survival orientation will be associated with greater family cohesion and stronger ethnic attachment.

Selection

Migrants are not a random subsample of the country-of-origin population, and the factors influencing the decision to emigrate may select for persons whose value orientations deviate from the average in the country of origin. The key question, however, is whether the selection is so extreme that the origin-level measures no longer provide meaningful information or whether the WVS context-of-emigration measure is a meaningful proxy for premigration value orientations, some degree of selection notwithstanding. The fact that on many of our dependent variables we find both statistically significant and substantively meaningful effects is certainly one indication that our context-of-emigration measures do capture some relevant variation between national-origin groups.

Furthermore, a number of other studies working with the basic human values developed by Shalom Schwartz generally find that, for the migrant generation, the country-of-origin value orientation is predictive of migrants' position, though the magnitude of the country-of-origin imprint appears to decline with time in the host country.[7]

In our case, we cannot empirically address the degree to which immigrant parents reflect country-of-origin value orientations, as this would require individual-level data on the value scores of immigrant parents (ideally at their time of arrival in the United States). Only then could we see how the value distributions of immigrants in the United States compare to the distributions of the origin country. Unfortunately, such data are not available for immigrants in the United States. As mentioned in the main text, similar research from Europe suggests that immigrants generally inhabit a "middle ground" in the value orientations between sending and receiving countries.[8] That said, the data we do have allow us to calculate some benchmarks to assess the role that selection might play. For these tests, we use the individual-level scores on the two values dimensions provided in the WVS. We note here that, as shown by Inglehart and Baker, these individual-level scores are not on the same metric as the country-level scores.[9]

Figure A.5 Importance of God in One's Life by Country and Education Level

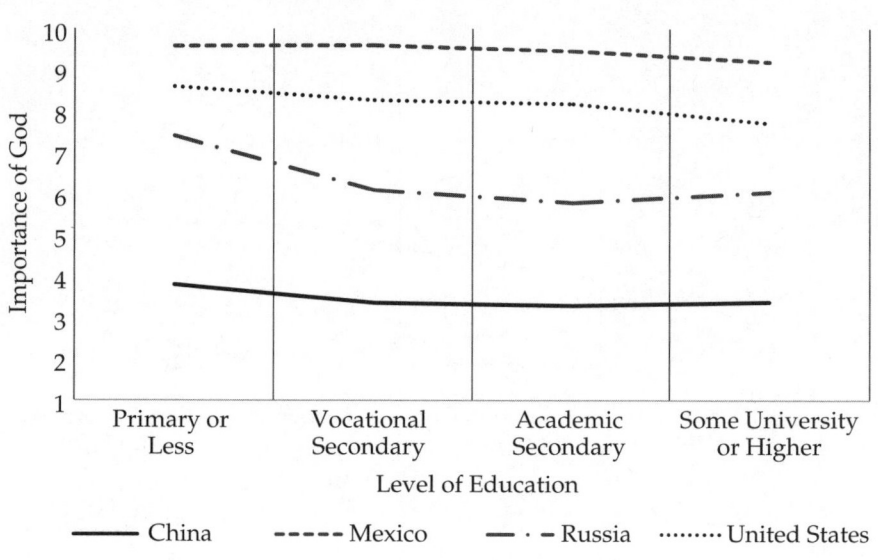

Source: WVS, wave 5.
Note: Scale goes from 1 to 10, with 1 being least important and 10 being most important. Adjusted for age.

Taking the combined individual-level file of the World Values Survey and partitioning the variation in these two value dimensions between individuals, countries, and survey years, we see that 40 percent of the overall variance on the traditional versus secular-rational scale is between countries, with most of the remainder falling on the individual (within-country) level and only a small fraction accounted for by survey year. For the survival versus self-expression scale, the between-country share is 30 percent—a bit smaller but still substantial.

Another way of looking at this question is to plot the within-country difference between WVS respondents with high and low levels of education; this comparison allows us to see, for instance, whether the more highly educated in a traditional country are more oriented toward self-expression than the low educated in a more secular-rational country. Given the strong correlation between education and values, this should give us a sense of the problem of selective migration with respect to values.

In figures A.5 and A.6, we plot one measure from each index across education levels for three main sending countries—China, Russia, and

Figure A.6 Acceptance of Homosexuality by Country and Education Level

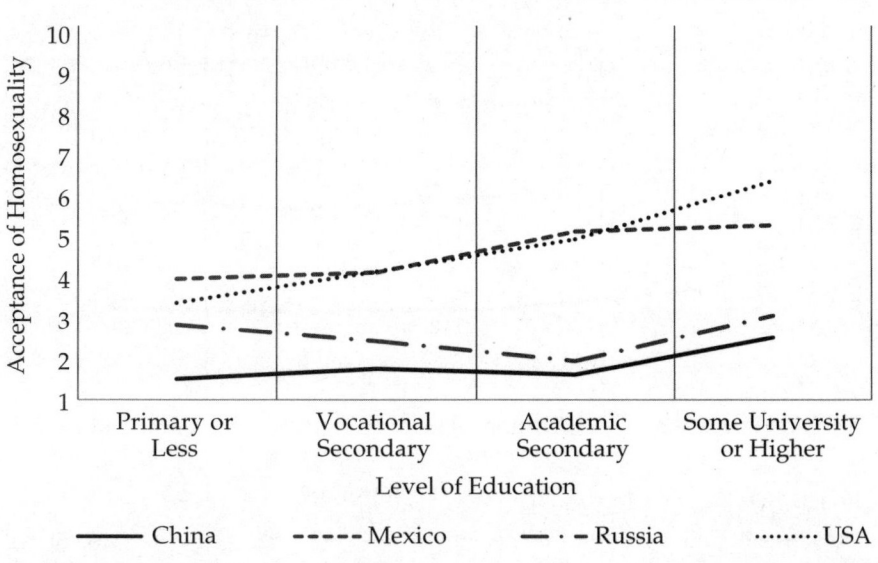

Source: WVS, wave 5.
Note: Scale goes from 1 to 10, with 1 being least accepting (homosexuality is never justifiable) and 10 being most tolerant. Adjusted for age.

Mexico: a measure of how important God is in one's life is a part of the traditional versus secular-rational index and acceptance of homosexuality is part of the survival versus self-expression dimension. Looking at figure A.5, we see that, in considering the importance of God in one's life by country and education, Mexico ranges highest on this measure, with China the lowest, across all education levels. There is no overlap whatsoever on this variable across any education level between China, Russia, and the United States. Although Mexico and the United States are closer, both being fairly traditional countries, even a U.S. resident with only a primary school education has a lower level of religiosity than a Mexican resident with a university degree.

Looking at acceptance of homosexuality (figure A.6), once again the United States and Mexico are closer, both being more self-expression-oriented countries, and this time there is little difference between the low-

and middle-educated groups. China and Russia also have very similar survival versus self-expression scores and so do not differ widely. However, it is clear that these two survival-oriented countries never overlap with the United States, not at any education level. To put it still another way, when looking at the traditional versus secular-rational value dimension, we see that only 12 percent of South Koreans are more traditional than the average American. Alternatively, we can compare two sending countries represented by respondents in our data sets: only 2 percent of the Koreans surveyed by the WVS were more traditional than the average Trinidadian respondent to the WVS.

Taken together, we think there is considerable evidence that the WVS scales do capture meaningful differences between countries of origin, that these differences are large enough to not be easily "erased" by migrant selection, and, most importantly, that our own results and those of other researchers strongly suggest that they do indeed matter for postmigration trajectories.

VALUE DIFFERENCES WITHIN THE UNITED STATES

Another concern would be that the native populations of New York City and Los Angeles are not at all reflective of the United States as a whole, especially considering that these cities have large immigrant populations.

The core of our argument about the exogenous effect of origin-country cultural orientations is that these orientations matter ipso facto and not in the first instance via creating social boundaries vis-à-vis natives. That said, the differences within the United States are probably not as enormous as we might think. Although the WVS data do not allow us to break out Los Angeles and New York, they do tell us about the size of the cities where respondents live. Figure A.7 shows the difference to the U.S. average in the two dimensions by size of city. The only unambiguous trend we can see is that those in small towns with less than 10,000 inhabitants are significantly more traditional and more oriented toward survival than the rest of the country. Small-town inhabitants account for just 18 percent of respondents in the United States.

Looking at the differences for cities with populations of 10,000 or more, the range is from about 0 (U.S. average) to 0.1 for the largest cities. In contrast, on the individual-level value scale the difference between China and Mexico on the traditional versus secular-rational dimension is eleven times as large (about 1.1).

Figure A.7 Difference from U.S. Average by Size of City for WVS Value Orientations

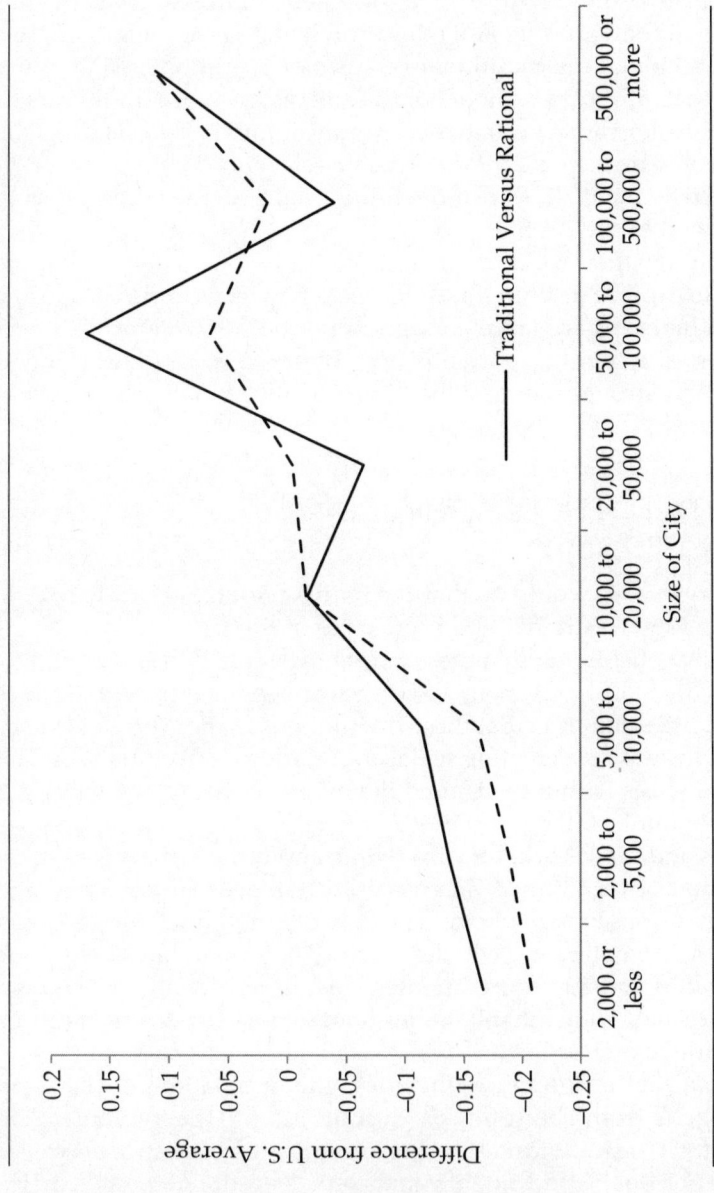

Source: WVS data set.

ITEMS USED TO CONSTRUCT VALUE SCALES

Traditional Versus Secular-Rational Values[10]

God is very important in respondent's life.

Respondent believes that it is more important for a child to learn obedience and religious faith than independence and determination.

Respondent believes that abortion is never justifiable.

Respondent has a strong sense of national pride.

Respondent favors more respect for authority.

Survival Versus Self-Expression Values

Respondent gives priority to economic and physical security over self-expression and quality of life (on the following four-item materialist versus postmaterialist values index):

Respondent describes self as not very happy.

Respondent believes that homosexuality is never justifiable.

Respondent has not signed and would not sign a petition.

Respondent believes that one has to be very careful about trusting people.

IMPUTATION ROUTINE FOR GROUP-LEVEL VARIABLES

We were able to obtain complete information on group-level legal status for all countries in the analysis. Information from the 1980 census on the mean level of education among the foreign-born in New York and Los Angeles was similarly available for most of the countries of origin; however, 11 percent of origins lacked a sufficient number of cases for stable estimates (N = 50). Skin color and the WVS index scores were missing for a larger proportion of origin countries: approximately one-third for the WVS scales (twenty-six of sixty-seven) and one-third for skin color scores (twenty-seven of sixty-seven). To preserve the full range of national-origin groups in our data, we use multiple imputation to fill in missing values. Using the imputation routines implemented in STATA Version 13, we create a set of fifteen imputed country-level measures that we then merge with the combined survey data.

All respondents are assigned group-level characteristics in accordance with the place of birth of their parent(s). Where the country of birth of one parent is missing, the respondent is assigned the country of birth of the parent with complete information. Where two foreign-born parents have different countries of birth, the mother's country of birth is assigned. Where one parent is U.S.-born, the foreign-born parent's country of birth is assigned.

To impute missing values in the skin-color variable we use an imputation model that includes the average skin color in the region (for example, the Caribbean). Since the scale ranges from 0 to 10, we truncate the imputation distribution for this variable to this interval. For the other context variables, we include a set of auxiliary variables in the imputation model: per capita GDP in 1975 and 2003 as measures of basic economic development, as well as the per capita GDP growth rate, the share of high-technology exports, and the share of exports of services. In addition, we use a variety of variables that index a more comprehensive perspective on development: the Human Development Index, the GINI Index of Inequality, the ratio of female-to-male income, the prevalence of contraceptive use, and the sending country's Polity score. Finally, to aid in the imputation of missing values for educational attainment, we draw on the Barro-Lee data and include three indicators of the sending-country education distribution: the share of the population ages twenty-five and older who have completed secondary education, the share who have completed tertiary education, and the average number of years of education completed.[11] For the WVS scales where all observed values are within the interval of −2 to 2, we truncate the imputation distribution to the −3-to-3 interval.

In all analyses, we use the Stata MI suite of commands to adjust standard errors for the multiply imputed data.

VARIABLES USED THROUGHOUT THE BOOK

The following variables are used throughout the book and are briefly described here. We introduce variables that are specific to chapters in the respective appendices.

Group-Level Variables

- Survival versus self-expression/actualization score
- Traditional versus secular-rational score
- Average group skin color
- Status prevalence scale
- Group years of education

Details on all group-level variables are found in chapter 3.

Individual-Level Variables

- Respondent's education: A continuous measure of years of completed schooling coded from categorical responses in the IIMMLA and ISGMNY
- Generational and legal status:
  - Foreign-born, noncitizen
  - Foreign-born, citizen
  - U.S.-born, two foreign-born parents (second generation)
  - U.S.-born, one foreign-born parent (2.5 generation)
- Language spoken in parental household:
  - Spoke only English at home
  - Spoke mainly English at home
  - Spoke English and another language at home
- Ability in parental language: A summary of scores from 1 to 4 on speaking, reading, writing, and understanding the foreign language spoken in the home
- Intact family: A variable indicating whether respondent lived with both biological parents from ages six to eighteen (ISGMNY) or six to sixteen (IIMMLA)
- Mixed parentage: A variable indicating the respondent had two foreign-born parents of mixed origins
- Separation from parent: A variable indicating whether the respondent was separated from a parent for a year or more during childhood
- Parent educated in the United States: A variable indicating whether the respondent had one, two, or no parents educated in the United States
- Parental occupational status: The International Socio-Economic Index of Occupational Status score for the respondent's mother or father, whichever is higher.[12] When information for either the mother or father is missing, the other parent is automatically used.
- Parental education: The years of education of the highest-educated parent. When information for either the mother or father is missing, the other parent is automatically used.
- Parental sent remittances: A variable indicating whether respondent's parents sent remittances currently (in the ISGMNY) or when respondent was growing up (in the IIMMLA)
- Respondent still enrolled in school full-time
- New York: An indicator for location of survey; Los Angeles is the omitted category

- Respondent's sex: An indicator for male; female is the omitted category
- Respondent's age in years

ISGMNY Only

- High school quality: New York City high school attended, anonymized and ranked into quintiles in terms of performance, based on a variety of indicators collected by the Division of Assessment and Accountability of the New York City Board of Education
- Use of public amenities: Respondents could answer that they used libraries or museums "a lot," "sometimes," or "never." We grouped together those who used both amenities "a lot" (8 percent) and those who used at least one "a lot" (41 percent), and we combined those who used libraries or museums only "sometimes" (49 percent) with the remaining 2 percent who never did.

IIMMLA Only

- Cross-border families:
  - All relatives in United States
  - Parent in the United States and relatives in origin country
  - Parents in origin country
- Visits during childhood:
  - Parent did not return to origin country during respondent's childhood
  - Parent returned to origin country
  - Parent returned to origin country and respondent joined parent
- Parent remitted in respondent's childhood
- Parental legal status at arrival: A variable indexing the legal status of respondent's parents when they arrived
  - One parent a U.S. citizen
  - Both parents legal permanent residents (LPR)
  - One parent an LPR and one not
  - Neither parent an LPR
- Arrived undocumented: A variable indicating that a respondent arrived without legal status
- Arrived with temporary status: A variable indicating that a respondent arrived with temporary status, such as a tourist or student visa or temporary work authorization

- Age at naturalization (the IIMMLA only): A variable measuring the age at which the respondent became a U.S. citizen
    - At birth; second-generation respondents are the omitted reference category
    - Naturalized before age sixteen
    - Naturalized between ages seventeen and twenty
    - Naturalized between ages twenty-one and thirty-eight
    - Not yet naturalized
- Language spoken in parental household: A more detailed version of the language variable available in the combined data set
    - Spoke only English at home
    - Spoke mainly English at home
    - Spoke both English and another language at home
    - Spoke mainly a language besides English at home

Notes

CHAPTER 1: ORIGINS AND DESTINATIONS

1. Morris 2002.
2. Rumbaut 2004.
3. Levels, Dronkers, and Kraaykamp 2008; Weldon 2006; Fleischmann and Dronkers 2010.
4. FitzGerald 2014, 116.
5. Portes and Zhou 1993.
6. Portes and Rumbaut 2001.
7. Alba and Nee 2003.
8. Kasinitz et al. 2008.
9. Bean, Brown, and Bachmeier 2015.
10. Lee and Zhou 2015.

CHAPTER 2: BRINGING THE INTERNATIONAL BACK IN: A NEW PERSPECTIVE

1. Katz 1993.
2. Portes and Rumbaut 2001, 49.
3. Portes and Rumbaut 2001, 102.
4. Portes and Rumbaut 2001, 88.
5. Portes and Rumbaut 2001, 98.
6. Portes and Rumbaut 2001, 102.
7. Haller, Portes, and Lynch 2011, 758.
8. Portes and Rumbaut 2001, 78.
9. For some earlier tests interacting community effects with individual- or family-level variables, see Xie and Greenman 2011; Kroneberg 2008.
10. Kasinitz et al. 2008, 22.
11. Kasinitz et al. 2008, 24.
12. Bean, Brown, and Bachmeier 2015.

13. Bean, Brown, and Bachmeier 2015, 7, 31, 56.
14. Bean, Brown, and Bachmeier 2015, 50.
15. Lee and Zhou 2015, 4.
16. Lee and Zhou 2015, 54.
17. Lee and Zhou 2015, 6.
18. Gordon 1964.
19. Alba 2016, 190.
20. Alba and Nee 2003, 57.
21. Alba and Nee 2003, 45.
22. Alba and Nee 2003, 66.
23. Alba and Nee 2003, 60.

CHAPTER 3: THE INTERNATIONAL PERSPECTIVE

1. See the appendix for a discussion of the empirical issues arising from this selectivity and about efforts to measure origin.
2. Röder and Lubbers 2016; Soehl 2017.
3. Inglehart and Baker 2000; Fuchs and Wössmann 2008.
4. Bjørnskov 2007.
5. Chua 2011.
6. Kalmijn and van Tubergen 2010; Levels, Dronkers, and Kraaykamp 2008.
7. Feliciano 2005.
8. Inglehart and Welzel 2005.
9. Louie 2012.
10. Foner and Alba 2008.
11. Kasinitz et al. 2008; Lee and Zhou 2015.
12. See the Welzel-Inglehart "Cultural Map" at the World Values Survey website, http://www.worldvaluessurvey.org/WVSContents.jsp (accessed December 10, 2017).
13. Inglehart and Welzel 2005, 65.
14. Lipset 1997.
15. Ocampo 2016.
16. Barro and Lee 2013.
17. Evans, Kelley, and Sikora 2014; Evans et al. 2010.
18. Ichou 2014; Feliciano 2005.
19. Inglehart and Welzel 2005, 220.
20. Reese et al. 1995.
21. Lee and Zhou 2015.
22. Tichenor 2009; Zolberg 2009; FitzGerald and Cook-Martín 2014.
23. Sassen 1996.
24. Neumayer 2006.
25. Zolberg, Suhrke, and Aguayo 1989.

26. Reher, Requena, and Sánchez-Domínguez 2013, 27.
27. Requena and Sánchez-Domínguez 2011.
28. Entchautegui and Menjivar 2015.
29. Smith 2005; Haikkola 2011.
30. Soehl and Waldinger 2012; Sears and Funk 1999.
31. Rumbaut, Massey, and Bean 2006.
32. Motomura 2014.
33. Motomura 2006.
34. Lockwood 1996.
35. Bloemraad, Korteweg, and Yurdakul 2008.
36. Arendt 1951.
37. Alba and Nee 2003.
38. Yoshikawa and Kalil 2011.
39. Bean, Brown, and Bachmeier 2015.
40. Wimmer 2008; Brubaker 2002.
41. Perlmann 1989.
42. As explained in Waldinger and Catron 2015.
43. Dribe and Lundh 2011; Ersanilli 2012; Levels, Dronkers, and Kraaykamp 2008; Van Tubergen and Kalmijn 2005.

CHAPTER 4: THE IMPORTANCE OF CONTEXT

1. Portes and Rumbaut 1990, 88, 89.
2. Mattoo, Constantinescu, and Özden 2008.
3. Portes and Rumbaut 2001, 46.
4. Roediger 2006.
5. Telles and Ortiz 2008.
6. Tuan 1998.
7. Portes and Rumbaut 2001, 55.
8. Branigan et al. 2013; Hersch 2011; Espino and Franz 2002.
9. Ortiz and Telles 2012; Hunter 2007.
10. Massey and Martin 2003.
11. Recognizing this difficulty, we replicate all the analyses to follow with an alternative measure of discrimination based on self-reports of each national-origin group. The effect of self-reported discrimination at the group level on educational attainment is consistently statistically indistinguishable from zero.
12. Ganzeboom 2010.
13. Exceptions are noted where appropriate when discussing the relevant analyses.
14. Respondents with Taiwanese and Hong Kong origins were included in the target samples of "Chinese" immigrants. For clarity, our analysis includes only mainland Chinese. We also included separate indicators for those of Taiwanese and Hong Kong origins. The coefficients for those with these

origins do not differ significantly from those for mainland Chinese, and their inclusion in the context scale do not alter our findings beyond the second decimal level.
15. Ganzeboom 2010.
16. Gelman 2006.
17. Levels and Dronkers 2008; Levels, Dronkers, and Kraaykamp 2008; Kanas and van Tubergen 2009.
18. Kalmijn and van Tubergen 2010.
19. Gonzales 2011.
20. As shown in table 4.3, the standard deviations of these variables are somewhat smaller in our sample.
21. We remind the reader that high scores on the traditional versus secular-rational axis denote origins in a society characterized by a secular orientation; high scores on the survival–self-expression axis denote origins in a society characterized by an orientation toward self-expression.
22. Moreover, we observed a stronger relationship between group average skin color and second-generation outcomes than between group-level reports of discrimination and second-generation outcomes.
23. Gonzales 2011.

CHAPTER 5: GETTING AHEAD: INSTITUTIONS, ETHNICITY, AND INTERNATIONAL INFLUENCES

1. Kasinitz et al. 2008; Kao and Thompson 2003; Kao and Tienda 1998; Hsin and Xie 2014.
2. Myers 2007.
3. Alba 2008.
4. It would be of interest to examine the hypothesis—put forward in *Inheriting the City* and other writings—that a cultural orientation toward multigenerational households also supports better educational or occupational outcomes. Unfortunately, only the IIMMLA contains the information necessary to identify second-generation respondents living with members of their extended family, and only the ISGMNY contains the detailed educational information necessary to see if this is associated with better high school quality. For this analysis, the best we can do is examine whether those currently residing with a family member (parent, aunt, cousin, and so on) have higher educational or occupational attainment. What we find is that those living with family are statistically indistinguishable in terms of educational attainment and have lower, rather than higher, occupational attainment. This is very likely a result of reverse causality, however, as those less well-off will be forced to reside with family even if they are already working. Thus, this is not very definitive evidence to bring to this question.

5. Portes, Guarnizo, and Haller 2002.
6. Portes and Rumbaut 2001, 47.
7. Kroneberg 2008; Xie and Greenman 2011; Greenman and Xie 2008.
8. Full results from all analyses in chapter 5 are found in the online appendix.
9. We also tested the regressions omitting respondents' own language ability, as this variable is potentially endogenous to educational and occupational attainment. The coefficients for educational attainment are virtually indistinguishable. However, the negative association between speaking English in the parental home and occupational status diminishes in size and becomes statistically insignificant when the language ability of the respondent is omitted from the regression.
10. This analysis was replicated using deciles rather than quintiles, but owing to heaping in parental educational attainment, some deciles were empty. However, there was not a significant jump from the ninth to the tenth decile for either average group education or parental education.
11. Kasinitz et al. 2008, 383.
12. Although we chose to omit from our analysis the children who did not report their parents' legal status, even if we had included them—and thereby might have captured more of the potentially undocumented parents—they did not differ significantly in education or occupation from the other parental status groups. Moreover, in a separate analysis of the 1.5 generation, when we interacted respondent citizenship with parent status at arrival, the strong positive effect of respondent citizenship held for the children of all parental legal statuses at arrival.
13. Portes and Rumbaut 2001, 82.

CHAPTER 6: ACQUIRING CITIZENSHIP

1. Ueda 1980; Schneider 2001; Bloemraad and Ueda 2006.
2. *The Economist* 2015.
3. Ian Haney Lopez 1996.
4. Rytina 2011; Lee 2011.
5. Aptekar 2012; Bibler Coutin 2003.
6. Bloemraad 2007.
7. Brubaker 1992.
8. Gilbertson and Singer 2003.
9. Gilbertson and Singer 2003.
10. North 1987.
11. Bloemraad 2006.
12. Alvarez 1987.
13. See USCIS 2016. However, the failure rate is twice the level recorded in the 1970s and 1980s (Waters and Gerstein Pineau 2016).
14. Stringer 2016, 6–8.
15. Rytina 2002.

16. Aptekar 2015; Ramakrishnan and Baldassare 2004; Wong et al. 2011.
17. Plascencia, Freeman, and Setzler 2003.
18. Kochenov and Henley & Partners 2016.
19. Syracuse University 2007.
20. Rytina 2005.
21. Cohn and Ruiz 2017.
22. Full results from all analyses in chapter 6 are found in the online appendix.
23. See, for example, Bloemraad 2006.
24. The coding of this variable varies across the two analyses. To ensure comparable answer categories we collapse this variable into three distinctions when using the combined data set but use the full range of four options when analyzing only the IIMMLA data.
25. Stringer 2016.

CHAPTER 7: EXERCISING CITIZENSHIP

1. Leal 2002.
2. Alba and Nee 2003, 156.
3. Alwin, Cohen, and Newcomb 1991; Merelman 1969; King and Merelman 1986.
4. Verba, Schlozman, and Brady 1995; King and Merelman 1986; Prior 2010; Stoker and Jennings 2008; Jennings and Markus 1984.
5. The results presented in the following pages derive from a series of regressions in which we entered variables for parents' legal status at the time of arrival; respondent's legal status at the time of arrival (separate dummy variables for entered undocumented and entered with a temporary visa); citizenship status (birth or alien) and age at naturalization; language spoken at home while a child; parents' English-language ability; whether a parent returned to the homeland when the respondent was a child; whether a parent sent home remittances when the respondent was a child; whether a parent never moved to the United States; years of education for the parent with the most years; respondent's years of education; and respondent's age. In addition, the regressions included six contextual variables, the nature of which is fully explained in prior chapters.
6. Rosenstone and Hanson 1993.
7. Hochschild and Mollenkopf 2009, 20.
8. Full results from all analyses in chapter 7 are found in the online appendix.
9. Pearson and Citrin 2007.
10. Pearson and Citrin 2007, 222.
11. Hajnal and Lee 2011.
12. Marwell 2009.
13. DeSipio 2005, 97.
14. DeSipio and De la Garza 1998.

15. Hajnal and Lee 2011.
16. Since the answer categories to the question about party registration were slightly different in the Los Angeles and New York City surveys, we restrict the sample to those who registered either for one of the major parties or as independents. This omits a small number of respondents in both surveys.

CHAPTER 8: CROSS-BORDER CONNECTIONS

1. Massey et al. 1987; Gabaccia 2013.
2. Ramakrishnan et al. 2012; Pew Research Center 2012 Asian-American Survey.
3. Soehl and Waldinger 2010.
4. See Hyman 1959; Jennings and Niemi 1968. On social learning theory more generally, see Bandura 1977.
5. Sapiro 2004, 6.
6. Verba, Schlozman, and Brady 1995; Jennings and Niemi 2015; Jennings, Stokers, and Bowers 2009.
7. Bandura 2002.
8. Haikkola 2011, 50.
9. Faist 2000, 191.
10. Guarnizo, Portes, and Haller 2003; Waldinger 2008.
11. Soehl and Waldinger 2010.
12. Mason 2004, 427.
13. Haikkola 2011, 1210.
14. Schuetz 1945, 108.
15. Brubaker et al. 2006, 254.
16. Full results from all analyses in chapter 8 are found in the online appendix.

CHAPTER 9: ETHNICITY: CROSSING BLURRY BOUNDARIES

1. Barth 1998.
2. Wimmer 2008.
3. Painter and Philo 1995.
4. Sarna 1978; Conzen et al. 1992; Lopez and Espiritu 1990; Zelinsky 2001.
5. Myrdal 1944.
6. Smith 1993.
7. The concept of an "ethno-racial pentagon" was coined by David Hollinger (2006, 25). On the possibility that these official classifications provide a poor fit with immigrants' own self-understandings, see Bloemraad 2006.
8. Weber 1978, 389.
9. On the distinction between an ethnic label and collective identity, see Phinney 1998 and Ashmore, Deaux, and McLaughlin-Volpe 2004.

10. Full results from all analyses in chapter 9 are found in the online appendix.
11. Alba and Nee 2003, 41.
12. Alba 1990.
13. For full elaboration of this model of language shift, see Fishman 1972. Applications to more recent trends can be found in David Lopez 1996 and Estrada 2007.
14. Kasinitz et al. 2008, 256.
15. Portes and Rumbaut 2001, 54.
16. Portes and Rumbaut 2001, 122.
17. Portes and Rumbaut 2001, 127.
18. Padilla and Borsato 2010.
19. Portes and Rumbaut 2001, 144.

CHAPTER 10: CONCLUSION: THE MAKING OF THE SECOND GENERATION

1. Kasinitz et al. 2008; Lee and Zhou 2015.
2. Gonzales 2011.
3. Kalter et al. 2016. See the CILS4EU website at: http://www.cils4.eu/ (accessed December 10, 2017).

APPENDIX

1. The WVS is a worldwide network of social scientists studying changing values and their impact on social and political life. In collaboration with the European Values Study, the WVS has carried out representative national surveys in more than one hundred countries containing almost 90 percent of the world's population.
2. Putnam 1993.
3. Guiso, Sapienza, and Zingales 2008.
4. Algan and Cahuc 2010.
5. Voicu and Tufis, 2015.
6. Evans et al. 2010.
7. Wimmer and Soehl 2014; Rudnev 2014.
8. Röder and Mühlau 2014.
9. Inglehart and Baker 2000, 24.
10. Inglehart and Baker 2000, 24.
11. Barro and Lee 2013.
12. Ganzeboom 2010.

References

Alba, Richard D. 1990. *Ethnic Identity: The Transformation of White America.* New Haven, Conn.: Yale University Press.
———. 2008. "Why We Still Need a Theory of Mainstream Assimilation." *Kölner Zeitschrift Für Soziologie Und Sozialpsychologie: Sonderheft* 48: 37–56.
———. 2016. "Assimilation in the Past and Present." In *The Oxford Handbook of American Immigration and Ethnicity,* edited by Ronald H. Bayor. Oxford: Oxford University Press.
Alba, Richard, and Victor Nee. 2003. *Remaking the American Mainstream: Assimilation and Contemporary Immigration.* Cambridge, Mass.: Harvard University Press.
Algan, Yann, and Pierre Cahuc. 2010. "Inherited Trust and Growth." *American Economic Review* 100(5): 2060–92.
Alvarez, Robert R. 1987. "A Profile of the Citizenship Process Among Hispanics in the United States." *International Migration Review* 21(2): 327–51.
Alwin, Duane F., Ronald L. Cohen, and Theodore M. Newcomb. 1991. *Political Attitudes over the Life Span: The Bennington Women After Fifty Years.* Madison: University of Wisconsin Press.
Aptekar, Sofya. 2012. "Naturalization Ceremonies and the Role of Immigrants in the American Nation." *Citizenship Studies* 16(7): 937–52.
———. 2015. *The Road to Citizenship: What Naturalization Means for Immigrants and the United States.* New Brunswick, NJ: Rutgers University Press.
Arendt, Hannah. 1951. *The Origins of Totalitarianism.* New York: Harcourt Brace and Co.
Ashmore, Richard D., Kay Deaux, and Tracy McLaughlin-Volpe. 2004. "An Organizing Framework for Collective Identity: Articulation and Significance of Multidimensionality." *Psychological Bulletin* 130(1): 80–114.
Bandura, Albert. 1977. *Social Learning Theory.* Englewood Cliffs, N.J.: Prentice-Hall.
———. 2002. "Social Cognitive Theory in Cultural Context." *Applied Psychology* 51(2): 269–90.
Barro, Robert J., and Jong-Wha Lee. 2013. "A New Data Set of Educational Attainment in the World, 1950–2010." *Journal of Development Economics* 104(C): 184–98.

Barth, Fredrik. 1998. *Ethnic Groups and Boundaries: The Social Organization of Culture Difference.* Long Grove, Ill.: Waveland Press.

Bean, Frank D., Susan K. Brown, and James D. Bachmeier. 2015. *Parents Without Papers: The Progress and Pitfalls of Mexican American Integration.* New York: Russell Sage Foundation.

Bibler Coutin, Susan. 2003. "Cultural Logics of Belonging and Movement Transnationalism, Naturalization, and U.S. Immigration Politics." *American Ethnologist* 30(4): 508–26.

Bjørnskov, Christian. 2007. "Determinants of Generalized Trust: A Cross-Country Comparison." *Public Choice* 130(1): 1–21.

Bloemraad, Irene. 2006. *Becoming a Citizen: Incorporating Immigrants and Refugees in the United States and Canada.* Berkeley: University of California Press.

———. 2007. "Much Ado About Nothing? The Contours of Dual Citizenship in the United States and Canada." In *Dual Citizenship in Global Perspective,* edited by Thomas Faist and Peter Kivisto. New York: Palgrave Macmillan.

Bloemraad, Irene, Anna Korteweg, and Gökçe Yurdakul. 2008. "Citizenship and Immigration: Multiculturalism, Assimilation, and Challenges to the Nation-State." *Annual Review of Sociology* 34(1): 153–79.

Bloemraad, Irene, and Reed Ueda. 2006. "Naturalization and Nationality." In *A Companion to American Immigration,* edited by Reed Ueda. Malden, Mass.: Blackwell Publishing.

Branigan, Amelia R., Jeremy Freese, Assaf Patir, Thomas W. McDade, Kiang Liu, and Catarina I. Kiefe. 2013. "Skin Color, Sex, and Educational Attainment in the Post–Civil Rights Era." *Social Science Research* 42(6): 1659–74.

Brubaker, Rogers. 1992. *Citizenship and Nationhood in France and Germany.* Vol. 21. Cambridge, Mass.: Harvard University Press.

———. 2002. "Ethnicity Without Groups." *European Journal of Sociology/Archives Européennes Sociologie* 43(2): 163–89.

Brubaker, Rogers, Margit Feischmidt, Jon Fox, and Liana Grancea. 2006. *Nationalist Politics and Everyday Ethnicity in a Transylvanian Town.* Princeton, N.J.: Princeton University Press.

Chua, Amy. 2011. *Battle Hymn of the Tiger Mother.* New York: Bloomsbury Publishing.

Cohn, D'Vera, and Neil G. Ruiz. 2017. "More Than Half of New Green Cards Go to People Already Living in the U.S." *FactTank: News in the Numbers,* Pew Research Center, Washington, D.C., July 6. http://www.pewresearch.org/facttank/2017/07/06/more-than-half-of-new-green-cards-go-to-people-already-living-in-the-u-s/ (accessed December 10, 2017).

Conzen, Kathleen Neils, David A. Gerber, Ewa Morawska, George E. Pozzetta, and Rudolph J. Vecoli. 1992. "The Invention of Ethnicity: A Perspective from the USA." *Journal of American Ethnic History* 12(1): 3–41.

DeSipio, Louis. 2005. "Building America, One Person at a Time: Naturalization and Political Behavior of the Naturalized in Contemporary American Politics." In

E Pluribus Unum? Contemporary and Historical Perspectives on Immigrant Political Incorporation, edited by Gary Gerstle and John Mollenkopf. New York: Russell Sage Foundation.

DeSipio, Louis, and Rodolfo O. De la Garza. 1998. *Making Americans, Remaking America: Immigration and Immigrant Policy.* Boulder, CO: Westview Press.

Dribe, Martin, and Christer Lundh. 2011. "Cultural Dissimilarity and Intermarriage: A Longitudinal Study of Immigrants in Sweden 1990–2005." *International Migration Review* 45(2): 297–324.

The Economist. 2015. "Paytriotism: Becoming British Is a Costly Business." *Economist*, April 18, 2015. https://www.economist.com/news/britain/21648699-becoming-british-costly-business-paytriotism (accessed December 10, 2017).

Entchautegui, Maria, and Cecilia Menjivar. 2015. "Paradoxes of Family Reunification Law: Family Separation and Reorganization Under the Current Immigration Regime." *Law and Policy* 37(1–2): 32–60.

Ersanilli, Evelyn. 2012. "Model(ling) Citizens? Integration Policies and Value Integration of Turkish Immigrants and Their Descendants in Germany, France, and the Netherlands." *Journal of Immigrant and Refugee Studies* 10(3): 338–58.

Espino, Rodolfo, and Michael M. Franz. 2002. "Latino Phenotypic Discrimination Revisited: The Impact of Skin Color on Occupational Status." *Social Science Quarterly* 83(2): 612–23.

Estrada, Vanesa. 2007. "Language." In *The New Americans: A Guide to Immigration since 1965*, edited by Mary Waters and Reed Ueda. Cambridge, Mass.: Harvard University Press.

Evans, M. D. R., Jonathan Kelley, and Joanna Sikora. 2014. "Scholarly Culture and Academic Performance in 42 Nations." *Social Forces* 92(4): 1573–1605.

Evans, M. D. R., Jonathan Kelley, Joanna Sikora, and Donald J. Treiman. 2010. "Family Scholarly Culture and Educational Success: Books and Schooling in 27 Nations." *Research in Social Stratification and Mobility* 28(2): 171–97.

Faist, Thomas. 2000. "Transnationalization in International Migration: Implications for the Study of Citizenship and Culture." *Ethnic and Racial Studies* 23(2): 189–222.

Feliciano, Cynthia. 2005. "Does Selective Migration Matter? Explaining Ethnic Disparities in Educational Attainment Among Immigrants' Children." *International Migration Review* 39(4): 841–71.

Finke, Roger, and Brian Grim. 2005. "Cross-National Socioeconomic and Religion Data, 2005." *The Association of Religion Data Archives*. http://www.thearda.com/Archive/Files/Descriptions/ECON2005.asp (accessed 15 September 15, 2013).

Fishman, Joshua A. 1972. *The Sociology of Language: An Interdisciplinary Social Science Approach to Language in Society.* Rowley, Mass.: Newbury House.

FitzGerald, David Scott. 2014. "The Sociology of International Migration." In *Migration Theory: Talking Across Disciplines*, edited by Caroline Brettell and James Hollifield. New York: Routledge.

FitzGerald, David Scott, and David Cook-Martín. 2014. *Culling the Masses: The Democratic Origins of Racist Immigration Policy in the Americas.* Cambridge, Mass.: Harvard University Press.

Fleischmann, Fenella, and Jaap Dronkers. 2010. "Unemployment Among Immigrants in European Labour Markets: An Analysis of Origin and Destination Effects." *Work, Employment, and Society* 24(2): 337–54.

Foner, Nancy, and Richard Alba. 2008. "Immigrant Religion in the U.S. and Western Europe: Bridge or Barrier to Inclusion?" *International Migration Review* 42(2): 360–92.

Fuchs, Thomas, and Ludger Wössmann. 2008. "What Accounts for International Differences in Student Performance? A Re-examination Using PISA Data." In *The Economics of Education and Training,* edited by Christians Dustmann, Bernd Fitzenberger, and Steve Machin. Heidelberg: Physica-Verlag HD and Co.

Gabaccia, Donna R. 2013. *Italy's Many Diasporas.* New Brunswick, N.J.: Routledge.

Ganzeboom, Harry B. G. 2010. "A New International Socio-Economic Index (ISEI) of Occupational Status for the International Standard Classification of Occupation 2008 (ISCO 08) Constructed with Data from the ISSP 2002–2007." Paper presented to the annual conference of the International Social Survey Program. Lisbon (May 1).

Gelman, Andrew. 2006. "Multilevel (Hierarchical) Modeling: What It Can and Cannot Do." *Technometrics* 48(3): 432–35.

Gilbertson, Greta, and Audrey Singer. 2003. "The Emergence of Protective Citizenship in the USA: Naturalization Among Dominican Immigrants in the Post-1996 Welfare Reform Era." *Ethnic and Racial Studies* 26(1): 25–51.

Gonzales, Roberto G. 2011. "Learning to Be Illegal: Undocumented Youth and Shifting Legal Contexts in the Transition to Adulthood." *American Sociological Review* 76(4): 602–19.

Gordon, Milton M. 1964. *Assimilation in American Life: The Role of Race, Religion, and National Origins.* Oxford: Oxford University Press.

Greenman, Emily, and Yu Xie. 2008. "Is Assimilation Theory Dead? The Effect of Assimilation on Adolescent Well-being." *Social Science Research* 37(1): 109–37.

Guarnizo, Luis Eduardo, Alejandro Portes, and William Haller. 2003. "Assimilation and Transnationalism: Determinants of Transnational Political Action Among Contemporary Migrants." *American Journal of Sociology* 108(6): 1211–48.

Guiso, Luigi, Paola Sapienza, and Luigi Zingales. 2008. "Social Capital as Good Culture." *Journal of the European Economic Association* 6(2–3): 295–320.

Haikkola, Lotta. 2011. "Making Connections: Second-Generation Children and the Transnational Field of Relations." *Journal of Ethnic and Migration Studies* 37(8): 1201–17.

Hajnal, Zoltan L., and Taeku Lee. 2011. *Why Americans Don't Join the Party: Race, Immigration, and the Failure (of Political Parties) to Engage the Electorate.* Princeton, N.J.: Princeton University Press.

Haller, William, Alejandro Portes, and Scott M. Lynch. 2011. "Dreams Fulfilled, Dreams Shattered: Determinants of Segmented Assimilation in the Second Generation." *Social Forces* 89(3): 733–62.

Hersch, Joni. 2011. "The Persistence of Skin Color Discrimination for Immigrants." *Social Science Research* 40(5): 1337–49.

Hochschild, Jennifer L., and John H. Mollenkopf. 2009. "Modelling Political Incorporation." In *Bringing Outsiders In: Transatlantic Perspectives on Immigrant Political Incorporation*, edited by Jennifer L. Hochschild and John H. Mollenkopf. Ithaca, N.Y.: Cornell University Press.

Hollinger, David. A. 2006. *Postethnic America: Beyond Multiculturalism.* New York: Basic Books.

Hsin, Amy, and Yu Xie. 2014. "Explaining Asian Americans' Academic Advantage over Whites." *Proceedings of the National Academy of Sciences* 111(23): 8416–21.

Hunter, Margaret. 2007. "The Persistent Problem of Colorism: Skin Tone, Status, and Inequality." *Sociology Compass* 1(1): 237–54.

Hyman, Herbert H. 1959. *Political Socialisation: A Study in the Psychology of Political Behaviour*. New York: Free Press.

Ichou, Mathieu. 2014. "Who They Were There: Immigrants' Educational Selectivity and Their Children's Educational Attainment." *European Sociological Review* 30(6): 750–65.

Inglehart, Ronald, and Wayne E. Baker. 2000. "Modernization, Cultural Change, and the Persistence of Traditional Values." *American Sociological Review* 65(1): 19–51.

Inglehart, Ronald, and Christian Welzel. 2005. *Modernization, Cultural Change, and Democracy: The Human Development Sequence*. Cambridge: Cambridge University Press.

Jaggers, Keith, and Ted Robert Gurr. 1996. "Polity III: Regime Type and Political Authority, 1800–1994." Ann Arbor, Mich.: Inter-University Consortium for Political and Social Research, November 21. DOI: 10.3886/ICPSR06695.v2.

Jennings, M. Kent, and Gregory B. Markus. 1984. "Partisan Orientations over the Long Haul: Results from the Three-Wave Political Socialization Panel Study." *American Political Science Review* 78(4): 1000–1018.

Jennings, M. Kent, and Richard G. Niemi. 1968. "The Transmission of Political Values from Parent to Child." *American Political Science Review* 62(1): 169–84.

——. 2015. *Political Character of Adolescence: The Influence of Families and Schools*. Princeton, N.J.: Princeton University Press.

Jennings, M. Kent, Laura Stoker, and Jake Bowers. 2009. "Politics Across Generations: Family Transmission Reexamined." *Journal of Politics* 71(3): 782–99.

Kalmijn, Matthijs, and Frank van Tubergen. 2010. "A Comparative Perspective on Intermarriage: Explaining Differences Among National-Origin Groups in the United States." *Demography* 47(2): 459–79.

Kalter, Frank, Anthony F. Heath, Miles Hewstone, Jan O. Jonsson, Matthijs Kalmijn, Irena Kogan, and Frank van Tubergen. 2016. Children of Immigrants Longitudinal Survey in Four European Countries (CILS4EU) – Reduced version. Reduced data file for download and off-site use. GESIS Data Archive, Cologne, ZA5656 Data file Version 3.1.0. DOI:10.4232/cils4eu.5656.3.1.0.

Kanas, Agnieszka, and Frank van Tubergen. 2009. "The Impact of Origin and Host Country Schooling on the Economic Performance of Immigrants." *Social Forces* 88(2): 893–915.

Kao, Grace, and Jennifer S. Thompson. 2003. "Racial and Ethnic Stratification in Educational Achievement and Attainment."*Annual Review of Sociology* 29: 417–42.

Kao, Grace, and Marta Tienda. 1998. "Educational Aspirations of Minority Youth." *American Journal of Education* 106(3): 349–84.

Kasinitz, Philip, John H. Mollenkopf, Mary C. Waters, and Jennifer Holdaway. 2008. *Inheriting the City: The Second Generation Comes of Age.* New York: Russell Sage Foundation.

Katz, Michael B. 1993. *The "Underclass" Debate: Views from History.* Princeton, N.J.: Princeton University Press.

King, Gary, and Richard Merelman. 1986. "The Development of Political Activists: A Model of Early Learning." *Social Science Quarterly* 67(3): 473–90.

Kochenov, Dimitry, and Henley & Partners, eds. 2016. *Henley & Partners–Kochenov Quality of Nationality Index (QNI): 2011–2015.* Zurich, Switzerland: Ideos. https://nationalityindex.com/ (accessed October 22, 2017).

Kroneberg, Clemens. 2008. "Ethnic Communities and School Performance Among the New Second Generation in the United States: Testing the Theory of Segmented Assimilation." *Annals of the American Academy of Political and Social Science* 620(1): 138–60.

Latinobarómetro. 2007. Latinobarómetro Survey 2007. Santiago, Chile: Corporación Latinobarómetro/Madrid, Spain: ASEP/JDS. http://www.latinobarometro.org (accessed August 1, 2018).

Leal, David L. 2002. "Political Participation by Latino Non-Citizens in the United States." *British Journal of Political Science* 32(2): 353–70.

Lee, James. 2011. "U.S. Naturalizations: 2010." *Annual Flow Report.* Washington: Department of Homeland Security, Office of Immigration Statistics (April). http://www.dhs.gov/xlibrary/assets/statistics/publications/natz_fr_2010.pdf (accessed December 10, 2017).

Lee, Jennifer, and Min Zhou. 2015. *The Asian American Achievement Paradox.* New York: Russell Sage Foundation.

Levels, Mark, and Jaap Dronkers. 2008. "Educational Performance of Native and Immigrant Children from Various Countries of Origin." *Ethnic and Racial Studies* 31(8): 1404–25.

Levels, Mark, Jaap Dronkers, and Gerbert Kraaykamp. 2008. "Immigrant Children's Educational Achievement in Western Countries: Origin, Destination, and Community Effects on Mathematical Performance." *American Sociological Review* 73(5): 835–53.

Lipset, Seymour Martin. 1997. *American Exceptionalism: A Double-Edged Sword*. New York: W. W. Norton & Co.

Lockwood, David. 1996. "Civic Integration and Class Formation." *British Journal of Sociology* 47(3): 531–50.

Lopez, David. 1996. "Language: Diversity and Change." In *Ethnic Los Angeles*, edited by Roger Waldinger and Mehdi Bozorgmehr. New York: Russell Sage Foundation.

Lopez, David, and Yen Espiritu. 1990. "Panethnicity in the United States: A Theoretical Framework." *Ethnic and Racial Studies* 13(2): 198–224.

Lopez, Ian Haney. 1996. *White by Law: The Legal Construction of Race*. New York: New York University Press.

Louie, Vivian. 2012. *Keeping the Immigrant Bargain: The Costs and Rewards of Success in America*. New York: Russell Sage Foundation.

Marwell, Nicole P. 2009. *Bargaining for Brooklyn: Community Organizations in the Entrepreneurial City*. Chicago: University of Chicago Press.

Mason, Jennifer. 2004. "Managing Kinship over Long Distances: The Significance of 'the Visit.'" *Social Policy and Society* 3(4): 421–29.

Massey, Douglas S., Rafael Alarcón, Jorge Durand, and Humberto Gonzalez. 1987. *Return to Aztlan: The Social Process of International Migration from Western Mexico*. Vol. 1. Berkeley: University of California Press.

Massey, Douglas S., and Jennifer A. Martin. 2003. "The NIS Skin Color Scale." Princeton, N.J.: Princeton University, Office of Population Research.

Mattoo, Aaditya, Neagu Ileana Constantinescu, and Çaglar Özden. 2008. "Brain Waste? Educated Immigrants in the U.S. Labor Market." *Journal of Development Economics* 87(2): 255–69.

Merelman, Richard M. 1969. "The Development of Political Ideology: A Framework for the Analysis of Political Socialization." *American Political Science Review* 63(3): 750–67.

Morris, Lydia. 2002. *Managing Migration: Civic Stratification and Migrants' Rights*. London: Routledge Press.

Motomura, Hiroshi. 2006. *Americans in Waiting: The Lost Story of Immigration and Citizenship in the United States*. Oxford: Oxford University Press.

———. 2014. *Immigration Outside the Law*. Oxford: Oxford University Press.

Myers, Dowell. 2007. *Immigrants and Boomers: Forging a New Social Contract for the Future of America*. New York: Russell Sage Foundation.

Myrdal, Gunnar. 1944. *An American Dilemma: The Negro Problem and Modern Democracy*. Vol. 2. New York: Transaction Publishers.

Neumayer, Eric. 2006. "Unequal Access to Foreign Spaces: How States Use Visa Restrictions to Regulate Mobility in a Globalised World." *Transactions of the British Institute of Geographers* 31(1): 72–84.

North, David S. 1987. "The Long Grey Welcome: A Study of the American Naturalization Program." *International Migration Review* 21(2): 311–26.

Ocampo, Anthony Christian. 2016. *The Latinos of Asia: How Filipino Americans Break the Rules of Race.* Stanford, Calif.: Stanford University Press.

Ortiz, Vilma, and Edward Telles. 2012. "Racial Identity and Racial Treatment of Mexican Americans." *Race and Social Problems* 4(1): 41–56.

Padilla, Amado, and Graciela N. Borsato. 2010. "Psychology." In *Handbook of Language and Ethnic Identity*, edited by Joshua Fishman and Ofelia Garcia. Oxford: Oxford University Press.

Painter, Joe, and Chris Philo. 1995. "Spaces of Citizenship: An Introduction." *Political Geography* 14(2): 107–20.

Pearson, Kathryn, and Jack Citrin. 2007. "The Political Assimilation of the Fourth Wave." In *Transforming Politics, Transforming America: The Political and Civic Incorporation of Immigrants in the United States*, edited by Taeku Lee, S. Karthick Ramakrishnan, and Ricardo Ramirez. Charlottesville: University of Virginia Press.

Perlmann, Joel. 1989. *Ethnic Differences: Schooling and Social Structure Among the Irish, Italians, Jews, and Blacks in an American City, 1880–1935.* Cambridge: Cambridge University Press.

Phinney, Jean S. 1998. "Ethnic Identity in Adolescents and Adults." *Readings in Ethnic Psychology* 108(3): 73–99.

Plascencia, Luis F., Gary P. Freeman, and Mark Setzler. 2003. "The Decline of Barriers to Immigrant Economic and Political Rights in the American States: 1977–2001." *International Migration Review* 37(1): 5–23.

Portes, Alejandro, Luis Eduardo Guarnizo, and William J. Haller. 2002. "Transnational Entrepreneurs: An Alternative Form of Immigrant Economic Adaptation." *American Sociological Review* 67(2): 278–98.

Portes, Alejandro, and Rubén G. Rumbaut. 1990. *Immigrant America: A Portrait.* 1st ed. Berkeley: University of California Press.

———. 2001. *Legacies: The Story of the Immigrant Second Generation.* Berkeley: University of California Press.

Portes, Alejandro, and Min Zhou. 1993. "The New Second Generation: Segmented Assimilation and Its Variants." *Annals of the American Academy of Political and Social Science* 530(1): 74–96.

Prior, Markus. 2010. "You've Either Got It or You Don't? The Stability of Political Interest over the Life Cycle." *Journal of Politics* 72(3): 747–66.

Putnam, Robert D. 1993. *Making Democracy Work: Civic Traditions in Modern Italy.* Princeton, N.J.: Princeton University Press.

Ramakrishnan, S. Karthick, and Mark Baldassare. 2004. *The Ties That Bind: Changing Demographics and Civic Engagement in California.* San Francisco: Public Policy Institute of California.

Ramakrishnan, Karthick, Jane Junn, Taeku Lee, and Janelle Wong. 2012. *National Asian American Survey, 2008.* ICPSR31481-v2. Ann Arbor, Mich.: Inter-university

Consortium for Political and Social Research, distributor (July 19). DOI: 10.3886/ICPSR31481.v2.

Reese, Leslie, Silvia Balzano, Ronald Gallimore, and Claude Goldenberg. 1995. "The Concept of Educación: Latino Family Values and American Schooling." *International Journal of Educational Research* 23(1): 57–81.

Reher, David, Miguel Requena, and Maria Sánchez-Domínguez. 2013. "Divided Families Among Latin American Immigrants in Spain: Just How Level Is the Playing Field?" *The History of the Family* 18(1): 26–43.

Requena, Miguel, and Maria Sánchez-Domínguez. 2011. "Las familias inmigrantes en España." *Revista internacional de sociología* 69(M1): 79–104.

Röder, Antje, and Marcel Lubbers. 2016. "After Migration: Acculturation of Attitudes Towards Homosexuality Among Polish Immigrants in Germany, Ireland, the Netherlands, and the U.K." *Ethnicities* 16(2): 261–89.

Röder, Antje, and Peter Mühlau. 2014. "Are They Acculturating? Europe's Immigrants and Gender Egalitarianism." *Social Forces* 92(3): 899–928.

Roediger, David R. 2006. *Working Toward Whiteness: How America's Immigrants Became White: The Strange Journey from Ellis Island to the Suburbs.* New York: Basic Books.

Rosenstone, Steven J., and John Mark Hansen. 1993. *Mobilization, Participation, and Democracy in America.* Basingstoke, U.K.: Macmillan.

Rudnev, Maksim. 2014. "Value Adaptation Among Intra-European Migrants: Role of Country of Birth and Country of Residence." *Journal of Cross-Cultural Psychology* 45(10): 1626–42.

Rumbaut, Rubén G. 2004. "Ages, Life Stages, and Generational Cohorts: Decomposing the Immigrant First and Second Generations in the United States." *International Migration Review* 38(3): 1160–1205.

Rumbaut, Rubén G., Frank D. Bean, Leo R. Chavez, Jennifer Lee, Susan K. Brown, Louis DeSipio, and Min Zhou. 2008. "Immigration and Intergenerational Mobility in Metropolitan Los Angeles (IIMMLA) 2004." Ann Arbor, Mich.: Inter-University Consortium for Political and Social Research. http://www.icpsr.umich.edu/DSDR/studies/22627/version/1 (accessed December 10, 2017).

Rumbaut, Rubén G., Douglas S. Massey, and Frank D. Bean. 2006. "Linguistic Life Expectancies: Immigrant Language Retention in Southern California." *Population and Development Review* 32(3): 447–60.

Rytina, Nancy. 2002. "IRCA Legalization Effects: Lawful Permanent Residence and Naturalization Through 2001." Washington: U.S. Office of Policy and Planning, Statistics Division, U.S. Immigration and Naturalization Service.

———. 2005. "Estimates of the Legal Permanent Resident Population and Population Eligible to Naturalize in 2003." *Population Estimates* (January). Washington: U.S. Department of Homeland Security, Office of Immigration Statistics. https://www.dhs.gov/sites/default/files/publications/LPR%20Population%20Estimates Population%20Eligible%20to%20Naturalize%20in%202003.pdf (accessed December 10, 2017).

———. 2011. "Estimates of the Legal Permanent Resident Population in 2010." Washington: U.S. Department of Homeland Security, Office of Immigration Statistics, Policy Directorate. https://www.dhs.gov/xlibrary/assets/statistics/publications/ois_lpr_pe_2010.pdf (accessed December 10, 2017).

Sapiro, Virginia. 2004. "Not Your Parents' 'Political Socialization': Introduction for a New Generation." *Annual Review of Political Science* 7: 1–23.

Sarna, Jonathan D. 1978. "From Immigrants to Ethnics: Toward a New Theory of 'Ethnicization.'" *Ethnicity* 5(4): 370–78.

Sassen, Saskia. 1996. *Losing Control? Sovereignty in an Age of Globalization.* New York: Columbia University Press.

Schneider, Dorothee. 2001. "Naturalization and United States Citizenship in Two Periods of Mass Migration: 1894–1930, 1965–2000." *Journal of American Ethnic History* 20(1): 50–82.

Schuetz, Alfred. 1945. "The Homecomer." *American Journal of Sociology* 50(5): 369–76.

Sears, David O., and Carolyn L. Funk. 1999. "Evidence of the Long-Term Persistence of Adults' Political Predispositions." *Journal of Politics* 61(1): 1–28.

Smith, Robert. 2005. *Mexican New York: Transnational Lives of New Immigrants.* Berkeley: University of California Press.

Smith, Rogers M. 1993. "Beyond Tocqueville, Myrdal, and Hartz: The Multiple Traditions in America." *American Political Science Review* 87(3): 549–66.

Soehl, Thomas. 2017. "From Origins to Destinations: Acculturation Trajectories in Migrants' Attitudes Towards Homosexuality." *Journal of Ethnic and Migration Studies* 43(11): 1831–53.

Soehl, Thomas, and Roger Waldinger. 2010. "Making the Connection: Latino Immigrants and Their Cross-Border Ties." *Ethnic and Racial Studies* 33(9): 1489–1510.

———. 2012. "Inheriting the Homeland? Intergenerational Transmission of Cross-Border Ties in Migrant Families." *American Journal of Sociology* 118(3): 778–813.

Stoker, Laura, and M. Kent Jennings. 2008. "Of Time and the Development of Partisan Polarization." *American Journal of Political Science* 52(3): 619–35.

Stringer, Scott M. 2016. "Opening the Golden Door: Lowering the Cost of Citizenship in the Immigrant Capital of the World." New York: Office of the New York City Comptroller, Bureau of Policy and Research (February). https://comptroller.nyc.gov/wp-content/uploads/documents/Citizenship_Report.pdf (accessed December 10, 2017).

Syracuse University, Transactional Records Access Clearinghouse. 2007. "Removal Orders Under Aggravated Felony Provisions." TRAC Immigration. http://trac.syr.edu/immigration/reports/175/include/table_graph1.html (accessed on 10 December 2017).

Telles, Edward M., and Vilma Ortiz. 2008. *Generations of Exclusion: Mexican-Americans, Assimilation, and Race.* New York: Russell Sage Foundation.

Tichenor, Daniel J. 2009. *Dividing Lines: The Politics of Immigration Control in America*. Princeton, N.J.: Princeton University Press.
Tuan, Mia. 1998. *Forever Foreigners or Honorary Whites? The Asian Ethnic Experience Today*. New Brunswick, N.J.: Rutgers University Press.
Ueda, Reed. 1980. "Naturalization and Citizenship." In *Harvard Encyclopedia of American Ethnic Groups*, edited by Stephan Thernstrom, Ann Orlov, and Oscar Handlin. Cambridge, Mass.: Belknap Press of Harvard University Press.
U.S. Citizenship and Immigration Services. 2016. "Applicant Performance on the Naturalization Test." Last modified October 13, 2017. https://www.uscis.gov/us-citizenship/naturalization-test/applicant-performance-naturalization-test (accessed October 20, 2016).
Van Tubergen, Frank, and Matthijs Kalmijn. 2005. "Destination-Language Proficiency in Cross-National Perspective: A Study of Immigrant Groups in Nine Western Countries." *American Journal of Sociology* 110(5): 1412–57.
Verba, Sidney, Kay Lehman Schlozman, and Henry Brady. 1995. *Voice and Equality: Civic Voluntarism in American Politics*. Vol. 4. Cambridge, Mass.: Harvard University Press.
Voicu, Bogdan, and Claudiu D. Tufis. 2015. "Migrating Trust: Contextual Determinants of International Migrants' Confidence in Political Institutions." *European Political Science Review* 9(3): 351–73.
Waldinger, Roger. 2008. "Between 'Here' and 'There': Immigrant Cross-Border Activities and Loyalties." *International Migration Review* 42(1): 3–29.
Waldinger, Roger, and Peter Catron. 2015. "Modes of Incorporation: A Conceptual and Empirical Critique." *Journal of Ethnic and Migration Studies* 42(1): 25–53.
Waters, Mary C., and Marisa Gerstein Pineau, eds. 2016. *The Integration of Immigrants into American Society*. Washington, D.C.: National Academies Press.
Weber, Max. 1978. *Economy and Society: An Outline of Interpretive Sociology*. Vol. 1. Berkeley: University of California Press.
Weldon, Steven A. 2006. "The Institutional Context of Tolerance for Ethnic Minorities: A Comparative, Multilevel Analysis of Western Europe." *American Journal of Political Science* 50(2): 331–49.
Wimmer, Andreas. 2008. "The Making and Unmaking of Ethnic Boundaries: A Multilevel Process Theory." *American Journal of Sociology* 113(4): 970–1022.
Wimmer, Andreas, and Thomas Soehl. 2014. "Blocked Acculturation: Cultural Heterodoxy Among Europe's Immigrants." *American Journal of Sociology* 120(1): 146–86.
Wong, Janelle, S. Karthick Ramakrishnan, Taeku Lee, and Jane Junn. 2011. *Asian American Political Participation: Emerging Constituents and Their Political Identities*. New York: Russell Sage Foundation.
World Values Survey (WVS). 2010–2014. Wave 5. Official Aggregate v.20150418. World Values Survey Association. Aggregate file producer: Asep/JDS, Madrid, Spain. www.worldvaluessurvey.org.

Xie, Yue, and Emily Greenman. 2011. "The Social Context of Assimilation: Testing Implications of Segmented Assimilation Theory." *Social Science Research* 40(3): 965–84.

Yoshikawa, Hirokazu, and Ariel Kalil. 2011. "The Effects of Parental Undocumented Status on the Developmental Contexts of Young Children in Immigrant Families." *Child Development Perspectives* 5(4): 291–97.

Zelinsky. Wilbur. 2001. *The Enigma of Ethnicity: Another American Dilemma.* Iowa City: University of Iowa Press.

Zolberg, Aristide R. 2009. *A Nation by Design: Immigration Policy in the Fashioning of America.* Cambridge, Mass.: Harvard University Press.

Zolberg, Aristide R., Astri Suhrke, and Sergio Aguayo. 1989. *Escape from Violence: Conflict and the Refugee Crisis in the Developing World.* Oxford: Oxford University Press.

Index

Boldface numbers refer to figures and tables.

acculturation: consonant, 240–41, **249–52,** 249–56, **254,** 271; defined, 71; dissonant, 32, 128, 240, 249–50, **249–52;** familial cohesion and, 121, 253; language use and, 239–40, 248–55, **249–52, 254;** selective, 31, 200, 240–41, **249–52,** 249–56, **254,** 271
adaptation, 44–45, 158, 171–72, 179, 185
Affordable Health Care Act (2010), 281
African immigrants, 94–95. *See also immigrants by country*
Alba, Richard. *See Remaking the American Mainstream*
Algan, Yann, 284
Antiterrorism and Effective Death Penalty Act (AEDPA, 1996), 163
Aptekar, Sofya, 162
Arendt, Hannah, 75
The Asian American Achievement Paradox (Lee & Zhou): coethnic communities and, 46; context for, **88,** 89–90; education and employment outcomes and, 122, 131–32, 148, 270; emigration context and, 52; intragroup differences and, 16; language use and, 241, 245; national origin comparisons in, 114, 139; overview, 39–41; parental hyperselectivity and, 129, 148; public institution use and, 78, 137, 149; survival orientation and, 62
Asian immigrants. *See also immigrants by country*: citizenship of, 156, 164; cross-border ties and, 206; discrimination and, 43; education outcomes for, 3, 39–41, 53, 130–32; emigration context and, 60, 89; employment outcomes for, 108; hyperselectivity of, 16, 39–40, 122, 129–30, 148, 241, 270; Mexican immigrants compared to, 3, 39, 41, 53; as model minority, 94; political participation of, 78, 162; skin-color stratification and, 95; stereotype promise and, 39–40, 89
assimilation. *See also* neo-assimilation theory; segmented assimilation theory: citizenship and, 156, 181–83, 185, 310n5; as continuous process, 78; downward, 29–34; individualistic adaptation and, 44–45; language and, 238; mainstream values, convergence with, 60; national origin and, 81; rates of, 3
asylum-seekers. *See* refugees

325

Bachmeier, James. *See Parents Without Papers*
Baker, Wayne E., 294
Barth, Fredrik, 226
Bean, Frank, 22. *See also Parents Without Papers*
bilingualism, 129, 239, 256. *See also* language
Bloemraad, Irene, 161, 167
Brown, Susan, 22. *See also Parents Without Papers*
Brubaker, Rogers, 159, 213

Cahuc, Pierre, 284
Cambodian immigrants, 64
Canada: emigration from, 94; naturalization rates in, 167
Caribbean immigrants. *See also immigrants by country*: cultural values of, 297; discrimination and, 43; education outcomes for, 108; heterogeneity of, 36; political participation of, 178; reception of, 104; skin-color stratification and, 94, 272
CBOs (community-based organizations), 194
Central American immigrants, 53, 105. *See also immigrants by country*
Chavez, Leo, 22
Children of Immigrants Longitudinal Study (CILS), 29, 250
Children of Immigrants Longitudinal Survey in Four European Countries (CILS4EU), 277
Chinese immigrants: citizenship of, 164; cultural values of, 295–96, **295–96**; education outcomes for, 3, 40–41, 108; exclusion of, 277; heterogeneity of, 36, 40; immigrant advantage and, 89; immigration context and, 64; language use and, 239; political participation of, 178; reception of, 89, 104; success of, 35–36, 40

Chua, Amy, 53
CILS (Children of Immigrants Longitudinal Study), 29, 250
CILS4EU (Children of Immigrants Longitudinal Survey in Four European Countries), 277
citizenship, exercise of, 19, 177–201; assimilation and exclusion, 181–83, 310n5; barriers to, 184, 193, 200; cross-border ties and, 180–81, 191, 200, 273; defined, 153; education levels and, 270–71; intragroup differences and, 191–92; legal status and, 186–91, 274–75; migration-status disparities and, 269; mobilization for, 190, 194; overview, 177–81; parental education and language ability, 185–86; partisanship and, 196–99, **197–98**, 268, 311n16; political identity and, 195–96; politics, formal and informal, 183–92, **186–89**; skin-color stratification and, **197**, 198–99, 200–201, 272
citizenship acquisition, 18–19, 153–76; barriers to, 155–58, **157**, 160–62, 174–75; citizen density and, **166**, 167, **168–70**; citizenship, exercise of, 182–83, 190–91; competencies and skills, 173–74; cross-border ties and, 223; emigration contexts and, 171; familial cohesion and, 268; fee and testing requirements for, 156, 161; history of, 155–56, 174, 277–78; immigration contexts and, 167–69, 172–73; migration control institutions and, 274; migration-status disparities and, 144, 269, 309n13; patterns and pathways to citizenship and, 163–74; perspectives on, 158–63; settlement and adaptation, 171–72
Citizenship and Immigration Services, 161. *See also* Immigration and Naturalization Service

citizenship density: familial cohesion and, 268; family-level, 172, 175, 269, 278–79; legal status and, 169; national origin groups and, 164–65, **166**; parental residency and, 172; reception context and, 165, **166**; speed of naturalization and, 167, **168**
Citrin, Jack, 192
civic engagement. *See* citizenship, exercise of
civic stratification, 9, 155, 263. *See also* legal status of immigrant parents
civil rights, 43, 177
coethnic communities: education outcomes and, 12, 112; ethnic capital and, 92; immigration context and, 32, **88,** 89, 270; national origin comparisons and, 97–99, **98,** 104, 113–14; political participation and, 194; segmented assimilation and, 30, 45–46, 253
Colombian immigrants, 104, 108
colorism, 94–95, 270. *See also* skin-color stratification
community-based organizations (CBOs), 194
cross-border ties, 19, 202–25. *See also* remittances; assimilation and, 44–45; citizenship, exercise of, 180–81, 191, 200, 273; disadvantages of, 123–24; education and employment outcomes and, 124, 141–42, **143,** 149, 204, 216, 271, 273; effect of, 3–4; foreign detachment and, 207–8, **209;** immigration context and, 67–72, **69,** 76–77; intergroup differences and, 213–16, **215;** intersocietal convergence and, 67, 70–72, 76, 205–8, 216–23, **217, 219;** intragroup differences and, 8–9, 49, 210–13, 263; language use and, 241, 246, 248; legal status and, 269, 275; resources and capacity, 220–23, **222;** selective process of immigration and, 4, 8, 67, 122–23, 223, 276; socioeconomic outcomes and, 123; transmitting to second generation, 208–16
cross-level interactions, 12, 32, 119
Cuban immigrants, 33, 63–64, 193, 279
Cultural Map (Inglehart & Welzel), 56, **57**
cultural values: citizenship and, 160; convergence with mainstream and, 60; cross-border ties and, 70, 210–11; defined, 54; education outcomes and, 58–60, **59,** 62, 91, 101, 110–11, 116, 121–22, 132, **133,** 136, 148, 267, 285, **288–89;** emigration context and, 52–58, 101, 262; ethnic capital and, 92; home-country benefits, 52, 54, 112, 264, 267–68; language use and, 240; legacy of, 38; motivation of migrants and, 44; resource deficiencies vs., 39; second-generation outcomes and, 52–58; selective acculturation and, 31; selective process for emigration and, 294–96, **295–96;** survey on. *See* World Values Survey; survival vs. self-expression. *See* survival vs. self-expression orientation; traditional vs. secular-rational. *See* traditional vs. secular-rational orientation; in United States, 38, 55, 56, **295–96,** 295–97, **298**

Dade County, Florida, study on second-generation children in, 29–34
data sources, 19–23
Deferred Action for Childhood Arrivals (DACA), 281
democracy, 53–56, 60–61, 177, 192, 285, **291, 293**
deportations, 163, 281
DeSipio, Louis, 22

discrimination. *See also* skin-color stratification: assimilation, effect on, 43; citizenship and, 72, 75, 175; in employment, 45, 93; legal status of immigrant parents and, 72, 75, 268–69; migration control institutions and, 45–46, 268–69; motivation and ambition vs., 30; national-origin group and, 116; partisanship resulting from, 193; protections against, 34–35, 75, 268; reception context and, 35

Dominican immigrants: language use and, 239; reception of, 99, 104–5; success of, 35; survey data on, 208, **209**

dual-nationality, 159

Ecuadorian immigrants, 104, 108

education of immigrant parents: acculturation and, 253–55, **254**; assimilation and, 52, 127–28; children's education outcomes and, 119, 127–32, **130, 133,** 269, 309*nn*10–11; citizenship acquisition and, 173–74; cross-border ties and, 220–21; ethnic identity and, 231; group-level resources vs., **130,** 130–36, **132, 134, 136**; group membership vs., 12; measurement of, 96

education outcomes: citizenship and, 162, 165, **168,** 270–71; cross-border ties and, 124, 142, **143,** 149, 204, 216, 271, 273; cultural values of origin countries and, 53, 58–60, **59,** 62, 91, 101, 110–11, 116, 121–22, 132, **133,** 136, 148, 267, 285, **288–89**; cultural values of United States and, 55; emigration context and, 54, 101, 110–11, 124, 133, **134**; employment outcomes and, 101, 127; ethnic capital and, 39–40, 89, 92–93, 122, 131–33, **133,** 148, 270; exceptional attainment and, 129–32, **133**; familial cohesion and, 54, 62, 121–22, 128–29, 148, 267, 268; group effect and, 113–16, **115,** 118, 135–36, 149–50, 192, 255, 270; high school quality and, 137–41, **138, 140,** 148–49; IIMMLA and ISGMNY data on, 131–32; immigration context and, 101–11, **102, 103–7,** 269; individual-level resources and, 114–16, **115,** 133, **134,** 138–39; intraclass variations in attainment, 109–11; intragroup differences in, 125, **126**; language use and, 139, 141, 148–49, 244, 267–68; legal status and, 91, 109, 124, 127, 142–44, **145,** 149, 274; multigenerational households and, 308*n*4; multi-level modeling for, 81–82; parent education levels and, 119, 127–32, **130, 133,** 269, 309*nn*10–11; reputational effect of, 93; right to, 109; skin-color stratification and, 101, 109–10, 271–72; stereotype promise and, 39–40; summary of findings on, 146–50, **147**; supplementary language schools and, 39, 89, 122, 131–33, **133,** 148

emigration context, 51–62; citizenship acquisition and, 171, 175; conceptualizing and measuring, 87, **88**; convergence with mainstream values and, 60; cultural values of origin countries and, 52–58, 101, 262; education and employment outcomes and, 58–59, **59,** 101, 110–11, 113, 124, 133, **134**; immigrant advantage and, 90; individual-level resources and, 114–16, **115**; parenting and, 52; selective process and. *See* selective process of immigration; socialization of immigrants and, 51, 171; World Values Survey and, 55–61, **57, 59**

Index 329

employment outcomes: cross-border ties and, 124; discrimination and, 45, 93; education and, 101, 127; emigration context and, 110–11, 124; ethnic capital and, 92–93; gender and, 52; immigration context and, 101–11, **102, 104–7**; individual-level resources and, 114–16, **115**; intraclass variations in outcomes, 109–11; intragroup differences in, 125, **126**; language use and, 309*n*9; legal status and, 63–65, 75, 109, 124, 127, 269, 274, 279; migrant worker demand, 7; skills and, 202, 255; skin-color stratification and, 109–10; summary of findings on, 146–50, **147**

ethnic capital. *See also* coethnic communities: Asian immigrant success and, 41; defined, 270; discrimination, effect of, 43; education outcomes and, 39–40, 89, 92–93, 122, 131–33, **133**, 148, 270; employment and, 92–93; IIMMLA and ISGMNY data on, 100, **100**; immigration context and, 109–10; national origin and, 80; political participation and, 194; segmented assimilation and, 91–93; social mobility and, 65; success and, 261; variations in, 7

Ethnic Differences (Perlmann), 80

ethnic identity, 19, 226–58; acculturation and, 249–55, **250–52, 254**; citizenship, exercise of, 192; citizenship acquisition and, 74; language retention and loss, 238–41, 238–49, **243, 247**; national histories and, 52; national pride and, 227–28, **228**; overview, 226–27; self-identification and, 231–38, **234, 236–37**, 257; social boundaries and, 227–38, 311*n*7

Europe, immigration to, 276

European immigrants. *See also immigrants by country*: citizenship of, 178; mass migrations and, 95–96, 277–78; skin-color stratification and, 94, 270

explanatory model, **5,** 5–6

Faist, Thomas, 211–12

familial cohesion and strategies. *See also* cross-border ties: acculturation and, 121, 253; benefits of, 30–31, 35–37; challenges to, 30–31, 34; citizenship acquisition and, 160; cultural values and, 54–55; education and employment outcomes and, 62, 121–22, 128–29, 148, 267, 268; immigrant advantage and, 90; income diversification and, 38, 44; language use and, 31, 121, 129, 240; parental authority and, 31, 54, 121; remittances and, 191; survival vs. self-expression orientation and, 56, 61

family reunification, 64, 67–68

Filipino immigrants, 3, 40, 58, 104, 108

Fishman, Joshua, 238–39

forms of capital model (Alba & Nee), 43–44

GDP, education outcomes and, 285, **286, 288,** 294

gender: employment and, 52; language competence and, 244; religion and, 52–53; survival vs. self-expression orientation and, 285, **290**; traditional vs. secular-rational orientation and, 285, **292**; UN Gender Empowerment Index, 285, **290, 292**

General Social Survey (GSS), 271, 284

Gilbertson, Greta, 160

globalization, 7, 53, 63, 80–81, 227

group effect and group resources. *See also* coethnic communities: acculturation and, 253, 255; acquisition

of citizenship and, 160; cross-border ties and, 208, 210; education outcomes and, 113–16, **115**, 118, 135–36, 149–50, 192, 255, 270–71; family resources and, 132–36, **134, 136**; immigrant education level vs., **130**, 130–36, **132, 134, 136**; language use and, 122, 244; list, 300; political participation and, **197**, 198, 200; second-generation advantage and, 35–36
GSS (General Social Survey), 271, 284
Guatemalan immigrants: citizenship density of, 164, 279; education outcomes of, 105; immigration context of, 63–64; reception of, 99, 104
Guiso, Luigi, 284

Hajnal, Zoltan, 193, 195
Hochschild, Jennifer, 184
Holdaway, Jennifer. *See Inheriting the City*
Hollinger, David, 311*n*7
home-country ties. *See* cross-border ties
homeland-oriented organizations, participation in, 205, 212, 214, 220–21, 275
homosexuality, 296, **296**
human capital, 30, 43–44, 92, 124
Human Development Index, 285, **291, 293**
hyperselectivity, 16, 39–41, 122, 129–30, 148, 241, 270

identity. *See* ethnic identity; political identity
IIMMLA. *See* Immigration and Intergenerational Mobility in Metropolitan Los Angeles
Illegal Immigration Reform and Immigrant Responsibility Act (IIRIRA, 1996), 163
immigrant advantage, 34–37, 89

immigrant parents. *See also specific countries of origin*: assimilation of. *See* assimilation; contexts for, 7; economic and cultural diversity of, 2; emigration context and, 49, 51–62; English proficiency of, 173, 181–82, 245–46, 248–50, **249**; intergroup differences in, 6–8, 11; intragroup differences in, 8–10, 11; legal status of. *See* legal status of immigrant parents; native-born parents compared to, 3, 6–7, 76–77; as political issue, 78; political membership of, 46; reasons for emigration, 27, 42, 44, 51; rights of, 9, 72–76, 78; selective immigration process for. *See* selective process of immigration; socialization of, 51, 58, 210–13, 227, 283; socioeconomic status and, 43, 51–52, 127; stigma for, 93; two-parent households and, 121, 129, 139, 176, 246
Immigrant Second Generation in Metropolitan New York (ISGMNY) survey: on acculturation, **249–52,** 249–55, **254**; on citizenship acquisition, 167, **170**; on citizenship density, 165, **166**; on cross-border ties, 68, **69,** 142, **143,** 149, 206–7, 214–16, **215**; on cultural values, 285–94, **286–93,** 297, **298**; data sources for, 97–98; descriptive statistics from, 100, **100**; on education outcomes, 101, **102,** 114, **115,** 125, **126,** 131–32; on employment outcomes, 101, **102,** 114, **115,** 125, **126,** 141; on high school quality, 137–41, **138, 140,** 149; on language use, 239, 241–50, **243, 249**; on legal status, 66, **66, 74, 145,** 146, **157,** 157–58, 223; national-origin diversity, 81–82, 283; on national pride, 227, **228**; overview, 19–23; on parental education vs. group resources, **130,** 130–36, **132,**

134, 136; on political participation, 196–99, **197–98**; on public resource use, 121, 137, 141, 149; on reception context, **98,** 99, 103–8, **104–7**; on skin-color stratification, 95; variables in, 302

Immigration and Intergenerational Mobility in Metropolitan Los Angeles (IIMMLA): on acculturation, **249–52,** 249–55, **254**; on Asian immigrants, 39–41; on citizenship, exercise of, 183–84, **186–89,** 190–91; on citizenship acquisition, 167, **170,** 172–73; on citizenship density, 165, **166**; on cross-border ties, 68, **69,** 137, 142, 205–8, **209,** 214–20, **215, 217, 219,** 273; on cultural values, 285–94, **286–93,** 297, **298**; data sources for, 97–98; descriptive statistics from, 100, **100**; on education outcomes, 101, **102,** 114, **115,** 125, **126,** 131–32; on employment outcomes, 101, **102,** 114, **115,** 125, **126**; on ethnic identity, 232–38, **234, 236–37**; on language use, 37, 241–44, **243, 247,** 248–50, **249,** 275; on legal status, 37, 66, **66,** 73–74, 137, 142–44, **145,** 146, 167–69, **168–69,** 223, 274; national-origin diversity of, 80–82, 97, 283, 307–8*n*14; on national pride, 227, **228**; overview, 19–23; on parental education vs. group resources, **130,** 130–36, **132, 134, 136**; on political participation, 196–99, **197–98**; on reception context, **98,** 99, 103–8, **104–7**; on remittances, 207; on skin-color stratification, 95, 272; variables in, 302

Immigration and Naturalization Service (INS), 66, 97, 99, 161, 174

immigration context, 18, 87–117; acculturation and, 253; citizenship, exercise of, 184; citizenship acquisition and, 167–69, **170,** 175; cross-border ties and, 213–16, **215**; education and employment outcomes and, 101–11, **102, 104–7,** 113; ethnic identity and, 231; household resources and, 91–97; individual-level resources and, 114–16, **115**; legal status and, 63–65; literature comparisons, 87–91, **88**; migration-status disparities and, 62–63, 66, **66,** 268–69; national origin and, 97–101, **98**; redefining, research outcomes and, 111–17

Immigration Reform and Control Act (IRCA, 1986), 64–65, 76, 161, 278, 281

Indian immigrants, 64

individual-level resources: acculturation and, 253; citizenship acquisition and, 269; cross-border ties and, 203, 224; education outcomes and, 114–16, **115,** 133, **134,** 138–39; political participation and, **197,** 198

Inglehart, Ronald, 55–56, **57, 59,** 294

Inheriting the City (Kasinitz, Mollenkopf, Waters, & Holdaway): assimilation and, 46; citizenship, exercise of, 78, 178; context for, **88,** 89–90; cross-border ties and, 203; emigration context and, 52; immigrant advantage perspective of, 121; language use and, 239; national origin comparisons in, 114, 139; overview, 34–37; positive forecast of, 15; public institution use and, 137, 149

INS (Immigration and Naturalization Service), 66, 97, 99, 161, 174

inter- and intragenerational differences, 87, 150, 250

intergenerational mobility, 121

intergroup differences: citizenship, exercise of, 178; citizenship acquisition and, 159–60, 164, 176; cross-border ties and, 213–16, **215**; emigration

context and, 6–8, 49, 51–62, **57, 59**;
ethnic identity and, 231; immigration context and, 6–8, 62–66, **66**;
international perspective and, 79–82;
language use and, 239–41; legal status, 49; scholarship on, 16–17; second-generation outcomes, 27; segmented assimilation and, 34; skin-color stratification and, 95; socioeconomic diversity and, 96
international perspective, 17–18, 49–83; application of, 77–82; assessment of, 263–75, **265–66**; citizenship, exercise of, 180; cross-border ties and, 67–72, **69,** 142, **143,** 204; emigration context, 51–62, 264–68; ethnic identity and, 231; immigration context, 62–66, **66,** 268–72; language use and, 240–41, 244; legal status of immigrants and, 72–76; overview, 49–51; summary of, **265**
International Socio-Economic Index (ISEI), 96, 101
intersocietal convergence, 67, 70–72, 76, 205–6, 216–23, **217, 219**
intragroup differences, 18, 118–50; citizenship, exercise of, 178, 191–92; citizenship acquisition and, 160, 176; cross-border ties and. *See* cross-border ties; ethnic identity and, 231; exceptional education outcomes and, 129–32, **130, 133**; family cohesion and, 128–29; high school quality and, 137–41, **138, 140**; home-society culture and, 44; international perspective and, 79–82, 272–75; language use and, 241; legal status and civic stratification. *See* legal status; overview, 125, **126**; scholarship on, 16–17; second-generation children outcomes and, 27, 43–44, 50; segmented assimilation and, 34;

skin-color stratification and, 95;
socioeconomic diversity and, 96;
sources of, 119–25, **120**; summary of findings on, 146–50, **147**
IRCA (Immigration Reform and Control Act), 64–65, 76, 161, 278, 281
ISEI (International Socio-Economic Index), 96, 101
ISGMNY. *See* Immigrant Second Generation in Metropolitan New York survey
Italian immigrants, 202

Kasinitz, Philip, 22. *See also Inheriting the City*
kinship ties. *See* cross-border ties
Korean immigrants: citizenship density of, 164; cultural values of, 297; education outcomes for, 108, 131; immigration context of, 64; reception of, 104

Labor Force Survey (United Kingdom), 276–77
language: acculturation and, 239–40, 248–55, **249–52, 254**; citizenship, exercise of, 179, 181–82, 186, 196, 200; competence in, 241–44, **243,** 248–49; cross-border ties and, 68–69, 71, 211, 213, 220–21, 225; education outcomes and, 139, 141, 148–49, 244, 267–68; emigration context and, 52; emotional connotations of, 213; employment outcomes and, 309n9; English citizenship requirements, 161–62; English usage in the home, 97, 173–74, 181–82, 245–46, 248–50, **249**; ethnic identity and, 231, 235, **236,** 238, 256; family cohesion and, 31, 121, 129; migration-status disparities and, 269; preference for, 244–48, **247**; retention and loss, 238–49, **243, 247**; success rates and, 36

Laotian immigrants, 64
Latin American immigrants. *See also immigrants by country*: cross-border ties of, 206, 212; emigration context and, 52–53, 60; Filipino immigrants compared to, 58; language use and, 239; political participation of, 178; skin-color stratification and, 94–95
Latino National Survey, 208
Lee, Jennifer, 22. *See also The Asian American Achievement Paradox*
Lee, Taeku, 193, 195
Legacies: The Story of the Second Generation (Rumbaut & Portes): acculturation and, 240–41, 249, 253; attitudes toward immigrants, 93–94; context for, **88,** 89–90; controversy of, 15; education and employment outcomes and, 148, 150; ethnic identity and, 231, 233; language use and, 240–41, 245; national origin comparisons of, 81, 97, 99, 108, 113, 114; overview, 29–34; reception context and, 46–48; refugee status and, 124
legal status of immigrant parents. *See also* citizenship acquisition; migration control institutions: barriers to, 45; challenges associated with lack of, 280–81; citizenship, exercise of, 180, 182–83, 185, 186–91, **187–89,** 274–75; citizenship acquisition and, 172; civic stratification and, 72–76; cross-border ties and, 269, 275; deportations and, 163, 281; discrimination and, 72, 75, 268–69; education outcomes and, 91, 109, 124, 127, 142–44, **145,** 149, 274; employment outcomes and, 63–65, 75, 109, 124, 127, 269, 274, 279; ethnic identity and, 231, 235, **236;** in Europe, 276–77; family reunification options and, 68; group effect and, 36, 46; immigration context and, 63–65; integration and, 37; language use and, 241, 244, 248; membership exclusion model and, 16, 37–38, 123; political identity and, 196; political participation and, 73–75, 77–78; refugees and, 65; rights and, 75; second-generation children, effect on, 7–10, 37, 49, 73–74, 76–77, 127, 281; skin-color stratification vs., 94–95; social mobility and, 65; societal perceptions and, 262; status prevalence scale, 66, **66**
legal status of second-generation. *See* second generation outcomes (1.5 generation)
literature review, 17, 27–48. *See also specific publications*; gaps in literature and, 47–48; immigration context, 87–91, **88;** membership exclusion, 37–38; minority cultures of mobility, 39–41; neo-assimilation theory, 41–46; overview, 28–29; second-generation advantage, 34–37; segmented assimilation, 29–34
The Long Grey Welcome (North), 161
Los Angeles, California. *See* Immigration and Intergenerational Mobility in Metropolitan Los Angeles

Massey and Martin Skin Color Scale (M&M Scale), 95
mass migrations, 80–81, 95–96, 156, 202, 277–78
membership exclusion model, 16, 37–38, 47, 123, **266**
Mexican immigrants: Asian immigrants compared to, 3, 39, 41, 53; citizenship density of, 164, 278–79; Cuban immigrants compared to, 33; cultural values of, **295–96,** 295–97; deportation of, 281; discrimination

and, 43; education outcomes of, 3, 105, 131; immigration context of, 64–65; membership exclusion and, 37–38; negative outcomes for, 53, 93, 112; reception of, 99, 104–5; resource acquisition and, 202; skin-color stratification and, 95; survey data on, 208, **209**

migration control institutions. *See also* legal status of immigrant parents: asylum, refusal of, 282; avoidance of, 161; border control and, 280; citizenship, exercising, 201; citizenship acquisition and, 274; discrimination of, 45–46, 268–69; domestic vs. international interests and, 62–63; early immigration law, 155–56, 277–78; exclusion from citizenship and, 72, 153, 155, 180, 278; monitoring and enforcement, 45–46; nationality-level differences created by, 76, 116–17, 279–80; national origin comparisons and, 97–99, **98**; as predictor of success, 112; purpose of, 262; reception, national origin comparisons, 103–8, **104–7**; refugees and, 64–65; second-generation outcomes and, 48; selective process of immigration and, 17, 67, 261

migration-status disparities, 7–8, 62–66, **66,** 268–69

minority mobility model, 39–41, **265,** 270

model and analysis: concepts of, 49; context for, **88,** 90; inter-and intragroup differences and, 79–82; multilevel, 81–82, 103, 108–9, 116; overview, 10–14; variables in, 50–51

model minorities, 94

modes of incorporation, 89

Mollenkopf, John, 22. *See also Inheriting the City*

Myrdal, Gunnar, 229

national origin: citizenship, exercise of, 192, 198, **198**; citizenship density and, 164–65; comparisons based on, 32–33, 50, 80–82, 90; data sources and, 21; discrimination and, 116; education outcomes and, 127, 135, 139; employment outcomes and, 127; immigration context and, 97–101, **98**; inter- and intragroup variations and, 79–80; pride and, 227–28, **228**; values and orientations from, 227

nativism, 155–56

Naturalization Acts (1870, 1906), 156, 174

Nee, Victor. *See Remaking the American Mainstream*

neo-assimilation theory: adaptation and, 158; citizenship, exercise of, 178–79, 181–82; citizenship acquisition and, 158, 175; education of immigrant parents and, 135; ethnic identity and, 231; immigration context and, 268–69; *Remaking the American Mainstream* on, 15, 41–46, 90; segmented assimilation theory vs, 15–16; socioeconomic resources and, 119, 127–28; summary of, **265**

New Immigrant Survey (NIS), 95

New York City, New York. *See Immigrant Second Generation in Metropolitan New York* survey

Nicaraguan immigrants, 64

North, David, 161

Ocampo, Anthony, 58

occupational outcomes. *See* employment outcomes

origin countries. *See* emigration context; national origin

Parents Without Papers (Bean, Brown, & Bachmeier): citizenship, exercise of, 180; context for, **88,** 90; legal status and cross-border ties, 46–48, 137, 149; membership exclusion model of, 16, 22, 37–38, 47, 123; socioeconomic mobility and, 77
partisanship, 193, 196–99, **197–98,** 200–201, 268, 272, 311*n*16
Pearson, Kathryn, 192
Perlmann, Joel, 80
Poland, cultural values from, 52
political identity, 192, 195–96
political participation. *See also* citizenship, exercise of: adaptation and, 179; citizenship and, 153–54; cross-country ties and, 210, 221; cultural values and, 53–54, 61; exclusion and, 46; incorporation and, 78, 181, 192; legal status and, 73–75, 77–78
Portes, Alejandro, 14. *See also Legacies*
post–civil rights era, 34–35, 43
protective naturalization, 160, 191
public goods and resources, 2–3, 78, 121, 137, 141, 149
Putnam, Robert, 284

racism. *See* skin-color stratification
reception context: Chinese and Vietnamese immigrants and, 89; Cuban vs. Mexican immigrants, 33; discrimination and, 35; education outcomes and, 133–36, **134**; effect on second-generation, 50; family-level resources and, 124; intergroup differences stemming from, 13, 46–47; national origin comparisons and, 97–99, **98,** 103–8, **104–7**; origin country vs., 32–33; as predictor of success, 112; segmented assimilation and, 30
Refugee Act (1980), 64

refugees: asylum, refusal of, 282; citizenship acquisition and, 160; communism and, 279; cross-border ties and, 202–3, 214; integration of, 214; language use and, 241; migration-status disparities and, 63–66, **66**; reception context for, 99, 108, 124
religion: communism and, 52; cultural values and, **295,** 295–96; gender differences and, 52–53; success rates of Asian immigrants and, 40; values of origin countries and, 52–55; World Values Survey and, 55
Remaking the American Mainstream (Alba & Nee): on citizenship, 75, 178; context for, **88,** 90; on cross-border ties, 203; neo-assimilation theory and, 15, 41–46, 90; on socioeconomic resources, 119
remittances: cross-border ties and, 45, 202, 206–8, 218, 224–25; education and employment outcomes and, 142, 149, 204–5, 221, 273; intergenerational behavior and, 207–8, 212; language competence and, 244; parental modeling of, 191
role reversal, 121, 250
Rumbaut, Rubén, 22. *See also Legacies*
Russian immigrants: cultural values of, **295–96,** 295–97; immigration context of, 63–64; language use and, 239; political participation of, 178; reception of, 99, 108, 112; refugee status of, 279, 282; success of, 35

Salvadoran immigrants: citizenship density of, 164, 279; education outcomes for, 105; employment outcomes for, 3; immigration context of, 63–64; reception of, 99, 104; refugee status and, 279; survey data on, 208, **209**

San Diego, California, study on second-generation children in, 29–34
Sapienza, Paola, 284
Schuetz, Alfred, 213
Schwartz, Shalom, 294
second-generation advantage, 15–16, 34–37, 89–90, 239, **266,** 282
second generation outcomes (1.5 generation): acculturation of, 251, **251**; citizenship, exercise of, 183, 184, 192, 200–201; citizenship acquisition of, 156, **157,** 161–63, 165, 167, **168,** 171–73, 175–76; civic stratification and, 73–74; cross-border ties and, 163; defined, 10; education outcomes and, 96–97, 139; ethnic identity of, 235, **237**; language use and, 242–44, **243**; legal status and, 73–74, 127, 309n13; socialization of, 52, 74
second generation outcomes (2 generation): acculturation of, 251, **251**; assimilation of, 3, 29–34, 239–40; birthright citizenship and, 73–74, 156, 175, 276; citizenship, exercise of. See citizenship, exercise of; civic stratification of, 9–10; cross-border ties and, 68–72, 204, 208–16, 263; education outcomes for. See education outcomes; employment outcomes for. See employment outcomes; employment outcomes of, **100,** 100–101; ethnic identity of, 235; legal status of parents, effect of, 7–10, 37, 49, 73–74, 76–77, 127, 281; minority status of, 76; native-born children compared to, 27–28; parents compared to, 27; skin-color stratification and, 94; socialization of. See socialization; socioeconomic resources and, 119, **120**; two-parent households and, 121, 129, 139, 176, 246; variations in, 2

second generation outcomes (2.5 generation): acculturation of, 251, **251**; citizenship density of, 164, 172; defined, 71; education outcomes of, 127–28, 144; language use and, 242–44, **243**; remittances and, 206
secular-rational orientation. See traditional vs. secular-rational orientation
segmented assimilation theory: acculturation and, 253; challenges to, 148; citizenship, exercise of, 179–80, 199–200; coethnic communities and, 30, 43–44, 253; controversy of, 14; critique of, 36; cross-border ties and, 224; education and employment outcomes and, 124–25; ethnic capital and, 91–93; ethnic identity and, 231; familial cohesion and, 128–29; language use and, 239–40; nationality comparisons, dependence on, 50, 112; neo-assimilation theory vs, 15–16; overview, 29–34; reception context and, 39, 46, 135–36; socioeconomic mobility and, 77; summary of, **266**
selective process of immigration: cross-border ties and, 4, 8, 67, 122–23, 223, 276; cultural values and, 58, 294–96, **295–96**; hyperselection and, 16, 39–41, 122, 129–30, 148, 241, 270; migration control institutions and, 17, 67, 261; national origin and, 50; second-generation advantage and, 15–16, 34
self-categorization, 231–38, **234, 236–37**
self-expression orientation. See survival vs. self-expression orientation
Singer, Audrey, 160
skin-color stratification: citizenship, exercise of, **197,** 198–99, 200–201, 272; colorism and, 94–95; cross-border ties and, 216; discrimination and, 94–95, 116, 307n11, 308n22;

education outcomes and, 101, 109–10, 271–72; emigration and immigration context and, 93–95; employment outcomes and, 109–10; high school quality and, 139; as variable, 95; variations in, 7, 33
social boundaries, 226–31, 246, 255–56
socialization: citizenship, exercise of, 184–85, 190, 193; education outcomes and, 93; emigration context and, 51, 171; of immigrant parents, 51, 58, 210–13, 227, 283; of second-generation children, 1–3, 10, 51–52, 74, 76–77
social mobility, 65, 77, 121, 179
social stratification, 119, 121, 176
societal membership, 16, 37–38
societal reception. *See* reception context
socioeconomic status: acculturation and, 253; citizenship acquisition and, 165, 174–75; cross-border ties and, 123, 203, 214, 220–23; diversity in, 96; group effect and, 36; intragroup differences and, 119, **120**; legal status and, 7–8, 87; reception and, 124; second-generation outcomes, 36–37; skin-color stratification and, 94; transmission of, 127
stereotype promise, 39–40, 89
surveys, 19–22. *See also specific surveys*
survival vs. self-expression orientation: citizenship acquisition and, 160, **169,** 171, 176; citizenship density and, 165, 171; city size and, 297, **298**; cross-border ties and, 67, 202, 214; education outcomes and, 58–60, **59,** 62, 91, 101, 110–11, 116, 136, 148, 267, 285, **288–89, 295–96,** 295–97; emigration context and, 54, 55–62, **57, 59,** 90, 101, 110; employment outcomes and, 110; familial cohesion and, 268;

individual- vs. group-level differences, 295; items used to construct value scales, 299; language use and, 241; score interpretation, 308*n*21

Taiwanese immigrants, 131
third generation, 13–14, 37, 195, 284
traditional vs. secular-rational orientation: citizenship, exercise of, 198, **198,** 268; city size and, 297, **298**; cross-border ties and, 214, 224; education outcomes and, 58–60, **59,** 91, 101, 110–11, 113–14, 116, 132–36, **133,** 267–68, 285, **286–87, 295–96,** 295–97; emigration context and, 55–61, **57, 59,** 90, 101, 110; employment outcomes and, 114; individual- vs. group-level differences, 295; items used to construct value scales, 299; language use and, 241; score interpretation, 308*n*21
transnationalism, 67, 203–4, 224. *See also* cross-border ties
two-parent households, 121, 129, 139, 176, 246

undocumented immigrants. *See* legal status of immigrant parents
uniform rule of naturalization, 155
United Nations, 285, **290–93**
United States. *See also* migration control institutions: cultural values of, 38, 55, 56, **295–96,** 295–97, *298*; education rights in, 109; history of immigration in, 155–56, 174, 277–78; increased diversity in, 227; national identity in, 227–29; religion in, 55

Vietnamese immigrants: citizenship density of, 164; educational attainment of, 131; education outcomes of, 40; heterogeneity of, 40; immigration

context of, 63; reception of, 89, 108; refugee status of, 160, 279, 282; success of, 40
voting rights, 78, 154, 162. *See also* political participation

Waters, Mary, 22. *See also Inheriting the City*
Weber, Max, 230
Welzel, Christian, 56, **57, 59**
white immigrants. *See* European immigrants
Wimmer, Andreas, 226
World Bank, 53
World Values Survey (WVS): defined, 312*n*1; on education outcomes, 110; emigration context and, 55–61, **57, 59,** 90; on homosexuality, **296,** 296–97; as measure of legacy effect, 267; migrant selection and, 294–97; national origin outcomes, 100–101; overview, 264, 284; on religion, **295,** 296; on survival vs. self-expression. *See* survival vs. self-expression orientation; on traditional vs. secular-rational. *See* traditional vs. secular-rational orientation
Worldwide Governance Indicators (WGI), 53

Zhou, Min, 14, 22. *See also The Asian American Achievement Paradox*
Zingales, Luigi, 284
zone of intersocietal convergence, 205–6, 223